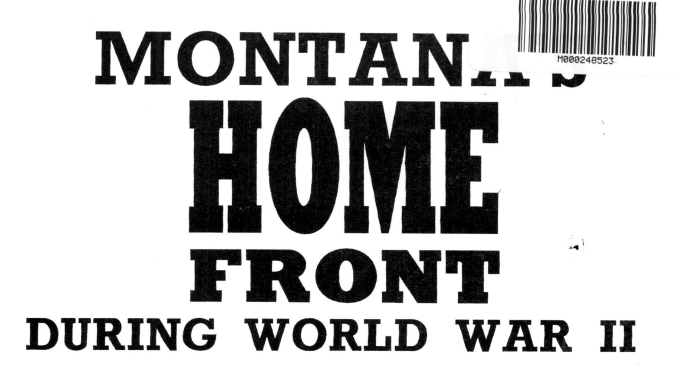

MONTANA'S HOME FRONT

DURING WORLD WAR II

By GARY GLYNN

PICTORIAL HISTORIES PUBLISHING COMPANY, INC.
Missoula, Montana

COPYRIGHT © 1994 BY GARY GLYNN
All rights reserved. No part of this book may be used
or reproduced without written permission of the publisher.

LIBRARY OF CONGRESS
CATALOG CARD NUMBER 94-67869

ISBN 0-929521-93-5

First Printing October 1994

Typography by Leslie R. Maricelli
Layout by Stan Cohen
Cover Layout by Mike Egeler

PICTORIAL HISTORIES PUBLISHING COMPANY, INC.
713 South Third West, Missoula, Montana 59801

⌒ Introduction ⌒

World War II was the most dramatic and all-encompassing event in the history of the human race. Although the state of Montana was extremely lucky in that the horrors of war took place thousands of miles away, not a single resident of the state escaped the impacts of the war. Forest fire lookouts scanned the skies for Japanese balloon bombs, sheepherders swore at rationing restrictions, small children collected rags, paper, and scrap metal, and farmers banded together to build prisoner of war camps intended for men from Berlin and Hamburg.

Montana history is overflowing with accounts of vigilantes and copper kings, cowboys and Indians, explorers and glory seekers. Academics have delved into the plight of the honyockers and the back-room machinations of the Anaconda Copper Mining Company, but the decade of the 1940s has been all but ignored.

Perhaps the history is too new, perhaps historians have been influenced by the opinion of their distinguished fellow, K. Ross Toole, who all but dismissed the period when he wrote, "Someday someone will write a monograph on that long sleep: Montana in the 1930's and 1940's. But it is apt to be a dull monograph. The New Deal came, the New Deal went, the war came, the war went. What the nation did, Montana did. Perhaps a fillip here, a fillip there. Still, what it really was was twenty years of deep somnolence." In general terms he may have been right, but this book is an attempt to demonstrate that during the war years Montanans were not asleep, were in fact, working so hard to win the war that all else fell by the wayside. The fact is, for four long years the residents of the Treasure State lead the nation in support of the war bond drives, collection of scrap metal and other vital materials, and enlistment rates. Only one state had a higher percentage of its population killed in World War II.

Much of the information in this book comes from the pages of 50 year old newspapers, specifically the *Billings Gazette*, the *Missoula Sentinel*, and most importantly, the *Great Falls Tribune*.

This book is about ordinary people doing extraordinary things. It was written to recognize all of the Montanans who played a part, no matter how small, in winning the war. Not all of the story is pretty, but it is a story that needed to be told.

Photo Sources

MHS – Montana Historical Society
UM – University of Montana Archives
HMFM – Historical Museum at Fort Missoula
LC – Library of Congress
SC – Stan Cohen Collection
USFS – United States Forest Service
USAF – United States Air Force
NA – National Archives
FDR – Franklin D. Roosevelt Presidential Library

*The author and publisher wish to dedicate this book to
all World War II veterans and especially to Hubert
"Hub" Zemke, who passed away in August 1994.*

ᑐ Contents ᑐ

☞ Shadows of War ☜

A nervous young Army captain slipped a package wrapped in plain brown paper to Burton K. Wheeler, Montana's senior U.S. Senator. It was the third of December 1941, four days before a Japanese attack on Pearl Harbor would propel the United States into World War II. In a suburb of Washington, D.C., Senator Wheeler held the U.S. War Department's top-secret plan for American entry into World War II in his hand. Dubbed the Victory Program, it predicted that Americans would soon be involved in the fighting in Europe, Africa and Asia, and called for an unprecedented expansion of the U.S. Army to 10 million men.

Wheeler immediately realized the Victory Program was a political bombshell. "The document undercut the repeated statements of Roosevelt and his followers that repeal of the neutrality acts, lend-lease, the destroyer deal, and similar measures, would keep us out of the European conflict."

Although a fellow Democrat, Wheeler was a vocal critic of President Franklin D. Roosevelt's interventionist foreign policy. A prominent isolationist, Wheeler was a powerful and ambitious senator who had considered leaving the Democratic party in 1940 because of its interventionist stand. Wheeler had opposed Roosevelt on such issues as the Lend-Lease Bill and the arming of American merchant ships, feeling these measures would only serve to draw the United States into World War II. Earlier in the year Wheeler had stated that he thought Roosevelt's foreign policy would "plow under every fourth American boy," to which the President replied, "That is really the rottenest thing that has been said in public life in my generation." Nevertheless, Wheeler, who had won reelection in 1940 by carrying every city and county in Montana, remained popular among his constituents.

What Wheeler didn't know was that British diplomat and spymaster William Stephenson (code name Intrepid) was responsible for leaking a sanitized version of the Victory Program to him, aided by a sympathetic captain in the U.S. Army. Stationed in New York, Stephenson was familiar with American politics and knew that Wheeler would probably release the plan to the media. Stephenson hoped that release of the President's top-secret war plans would both embarrass Senator Wheeler and further strain relations between the United States and Germany, so that Roosevelt would enter the war on the side of the British. He was partly right.

Wheeler immediately showed the plan to reporter Chesly Manly and by the following morning the headlines of the *Washington Times-Herald* revealed the details of "FDR'S WAR PLANS." The story threatened to set off a major scandal in Washington, D.C., and defense officials were both stunned and furious about the release of major details of their war plans. Secretary of War Henry Stimson said, "Nothing more unpatriotic or damaging to our plans for defense could very well be conceived of." A massive FBI investigation began but Senator Wheeler's role in the bizarre episode of the Victory Program wasn't revealed until many years later.

Like Wheeler, Montana's Republican Congresswoman Jeannette Rankin also opposed war-related measures such as the Lend-Lease program and the proposed arming of American merchant ships. The first woman ever elected to the U.S. Congress in 1916, Rankin was reelected in 1940 after more than a 20-year absence.

Her colleague from the Eastern District was Montana Congressman James F. O'Connor of Livingston, elected in 1937 and an ally of Senator Wheeler. Montana's second senator, James Murray, was a strong labor supporter from Butte who often opposed Wheeler and his isolationist allies. Murray, who had been elected in 1935, was of Irish descent and had previously served as Silver Bow County attorney. As a member of the Senate Foreign Relations committee, Murray often attacked America Firsters and isolationists. Although he opposed Roosevelt's peacetime conscription, he generally supported the President's other positions prior to the war.

Statewide, a close balance between Democrats and Republicans had existed in the Montana state legislature since the election of 1940, when former Attorney General Sam "Model T" Ford was chosen for the first of his two terms as governor. Ford had been the state's attorney general during World War I. The dominant force in Montana politics during the 1940s was the so-called "Wheeler-Rankin-Ford Axis" a marriage of convenience attacked by both the right and the left. According to Montana historian Joseph

The 1930s

- January 29, 1933. Amelia Earhart pilots a Ford Trimotor into Helena.
- 1933. Going-to-the-Sun Highway dedicated.
- October 1933. Construction begins on Fort Peck Dam.
- 1935. Montana Highway Patrol is formed.
- October 1935. A series of earthquakes kills four people, damages Helena High School and causes $4 million in damage.
- December 15, 1935. Bill Holt named governor after Gov. Frank Cooney dies in office.
- 1936. Oil discovered south of Baker.
- November 23, 1936. Fort Peck Dam featured on the cover of the first issue of *LIFE* magazine.
- 1937. Roy Ayers begins term as governor.
- June 12, 1937. Two-and-one-half inches of rain and hail fell in one hour, causing a major flood in the Billings area when an irrigation canal ruptured and flooded the northside and downtown. The railroad washed out, the Midland Empire fairgrounds were damaged by hail, and other buildings in downtown Billings had their basements flooded. The *Billings Gazette* called it "the greatest catastrophe in the city's 54 year history" and damage was estimated at $2 million.

Montana Governor Sam C. Ford (right) and New York Governor Thomas E. Dewey. UM 88-0049

Congressman James O'Connor at his ranch near White Sulphur Springs. UM 83-25

Radio

Although some regions in the state did not yet have electricity, nearly every household had some kind of radio. According to the U.S. Census Bureau, there were 135,500 radios by 1940, a huge increase from the 15 radio sets in the state when KDYS, Montana's first radio station began broadcasting in 1922 from the offices of the *Great Falls Tribune*. KDYS could be heard throughout the Intermountain West and its remote broadcast of the Dempsey-Gibbons boxing match in Shelby was the first sporting event broadcast in the state. KDYS closed its doors 18 months after opening, but it was soon replaced by KFBB, which began transmitting in Havre in 1922, then moved to Great Falls. There were 10 radio stations operating in the Treasure State by 1941, providing listeners with unprecedented access to world news through shows such as Lowell Thomas' daily radio program. CBS newsman Howard K. Smith reported from Berlin while Edward R. Murrow's reports from London brought the horrors of the Battle of Britain into even the most remote Montana households.

1938-1940

· January 1938. Northwest Airlines flight crashes near Bozeman.
· April 22, 1938. Lewis and Clark Caverns becomes the first Montana state park.
· April 1938. Kerr Dam begins operations.
· June 19, 1938. 47 die when Milwaukee train "Olympian" crashes near Miles City.
· 1939. Fort Peck Dam completed. Custer County Community College founded in Miles City.
· 1940. Bob Marshall Primitive area set aside. Dawson County Community College founded in Glendive. 55 mile per hour night-time speed limit established.
· July 12, 1940. First smokejumper fire jump made by Earl Cooley and Rufus Robinson at Martin Creek in the Nez Perce Forest.
· September 11, 1940. The 38-year-old Northern Hotel in Billings gutted by fire. The four-story, 200 room hotel was a total loss and damage was estimated at $750,000. Thirteen other businesses also burned, including the Buy for Less Drug, the Jane Drake Dress store, and the Oak Tavern, which displayed a number of relics which once belonged to Bill Cody. Electricity to much of downtown Billings was cut.

The Civilian Conservation Corps camp at Nine Mile as it appeared in August 1941. This was the largest CCC camp in the United States. USFS 413859

During the early 1940s, Region One of the U.S. Forest Service established national defense training schools in Montana. Here a student is being trained in auto mechanics. USFS

K. Howard, both Wheeler and Ford were "tired radicals" by 1941.

The third member of the group was not Jeannette Rankin, but her brother Wellington, the richest man in Montana and a major political player in Montana. Although he held no elective office in 1941, he had previously served as state attorney general, state Supreme Court justice, and U.S. district attorney. A Harvard Law School graduate, World War I veteran and son of a cattle rancher, he had amassed a fortune by purchasing bankrupt ranches in the 1930s.

The 1940 census counted just over half a million Montanans, 62 percent of them rural dwellers. Of that total, 16,841 were Native Americans and 1,120 were African-Americans. One out of every 10 Montanans had been born in a foreign country, and the total included 508 people of Japanese ancestry as well as 258 Chinese.

As the last months of 1941 came to a close, Montana's economy was still not fully recovered from the lingering after-effects of depression and drought, and like most Americans, Montanans were more concerned about matters at home than they were about events in far-off Europe and Asia. Half of all the banks in Montana had failed in the early '20s, years before the stock market crash of 1929 set off the Great Depression. By the early '30s, Montana farmland was selling for 50 cents an acre and cattle prices had plummeted to 5 cents per pound, and by the middle of the decade one quarter of all Montanans were on relief. New Deal programs like the Works Progress Administration (WPA), the Civilian Conservation Corps (CCC), and the National Youth Administration (NYA) did little to ease the suffering of many people, but they did have a lasting effect on Montana. By 1940, WPA workers in Montana had built 7,239 miles of highway, 1,366 bridges, 301 schools, 31 stadiums, 81 athletic fields, 30 swimming pools, 40 skating rinks, 16 golf courses, 10 ski jumps, and 10,000 outhouses. Two hundred people worked at the state headquarters of the WPA in Helena, and 275 others worked on projects in the Capital City. Another New Deal program was the National Youth Administration, which taught young men and women (aged 16-25) the fundamentals of stenography, auto mechanics, welding, and radio repair. The Helena branch of the NYA had a dining hall and barracks facilities for 70 women and 120 men. Beginning in 1933, the CCC had employed many young Montanans in the woods of the Forest Service's Region One, and also brought many young men from Eastern cities to the state. A CCC recruitment office was opened in Helena, and Fort Missoula became a supply center for the organization. During 1933, 67 CCC camps were built in the state. One of the largest of these was Camp Nine Mile, near Alberton, which housed up to 500 people during its peak. In the years prior to the war, 105,000 CCC enrollees worked in the forests of Region One. They constructed roads, bridges, trails, campgrounds, and forest lookouts, and also fought fires, planted trees, and worked on projects intended to eradicate

The "America First" committee meeting in Washington, D.C., during December 1940, just one year before the Pearl Harbor attack. FDR 74-20 (129)

Senator Burton K. Wheeler of Montana was a leader of the "America First" organization prior to America's involvement in World War II. FDR 74-20 (182)

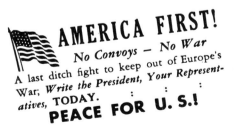

1941

- April 6. Germany invades Greece and Yugoslavia.
- April 13. Japan and Russia sign non-aggression pact.
- April 17. Yugoslavia surrenders to the Axis and Tito begins to organize guerrilla forces.
- June 22. Germany invades Russia in operation Barbarossa.
- July 13. England and Soviet Union sign a mutual aid agreement.
- August 14. Atlantic Charter agreement signed.
- August 25. British and Soviet troops occupy Iran.
- October. German forces on the outskirts of Moscow and Leningrad.
- November 17. Admiral Yamamoto and elements of the Combined Fleet leave Saeki Bay, Japan.
- November 29. Governor Ford addresses a convention of Native American leaders in Havre, telling them he thought that their treatment by the Federal government had been "shameful."
- December 3. "Victory Program" leaked to Sen. Burton K. Wheeler.
- December 4. Japanese fleet changes course towards Pearl Harbor.
- December 6. The British declare war on Finland, Hungary, and Rumania.

threatened to strike, and United Mine Workers in the state's coal mines did strike. Although wages in the state were low, (highly paid miners and smelter workers made $7.50 per day) so were prices. A new coal-wood range sold for $79.95. Electric vacuums (for those who had electricity) cost $9.95. Used appliances could be picked up for $5 to $20. Even houses in major Montana cities rarely cost more than $3,000 or $4,000.

Although America was still neutral in the war that was raging across Europe and Asia, the war's effects were reaching as far as Western Montana. In the Garden City of Missoula, 1,200 Italian citizens, most of them merchant seamen, were being detained at the frontier military post at Fort Missoula. Held by the U.S. Immigration and Naturalization Service for overstaying their visas, most of these men were crewmen from the luxury liner *Conte Biancamano*, which had been stranded in the U.S. Panama Canal Zone for 18 months after a Central

white pine blister rust. The largest New Deal program in the state was the construction of Fort Peck Dam, the largest earth-filled dam in the world, which employed 10,000 men.

By 1939 there were 12,000 manufacturing jobs in the state. The state's largest employer, the Anaconda Copper Mining Company had recently purchased mines in Chile and Mexico, and Montana workers feared that A.C.M. might close or cut back the Butte and Anaconda operations, eliminating some of the state's best jobs. One-third of all Montana workers were employed in agriculture and the state's farmers were still heavily dependent on the Federal government. Federal money was being used in the construction of many new dams around the state for flood control and irrigation, and Federal funds were also being used to reseed 1.5 million acres of the state with crested wheatgrass.

Logging began to improve in the late 1930s when several smaller lumber mills moved into the state and began competing with the larger concerns. As Montana's economy improved slightly during the late 1930s, labor unions began to exert their strength. In the waning months of 1941, railroad workers

Postal items of the Italian internees at Fort Missoula. SC

An aerial view of Fort Missoula showing the Italian barracks to the right. Only a few crumbling foundations remain at this site today. The Missoula Country Club golf course is in the bottom left. sc

This letter was mailed to an Italian detainee at Fort Missoula from Italy via neutral Portugal. Note the censor strips on each end of the envelope.

Italian detainees in the yard at Fort Missoula. The building in the background on the access road was the Fort's fire station and is still in existence. UM 84-294

Main entrance of the Fort Missoula Italian camp, 1942. UM 84-291

New arrivals to the Italian camp, 1942. UM 84-297 AND 298

American cruise. Many of her sailors had been indicted for damaging the ship's mechanisms, to prevent the ship from being seized and turned over to the British Navy. On the other hand, some of the sailors claimed the sabotage was to prevent their ship from returning to Benito Mussolini's fascist Italy. The Italians, many of whom were entertainers in a band and symphony, brought their musical instruments and three dogs with them when they began arriving in Missoula in mid-August of 1941. The performers from the *Conte Biancamano* included a string quartet, a musical trio, and a full-fledged symphony. They entertained their fellow prisoners and soon held regular public concerts for a small fee. Ten percent of their earnings were donated to a Missoula charity.

Missoula residents grew to like the Italians but during the first few months they were relieved to see the high fence going up around the perimeter of the Fort. Sixty-foot guard towers were constructed at the north and south gates and a dozen guards patrolled the grounds on foot and on horseback at all times. All visitors had to register at the gates, which were linked by telephone to the main office.

The Italian consul from Seattle visited Fort Missoula and told the men to be on their best behavior. Besides sailors, 62 Italians who had worked at the Italian pavilion at the 1939 New York World's Fair were also sent to Missoula for overstaying their visas. One of their fellow workers, Armando Tosi, managed to return to Italy, and gave an interview in which he characterized Fort Missoula as a concentration camp. Two Italian newspapers investigated his charges but found that the detention center at Fort Missoula had "...all the characteristics of a summer resort."

Camp administrators reported that while the Italians were generally poor housekeepers, they had several excellent cooks among them and the prisoners were soon enjoying spaghetti and fresh-baked bread. The Italians resented the ban on alcohol and it didn't take long before they were brewing wine out of raisins and figs. Reveille at the camp was at 6:00 a.m., followed by two roll calls at 8:00 a.m. and 8:00 p.m. For recreation the Italians played soccer and bocci ball, put on several plays, and showed off their artistic skills at an exhibit of their paintings in downtown Missoula. Building ship models became a popular pastime and there were religious services on Sundays. In an effort to increase attendance, the weekly ration of tobacco was given out at the end of the church services, and from then on attendance was nearly 100 percent.

Mario Cananero, one of the Italian detainees, in front of the Fort Missoula rec hall, 1942. UM 84-290

The kitchen crew at Fort Missoula, 1942. A U.S. Border Patrol guard appears to be fourth from left. UM 84-292

Mess hall for the Italian detainees at Fort Missoula. Notice the portraits of King Victor Emmanuele III (left) and Benito Mussolini (right) on the back wall. MHS PAC 84-34

Guards at Fort Missoula. MHS PAC 84-34

Not knowing that world events would soon shatter the peace of the holiday season, Montanans recuperating from the Thanksgiving weekend began to prepare for the Christmas season.

The society pages of local newspapers were filled with accounts of prominent citizens who had entertained guests for Thanksgiving dinner. Fancy restaurants offered full course meals for a dollar. In fashion news, shorter skirts and more revealing necklines were all the rage. At Montana State University in Missoula (hereafter referred to as the University of Montana) Coach George Dahlberg and his squad of 10 Grizzly basketball players (including future Grizzly coach Jack Swarthout) were practicing for their first road game of the season at Moscow, Idaho (they won 16-0). Adventurous souls were finding good skiing conditions at the rope tows near Red Lodge and Bear Canyon in Gallatin County.

Despite the upcoming holiday, the ominous threat of war hung over the country. Strategic materials and metals were being collected in Montana, mines were opening, and the FBI was training local policemen to detect saboteurs. Many people believed it was only a matter of time before President Roosevelt joined with Churchill and Stalin in opposing Hitler and his seemingly invincible Nazis. The war in Europe was on everyone's mind. The British, fighting desperately in North Africa against Rommel's tanks, had just widened the conflict by declaring war against Finland, Hungary, and Rumania. In the brutal cold of the Eastern front, German Panzer divisions had taken Rostov and were threatening Moscow. Hitler's ally Benito Mussolini had just survived an assassination attempt in Italy and was struggling to suppress dissent.

Tensions were also high on the other side of the globe as Japanese troops fought on the outskirts of Shanghai and were threatening to invade Thailand. U.S. Marines were being evacuated from that Chinese city, and high level talks were in progress between Washington and Tokyo in an attempt to prevent war.

President Roosevelt, who had spent Thanksgiving at his "Little White House" in Georgia, had little faith in the negotiations with the Japanese and publicly questioned their sincerity. A few days before Senator Wheeler released the Victory Program, Roosevelt expressed the opinion that in one year, "our boys in the military and naval academies may be fighting for the defense of American institutions."

Above: This model of a small fishing boat made by one of the Italian detainees, now in the possession of Mr. and Mrs. Norman Swanson of Missoula.
Below: This miniature life preserver was made by one of the Italian detainees. The Italians named Fort Missoula—Bella Vista for the beautiful view of the mountains from their location. HMFM

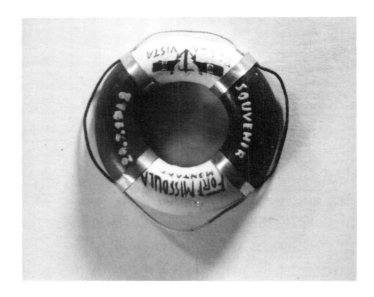

Some of those boys in the military were the 100 officers and 1,500 men of the Montana National Guard, who had been called to active duty in the fall of 1940. Along with members of the Idaho National Guard, they formed the backbone of the Army's 163rd Infantry Regiment stationed at Fort Lewis, Washington. After more than a year of intensive training, the men of the 163rd, who much to their dismay were known as the "Sheepherders," were highly trained infantrymen itching for a change in

THREE COMPANIES OF FORT MISSOULA SOLDIERS DEPART FOR UNANNOUNCED STATION

Three companies of soldiers of the First battalion of the Fourth infantry, commanded by Lieutenant Colonel Earl Landreth, left Fort Missoula by special train at 11:55 o'clock this morning for an unannounced port on the West coast. Three hundred and forty-nine men and seven officers were included in the force, composed of Companies A, B and C.

According to information from Fort Lewis, Wash., carried by the Associated Press, the troops are part of approximately 570 soldiers who will go to Anchorage, Alaska, "to provide protection for new airbases established in Alaska." On Tuesday, Company D, of the First battalion and the First battalion section of the service company, consisting of 132 men and two officers, left Fort Missoula by motor transport for Fort Lewis.

Officers on the staff of the force which left today, besides Colonel Landreth, were Captain E. H. Pulliam, supply officer; Captain M. C. Shattuck, adjutant; Captain John G. Hill; Captain Silas W. Hosea, commanding Company C; Captain R. G. Emory, commanding Company B; Lieutenant Robert P. Hagen, commanding Company A, and Lieutenant Samuel E. Shoemaker, attached to Company B.

Remaining at the post are Company G and a platoon of Company H, from Fort George Wright, Wash., which observers said may form the nucleus of a new force equalling or exceeding the force which has been moved.

Major Ednie in Command.

With the departure of Colonel Landreth, who has been in command of Fort Missoula since August 1, 1939, Major Alfred V. Ednie, executive officer, took command of the post. The medical detachment, under Colonel C. L. Vanderboget, and the quartermaster corps also are still stationed at the post. Colonel Landreth is to be replaced as commander of the Fort Missoula CCC district.

The troops which left today were transported by truck from the post to the Milwaukee railroad station, where a special train of 10 passenger cars and three baggage cars stood waiting. A large crowd, including wives, children and friends of the soldiers, was gathered at the station when the train pulled out.

Colonel H. F. Sykes, adjutant general of the Ninth Corps area and chief assistant to the commanding general of the area, has been at the fort to confer with officers on the troop movement.

At the post this morning, final preparations were being rushed for moving the troops. Stacked arms and full field equipment of the soldiers were standing on the drill ground, while duffle bags were piled in front of the barracks buildings. Trucks of the quartermaster corps, including new equipment recently issued to the unit, moved about hauling baggage and equipment or waiting in readiness to transport the men to the railway station.

Headquarters was a scene of intense activity as staff officers completed final details for the move.

Missoula Sentinel
June 20, 1940

Former Soldiers At Fort Thought To Be in Pacific

Names of 19 Listed; One Reported Killed in Action In War Zone.

At least 19 soldiers formerly stationed at Fort Missoula when the place, now an alien detention camp, was an Army post garrisoned by a battalion of the Fourth infantry, are now in the Philippines, Panama or Hawaii, it was learned last night.

A Missoula resident who was in the Army at Fort Missoula said 14 of the men were last reported to be in outfits stationed at various Army posts in several parts of the two groups of islands now under enemy attack.

Reported to be in the Philippines are First Sergeant John J. Dominquez, former "top kick" of Company C, Fourth infantry; Joe Banas, Otto Gebel, Edwin T. Dudley, Henry E. Sellers, Robert C. Milks, Allen T. Hendricksen and John J. Whitson.

Reported stationed in Hawaii are Jack Paich, well-known in Missoula as a baseball and basketball player on Fort Missoula teams; Frank Hynick, Henry Johnson, Robert Cory, Alvin Stiffler.

Men thought to be in Panama are Sergeant Gilbert Thrasher, Sergeant John J. Elias, Patrick Sullivan, Leonard Long and Floyd McMaster.

Appearing on the first casualty list, released Tuesday, was the name of Robert L. Schott, private first class, who was stationed at Fort Missoula for several months. Schott, son of Mrs. Hazel C. Schott of Elkhart, Ind., was killed in action.

December 11, 1941
Missoulian

routine. They were looking forward to Christmas leave, not knowing that a Japanese fleet was at that moment steaming across the Pacific.

Traveling under strict radio silence, the Japanese battle fleet was several hundred miles north of Midway Island when Admiral Yamamoto ordered a course change. On Thursday, December 4th, the same day that the release of the Victory Program caused such a stir in Washington, D.C., five Japanese aircraft carriers turned south, towards the Hawaiian Islands and the American naval base at Pearl Harbor.

The 163rd Infantry Regiment

The Montana National Guard made up the core of the 163rd Infantry Regiment, which in turn was a part of the 41st Division, originally composed of National Guard units from Idaho, Oregon, Washington, Montana, and Wyoming. When they were inducted into the Regular Army in 1940, the 163rd Infantry was comprised of men from these cities.
- 163rd Headquarters Company, Helena.
- 163rd band, Bozeman.
- 163rd Service Company, Bozeman
- 163rd Medical Detachment, Whitefish.
- Headquarters Company, First Battalion, Whitehall.
- C Company, First Battalion, Bozeman.
- D Company, First Battalion, Harlowton and Whitehall.
- Headquarters Company, Second Battalion, Bainville.
- E Company, Second Battalion, Culbertson and Wolf Point.
- F Company, Second Battalion, Kalispell.
- G Company, Second Battalion, Glasgow.
- H Company, Second Battalion, Billings.
- Headquarters Company, Third Battalion, Billings.
- I Company, Third Battalion, Great Falls.
- K Company, Third Battalion, Lewistown.
- L Company, Third Battalion, Billings.
- M Company, Third Battalion, Chinook, Bainville and Harlem.
- 163rd anti-tank platoon, Livingston.
- 116th Quartermaster Detachment, National Guard reserves from Bozeman and Malta.
- 116th Medical Detachment, Great Falls.

The Montana National Guard was organized 1884-1887 as the 1st Regiment of Infantry. It was redesignated the 1st Montana Volunteer Infantry and was mustered into Federal service in May 1898 at Helena. After serving in the Philippines during the Spanish-American War, the unit was mustered out October 17, 1899, at San Francisco. From 1901 to 1903, it was reorganized as the 2nd Infantry, Montana National Guard. It was again mustered into Federal service June 27, 1916, at Fort Harrison and was stationed at Douglas, Arizona, during the Mexican border troubles. The unit was mustered out of Federal service in November 1916, but was mustered back on April 7, 1917. It was combined with elements of the District of Columbia National Guard and was redesignated the 163rd Infantry Regiment of the 41st Division in September 1917. At the end of World War I, the 163rd was mustered out of Federal service once more, and reverted to the 2nd Infantry, Montana National Guard during 1921 and 1922. In May 1922, it was redesignated the 163rd Infantry, 41st Division, with headquarters at Helena. The headquarters was relocated to Billings in 1939. On September 16, 1940, the 163rd Infantry was once again mustered into Federal service as part of the 41st Infantry Division. After serving in the Southwest Pacific theater throughout World War II, the unit was deactivated in Japan on December 31, 1945. Six months later it became the 163rd Regimental Combat Team. In 1953 the Montana National Guard was redesignated as the 163rd Armored Cavalry.

Black Horse Shrine Patrol, Western Days Parade, Billings, 1940. MHS 941-111

Billings

As the end of 1941 approached the 42,000 residents of Yellowstone County were watching with interest as the 10-story brick exterior of the 205 ultra-modern Northern Hotel neared completion. L.W. Carter managed the Northern, as well as the 100 room Grand Hotel in Billings. In April 1943 another fire destroyed the Montgomery Wards building, causing $143,000 in damage.

H.E. Biddinger, mayor of Billings, was re-elected in 1945. The *Billings Gazette*, which like most of the other daily newspapers in the state was partially owned by the Anaconda Company, kept Billings residents informed about national news and updates on the war raging across Europe and Asia, but provided little local news, although it did report on the major crack-down on crime mounted by Billings police, who confiscated the bicycles of 13 boys and girls found guilty of traffic violations. Those seeking local information and entertainment often turned to the radio dial and NBC affiliate KGHL, which had been broadcasting in Billings since 1928.

Billings theatres in the 1940s included the Fox, the air-conditioned Rio and the rebuilt Babcock, which had been gutted by fire in 1935. Billings (Senior) High was built in 1941 to serve 1,500 students, and three years later construction of a Catholic high school (Billings Central) was being planned in the Magic City. Eastern Montana Normal College was founded in 1927 after Billings residents donated 52 acres for the campus. The Administration building, built in 1935, housed most of the departments, while classes were held in downtown Billings. Many of the current buildings on the campus were built in the years after the war. Eastern Montana Normal, which had 118 students in 1942, saw a precipitous decline during the war as enrollment fell to 47 students in 1943.

Billings had one other college, Billings Polytechnic, which was 33 years old in 1941. Dr. Ernest T. Eaton, founder and president of the college, also served as the state's lieutenant governor.

The war brought many changes to the Magic City. From July 1942 to November 1943 Northwest Airlines conducted a training center for the Air Transport Command at Logan Field. M-26 tank recovery vehicles and pontoons for Navy float planes were manufactured at assembly lines in Billings, and during the last year of the war Italian and German prisoners of war worked nearby sugar beet fields during the day and were held at a makeshift camp at the Great Northern sugar factory at night. Billings men made up the core of two companies (H and L) of the Army's 163rd Infantry Regiment.

2

☞ Montana Goes To War ☜

Most of the men on the light cruiser *USS Helena* were still in their bunks at 10 minutes before 8:00 a.m. on the fateful morning of December 7, 1941. The men of the ship's Marine detachment were warming up for a softball game on a nearby dock, while other members of the crew were preparing to go to church. The *Helena*, named for Montana's capital city, was tied up at the dock normally used by the flagship of the Pacific fleet, the *USS Pennsylvania*. An old minelayer, the *USS Oglala* was tied up on the far side of the *Helena*, directly across a narrow channel from Ford Island, where seven battleships of the Pacific fleet were moored.

A lookout on deck watched as five low-flying planes dived out of the sun. He assumed they were American planes until the last plane peeled off and dove straight for the *Helena*, releasing its torpedo in midchannel. The torpedo passed under the ancient *Oglala* and tore into the engine room of the *Helena*. The resulting blast ripped a 40-foot hole in the *Helena*'s hull and roared through the open passageways of the ship, incinerating 40 sailors and wounding 90 more. "There was guys on the docks stacked up like cordwood" reported Bill Sundermeyer of Darby, one of the Montanans aboard. The *Helena*'s forward main reduction gear, 21 tons of metal, was ripped from its moorings, damaging the massive propeller and turbine shafts of the cruiser.

It was 7:55 a.m. and the day that "would live in infamy" was just beginning. Suddenly the air was filled with darting Japanese planes, bursts of antiaircraft fire, and the oily black smoke of burning ships. On the shattered deck of the *Helena*, machine gunners began firing back at the Japanese planes while engineers frantically worked to pump out the water that was pouring into the engine room. The gun crews of the *Helena* shot down several Japanese planes, put a hole in the smokestack of a neighboring ship and nearly shot Rear Admiral Furlong off the deck of the *Oglala*. When a bomb destroyed a snack wagon on the adjacent dock, some of the *Helena*'s gunners took advantage of a lull in the fighting and dashed ashore to fill their pockets with candy bars. The torpedo explosion had burst the seams of the *Oglala* and the old ship was towed to deeper water

where it capsized and sank two hours after being hit.

Thirteen minutes after the *Helena* was struck, a bomb set off a massive explosion in the *USS Arizona*'s boilers and forward ammunition magazine, sealing the fate of 1,100 sailors.

Two hours after it began, the attack was over and the Japanese planes were on their way back to the carriers. Twenty-four hundred Americans lay dead, including 68 civilians. The huge base at Pearl Harbor was a smoking shambles. Eight ships had been sunk and 13 more, including the *Helena*, had been badly damaged. Capt. James D. O'Brien of Billings, operations and training officer of the 24th Division, and Sgt. John A. Heisler of Billings were both awarded the Legion of Merit for their actions at Pearl Harbor. Capt. James Shoemaker of Helena commanded the Pearl Harbor Naval Air Station during the attack, and later commanded the Norfolk Naval Air Station.

Montanans, like most Americans, heard the news over the radio, and the news was all bad. Reports of Japanese air raids began coming in from American forces in the Philippines, Guam, Wake, and Midway Island. Japanese attacks were also reported in Hong Kong, Singapore, Thailand, and Shanghai. The news was greeted with stunned silence at first, then increasing anger. Sen. Burton K. Wheeler, one of the most prominent isolationists in the country was staying at the B.R. Albin home in Billings where a *Gazette* reporter found him very agitated and walking in circles. Asked for his reaction, Wheeler called for an immediate declaration of war. "Let's lick hell out of them," he said. "We must now exert our every energy not only to win but to give the Japanese such a whipping that they will not want war again."

Gov. Sam Ford was in Missoula for the welcoming ceremony of the University's new president, Dr. Ernest Melby. Ford told reporters he was "...still about half-stunned by the sudden amazing news." He asked police to be extra vigilant and called an emergency meeting with other state officials to coordinate the defense of the state's airfields, dams, refineries, bridges and highways. Since the entire Montana National Guard was serving with the 163rd Infantry Regiment, American Legion members volunteered to guard the smelters at Anaconda, East

USS Helena (CL-50). MHS 951-399

The scene at 1010 dock at Pearl Harbor on December 7, 1941. Men from the capsized *USS Oglala* set up a first aid station and mounted four .30-caliber machine guns (salvaged from the *Oglala* before she rolled over) on the dock. The *USS Helena* is just ahead of the *Oglala*. NA 80-G-464887

14

The Oregonian

ESTABLISHED BY HENRY L. PITTOCK
An Independent Republican Newspaper
Published Daily, Except Sunday, by The Oregonian
Publishing Company, Oregonian Bldg., 537 S. W. Sixth
Ave., Portland, Oregon. Telephone AT 2121.
Sole ownership of The Oregonian resides in the
H. L. Pittock Family and the Scott Company
CAROLINE P. LEADBETTER,   PALMER HOYT,
President   Publisher
The Oregonian is a member of the Associated Press.
The Associated Press is exclusively entitled to the use
for publication of all news dispatches credited to it or
not otherwise credited in this paper, and also the local
news published herein. All rights of publication of spe-
cial dispatches herein are also reserved.
National Advertising Offices—Paul Block and Asso-
ciates, 400 Madison ave., New York city; Detroit; 1420
igan ave., Chicago; General Motors bldg., San Fran-
Walnut, Philadelphia; Monadnock bldg., Los Angeles; 1411
cisco; Chamber of Commerce bldg., Seattle; Little bldg., Boston.
Fourth Avenue bldg., Seattle; Little bldg., Boston.

DECEMBER 10, 1941

Remember Pearl Harbor!
The reactions of the American citizen of the
Pacific coast to the opening of war with Japan
are not different from those of his fellow citizen in another part of the country, except that

The first mention of "Remember Pearl Harbor" was in *The Oregonian*, December 10, 1941.

Sam C. Ford, governor of Montana from 1941 to 1949.
MHS 942-245

December 1941

- December 7. Japanese attack Pearl Harbor, eight battleships sunk or put out of action, 3,000 casualties.
- December 8. Jeannette Rankin casts only dissenting vote in Congress on entry into WWII.
- December 9. Air raids reported in San Francisco.
- December 10. The *Billings Gazette* begins carrying pictures of aircraft insignia to aid in identification of American planes.
- December 12. Train collision in Great Falls leads some residents to believe an air raid is underway.
- December 13. Soviets claim to have killed 85,000 Germans in front of Moscow. The British attack west of Tobruk.

Killed at Pearl Harbor

- Yeoman 1st Class Lloyd M. Daniel of Livingston, private secretary to Admiral Kidd, *USS Arizona*.
- Shipfitter 2nd Class Harold H. Scilley, Butte, *USS Arizona*.
- Radio Technician Charles P. Fisk III, Hysham, *USS Arizona*.
- Electricians Mate 3rd Class Gerald Fraser Dullum, East Helena and a 1939 graduate of Helena High, *USS Arizona*.
- Corporal Donald L. Meagher, 1939 graduate of Great Falls High. He was killed manning a machine gun in a parked bomber.
- Seaman Earl L. Morrison, Sidney.
- Sergeant Carlo A. Micheleto, Sidney.
- Coxswain George D. Smart, Polson.

Sports

Early in 1942, Ben Hogan and Sam Snead were battling for the lead in the Miami Open Golf tourney. Boxer Joe Louis and American League batting champ Ted Williams passed their physicals and were inducted into the army as privates earning less than a dollar a day.

Former Montana Grizzly football standout Eso Naranche intercepted a pass in the Shriner's East-West All Star Game, held in New Orleans on January 4.

In other news, the Montana Grizzlies provided some relief from the dismal world situation by racking up 13 straight victories on the basketball court, including two hotly contested games against the Bobcats, before traveling to Idaho to play the Vandals, where they were defeated 49 to 28. The Bobcats retaliated for their earlier losses by defeating the Grizzlies in the last two games of the season.

Missoula

A city of 29,000 residents in the early 1940s, Missoula was destined to lose 13 percent of its population in just two and a half years. Missoula had two newspapers, The *Daily Missoulian*, edited by French Ferguson, and the afternoon *Missoula Sentinel*, both of which were wholly owned by the Anaconda Copper Mining Company. A better source of local news was the radio station. A radio station had operated in the Wilma Building as early as 1923-24. The equipment from this station was eventually transferred to the University, where it was used to operate KUOM, which began transmitting in 1925 with a Missoula symphony broadcast which was heard from Florida to Alaska. KUOM featured local programming and talent but was forced to shut down four years later because of poor equipment, leaving Missoula without a local station until CBS affiliate KGVO began broadcasting in 1931. Movie goers patronized the Wilma, Rio and Rialto. Missoula groceries included the Stop N' Shop across from the Post office at Pattee and E. Broadway, the SuperSave on Alder and the Red and White Food Stores. Buttreys was a woman's clothing store on N. Higgins, and the Mercantile was a local landmark.

Missoula underwent a rash of fires in early 1942, starting with a New Year's Day blaze on North Higgins that destroyed or damaged several businesses. In February a fire destroyed a warehouse at Swanberg Lumber Company, and one of the fire engines called to the scene unwittingly carried a live spark back to the Orchard Homes volunteer fire department. During the night, the fire station and the fire engine went up in flames. In other Missoula news, School District 1 officials postponed a $40,000 addition to Paxson school because of war-related shortages in construction materials. C.S. Porter was the superintendent of Missoula schools, and Missoula High graduated 169 students in 1945. By the spring of 1945 2,500 Missoula residents were serving in the armed forces. The county would lose 166 men during the war.

Broadway Street in Missoula, looking east (southside) April 1942. LC USF34-65649

Broadway Street in Missoula, looking east (northside) April 1942. LC

Jeannette Rankin made headlines around the country for her vote against America's entry into World War II as she had also done in 1917.

Monument to Jeannette Rankin in the Jeannette Rankin Peace Park in Missoula.

Helena, Great Falls, and the mines at Butte.

Most of the 1,500 Montanans in the 163rd Infantry Regiment had been issued weekend passes and only heard of the Japanese attack when they returned to Fort Lewis, Washington on Sunday night. They were immediately trucked to the Olympic Peninsula to guard against an anticipated Japanese attack on the West Coast.

National hysteria set in. The *Missoulian* headline on December 9 read "Unidentified Planes Approach Southern California!" "Frisco Repulses Jap Raid" read the *Billings Gazette* headlines.

In Washington, D.C., Montana Congresswoman Jeannette Rankin heard the news of the attack on Pearl Harbor at her sister's house. She boarded a train from Washington to Detroit, and on the train, she heard that Congress would meet the next day in emergency session. She left the train at Pittsburgh and returned to Washington, then spent much of the next morning driving around the capital alone so that no one, not even her brother Wellington, could reach her. A dedicated pacifist who had campaigned for her seat on a peace platform, she wanted to speak to no one who might try and influence her vote. When the U.S. House met on the afternoon of the eighth, she tried to get other congressmen to debate the war resolution, but Speaker Sam Rayburn would not allow it and told her to sit down. At the vote, she spoke up in violation of protocol. "As a woman I can't go to war, and I refuse to send anyone else." She was hissed and booed by the gallery as well as by her fellow congressmen, who voted 338 to 1 for war. She cast the sole dissenting vote. In the Senate, the vote for war was unanimous, leaving Jeannette Rankin in a very lonely position.

William Allen White, editor of the *Emporia Gazette* wrote that, "Probably 100 men in Congress would have liked to do what she did. Not one of them had the courage to do it. The *Gazette* entirely disagrees with the wisdom of her position. But Lord, it was a brave thing!....When in one hundred years from now, courage, sheer courage based on moral indignation, is celebrated in this country, the name of Jeannette Rankin who stood firm in folly for her faith, will be written in monumental bronze not for what she did but for the way she did it."

For the moment though, the congresswoman from Montana was so hounded by hostile onlookers that she was forced to seek refuge in a phone booth, where she finally called the Capitol switchboard. Capitol police thought she might be in danger and

they arrived to escort her home past the reporters snapping her photo. Her brother Wellington phoned her that night to tell her, "Montana is 110 percent against you." Within days, the commander of the Montana American Legion called for her resignation, and she was vilified in angry letters from Montanans and others around the country. She also received many letters supporting her stand. On the 11th of December, she voted "Present" during the declaration of war on Germany and Italy.

Everyone's nerves were on edge. Great Falls residents were sure an air raid was underway one day when a loud crash echoed through town. It turned out to be a train collision. The reality of war had thrown a wet blanket over the entire Christmas season. Movies starring Bob Hope, Abbott and Costello, and W.C. Fields were playing at local theaters, but in those final dark days of 1941, most people were in no mood for comedy. Instead, people all around the state gathered around their radios, listening to the steady stream of bad news.

Some semblance of normalcy remained in the state however, and a few loggers working in remote areas of Western Montana emerged from the woods just before Christmas and were shocked to learn that their country had been at war for two weeks.

Throughout December, the Army and Navy recruiting offices in Butte, Helena, and Missoula were jammed with young men wanting to enlist, and the recruiters were apparently not too picky about who they signed up. Officials in Helena were willing to accept a nine-year-old boy as a bugler, but the boy's mother refused to give her permission. Fourteen-year-old Leo Peltier of Eureka was allowed to enlist, however. (PFC Peltier served for four years. He celebrated his 18th birthday four days after VE Day.)

Fifty-seven hundred Montanans joined the armed forces in 1941, and although two-thirds of them were draftees, some 1,600 men enlisted in the state in the weeks following Pearl Harbor. More than $9 million worth of war bonds were sold in the state by the end of the year.

The Army induction center in Missoula was damaged in a New Years Day fire which also destroyed the Shapard Hotel and Gambles Auto supply, but the fire damage didn't stop another 800 Montanans from signing up in January. The Missoula enlistees were sworn in at the Higgins Building, then marched to the railroad station where they boarded the Northern Pacific Railroad for Fort

Douglas, Utah, or Fort Lewis, Washington.

Newspapers across the state scrambled to identify Montanans known to be in the war zone, and several men from Helena and Townsend were reported to be prisoners of the Japanese on Wake Island. Dr. and Mrs. Chester Lawson (Dr. Lawson was born in Kalispell and lived in Havre) were missionaries in China who were captured by the Japanese in China immediately after the attack on Pearl Harbor. They were repatriated on the *SS Gripsholm* two years later.

A week after the attack on Pearl Harbor, Montanans learned that Pvt. Leroy Carpenter of Butte had been killed in the fighting in the Philippines, the first reported death of a Montana man during World War II.

In the weeks following Pearl Harbor, several racially motivated attacks against Asians were recorded in the state, forcing the Missoula County Sheriff to take five men of Japanese ancestry into protective custody after a train crew threatened to lynch them near Superior. The state attorney general finally warned Montanans to be tolerant of the estimated 17,000 foreign nationals living in the Treasure State. All Japanese, Italian, and German nationals in the U.S. were ordered to turn in their cameras, shortwave radios and firearms. Refusal to do so was punishable by imprisonment. Prior to Pearl Harbor, the FBI had classified some of the Japanese nationals and Japanese-Americans living on the West Coast by their perceived threat. Diplomats, fishermen and fish producers, Shinto and Buddhist priests, and community leaders were des-

---

Shep: The Faithful Collie

On January 12, 1942, one of Montana's best known residents was killed in Fort Benton. Shep was a part collie who had been meeting the train in Fort Benton every day since 1936, searching for the sheep-herder master who had died and whose body had been shipped east on the train. Trainmen took care of the dog and Shep was well-known to frequent travelers. Several national publications had featured stories on the dog, and the townspeople of Fort Benton and the train conductors were heartbroken when he was struck by a train and killed. Shep is still fondly remembered in Fort Benton, and in 1992, on the 50th anniversary of his untimely demise, 200 people gathered to honor the faithful collie. Fort Benton residents are planning to erect a statue of Shep near the train depot where he died.

---

ignated "A" or Known Dangerous. Others who might be dangerous but who had not yet been investigated were given a "B" rating. Japanese language teachers, editors, and martial arts instructors were classified "C" for being pro-Japanese. Within hours after the attack on Pearl Harbor, more than 600 people on this ABC list were rounded up, despite the fact that some were loyal citizens of the United States. The place chosen to house these first Japanese internees was the Immigration and Naturalization facility at Fort Missoula.

The Japanese men began arriving in Missoula 11 days after Pearl Harbor. A Korean who was traveling on the same train was beaten at the Missoula train depot because he looked oriental. Before the beating he had been planning on enlisting in the Army. The Japanese internees averaged 60 years of age and several died almost immediately, one on the first day in Missoula. In the next few weeks hundreds of Japanese began arriving, as well as a few more Italian nationals who had been rounded up. The Italians, most of whom had overstayed their visas, were now reclassified as enemy aliens. Even so, they were treated better than the Japanese. The Japanese detained at Fort Missoula were kept separate from the Italians and the two groups did not mix. By the end of December, 650 Japanese and Japanese-American community leaders from the West Coast states were being held at Fort Missoula.

Despite America's declaration of war against their country, five of the Italian officers interned at Fort Missoula occupied their time repairing toys to

---

January 1942

- January 1. New Years Day fire in downtown Missoula destroys Shapard Hotel, Gambles Auto Supply, and damages Yandt's Men's Store and the Army induction center.
- January 2. Manila falls to the Japanese.
- January 8. Soviet offensive begins at Sevastopol.
- January 11. Japanese land in the Dutch East Indies.
- January 12. Collie "Shep" killed at Fort Benton.
- January 23. Montana Grizzlies defeat Western Montana Normal 57-35.
- January 30. Montana Grizzlies defeat the Bobcats 47-44. The following day the Grizzlies again beat their arch-rival, 44-43 on a free throw in the final seconds.

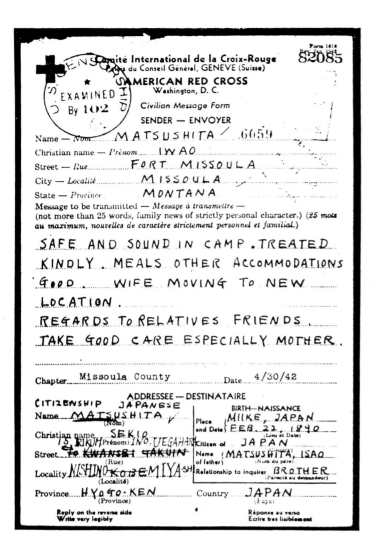

be given as Christmas presents to Missoula children. Mrs. Russell Neal, the community chest officer who organized the repairs, thought the seamen were doing a "splendid and careful job." The Immigration and Naturalization Service hired other sailors to do construction work, weaving, sewing, furniture making, and blacksmithing. They were paid 80 cents a day. The major problem reported among the Italians was inactivity, and the camp doctor reported a significant rise in "neuroses" due to the boredom of incarceration.

In the early days of 1942 the news from the various war fronts was all bad. Manila had fallen to the Japanese and the surviving American troops in the Philippines were retreating into the Bataan Peninsula and the island fortress of Corregidor, where they would make their futile last stand. The Japanese Imperial Army landed in the Dutch East Indies, and a month later in Burma. Singapore soon fell, and at the end of February Allied Naval forces lost the battle of the Java Sea. The Nazis were rolling across the Soviet Union, and closer to home, German and Japanese submarines were preying on U.S. shipping only a few miles from the American coasts.

Everyone in the state seemed to be doing something for the war effort. Those too old for the military joined rifle and pistol clubs. Since the men of the Montana National Guard were serving with the Regular Army on the west coast, a battalion of the 164th Infantry (the North Dakota National Guard, which had also been sent to Montana during World War I) was sent to Montana in January and February to guard the state's vital industries against sabotage. This made some long-time residents wonder which was worse, the threat of Nazi paratroopers or the reality of armed North Dakotans.

Montana women collected thousands of books

Postal items to and from Iwao Matsushita, a Japanese-American internee at Fort Missoula.

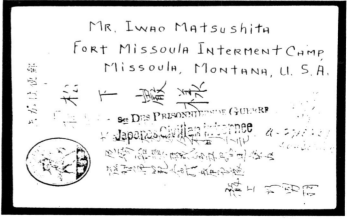

Japanese-American internees display their creations from stones picked up in their confinement area at Fort Missoula, 1942.
MHS 84-34

A baseball team at Fort Missoula made up of Japanese-Americans from Hawaii. Left to right, front row: Tomoichi Hayashi, Ryuichi Kashima, Kazumi Matsumoto and Shujiro Takakuwa. Center row: Masayuki Iwata, Kumaji Furuya, Goki Takiguchi, Yoshinobu Sasaki and Masahiro Himeno. Third row: Soichi Obata, Akio Kimura, Isaku Orita, Tamaki Arita, Masato Kiyozaki and Suijo Kabashima.

(15,000 by the end of February) and sent them to servicemen. At the request of the Army, school children around the state donated 2,000 airplane models for use in aircraft identification. They also went door to door collecting tin and scrap metal. On several of the state's Indian Reservations, Native Americans were learning the fundamentals of welding and metal fabrication, skills that were in short supply. Thirteen hundred students were attending Montana State University at Missoula and many were taking the new course in radio repair. Montana State College at Bozeman added courses in farm machinery repair to meet the expected demand in that field.

In an effort to combat venereal disease, Gov. Sam Ford urged men to observe a Social Hygiene Day. Girl Scout leaders met in Billings to decide how they could best help the war effort, and in January Cascade County veterans began lobbying Congress for an air base and war plants based in Great Falls.

With so many men enlisting, state agriculture officials were becoming worried about labor to pick the sugar beets and were trying to get approval to bring in migrant workers. The impending labor shortage soon came to the attention of Senator Murray, chairman of the Senate Small Business Committee, and he promised to bring more Mexican and Japanese farm laborers into the state. Murray also tried to ease the burden of car dealers and others hurt by the rationing programs that were being drawn up, and pushed to get more gas for Montana's farmers and loggers.

With the Japanese firmly in control of much of the Pacific, America was cut off from its major suppliers of oil and rubber. German submarines operating in the Caribbean greatly reduced the amount of sugar reaching the U.S. Shortages of these items became apparent almost immediately, and the lack of tires and sugar caused a good deal of concern in Montana. Tires were strictly rationed and each county was allotted a certain number. Very few were available to the public, although clergymen were exempted from the ban on tire buying. Even retread tires were rationed, and the shortages resulted in a wave of tire thefts. In an attempt to reduce wear on tires, the state set a speed limit of 50 miles an hour, 45 miles an hour for state vehicles (this was later reduced to 35 miles an hour). The military allocated $5 million in emergency funds to improve Montana highways even though the production of family cars was ordered halted on February 1. Cattle ranchers predicted that if the transportation situation got any worse, they would have to resort to old fashioned cattle drives.

The supply of sugar was controlled even more tightly than the supply of tires. Rationing cards were issued and each person was restricted to three quarters of a pound of sugar each week. Shoppers were required to report how much sugar they had at home before they could buy any more, and hoarding sugar was punishable by a $10,000 fine or 10 years in prison.

Navy officials were deciding the fate of two ships with Montana connections. One was the battleship *USS Montana*, under construction at a shipyard. The other was the badly damaged *USS Helena*. It was finally decided to scrap the *USS Montana* because new developments had made the 903-foot long, 58,000-ton battleship obsolete even before it was finished. The *Helena*, on the other hand, was vitally needed for the war effort and it was decided to tow the damaged cruiser to Mare Island, California, for major repairs. Work crews at Pearl Harbor began readying the *Helena* for a long and dangerous sea voyage.

February 1942

· February 1. Blackfeet tribal leader Mountain Chief died in Browning at age 94.
· February 8. Burma invaded by the Japanese.
· February 9. "War Time" instituted to save electricity.
· February 15. Singapore falls to the Japanese.
· February 19. Federal inspectors begin visiting junkyards to survey them for usable scrap metal.
· February 20. Delegates to 1942 High School week focused on the opportunities for war time training at Montana colleges.
· February 22. Grizzlies win 13th consecutive game 75-49 over Whitman College.
· February 23. Missoula Spartans led the state with 12 wins and three losses.
· February 26. The Bobcat basketball team defeats the Grizzly basketball team twice in two days 44-30, 46-42.
· February 27. Allies lose the battle of the Java Sea.

3

☞ The National Guard Goes Down Under ☜

As the snow began to melt on the Montana prairie, the 135,000 radios in the state kept blaring out bad news from the Pacific. Singapore had fallen, American forces in the Philippines were retreating further into the Bataan Peninsula, and the Japanese had landed in New Guinea. This latest attack by the Japanese threatened northern Australia, where most of the men were away fighting in North Africa, and the Australian government called for help. President Roosevelt agreed to send two divisions of American troops to guard Australia, and the "Sheepherders" of the 163rd Infantry Regiment finally received their marching orders. After a stint guarding Washington state beaches against an anticipated Japanese attack, they left Fort Lewis aboard a train bound for San Francisco. Three to four hundred of the former National Guardsmen were transferred to other duties at this time, including a number of World War I veterans considered too old for the rigors of combat. On arrival in California, the National Guardsmen were immediately hustled aboard the troopship (luxury liner *Queen Elizabeth*) which would carry them across the submarine-infested waters of the Pacific. They were among the first Army troops sent overseas during World War II.

They were at sea two-and-a-half weeks before the *Queen Elizabeth* docked in Sydney, Australia, where a Japanese invasion was expected at any moment. Relieved to be on solid ground again, hundreds of Guardsmen trooped down the gangway during the first week of April. As they began training for jungle warfare at their new camp north of Brisbane, their understandable nervousness deepened as radio bulletins from the Philippines confirmed that 12,000 starving Americans and more than 60,000 Filipino soldiers had just surrendered to the Japanese. Within days, shocking reports began filtering out of the Philippines, accounts of Japanese atrocities committed on American prisoners of war during what would soon be called the Bataan Death March.

Dozens of Montanans were captured in the Philippines, including several doctors, among them Dr. William B. Dineen of Missoula, and Dr. Charles Leach, the son-in-law of Joseph Dixon, a former Governor and U.S. Senator. A number of missionaries from Montana were also captured by the Japanese, and in several cases whole families were interned under brutal conditions.

A week after the Montana National Guardsmen arrived in Australia, Col. Jimmy Doolittle led a daring raid of 16 B-25 bombers which took off from an aircraft carrier and bombed Tokyo. Two of the 80 "Raiders" were Montanans, David Thatcher of Billings and Edward Saylor of Brusett. Both survived the raid and the subsequent crash-landings in China and returned to Montana as heroes. Thatcher, a modest man who saved the lives of the other four members of his crew, suddenly found himself a celebrity. "When we were first told what the 'special mission' was to be, I just thought it would be a lot of fun, but I honestly never expected to come back." After a harrowing take-off from the deck of the *USS Hornet*, Thatcher watched as his B-25, piloted by Lt. Ted Lawson, skimmed over the ocean. They were flying so low that Japanese swimmers waved as they passed over the beach and headed for their target, the Nippon machinery works and steel factory. "As we let go our first load I saw a great column of black smoke and debris shoot into the air....the antiaircraft fire was pretty heavy. It jarred the plane around it was so close, but I'm sure we weren't hit." Flying on, their B-25 eventually ran short of fuel and crashed in the ocean just short of the China coast. All five members of the crew made it to shore, but they were all badly injured except Thatcher. The young corporal from Billings bound their wounds and helped find shelter. According to an official War Department release, "All this plane's crew were either saved from capture or death as a result of Corporal Thatcher's initiative and courage in assuming responsibility and tending the wounds himself day and night and arranging for the transportation of his companions." Chinese guerrillas helped them elude the Japanese patrols sent to find them and all of the men eventually reached safety, but Lawson's leg was so badly infected that it had to be amputated along the way. Lawson wrote down his experiences in the best-selling *Thirty Seconds Over Tokyo*, which was soon made into a major Hollywood film starring Spencer Tracy and Robert Mitchum. Robert Walker

Philippines

· Lt. William M. Raining, Billings, posthumously won two Silver Stars and the Distinguished Flying Cross for his part in evacuating Americans from the Philippines. He was killed in a plane crash in Australia in 1942.
· Kenneth I. Scott of Great Falls was a crewmember of the *USS Trout* in February 1942 when the submarine evacuated the Philippine treasury, some two tons of gold and 18 tons of silver from Corregidor. Scott and the other members of the crew were awarded Silver Stars for their part in this mission. Scott was still with the Trout on her 11th war patrol, when on February 29, 1944 she was sunk with all hands off Okinawa after torpedoing two Japanese transports, sinking one.
· Sgt. Russell Huffman of Highwood was a gunner aboard the B-17 that evacuated Gen. Douglas MacArthur and family from Del Monte airfield in the Southern Philippines in mid-March. After flying the commander of the Southwest Pacific theater to Australia, Huffman's crew returned to Del Monte and flew three more missions, including evacuating 16 members of the PT boat crew that had taken MacArthur from Corregidor to Mindanao. Huffman, who had lost all of his belongings when his barracks at Clark Field in the Philippines had been bombed during the first hours of the war, later chronicled his amazing experiences throughout the Southwest Pacific in a series of articles entitled "A Montana Gunner in Pacific Skies" which appeared in the *Great Falls Tribune* during the spring of 1944. Huffman survived several crash-landings, bailed out at 32,000 feet off the New Guinea coast, and once crash-landed a riddled B-17 after all of the officers had been killed or wounded. Huffman participated in raids on Java, Rabaul, and New Guinea. During the first year of the war Huffman shot down 19 Japanese planes, spent three terrifying nights as an infantryman on Bataan, encountered cannibals and sharks, and witnessed more history in a few months than most people do in a lifetime. He was awarded the Silver Star with three oak leaf clusters, as well as a Purple Heart.

Bataan

· Sgt. George Banfield of Butte was captured at Marivales on Bataan. After he was liberated from Bilibid prison almost four years later, he said, "Two things stand out as nothing less than amazing in connection with the death march. The first is that human beings could undergo such physical and mental punishment and the second is that so-called human beings could be as brutal as the Nips proved themselves to be during the march."
· Col. Carlton L. Vanderboget, the senior medical officer at Clark Field, was wounded in Bataan March 26, 1942 when a shell hit the vehicle he was in, killing several of his comrades. He was sent to Bilibid prison, where he described the conduct of the Japanese, "there are no words in the English language that could exaggerate or fully express the extent and nature of the atrocities they have committed." By the time he returned to his home in Missoula he had lost nearly 100 pounds.
· Tech. Sgt. Tracey Tucker spent 19 months in a Japanese prison camp in the Philippines before escaping. He claimed that a Japanese student he knew at Whitefish High was serving as a Japanese officer in the prison camp.
· Mr. and Mrs. Paul Fourtner of Butte were informed twice in one day that two of their three sons had died in Japanese prison camps after being captured in the Philippines.

March 1942

· March 6. Distribution of sugar rationing books begins at local grade schools.
· March 8. Japanese forces land in New Guinea.
· March 13. Washing machine production halted, bicycle production curtailed, typewriters rationed.
· March 14. Abandoned Civilian Conservation Corps camps in Montana turned over to the military.
· March 15. Missoula Spartans beat Helena 53-22 in the Northern Division Championships.
· March 19. Luxury liner *Queen Elizabeth* leaves San Francisco with Montana National Guardsmen aboard.
· March 21. Train collision in Missoula.
· March 23. Japanese troops occupy the Andaman Islands.

Crew of plane #7 on the Doolittle Tokyo Raid. Left to right: Lt. Charles L. McClure (navigator); Lt. Ted W. Lawson (pilot); Lt. Robert S. Clever (bombardier); Lt. Dean Davenport (co-pilot); Sgt. David J. Thatcher (engineer-gunner). Thatcher was originally from the Billings area, and now lives in Missoula. USAF 94606

Butte

Population of Silver Bow County 53,207 (1940 census). Mayor Barry O'Leary served throughout the war years, and was re-elected to a third term in the Spring of 1945.

As it had been for many years, the Mining City of Butte was dominated by the Anaconda Copper Mining Company, and the hill beneath Butte was honeycombed with 2,000 miles of tunnels. Most of the miners lived in three suburbs in northeast Butte, Centreville, Walkerville, and Meaderville, home of the famous Leonard Mine, which was open to visitors before the war. Because of its mines, Butte was declared a vital defense area within days after Pearl Harbor. Rents were frozen and air raid shelters were set up in some of the abandoned mines beneath the city. More than 100 men joined the local chapter of War Dads. The Montana School of Mines started in 1900 and had a student body of 450 by the 1940s. Professor A.E. Adami was appointed Dean of the Montana School of Mines in 1943. The school, which consisted of six brick buildings, was the smallest unit of the state university system and offered courses in mining, metallurgy, geology and petroleum engineering. Throughout the war years virtually the entire student body at Mines consisted of Navy engineering students.

Butte boasted four theaters, as well as the Art Center on Montana Street, which was founded in 1938 as part of a Federal Art Project. The Columbia Gardens amusement park, built by copper king W.A. Clark in 1898, was a popular entertainment center among Butte residents which featured a roller coaster, playground, pansy gardens, picnic grounds and a pavilion where dances were held every summer night.

The news media in Butte consisted of NBC affiliate KXLF, which had operated since 1929, and the *Montana Standard* and the evening *Butte Daily Post*, both owned by the Company. More than 40 hotels and countless rooming houses dotted the hill. St. James Hospital was newly remodeled and boasted 210 beds. After a fire damaged the army induction center and x-ray machines in Missoula, the center was moved to Butte early in 1942, partly because Butte was a hub of railroading, with the Northern Pacific, Union Pacific, Milwaukee Road, Great Northern, and the Butte, Anaconda, and Pacific passing through town. The railroads brought approximately half a million servicemen through town each year.

played the part of David Thatcher, the teenage flyer from Billings.

Many Montanans escaped the depressing war news for a few hours each week by joining 50 million other Americans in attending the movies. After only a few months the war was already having a detrimental affect on the number of new Hollywood films being released, and the popularity of gangster movies gave way to war films. One of the first of these to reach Montana theaters was the Ronald Reagan film, *International Squadron*. *Dive Bomber* starred Errol Flynn, Fred MacMurray, and Ralph Bellamy and was described as "Rowdy, Reckless, and Romantic." More notable releases of 1942 were *Wake Island* and Alfred Hitchcock's *Saboteur*. Even the Saturday morning cartoon features, (referred to in some theaters as the "Slap the Jap" shows), reflected the country's obsession with the war. *Donald Duck Gets Drafted* shared the bill with Popeye features like *Many Tanks* and *Fleets of Strength*. Hollywood stars with Montana connections included actress Myrna Loy, originally from Radersburg, and actor George Montgomery, who owned a cabin near Lincoln.

In May, Allied airpower defeated the Japanese fleet in the Battle of the Coral Sea, although the carrier *USS Lexington* was lost with several sailors from the Treasure State aboard. At the same time, Japanese troops overran the fortified island of Corregidor in Manila Bay, the last American stronghold in the Philippines. At home, the casualty lists of Montanans killed or missing in the Pacific began to mount.

In Montana the war was beginning to affect every facet of life. All lumber sales in the state were diverted to military use and several large war-related construction projects were announced. Momentum had been building in the lobbying effort to bring an Army Air Force base and defense jobs to Great Falls, and Congress set aside $3 million to begin construction of a base just outside of the Electric City. Congress announced in March that the proposed new highway to Alaska would run through the tiny town of Sweetgrass, and a huge irrigation and hydropower dam was planned for Canyon Ferry on the Missouri River (it would not be built until after the war). The threat of sabotage to the hydroelectric dams in the state was taken so seriously that an unidentified plane flying near Kerr Dam was fired on by military guards, and fishermen were disappointed to learn they would no longer be allowed to

wet a line within a mile of the dams.

Delegates to the 1942 High School Week focused on the opportunities for wartime training at the state's colleges, including the new crash courses in radio repair that were being offered at the University of Montana and Montana State College. Local school districts were also feeling the impact of wartime shortages, and in March the Montana High School Association voted to cancel all football, basketball, and track championships for the duration of the war. In Missoula, School District 1 postponed a $40,000 addition to Paxson School, and the Fair Board voted to put off planned repairs to the fairgrounds, damaged in a fire the year before. They also voted to cancel the 1942 Western Montana Fair, an action copied by many of the other fair boards around the state.

Anti-Japanese sentiment was already running high in the state when University President Ernest Melby set off an uproar. Melby agreed to admit several Japanese-American students who were being forced to leave the Seattle area, but suspicious residents charged that the students might set forest fires or engage in sabotage, and a special meeting of the Board of Education was finally called to study the matter. Bowing to public pressure, the Board turned down the 12 Japanese students who had already applied, and deferred the entry of any other Japanese students for the rest of the year.

There were nearly 1,000 Japanese held behind barbed wire at Fort Missoula by April. The Japanese, most of them respected citizens from the Japanese-American communities in Hawaii and California, were considered a threat to national security despite the fact that some were American citizens and almost all were elderly. The men were fed rice, soy, and fish, and according to the camp administrators, they were better housekeepers than the Italians, with whom they rarely mixed. There was little for the prisoners to do at Fort Missoula, and several of the prisoners spent their time gathering tiny pebbles and cementing them into vases and bowls. Some of the Japanese who had been common laborers said they preferred life at Fort Missoula to the work they had been doing before the war. The prisoners were allowed to write letters and could receive visitors at any time as long as they spoke in English. Both the Italians and the Japanese were allowed passes to go into Missoula but during the first months they were always accompanied by guards.

After several months of being held without trial,

April 1942

- April 1. Mass evacuation of all people of Japanese ancestry begins on the West Coast.
- April 5. Great Falls native George Montgomery marries Hedy Lamarr.
- April 7. 163rd Infantry Regiment, Montana National Guard, arrives in Australia.
- April 8. WPB announced that the mines in Sweetgrass and Stillwater counties make Montana the largest chromium producer in the world.
- April 9. Bataan Death March begins in Philippines.
- April 10. Production of golf clubs and balls halted.
- April 18. Doolittle's Raiders bomb Tokyo.
- April 23. Sugar rationing stamps go into effect in May.
- April 29. Price ceilings fixed on all food and clothing.

May 1942

- May 4. Battle of the Coral Sea begins.
- May 6. American forces on Corregidor surrender. Shut Out wins Kentucky Derby.
- May 8. The aircraft carrier *USS Lexington* is sunk at Coral Sea.
- May 9. Construction begins on an Army Air Force Base at Great Falls.
- May 14. Five hundred athletes from 77 schools begin arriving in Missoula for the Montana State High School Track championships,.
- May 16. Missoula Spartans win their fourth straight Interscholastic Track and Field title, edging out Butte.
- May 17. "I Am An American Day" proclaimed by Governor Ford.
- May 26. Four Japanese carriers leave the Inland Sea, bound for Midway.
- May 29. Germans and British fight a tank battle near Tobruk.

Sports

Even local sports were affected by the war raging halfway around the globe. The Missoula Spartans had the best high school record in the state after winning the Northern Division basketball tournament, but they lost to Butte in the first round of the state meet in Livingston. The Billings Broncs won the 1942 State championship in a blowout against a team fielded by the tiny mining community of Klein. Later in the spring, Missoula welcomed 500 student athletes from 77 different schools for the State High School Track championships. It was to be the last major high school sporting event held in Montana for more than a year, and the Missoula Spartans won, edging out Butte High for their fourth straight title. With tire shortages and gasoline rationing putting a crimp in state sporting events, the Montana High School Association met in late March and decided to cancel all state football, basketball, and track championships for the duration of the war.

the fate of the Japanese prisoners was put in the hands of Enemy Alien Hearings Boards. The man in charge of the hearings was Democratic Congressman John Tolan of California, who had once been the county attorney in Anaconda and had practiced law in Missoula from 1906 to 1915. Several local citizens served on the Montana Board, including Mike Mansfield, a young university professor with political ambitions. Each Japanese man was given a hearing to determine his fate. The men were supposed to be interviewed by residents from their home states, but the Montana Board wound up doing many of the interviews. Although the Japanese were not allowed to have lawyers, friends and relatives could testify in their behalf.

Some of the Japanese tried to protect each other by claiming that they had all been in the country since before 1924, when Japanese immigration had been halted. This led to conflicting stories told by some of the internees and caused hard feelings among the prisoners when some were accused of perjury. Inspectors claimed that the Japanese were conspiring among themselves to lie to the Board.

By the spring of 1942, wartime rationing and shortages of even the most mundane household items were beginning to affect all Montanans, especially those with a sweet tooth. The shortage of sugar which had existed for months became so severe that long lines formed at local grade schools as residents picked up Ration Book Number One. Each of the new ration books contained four coupons, entitling the bearer to purchase just one pound of sugar every two weeks.

Montana sugar beet farmers were becoming worried by early spring. In 1941 they had produced 250,000,000 pounds of sugar, enough to supply 10 million people. In the war hysteria following Pearl harbor, the farmers had promised to increase their production by 25 percent but had not accounted for the fact that most of their farm workers had enlisted. Now they had 86,000 acres of sugar beets under cultivation and no one to thin, weed, and harvest the precious crop. Fearing their crop might rot in the ground if workers weren't found, the farmers saw a golden opportunity to save their beets if the hundreds of thousands of Japanese-Americans who were being forced to evacuate the West Coast were brought to the Treasure State. Montana farmers began pressuring Senators Wheeler and Murray to cut the red tape necessary for obtaining Nisei.

Sugar was only one of the items in short supply during the spring of '42. The dreaded War Production Board (WPB) had assumed dictatorial powers and it daily set forth new restrictions on items large and small. Automobile assembly lines were no longer allowed to produce passenger cars, only military vehicles, and the production of radios, phonographs, refrigerators, washing machines, and musical instruments was halted altogether. Tea, coffee, cocoa, and typewriters were suddenly hard to find, and inflation rose steadily (hotdogs reached a shocking 7 cents apiece and Pepsi-Cola was 5 cents a bottle), prompting the government to freeze prices on all food and clothing.

The rubber shortage was considered at least as critical as the scarcity of sugar, and scientists were frantically trying to come up with new ways to make synthetic rubber. The supply of rubber was so low that a special permit was needed just to buy old retread tires, and between the rubber shortage and the three gallons of gas per week that motorists with nonessential jobs were allowed, it came as no surprise when there was a sudden boom in bicycling.

The WPB went so far as to decree the length of women's hemlines and the amount of fabric that could be used in each type of garment. Synthetics were being designed to replace wool and tailors were ordered to cut off cuffs rather than repair them. Metal zippers were banned altogether because they contained copper.

Products made of copper and brass, toy soldiers containing lead, and many other metal items were restricted by the WPB. Even products like toothpaste and shaving cream, packaged in metal tubes, could only be purchased if an empty tube was returned to the store. The shortage of metal gave a big boost to Montana's mining industry, however, and by May hundreds of miners were at work at the new Mouat Mine high above the Stillwater River in central Montana, soon to become the nation's largest supplier of chromium.

4

☞ Helena Welcomes The Devil's Brigade ☜

As wildflowers and green grass began appearing in western Montana, nearly 1,000 men of Japanese ancestry were still being held in the detention camp at Fort Missoula, waiting as the Enemy Alien Hearing Boards determined their fate. The proceedings were little better than a farce and the Japanese were considered guilty until they could prove their innocence. Agents from the Internal Revenue Service sat in on the hearings to examine the tax status of the prisoners and found that some of the men owed as much $12,000 in back taxes. Assistant U.S. Attorney Gerald Hile declared that even though most of the Japanese posed no threat to the United States, "a few of them are not hesitant to let it be known that they hope Japan wins the war."

The Hearings Boards wrapped up their work at the Fort in mid-June, about the same time that the Swiss Red Cross and the Spanish Consulate in San Francisco filed a complaint with the State Department alleging mistreatment of the Japanese prisoners at Fort Missoula. A subsequent investigation revealed that some of the prisoners had been singled out for punishment by the Immigration Service guards and their Korean interpreters. Prisoners had been slapped, kicked, had their feet stepped on and their hair pulled. Objects had been thrown at them and some had been confined in the guardhouse for up to a month at a time. Elderly Japanese men had been made to stand outside in freezing weather for several hours before their hearings, and verbal abuse of the prisoners was widespread. Inspector Herman Schwandt testified he had overheard a guard threaten one of the Japanese prisoners. "You lying yellow son-of-a-bitch, you have been lying long enough. If you don't tell the truth now I am going to knock your teeth down your throat."

Two Korean interpreters were described as particularly cruel towards the Japanese and were eventually fired for striking the prisoners. Three Immigration inspectors were demoted and suspended for 90 days due to their treatment of the prisoners.

After the hearings, some of the Japanese were sent to Fort Sill, Oklahoma while others were reunited with their families at detention camps like the one that a Billings construction company was building near Heart Mountain in northern Wyoming. Despite their mistreatment at the hands of the Immigration Service, some of the Japanese leaders wrote to Supervisor Collaer telling him how much they missed Missoula, and to thank him for his efforts on their behalf. By the end of the year only 29 of the Japanese detainees remained at the Fort, although more were sent there later in the war.

Despite the crucial shortage of available farm laborers, farmers in the state looked forward to a record crop. After several months of wrangling, the government relaxed the rules and Japanese-Americans who had been born in the U.S. (Nisei) were allowed to volunteer for farm labor. With $10,000,000 worth of sugar at stake, Montana's sugar beet growers were delighted, even though they feared that the Nisei might be Japanese sympathizers. Their fears were groundless, however, and for the most part the Nisei were excellent workers. Arthur Deschamps of the American Crystal Sugar Company imported 25 Nisei laborers from California to work in the sugar fields in the Bitterroot Valley, 65 internees volunteered for labor from Fort Missoula, and other Japanese-Americans came from Washington state to work the fields. Although only a small percentage of the requested 5,000 laborers ever arrived, the farmers were pleased with the Nisei who did come. The Nisei, on the other hand, were not always pleased with their working conditions. Temporary camps were set up in Stevensville, Corvallis, Townsend and other locations in the state, yet despite the fact that the Nisei were American citizens, the camps were policed by armed guards, as much for the farmer's protection as for the laborer's safety. The Nisei resented the crudely furnished camps, and the backbreaking labor for low pay.

The wounds of Pearl Harbor still ran deep, and many Montanans were angry about the presence of the farm workers, the Japanese internees at Fort Missoula, and the 50 Nisei who were employed by the Northern Pacific railroad.

Warm June weather brought a sense of optimism to the state of Montana. Although no one really knew it at the time, a turning point was reached in the Pacific War. The news that four Japanese aircraft

Montana Newspapers

"Marines Land on Guadalcanal" screamed the bright red headlines of the *Missoula Sentinel*, the afternoon version of the *Daily Missoulian*. Like most of the 14 dailies and 120 smaller newspapers in the state in 1942, both papers were owned by the giant Anaconda Company. Through its holding company the Fairmont Corporation, Anaconda owned an interest in the *Anaconda Standard*, the *Billings Gazette*, the *Montana Standard*, the *Butte Daily Post*, the *Livingston Enterprise*, the *Missoula Sentinel*, the *Daily Missoulian*, and the *Helena Independent*. The "Company" papers in Montana were notorious for concentrating on national and international affairs to the exclusion of local issues and controversies. Senator Murray blasted the state's Anaconda-owned newspapers because they refused to cover his activities. "Only in a few cities in our state have we an honest press publishing news free from propaganda." Clearly the best of the state's large newspapers was the *Great Falls Tribune*. According to Fred Martin, "The *Tribune* was not anti-company or anti-labor, but it operated as a newspaper, recognizing that news was a free-flowing commodity. The staff didn't have to fit into a mold; one could think for himself. Staffers didn't have to worry about the business office policy on any reasonable news story." The *People's Voice*, a politically oriented weekly from Helena, vigorously attacked Sen. B.K. Wheeler, Charles Lindbergh and the America First movement, while expressing support for President Roosevelt and his war policy. Including ads, a full page of sports, and a page of funnies, a normal weekday newspaper was only six pages long. Cartoons were twice as large as they are today, but even after 50 years, some of the titles remain the same. "Out Our Way," "Little Orphan Annie," "Our Boarding House," "Alley Oop," and "Gasoline Alley" were all popular, as were "Moon Mullins," "Kitty Higgins," "Sergeant Stony Craig," "Mutt and Jeff," and "Don Winslow of the Navy". Cigarette and bourbon ads competed for space in the paper with such popular features as "News of Montana Men in the Service" or "How to feed a Family of Four for $13 a week." Reflecting the changes that the war had brought to Montana society, the *Great Falls Tribune* printed fashion and beauty tips for women working in grimy defense plants, and also ran a photo feature showing women how to roll their own cigarettes. Most newspapers across the country battled wartime shortages of newsprint, lead, and ink, and most raised their prices in 1942 to a nickel per issue.

Midway

· Charles M. Mason, the son of Missoula's mayor, and Wayne Daigle, also of Missoula, were rescued from the *USS Yorktown* when it sank.
· Ens. James Shelton of Denton was killed attacking the Japanese fleet at Midway. He was a member of Scout Squadron Six, based on the *USS Enterprise*. His squadron of Dauntless bombers attacked and sank the Japanese carrier *Kaga* at Midway. He was posthumously awarded the Navy Cross for his actions, and a destroyer escort, the *USS Shelton*, was named after him.

June 1942

· June 3. Japanese bomb Dutch Harbor, Alaska.
· June 4. Four Japanese aircraft carriers are sunk at Midway.
· June 5. Governor Ford commutes the sentence of 24 inmates at Montana State Prison so the men could enlist.
· June 7. *USS Yorktown* is sunk by a Japanese submarine.
· June 10. Nazis destroy Czech town of Lidice.
· June 11. Six drown at Fort Peck Reservoir.
· June 12. Japanese begin occupying the Aleutian Islands of Attu and Kiska.
· June 21. Germans seize Tobruk from the British.
· June 25. Governor Ford reduces state speed limit to 40 miles per hour.
· June 28. David Thatcher and Edward Saylor are awarded the Distinguished Flying Cross in Washington, D.C.
· June 30. Funding is cut off for the Civilian Conservation Corps (CCC). A flying instructor and student are injured in a plane crash west of Billings.

carriers had been sunk in the Battle of Midway, balanced by the loss of the *USS Yorktown*, came as a welcome ray of hope after the military reverses of the previous winter and spring.

Things were not going quite so well in North Africa, where the Afrika Korps seized Tobruk from the British in mid-June. The British, commanded by General Montgomery, barely managed to halt the German offensive at El Alamein. On the Eastern Front, the beleaguered Soviets desperately needed whatever help America could provide. Since the U.S. Army was woefully unprepared to take the offensive against the Nazis in 1942, the only help that President Roosevelt could provide was to send as many war supplies as possible to the Soviet Union through the Lend-Lease program. German and Japanese submarines were preying on shipping off both coasts of the U.S. and the only safe supply route to the U.S.S.R. was by air, via Alaska and Siberia. Lend-Lease officials began searching for a suitable airfield in the northern United States within flying range of Alaska.

They finally settled on Great Falls, a city with 300 clear flying days per year and on a direct line along the Alaska-Siberia Air Route (ALSIB). In June 1942, 170 officers and men of the 7th Ferrying Group of the Air Transport Command (ATC) were transferred from Long Beach, California, to Great Falls, where construction had begun the month before on a new Army Air Force base. The base was 65 percent completed by the time the Headquarters Squadron arrived on August 20, 1942. On that day, soldiers fought a brush fire which threatened the new buildings. At first the airmen were stationed at Gore Field (the Great Falls municipal airfield) while construction continued at East Base, six miles from town. The Great Falls Civic Center and Ice Arena served as barracks and mess hall for the enlisted men, while officers stayed at local hotels. The mayor and other city officials were temporarily displaced from their offices to make room for the Army. The Fine Arts Building at the fairgrounds was used for the air base administration, while the Mercantile Building was filled with spare aircraft engines. The Dining Pavilion served as a mess hall. Major Eaton was in charge of the air base, while Col. Ponton D'Arce commanded the 7th Ferrying Group.

An appeal to patriotism saved the fireworks display on the Fourth of July. Fearing forest fires, Gen. John DeWitt had earlier banned the sale of fireworks in Montana but he rescinded his order at the request of local citizens who felt that celebrating the Fourth was more important than fire prevention. Arriving home in time for the Independence Day celebrations were two local war heroes, veterans of the celebrated Doolittle bombing raid on Tokyo. Sgt. Dave Thatcher of Billings and Sgt. Edward Saylor of Brusett returned to Montana wearing shiny new Distinguished Flying Crosses, presented to them by Gen. Henry "Hap" Arnold, chief of the Army Air Forces.

Edward Saylor received a warm welcome as the guest of honor at a Heroes Day parade and war bond rally at Dornblaser Field in Missoula. One thousand people gathered on the Billings courthouse lawn as Thatcher was awarded the Silver Star for saving the life of four members of his aircrew after their B-25 crashed in China. "Real heroes, it seems, are always modest," said the *Billings Gazette*. "For the uncrowned champion of the Modest Heroes League, we raise to nominate Sergeant David J. Thatcher, late of Shangri-la and Tokyo." Thatcher replied that, "It's funny to see my name in the paper. We saw plenty of action over Japan, all right," but added that he would like to, "go over again."

Montana's Capital City of Helena also became the site of a military buildup during the summer of 1942. "Project Plough" was a top-secret plan to drop commandos into German-occupied Norway and disrupt that country's industry. It was to be a joint U.S. and Canadian operation, and Col. Robert T. Frederick was chosen to lead it. He was authorized to recruit 133 officers and 1,688 men of both countries for what was widely regarded as a suicide mission. He chose to name his commandos the First Special Service Force, in hopes that they would be confused with the Army detachments in charge of recreation and leisure.

Frederick put out a call for officers under 35 years of age and in excellent condition who were willing to learn parachute training and had experience living in the arctic or mountainous regions. Officers were told they would have "a short and exciting life" if they volunteered. Each day, trains brought more soldiers into Helena, but not all of the volunteers were accepted. Enlisted men were required to have at least three years of grammar school and preference was given to: "Lumberjacks, Forest Rangers, Hunters, Northwoodsmen, Game Wardens, Prospectors, and Explorers."

Many army commanders simply cleaned out the troublemakers from their post stockades and sent

Aerial view of East Base, the Army Air Force facility built at Great Falls during 1942 and 1943. During the war years, the Army also took control of Gore Field, the Great Falls municipal airport. USAF

Hangar at East Base. Construction continued at the base throughout the war. USAF

An American soldier paints the red star of the Soviet Union on a war plane. Approximately 8,000 aircraft were shipped to the Soviet Union along the Alaska-Siberia Air Route (ALSIB) as part of the Lend-Lease agreement. USAF

A P-39 Airacobra flies north from Great Falls along the ALSIB route. The Soviets found the P-39s particularly valuable for supporting ground troops. They dubbed the planes "cobrastochkas," or dear little cobras. USAF

A Douglas C-47 cargo plane awaits delivery to Soviet pilots. USAF

Enlisted men's barracks in
the Great Falls Civic Center.
USAF

Officer's club at Great Falls.
USAF

Original dance band at Gore
Field. The new air force
facility in Great Falls brought
a number of nationally
known sports and entertainment figures to the Electric
City during the war years.
USAF

Maj. Gen. Slavin of the Soviet army boards a plane at Great Falls. A number of Soviets were stationed in Great Falls, representing the Soviet Air Force and the Soviet Purchasing Commission. Many more Soviet ambassadors, military men and spies passed through Great Falls on their way from Moscow to Washington, D.C. USAF

A military formation at East Base. Note the hastily constructed buildings in the background. USAF

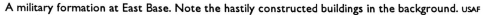

An AT-6 Texan, one of the
best trainers used by the
U.S. Army Force.Turk
Harshbarger, Jerome, Idaho

A P-38 Lightning, victim of
an icy runway in Alaska. Turk
Harshbarger, Jerome, Idaho

An A-20 Havoc crashed on
the runway at Great Falls.
The Soviets received 3,125
Havocs, and most passed
through Great Falls. The
ALSIB route from Great
Falls to the Soviet Union
was extremely hazardous.
Remote terrain, arctic
weather conditions and
inexperienced pilots were
responsible for a large
number of crashes. A major
effort was made to rescue
downed pilots in the remote
bush of Canada and Alaska.
Rescue parachutists were
trained at Camp Paxson,
Montana, while sled dogs for
rescue crews were trained
at Camp Rimini, Montana.
Turk Harshbarger, Jerome, Idaho

A row of P-39s wait on the runway at Great Falls. Many of the planes were ferried from aircraft factories to Great Falls by WASPs, Women Air Service Pilots. At Great Falls, the planes were prepared for cold weather flying and were painted with Soviet insignia. USAF

Helena

The state capital and county seat of Lewis and Clark County (pop 22,131), Helena was a trade and service center which had seen steady growth throughout the 1930s and had a population of 15,000 in 1940. Like most other cities in the state, it saw a dramatic loss of population during the war years, losing more than 4,000 people in two-and-a-half years.

The city had two radio stations, KPFA and KXLJ, an NBC affiliate. Two newspapers, the *Helena Independent* and the *Montana Record* existed in the capital city, and both were founded in 1866. In the fall of 1943, the Montana Record Publishing Company bought the Independent Publishing Company and began producing just one paper, the *Helena Independent-Record*, an afternoon and Sunday morning paper. In early 1943 L.A. Riskin, editor of the *Helena Independent*, became editor of the Post Publishing Company in Butte, and he was replaced by E.A. Dye. Helena was served by the Great Northern and Northern Pacific railroads, and boasted six hotels, including the Placer. There were three movie theaters and the Little Theater Group put on many live productions during the early 1940s.

Operated by the Catholic Church, Carroll College was one of the oldest private colleges operating in the state. Throughout the war years Carroll College hosted two Navy programs, the V-12 program which trained students in basic training and pre-med, and the V-5 program which trained 550 aviator cadets in conjunction with the Morrison Flying Service. By July of 1944, 100 V-12 trainees had graduated from Carroll and 140 more had arrived in Helena. The V-5 program ended in August of 1944.

Fort William Henry Harrison, an old frontier military post just northwest of Helena, had been under the jurisdiction of the Veterans Administration until July 1942, when the old fort was returned to the U.S. Army. Hundreds of large four-man tents suddenly sprouted at the Fort as teams of carpenters and electricians began building more permanent structures to house the First Special Service Force, a new unit composed of 1,800 volunteers chosen from the Canadian and U.S. Armies. Later in the war, the 464th Quartermaster Corps was stationed at the Fort. After the war, federal funds greatly expanded the Veterans Administration Hospital at Fort Harrison.

Fort Harrison, located just a few miles from downtown Helena, became the scene of a major military buildup upon the arrival of the First Special Service Force during the late summer and fall of 1942. Today the fort is occupied by the Montana National Guard and a Veteran's Administration Hospital.

FORT HARRISON

Fort Harrison has had a colorful history dating back to the 1880's. It was established as a military fort and named Fort William Henry Harrison in honor of the 9th President of the United States. U.S. Army troops were stationed here from 1892 until 1912. In 1919 the U.S. Public Health Service then took possession of the military reservation and operated a hospital here until 1922. The Veterans Bureau took over the hospital in 1922 and on June 1, 1929 the regional office was moved from Helena to Ft. Harrison. A new hospital and clinical building was constructed in 1932 and rebuilt in 1936 after a series of severe earthquakes destroyed many buildings and caused extensive damage to the hospital. On October 1, 1948 the hospital and regional office were consolidated and became known as the VA Center. The present 160 bed hospital was constructed in 1963 and in 1964 the former hospital was remodeled to house the VA Regional Office.

GILL

BICENTENNIAL MEMORIAL
1776 - 1976
Donated by
Veterans Administration Employees

them to Helena. In at least one case, Frederick was requested to send the armed guards back as soon as his "volunteers" had been delivered. Enlisted man Conrad Legault said, "When they interviewed me for the Force, they took me, even though I had no jail record."

While 600 construction workers built permanent housing at Fort Harrison, large four-man tents were pitched for the men. Two Americans and two Canadians were assigned to each tent. The Americans and Canadians wore a variety of different uniforms, and the situation got worse when they began swapping uniforms. Ranchers and miners in Helena stared in amazement when they suddenly found their favorite bars along Last Chance Gulch crowded with Canadian soldiers wearing kilts and berets, but the residents soon grew accustomed to the highly-trained Canadian volunteers.

Friday nights in Helena were somewhat boisterous when the Forcemen came to town, as the soldiers from Fort Harrison practiced their hand-to-hand combat skills during wild bar fights with the local cowboys and miners. The Forcemen soon learned they could hock their hard-earned paratrooper wings for drinks in the Helena bars. The Gold Bar was a favorite of the enlisted men while their officers preferred the Montana Club.

Despite persistent rumors that some of the American soldiers had criminal records, the people of Helena soon adopted the Forcemen as their own. Many went so far as to invite the soldiers home for Sunday dinner, and nine Helena women found employment as chauffeurs for the men of the First Special Service Force.

Helena residents discovered a new spectator sport in August when the Forcemen began parachute training. Crowds of people lined the jump zone as the skies around the Capital City bloomed with hundreds of parachutes. Besides hours of calisthenics, parachute training, and hand-to-hand combat drills, the Forcemen also spent considerable time honing their demolition skills. They usually used an excessive amount of explosives and wound up shattering many of the windows in Helena, but the mayor refused to bill the Army. Broken glass was only one of many contributions Helena residents would make for the war effort. The irrepressible Forcemen blew up old mines, bridges and houses in the area, sometimes with permission from the owners, sometimes without, and the demolition practice led to several lawsuits after the wrong buildings were blown up.

Members of the First Special Service Force practice skiing near Blossburg, on the Continental Divide west of Helena. Twelve Norwegian ski instructors trained the Forcemen, who were preparing for Project Plough, an invasion of Nazi-occupied Norway. Project Plough was widely considered to be a suicide mission.

Training of the First Special Service Force at Fort Harrison. The U.S. and Canadian members of the Force were some of the most highly trained soldiers of World War II.

Maj. John Shinberger was responsible for much of the training. Nicknamed "The Prussian," veterans remembered he kept a footlocker of live rattlesnakes under his cot, mainly because he was afraid of them and felt that familiarity was the best way to overcome his fear. Almost from the beginning it became obvious that this was no ordinary Army unit, and one Montana newspaper reported that the Forcemen were "Super-Specialists in offensive warfare." The Germans would call them the "Devil's Brigade."

As more and more men enlisted in the armed forces, women began moving into the work force in record numbers, taking jobs previously held only by men. There were other changes in society as well. Mrs. Patricia O'Connell of Polson was a student at the University of Montana during the war. She reported that, "I found the University to have almost a completely female student body. The teachers were all old men—over fifty at least." In the June primary in Montana, almost half of the candidates running for state and local offices were women. In August the Navy began recruiting WAVES, "Women Accepted for Volunteer Emergency Service," and the program was so successful that the Army and the Coast Guard quickly adopted their own women's auxiliary corps, WACs and SPARS. The lumber industry in the Northwest employed 4,000 women during the summer of 1942, and the Forest Service hired women cooks and timekeepers to serve in fire camps. Women trained to coach high school athletics, and many Montana women flocked to fill the new high-paying jobs in the West Coast aircraft and ship factories, where they sometimes bewildered their male employers. One exasperated aircraft executive complained to a reporter, "girls are a little more independent and harder to discipline than men."

Even those women who remained at home faced war-related hardships. The *Daily Missoulian* reported that "sugar madness again swept through the ranks of Missoula housewives Wednesday when it was estimated at least 1,000 appeared at the rationing board headquarters in the Federal building to make application for their canning sugar." In a scene repeated throughout the state, the crowd of women seeking sugar in Missoula was so great that two auxiliary sugar rationing stations were opened in Bonner and Orchard Homes, staffed by 100 volunteers who helped clerks with the required government paperwork. Others found innovative ways to cope with the shortages. A Helena restaurant owner

The First Special Service Force memorial, located in Memorial Park on Last Chance Gulch in Helena, directly across the street from the headquarters of the Montana National Guard.

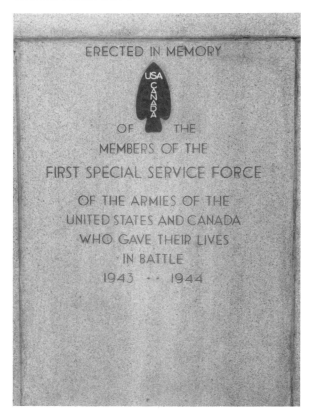

July 1942

- July 2. British General Montgomery halts German offensive at El Alamein.
- July 7. The Blue Fountain Room (soda fountain) opens at the Florence Hotel in Missoula.
- July 10. Dave Thatcher is awarded the Silver Star in Billings.
- July 21. Montana primary election is held, (nearly half of the candidates are women).
- July 22. Japanese students are denied entry to state universities.
- July 28. Soviets announce that Rostov has fallen to the Germans.

August 1942

- August 2. Miners Field Day celebrated in Butte.
- August 7. U.S. Marines land on Guadalcanal. Vern Haugland, former *Missoulian* and *Sentinel* reporter, parachutes from a crippled bomber over New Guinea. Frances Corbin, former UM literature professor and Dean of Women, is buried in Missoula.
- August 9. Japanese sink four American cruisers at Savo.
- August 17. U.S. Marines raid Makin Island.
- August 19. Allied and Canadian soldiers mount an abortive raid against the French port of Dieppe.
- August 21. Marines on Guadalcanal withstand a major Japanese attack across the Tenaru River.
- August 23. Doolittle Raider E.J. Saylor of Brusett is the guest of honor at Missoula Heroes Day Parade.
- August 25. Japanese forces begin landing at Milne Bay, New Guinea.
- August 26. Soviets counterattack at Stalingrad.

Guadalcanal

- Lt.(jg) William Holt of Great Falls, a Wildcat pilot from the aircraft carrier *USS Saratoga*, was posthumously awarded the Distinguished Flying Cross for "Heroism and extraordinary achievement." On August 7, 1942 he and another fighter pilot attacked 27 Japanese bombers near Guadalcanal, but were in turn attacked by Japanese Zeros. Holt was credited with destroying five Japanese bombers, but he and his wingman were both shot down and killed. In early 1944 a Destroyer Escort was named after Lieutenant Holt.
- Marine Lt. Gen. Albert D. Cooley of Billings was a major stationed at Quantico, Virginia when the war began. In September of 1942 he was sent to Guadalcanal as commander of Marine Air Group 14 (MAG-14), and was put in charge of all bombers flying from that island. He was awarded the Navy Cross for his actions in the Solomons. He then commanded the Marine Air Support Group and was active in training Marine pilots to fly off of aircraft carriers.
- Capt. Gregg Lash of Montana was one of the fliers of the Cactus Air Force on Guadalcanal.
- Lt. John Zuber of Missoula was a flier shot down near Guadalcanal in August 1942. He spent five days marooned in his life raft before being rescued.
- Sgt. Berk MacPherson and PFC Don Bowcutt, both of Great Falls were part of the elite Carlson's [Marine] Raiders who were landed on Makin Island by submarine as part of a diversion to the Guadalcanal landings. MacPherson later transferred to Edson's Raiders. He fought on New Georgia and was wounded in the foot on Guam.
- PFC Floyd A. Durfey of Richey was awarded the Silver Star at Fort Harrison for his actions on Guadalcanal. He was later made the honorary chairman of the Montana scrap metal drive.
- Capt. Thomas C. Mather of Great Falls served with the Marine Corps on Guadalcanal, where he won the Navy Cross for his actions on October 23 and 24, 1942. A graduate of the University of Montana, he was knocked out by a mortar shell but recovered in time to lead an attack that destroyed five Japanese tanks.

put tiny American flags in his sugar bowls, hoping an appeal to patriotism would limit consumption. Although his customers kept stealing all of the little flags, they used a lot less sugar.

By 1942, more than a third of Montanan residents had replaced their old iceboxes with mechanical refrigerators, but the cost of filling their new appliances kept going up. A six-pack of soda pop cost a quarter while steak ran as high as $.35 per pound. Pot roast was $.27 per pound, and a bottle of Old Hickory whiskey sold for $2.35 per quart. Coffee, soon to be rationed, was selling for more than $.25 per pound.

Clothing prices at the Missoula Mercantile and Great Fall's Paris Fligman Company were also up. Men's sport shirts and women's hats averaged $3.00 apiece, and neckties cost $1.00. The price increases also affected the real estate market in the state. Large homes in Missoula's University district were going for as much as $5,000, although a few bargains could still be found for less than half that. The large Clark Hotel in Butte sold for $200,000. Severe housing shortages began to develop in Helena, Great Falls and Butte as large number of military personnel, construction workers and miners flocked into those cities.

The new V-mail letter forms to send letters to servicemen became available about the same time that news from some Montanans overseas began to filter back home. Because of the strict censorship rules in effect, few residents were aware that the 163rd Infantry Regiment had been sent "down under" for jungle warfare training. That changed when an Australian citizen wrote a letter to General Marshall praising the good conduct of the Montana National Guardsmen in Australia and claiming that, "a finer lot of well-behaved young men never represented any country." General Marshall passed the letter on to Governor Ford and it was subsequently printed in newspapers statewide.

On August 7, 1942 U.S. Marines invaded a little-known island in the Solomon chain by the name of Guadalcanal. Stretched to the limit, American forces fought desperately in the air, on the sea, and in the jungles to hold the crude airstrip on Guadalcanal. Col. Lawson H.M. Sanderson of the First Marine Air Wing was the first Montana awarded the Legion of Merit for his actions in the air over Guadalcanal. "Sandy" Sanderson had played for the Montana Grizzly football team in 1916, and had lettered in football, track, basketball and baseball. He is credited with inventing the technique of dive-bombing. Using a homemade bomb release made from a flour sack, he made the first dive-bombing run over Haiti in 1919. He won the Distinguished Flying Cross over Nicarauga and set world air speed records in 1925 and 1926. He also won several major air races. During World War II he served in the Solomons and New Guinea.

In August, newspaper readers around the country followed the story of Vern Haugland, a reporter who had grown up on a ranch near Bozeman, and a 1931 graduate of the University of Montana. Haugland worked for the *Missoula Sentinel*, the *Daily Missoulian*, and the *Montana Standard* before being hired by the Hollywood desk of the *Associated Press* in 1936. On the morning of August 7, 1942, Haugland left Townsville, Australia, in a B-26 bomber to cover the fighting on Guadalcanal. On the return flight, the plane encountered heavy cloud cover and ran out of fuel while searching for Port Moresby, New Guinea. The eight men aboard were forced to parachute at night from an altitude of 13,000 feet.

Several members of the plane's crew staggered out of the jungle, but weeks went by and the search was called off when no sign of the reporter was found. Haugland had in fact landed safely in a tree, then set off walking downhill. On the following day he met the plane's copilot, Lt. James "Mike" Michael. The two men hiked for several days through an extremely rough river canyon, and were forced to swim through rapids after heavy rains made the river rise unpredictably. On August 16, the two men separated. Mike climbed the canyon while Haugland, who was too weak to climb, used his life jacket to float the river. Several days later Haugland encountered a massive mountain range. "I had seen breathtaking vistas back home, but nowhere—not in Glacier Park or Yellowstone or at Lake Louise, Yosemite, or Bryce or Zion or even Grand Canyon National Park—were there views to match this for sheer fantasy." He was in no condition to enjoy the view, however. Starving and soaked by constant downpours, Haugland fell victim to tropical diseases and was on the verge of giving up. After a week-and-a-half of resting in one place, he finally gathered the strength to continue.

5

⪢ Red Stars Over Montana ⪡

Stumbling through the thick jungle, high mountains, and extremely broken country of the Papuan region of New Guinea, reporter Vern Haugland grew increasingly weak from lack of food. On the first of September he spotted a large valley in the far distance. Eight days later he was still trying to reach the valley when he noticed signs of human habitation. He followed a trail to the village of Obea, near the Ibinambo River, where he met natives who appeared friendly. Although the Papuans provided Haugland with food, he was very ill and becoming increasingly delirious, so the natives guided him to the larger village of Sirimidi. When Haugland arrived at Sirimidi on September 11, he met two missionaries, Australian Luscombe Newman and Englishman Jack Salzman. The missionaries realized that Haugland needed immediate medical attention, and they hired natives to carry him on a rough stretcher over the Owen Stanley Mountains to Abau, where he was flown in an open two-seat airplane to Port Moresby. By the time Haugland finally arrived in a hospital on September 23, he weighed only 90 pounds, a loss of nearly 70 pounds during his 47 days in the jungle. His friend Mike and the plane's navigator were never heard from again.

Much to Haugland's dismay, the diary he had kept of his ordeal was printed in newspapers at home while he was still delirious, and the diary was soon published in book form, making him an instant celebrity. Never one to miss a photo opportunity, Gen. Douglas MacArthur visited Haugland in the hospital on October 3, and awarded him the Silver Star for heroism, the first ever given to a civilian. On October 10, Haugland was flown in an American bomber to Australia, where he spent another month in the hospital before returning to work. The University of Montana journalism school issued a pamphlet on his adventures, and in 1943, Haugland's account of his experiences, *Letter From New Guinea* was published in New York. Haugland returned to work as a war reporter and eventually published two books on the air war in Europe and the Pacific. He died in 1984.

In September of 1942, strange rumors began circulating around Cascade County. Puzzled farmers reported that dozens of warplanes bearing the red star of the Soviet Union were flying north from the Great Falls municipal airport. Uniformed Russian soldiers were seen on the streets of the Electric City, and the American military presence in Great Falls was mushrooming.

With strict wartime security in place, local citizens had no way of knowing that their city had been chosen as the southern hub of a major military link with Russia. As American involvement in World War II entered its 10th month with few successes, supplying our Soviet allies with new aircraft became one of President Roosevelt's top priorities. A Montana-Alaska-Siberia air route was mapped out, and a group of Red Army soldiers arrived quietly in Great Falls, ready to oversee the Soviet end of the operation. Head of the Soviet contingent was Col. A.M. Kotikov, who along with his wife took up residence in the Pennsylvania Apartments. Anatoli Kotikov had previously pioneered an air route from Moscow to Seattle over the North Pole. He had 38 parachute jumps and 17 years in the Red Army to his credit.

The new warplanes arriving in Montana were prepared for cold-weather flying, were painted with the red star of the Soviet Union, and were officially turned over to the Soviets, even though American pilots ferried the planes as far as Fairbanks, Alaska, where Russian pilots took over. The dangerous journey to Fairbanks covered nearly 2,000 miles, and with intermediate stops in Edmonton, Fort St. John, Fort Nelson, and Whitehorse, it usually took six days of flying through intense cold and blinding snowstorms. A large number of the planes crashed but every one that got through strengthened the Soviet military at a time when a decisive and massive battle was shaping up around Stalingrad.

The man responsible for turning the planes over to the Soviets was the United Nation's representative in Great Falls, Maj. George R. Jordan. Jordan had been a sergeant gunner in Eddie Rickenbacker's pursuit squadron during World War I, and before the U.S. entry into World War II he had observed the bombing techniques of the Royal Air Force by going along as an observer during bombing raids over

Germany.

A Presidential order ensured that planes bound for the Soviet Union took priority over everything else at the Great Falls Air Base. In the first month of operation at the new base, 50 planes left on the first leg of their long journey, and it wasn't long before 400 Airacobras (P-39s), 80 medium bombers (A-20s), and 15 cargo planes (C-47s) left Great Falls every month. According to one officer, there was always a plane on the runway preparing for takeoff. During the war years, at least 7,000 airplanes left Great Falls for the 8,800-mile journey to the Eastern Front. The Soviets were particularly pleased with the P-39 Airacobras, and affectionately called the pursuit planes "Cobrastochkas" (dear little Cobras). The new base at Great Falls was also being used to train American bomber crews, and the first bomber squadron, commanded by Col. Ford J. Lauer, arrived in Great Falls on November 20, 1942. The 385th, 390th, and 401st squadrons of the Second Bombardment Group eventually trained in Montana.

Long before the Soviets arrived in Montana, 1,200 Italian citizens had been detained at Fort Missoula. Although the Italians were usually model prisoners, the detainees did not always agree on political matters. In early September 1942, fighting broke out between fascists and anti-fascists. Dr. Orvall Smiley, the camp doctor, provoked a riot when he posted a letter written to him by one of the prisoners, an anti-fascist. A fascist among the prisoners took offense at the letter and assaulted the letter-writer. Then other anti-fascists in the camp were attacked, which evolved into a riot in which five men were hospitalized. Guards stormed into the camp and broke up the fight with tear gas.

Missoula police were also busy in September. In raids on nine local bars and restaurants, they seized illegal pinball machines, slot machines, punchboards and blackjack tables. Other than illegal gambling, there was little crime in 1942, perhaps because county sheriffs often escorted troublemakers, hoboes, and gypsies to the county line, and left them with a warning not to return.

The fall of 1942 brought a return to school for Montana's teachers and students. Administrators soon discovered that school enrollment across the state had dropped by 10,000 students from the previous year. Much of the decrease was due to the large numbers of families leaving the state to work in high-paying defense industries on the West Coast. Few of

Missoula's students complained when Missoula High (now Hellgate) opened a week late in an effort to save money. The school had just completed a new gymnasium, but Missoula's best athletes got little opportunity to use the facility. By the end of the school year, every Spartan letterman had enlisted in the armed forces. The same situation existed at nearly every school in the state, and because of wartime travel restrictions, no state football championship was held in 1942.

Montana's University system was also undergoing change. A.L. Strand, president of Montana State College in Bozeman, left in October to take over the helm of Oregon State College. He was temporarily replaced by the Dean of Engineering, William Cobleigh, who severely disrupted fall quarter in 1942 by releasing all male students and faculty from classes for three weeks so they could help pick the sugar beet crop. The College's new nursing program attracted 163 students that first year, and for only the second time ever, enrollment at Bozeman (1,428) was greater than at Missoula (1,118). The University population had dropped 25 percent in the past year, compared with a 16 percent drop at the College.

The Sigma Phi Epsilon fraternity house in Missoula was forced to close its doors because all 40 of the fraternity members had enlisted. Many of the students returning to the University were enrolled in the new officer training programs sponsored by the Army, Navy, and Marines, but they still had time to catch an occasional football game. The Montana Grizzlies were the only Montana college team in 1942, as the Bobcats and teams from the smaller schools had opted to cancel their football programs due to the war.

Grizzly head coach Doug Fessenden was already serving in the Army, so assistant coach George P. Dahlberg directed the Montana program. The Grizzlies tried out the "Minnesota shift," a new offense that proved ineffective against Brigham Young University, where the Grizzlies were defeated 12-6 in their season opener. Dahlberg received orders to report to the military in mid-season, and was replaced by Clyde Carpenter, who was shortly inducted himself. Devastated by the loss of three head coaches to the armed forces in as many months, the Grizzlies had a dismal season, losing all eight games. After losing their final game 38-0 against UCLA, Montana was declared, "the undisputed holders of the Pacific Coast conference cellar." Crippled by wartime shortages and the enlistment of players and

Representative Prices 1942

- milk - $.14 per quart
- hamburger - $.23 per pound
- flour - $1.73 for 49 pounds
- beef roasts - $.27 per pound
- ham - $.37 per pound
- Coffee - $.35 per pound
- eggs - $.30 per dozen
- Campbell's tomato soup - 3 cans for $.25
- peanut butter - 25 ounces for $.37
- Spam - $.39 for a 12 ounce can
- cigarettes - $.10 per pack of 24
- cigars - $.03 to $.06
- beer - $.10 per bottle
- electric train sets - $8.79
- dolls - $2.49
- playsinks - $2.98
- Scout trainer machine gun toy - $2.49
- *Great Falls Tribune*, one year subscription - $20
- hardback books - $2 to $5
- First-class letter - $.02 (this increased to $.03 in 1944)
- men's suits - $30 to $40
- Stetson hats - $7.50 to $25
- Winchester Model 92 pump shotgun - $56.70
- 12-gauge shotgun shells - 24 for $1.20
- 100 Anacin - $.78
- Carter's Pills - $.19
- enamel paint - $1.55 per quart, $2.69 per gallon
- tires - $12 to $22

September 1942

- September 1. Five planes lift off from Great Falls, bound for the U.S.S.R., where German troops have reached the suburbs of Stalingrad.
- September 12. Japanese attack "Bloody Ridge" on Guadalcanal.
- September 14. Japanese torpedo sinks *USS Wasp* in the Solomons. *USS Helena* rescues 400 survivors.
- September 15. Search for reporter Vern Haugland is abandoned in New Guinea.
- September 16. Australian troops in New Guinea halt Japanese advance only 30 miles from Port Moresby.
- September 23. After 47 days wandering in the New Guinea jungle, AP reporter Vern Haugland is flown to Port Moresby.
- September 26. Bird hunting begins.
- September 27. Brigham Young University football team defeats Montana Grizzlies 12-6 in Missoula.

coaches, two-and-a-half years passed before the next Grizzly football team took the field.

Montanans mourned the passing of Will James, the noted cowboy artist and author who had been born near Great Falls in 1892, and who died in Hollywood in early September 1942. Arthur L. Higgins, another prominent Montanan, also died in September. Higgins, age 69, was the son of Missoula founder C.P. Higgins and had been one of the first children born in Missoula.

In business news, theaters in Butte reopened after a three-week strike by ushers and other employees, and Billings became home to a Northwest Airlines pilot training program that had been previously based in Minnesota.

Many Montanans grumbled about the new 35 mile an hour speed limit which went into effect nationwide on the first of October. The new speed limit, a further attempt to conserve precious gasoline and rubber tires needed for the war effort, was very unpopular in the wide open spaces of the Big Sky country. Rubber, crucial in the manufacture of all kinds of military supplies, from truck tires to aircraft parts, was in especially short supply because 90 percent of America's rubber had been imported from Southeast Asia before the war. By the fall of 1942, the shortage of rubber was so severe that it became a criminal offense to own more than five tires per vehicle. A person who wanted to purchase a pair of rubber overshoes had to turn in a used pair first, and the government tried several far-fetched ideas in an attempt to find an alternate source of rubber. Several of these schemes were carried out under the auspices of the U.S. Forest Service.

Dozens of the Forest Service's Northern Region employees from Missoula were temporarily transferred to Salinas, California, where the government established large plantations of guayule, a latex-producing plant that the government hoped would help ease the severe shortage of rubber. Regional Forester Evan Kelley was put in charge of the guayule project, which was curtailed in the fall of 1943 because of the increased production of synthetic rubber.

Some of the remaining Forest Service workers in Montana planted 30 acres of Russian dandelions (kok-sagyz), in the Target Range area outside of Missoula, and at two other test sites near Miles City and Lewistown. The sap of the dandelions contained small amounts of latex, and the government was interested in finding out if the weeds could be used

Planting guayule seeds in a nursery at Salinas, California, in May 1942. The fine seed is planted with a mixture of sawdust and sand. LC-USW3-35374-D

Many of Montana's Forest Service personnel were sent to Salinas, California, during the fall of 1942 to supervise the government's rush program to produce rubber from the guayule plant. Bales of guayule are stacked in a California barn. LC-USF 34-72532-D

Dr. William B. McCallum of Intercontinental Rubber Producers, manager of the guayule project in Salinas, had been with the company since 1910 and was reputed to be the world's expert on guayule cultures. LC-USF34-70977-D

Bozeman, population 8,665, was the seat of government for the 17,500 residents of Gallatin County. In 1942 Bozeman was an agricultural, tourism and trade center, as well as being home to Montana State College, the largest unit of the state university system. With the exception of army aviation cadets who trained at Montana State College, the war brought few changes to the Bozeman area. Tourism in nearby Yellowstone National Park dropped off dramatically during the war years, which hurt the Bozeman economy. Media outlets included the *Bozeman Daily Chronicle* and KXLQ radio, an NBC affiliate. During the summer months the Bobcat Drive-In was a popular hangout. A warehouse in Bozeman shipped seed peas all over the country, and the surrounding area boasted large numbers of purebred cattle. The college's annual livestock show was canceled due to the war. Most of the men of Company C, 163rd Infantry Regiment, as well as the 163rd band were from Bozeman. One of those serving with the 163rd was Bozeman City Manager M.E. Henderson, whose job was held open for him until he returned after a seven-year absence. H.B. Landoe served as mayor until he was granted leave by the city council during the spring of 1945 in order to enlist in the military. He was replaced by Harry L. Healy.

Pacific

- William Dreidlein of White Sulphur Springs was on the *USS Wasp* when it sank. He spent several hours in the water before being rescued.
- Lt. Cmdr. Lee S. Pancake of Malta, the staff commander of a destroyer squadron, was killed in action October 26, 1942 in the Pacific. He was awarded the Navy Cross for his actions. Phillips County later named a B-29 bomber after him.
- Lt. Stanley W. "Swede" Vejtasa of Circle was a F4F pilot with Fighting Squadron Ten aboard the *USS Enterprise*. A former University of Montana student, Vejtasa shot down 11 Japanese planes, sank a cruiser, damaged a carrier, and participated in the battles of Coral Sea and Santa Cruz. At Santa Cruz he singlehandedly shot down two Japanese dive bombers and five torpedo planes which were attacking the damaged *Enterprise*, the only American carrier still afloat in the Pacific. Credited with saving the *Enterprise* from further damage, he was awarded a gold star in lieu of his third Navy Cross.
- Walter Johnson of Turner, chief torpedoman, was on the *USS Guardfish* when the submarine approached so closely to the Japanese Coast that the crewmen were able to take photos of a horse race held on shore. *Guardfish* became the first submarine awarded a Presidential Unit Citation.
- Richard Purdum of Bozeman was awarded the Air Medal after attacking a Japanese carrier and destroying three planes.

to produce commercial amounts of rubber. An additional 30 acres of Russian dandelions were planted near Missoula and Frenchtown in 1943, and 1,200 pounds of seed and 5,000 pounds of dandelion roots were sent to Philadelphia to be tested for rubber content. The dandelions yielded between 50 and 60 pounds of rubber per acre, but, like the planting of guayule, the Russian dandelion project was deemed unsuccessful and was dropped during the summer of 1944.

Forest Service workers were already overworked without the added burden of planting dandelions. Four hundred former Region One employees were serving with the armed forces by the fall of 1942, and the war effort had greatly added to the duties of the remaining workers. Employees of Missoula's smokejumper center taught soldiers the art of parachute rigging while forest engineers were kept busy building roads into several new mines which were being rushed into production around the state. Although more than $3,000,000 was allocated for Forest Service projects in Montana during 1942, the same year saw funding dropped for the Civilian Conservation Corps (CCC), a program which the Forest Service had administered for the past nine years. In September 1942, the Army took over the administration of 38 CCC camps from the Forest Service. The Army intended to use the camps to house conscientious objectors to the draft. One hundred and fifty conscientious objectors were sent to Glacier Park to help fight fires and do maintenance work in the Park. They were part of the Civilian Public Service (CPS) program. Most of the men were Quakers, Amish, Hutterites, and Mennonites who objected to serving in the military due to religious reasons. Although the program fell under the auspices of the Selective Service, it was administered by the Mennonite Church. The CPS men in Glacier Park were housed at Camp 55, near the western entrance of the park. The camp housed some 200 men, who were paid $5.00 per month, received no benefits, and pretty much stayed to themselves. Since 1970 the CPS men have held a number of reunions at Glacier Park.

Other CPS men were sent to Missoula for smokejumper training, and throughout the war years most of the Region One smokejumpers were conscientious objectors. One of the CPS smokejumpers was a Pennsylvania Quaker named David Flaccus. After the war Flaccus remained in Montana, where he founded Mountain Press Printing in Missoula, and along with Bob Johnson, built the Snowbowl Ski

Members of the Civilian Public Service (CPS) smokejumper unit at Camp Paxson, near Seeley Lake, 1943. These conscientious objectors spent the war years fighting forest fires in the west. EARL COOLEY, MISSOULA

Area.

Due to wartime shortages of supplies, money, and manpower, the National Park Service considered closing Glacier and Yellowstone National Parks for the 1943 season. Park officials at Yellowstone had experienced bear trouble throughout the summer, with one human fatality and 200 bear-related injuries in the park. Park rangers killed 83 bears during the summer.

Badly damaged by torpedoes during the Japanese attack on Pearl Harbor, the *USS Helena* had undergone several months of repairs and refitting at Mare Island, California, before leaving for the dangerous waters surrounding the Solomon Islands in mid-July 1942. On one of the *Helena's* first missions in the South Pacific, the light cruiser was escorting the *USS Wasp* when the aircraft carrier was struck by three torpedoes fired by a Japanese submarine. *Helena* picked up 400 men from the sinking *Wasp* and carried them to safety. *Helena* herself was nearly struck by two torpedoes launched by two different submarines, one of which hit another cruiser. On September 23, Capt. Oliver Read was reassigned and Capt. Gilbert C. Hoover, who held the Navy Cross, took command. Boasting an extremely well-trained crew and a band that was a popular attraction for sailors from other ships when they were in port, the cruiser named for Montana's capital city was known as the "Happy *Helena*."

Much of the war news in October 1942 centered on the island of Guadalcanal and the vicious sea battles occurring offshore between the U.S. Navy and the Japanese fleet. It was in the waters off Guadalcanal where the crack gun crews of the *USS Helena* began taking their revenge for Pearl Harbor. In mid-October, the *Helena* and eight other ships set off to meet an approaching Japanese fleet. It was a pitch-black night, but the *Helena* was equipped with the most modern radar set available. The *Helena* detected the oncoming Japanese force before any of the other American ships and Captain Hoover requested permission to open fire. Admiral Scott on the *USS San Francisco* told him to wait. A few minutes later Hoover again requested permission. "Roger" came the reply, acknowledging receipt of the message, but signal officer Lt. W.D. Fisher erroneously reported to Hoover that permission had been given, and *Helena* opened fire with her 15 main guns at 11:46. According to radio officer C.G. Morris, "in the radio shack and coding room we were sent reeling and stumbling against the bulkheads, smoth-

ered by a snowstorm of books and papers from the tables. The clock leaped from its pedestal. Electric fans hit the deck with a metallic clatter. Not a man in the room had a breath left in him."

The *Helena's* six-inch shells slammed into a Japanese ship and set it ablaze. In the flickering light of the burning vessel, more than a dozen warships on both sides opened fire. A Japanese destroyer sank in less than two minutes of combat, and *Helena* turned her guns on the Japanese cruiser *Aoba*, mortally wounding Admiral Goto. A hot shell-case ejected from turret #5 started a small fire on the main deck, but it was quickly extinguished. A hang-fire in turret #4 caused some concern on-board, but the defective shell was ejected and thrown overboard without incident. Swerving wildly to avoid Japanese torpedoes and burning ships, *Helena's* expert gun crews kept up a steady barrage as the battle of Cape Esperance degenerated into a confused melee. By the time dawn broke, the sea was littered with smashed and sinking ships. The *Helena* however, emerged unscathed from the thick of the battle.

Closer to home, 1,500 Japanese-Americans who had been displaced from their West Coast homes were helping pick the vital sugar beet crop, as were some of the Italian prisoners from Fort Missoula. Even so, there were not enough workers to get the crop in before the ground froze, and Gov. Sam Ford appealed to President Roosevelt to send soldiers to help harvest the 65,000 acres of beets. He was turned down, but local businessmen, Boy Scouts, college and high school students and other ordinary citizens stepped forward to help save the precious crop.

At the Great Western Sugar refinery in Billings, the Utah-Idaho Sugar Company in Chinook, and at the plants owned by the Holly Sugar Company in Hardin, Sidney and Miles City, employees worked overtime to cook the record 915,000 tons of beets that had been picked. The American Crystal Sugar Company in Missoula processed some 2,200 freight cars full of beets, an increase of 60 percent from the year before. In all, 141,000 tons of processed sugar were produced in the Treasure State in 1942, and Montana farmers enjoyed a sharp rise in income from the previous year.

The total value of all of the state's agricultural crops reached $134,000,000 in 1942. The cattle industry also had a banner year, but the sheep industry, which brought in only $13,000,000 during 1942, experienced the beginning of a decline which would extend throughout the war years.

The Great Western Sugar Company in Billings. MHS 941-126

The labor shortage also took a toll on the state's mining industry. All gold mines were ordered closed so that the miners and their equipment could be used to produce more strategic minerals, like chromium from the large Mouat Mine near Columbus, and copper from the mines at Butte. In November, 500 black soldiers arrived in Butte to help work in the mines. The city was rocked by rumors that local miners would rather strike rather than work with the blacks, but union leaders in Butte called this charge completely false and the soldiers went to work without incident. The blacks were soon discharged from the Army, but continued to work in the mines throughout the war.

Spurred by the example of the Smithsonian Institution, which donated their collection of World War I cannon and armaments to the war effort, the University of Montana Journalism School donated their historic linotype machine as part of a nationwide scrap drive. A Civil War cannon at the Northern Pacific Railroad depot in Missoula also went into the scrap heap. Ravalli County residents turned in nearly 1,000 tons of scrap metal by December. Students at Big Sandy School collected an average of 760 pounds of scrap metal apiece, while other school-children around the state went door to door collecting old brass keys, a drive that yielded 7,400 pounds of high-quality metal. With 200 rail cars of scrap leaving the state each month, Montana's scrap metal goal for the upcoming year was set at 32,000 tons. The U.S. Forest Service identified some 6,000 tons

of metal available for scrap on federal land in Montana. Most of the metal was located in old abandoned sawmills around the region, and one of the first shipments of scrap metal came from an old tepee burner located at the original Bonner Mill. It was dynamited and loaded aboard rail cars. Montana became the first state in the union to reach the federally mandated quota.

Family pets also played a part in the war effort and the "Dogs for Defense" program accepted donated Siberian Huskies, Alaskan Malamutes, and Eskimo dogs for military use. George McCole served as the state director of the program. The Army's War Dog Reception Training Center was set up at Camp Rimini, in the mountains near Helena, to train the dogs for sled pulling, packing, and search and rescue work. More than 600 Montanans donated their dogs. The majority of the dogs were sent to Camp Robinson, Nebraska, but some went to Camp Rimini. Although most were eventually used in rescue operations in Alaska and Canada, some of these dogs saw action in combat situations in Europe and the Pacific islands.

Once hunting season began, Montana hunters began flocking to the woods. Shortages of meat were expected and many people who had never hunted before took up the sport. Surprisingly, despite rationing and shortages of all kinds of products, the sale of firearms and ammunition was not yet restricted. Gambles Hardware stores did a brisk business selling Winchester pump shotguns for $56 apiece,

Government-built housing at the Mouat mine, near Columbus, Montana. This mine, and the nearby Benbow, contained much of the nation's known reserves of chromium. The mines were operated by the Anaconda Copper Mining Co. They were ordered closed later in the war in order to shift miners and equipment to the Butte mines.
LC-USW3-9000-E

and a box of 12-gauge shells cost just $1.00. Unfortunately for hunters, the weather didn't cooperate. A warm, dry fall in 1942 kept the harvest low. A severe snowstorm in early November left 10-foot-high drifts which trapped 23 hunters in backcountry camps on the Powell Ranger District.

The meat shortage quickly became a reality for many people, and catfish stew, hotdogs and horsemeat were promoted as alternatives to the increasingly scarce beef, chicken and turkey. Housewives learned to stretch hamburger by adding Quaker Oats. Although Montana cowboys were vehemently opposed, horses were shipped from the Drummond area to a meat packing plant.

At the same time, the government revealed that household cooking fats like bacon grease were desperately needed for the production of urgently needed defense materials like nitroglycerine, lubricants, medical supplies, textiles and adhesives. Montana households, restaurants, and grocery stores were

urged to save the cooking fats, and Camp Fire Girls, 4-H Clubs, and the Girls Reserve began collecting tons of grease. They collected a record 27 tons of bacon grease and household fats by April of 1943.

Coffee was added to the list of restricted products in November, and shoppers were only allowed to buy a pound of brew every five weeks, approximately one cup of coffee per day. A shortage of dress material resulted when the army bought up millions of yards of fabric to give to North African women as a goodwill gesture. Cigarettes were not yet rationed, but the production of hard liquor was halted completely in November. Although distillers reported they had enough bourbon on hand to supply the country for five years, shortages of gin and vodka were predicted, and some liquor stores around the state were cleaned out.

Inflation rose steadily throughout the war years, despite government price controls on rent and food. Firewood prices skyrocketed in western Montana,

Dogs For Defense

• "Mae West," a dog donated by Reverend Traweek of Lewistown, was killed in action.
• "Rock," a black lab donated by Mr. and Mrs. John Williams of Washoe, was killed in action. The William's other dog, "Blackie," served for 13 months before receiving an honorable discharge.
• "Brownie," a collie donated by Richard Hollenback of Gold Creek, was killed in action in Europe.
• "Moocher," a war dog donated by Ben P. Watkins of Chinook, was killed in action.
• "Kappy," a doberman donated by Lester F. Bishop of Butte, was credited with saving the lives of several Marines on Iwo Jima.

The Army's War Dog Reception Center was established at Camp Rimini in 1942 in order to supply pack dogs for the First Special Service Force. Once Project Plough was canceled, however, officials at Rimini concentrated on producing trained sled dogs. The sled dogs were primarily used by rescue crews in Alaska, Canada and Greenland. The dog kennels shown here were constructed of crates used to ship equipment to the First Special Service Force at Fort Harrison. MHS 83-45

the price of paperback books went up to 49 cents apiece, and bus fares in Missoula rose from a nickel to seven cents. Marriage licenses increased $.25 to $2.25. A shave-and-a-haircut went from $1.00 to $1.25, and the weekly newspaper column entitled "How a family of four can eat well on $13 a week" changed to $14 a week.

As the November elections approached, senatorial candidate Wellington Rankin deftly mixed patriotism, family values and the economy in his 1942 campaign for the senate seat held by James Murray. He pledged to "vigorously support every measure to win the war and crush the Axis military powers forever, furnish care for families dependent upon those in the military and secure a fair share of war industries for Montana."

Murray alienated many voters in Montana after he wrote several articles for the magazine *Soviet Russia Today*, in which he praised V.I. Lenin, the Red Army, and the Soviet government. Fellow Democrat, Sen. B.K. Wheeler opposed Murray's reelection during the primary, but remained quiet during the main election against Wellington Rankin. Despite Rankin's promises, voters narrowly reelected Murray, perhaps because many were still angry at Rankin's sister, Jeannette, the only member of Congress to oppose the United State's entry into World War II. The race was so close that Murray was not declared the winner until the Friday after the election.

Howard A. Johnson was elected chief justice of the five-member Supreme Court, and Republicans gained a majority in both houses of the state legislature. Voters in eastern Montana reelected Democratic Congressman James O'Connor over Republican challenger F.F. Haynes. O'Connor was a friend and ally of Wheeler who had previously served three terms in the House. Jeannette Rankin, who had chosen not to seek reelection, had worked on several bills during the past year, one to provide aid for Indians dependent on men in the military and another to extend the statute of limitations on crooked war contractors. Neither of these bills were passed. She also published a book entitled *Some Questions About Pearl Harbor*.

Montana voters sent a political newcomer to replace Jeannette Rankin in Congress. University professor Mike J. Mansfield easily defeated Republican Howard K. Hazelbaker, the owner of the *Flathead Courier* newspaper in Polson. Mansfield grew up in Great Falls, then joined the Navy at age 14. He also served in the U.S. Marines and the Army for a period before going to work in the Butte mines for eight years. After receiving a Masters degree, he taught history at the University of Montana from 1933 until his election to Congress. Other prominent state politicians included Superintendent of Public Instruction Elizabeth Ireland, who served from 1929-1937 and from 1941 to 1949. Postmaster General Frank Walker was the first Montanan to hold national cabinet rank, and he became involved in a major controversy when he suspended the 2nd class mailing privileges of *Esquire* magazine, after the magazine printed "obscene" paintings of half-dressed women.

Allied forces all over the world took the offensive during the fall of 1942. In October the British army attacked German troops at El Alamein, while the Soviets were preparing to spring a giant trap on the unsuspecting German forces at Stalingrad. On November 8, 1942, American soldiers landed at several places in North Africa. In the Pacific, thousands of U.S. Marines desperately hung on to a tiny beachhead on the island of Guadalcanal. The light cruiser *USS Helena* continued to protect the Marines from the Japanese fleet. At the end of October, the *Helena* bombarded Japanese positions on Lunga Point and Kokumbona on Guadalcanal, and a few days later fired on Japanese soldiers at Koli Point. In November 1942, the *Helena* played a prominent role in what one American admiral called, "the fiercest naval battle ever fought." The *Helena* entered Lengo channel early on November 12 and bombarded Japanese positions on Guadalcanal. The American ships were attacked by Japanese bombers, one of which hit the heavy cruiser *USS San Francisco*. Late that night the American fleet went searching for Japanese warships bringing reinforcements and supplies to the embattled forces of the Imperial Army.

Thirteen American ships moved stealthily toward the suspected position of the Japanese ships. During the early morning hours of Friday the 13th, a night so dark that *Helena*'s lookouts reported they could not see their hands in front of their faces, the *Helena*'s modern radar detected the oncoming Japanese ships long before the rest of the fleet. According to a U.S. Navy release, "A cruiser stabbed the darkness with her searchlight, found the *Helena* and opened fire. The *Helena*'s main battery, meanwhile, had been trained on the same cruiser and had gotten the range. The *Helena*, as in the Battle of Cape Esperance, was the first United States ship to fire."

Cpl. Fred Svennson of Great Falls drew this cartoon of life in England for the typical American soldier. Svennson was later killed in action.

DARLAN ASSASSINAT

GREAT FALLS TRIB

MONTANA'S BEST NEWS GATHERER

United Press

Fifty-Eighth Year

GREAT FALLS, MONTANA, FRIDAY MORNING, DEC. 25, 1942

Soldiers Send Greetings to Tribune Readers

Corporal Fred Svensson, formerly of Dutton and Great Falls, sent the above cartoon to The Tribune. Svensson formerly drew some cartoons for The Tribune and for several years had his art reproduced by The Montana Famer. In his letter, Svensson says Montana boys in his battalion in Britain enjoy reading The Tribune and suggests they wished to send greetings to their home folks in the Christmas edition of this newspaper. The card bore the names of the following Montanans serving with Svensson in Britain: Lieut. J. C. Walters, Whitefish; Corporal M. E. Berget, Shelby; Corporal G. A. Burgoyne, Hamilton; Serg. E. C. Burmeister, Billings; Serg. P. Dahlman, Great Falls; Private T. Finkbeiner, Terry; Corporal Harold Jensen, Chester; Corporal L. C. Johnson, Valier; Serg. P. J. Murphy, Nashua; Serg. J. F. Petit, White Sulphur Springs; Serg. P. B. Sheets, Shelby; Serg. N. Shotnakoff Jr., Fort Peck; Corporal Fred Svensson, Great Falls; Serg. W. A. Martin, Conrad; Corporal Benjamin Annis, Billings; Corporal H. R. Warren, Dodson; Serg. Alfred Rud, Conrad; Private Carl Haglund, Eureka; Corporal J. W. Grady, Livingston; Corporal M. J. Hull, Chester; Private Ed Lenning, Avon; Private C. F. Chapman, Malta; Serg. W. W. Hatcher, Belgrade; Corporal T. Knapp, Philipsburg; Serg. George McFarland, Billings; Private S. A. Sungren, Joplin; Corporal C. W. Adams, Galata; Private W. C. Buklis, Eureka; Private H. C. Mainard, Conrad; Corporal J. H. Myrvang, Dodson; Private Willis Porter, Absarokee; Corporal H. D. Shea, Walkerville; Serg. A. Panauuk, Miles City.

Harlem Boy, 16, Captured at Chinook After Fatal Shooting of Girl Friend

CHINOOK, Dec. 24.—(AP)—After saying he knew "nothing"

Allies Sink 3 Jap Ships In Big Sweep

Ground Forces Pierce Enemy's Last Line of Defense in Buna Area

MELBOURNE, Dec. 25.—(AP) —Allied airmen have sunk a Japanese destroyer, a transport and a cargo ship to the north of New Guinea in the most widespread air sweeps in the southwest Pacific in many weeks, while American and Australian ground forces have penetrated to what an official communique today described as "the last line" of Japanese defenses in the Buna area.

Ranging over the waters to the northwest and north of Australia, Gen. Douglas MacArthur's airmen shot down six Japanese planes and damaged five others in nine separate sorties. These attacks carried the Allied planes over the principal enemy operational bases in the islands from Timor to New Ireland.

Attacking from both flanks, Australian and American infantry, backed by tanks, artillery and mortars, Thursday smashed through the enemy's outer defenses around the Buna government station. At nightfall the Allies controlled practically all of the main airfield at Buna and had the Japanese pinned down to a coastal strip about a mile long and between 500 and 600 yards deep.

The communique warned, however, that this confined space was "a prepared and fortified citadel of resistance."

In a series of hard-hitting attacks at Japanese shipping north of New Guinea, Consolidated B-24s sank a Japanese cargo vessel off Arawe, a port on the south coast of New Britain, destroyed a 5,000-ton transport near Gasmata, and medium bombers sank a destroyer off the New Guinea coast near Salamaua.

The B-24s fought off 15 Zero fighting planes which made an unsuccessful effort to screen the transport near Gasmata. One of the Zeros was shot down and two others were damaged.

Over Kavieng, New Ireland, one B-24 bomber shot down two Japanese fighters and damaged two others which attempted to inter-

Dies in

R. E. MOR

Lieutenant Morrison state senator from county, who had entered the army first lieutenant last Thursday morning a medium bomber near Tampa, Fla. Press reported. Lieutenant rison was stationed Field, Tampa.

Red Mo Dies in At Tamp

Flying State Was Leading In Montana

HELENA, Dec. Morrison died today lived for much of in the air.

The war departm nounced that Lieut. son, 42, of MacDill was killed in the c ium bomber on the park.

-56-

Training exercises of the First Special Service Force at Fort Harrison, 1942. Bob Durkee, Helena

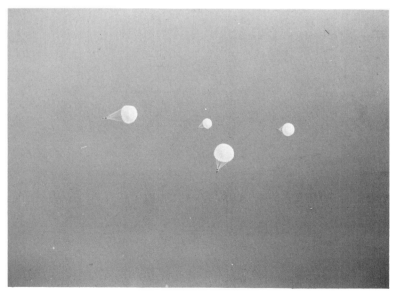

Esperance, was the first United States ship to fire." One sailor said it was "like sitting in the front row of a theater with your pants off when the house lights are switched on." *Helena*'s crack gunners opened fire with devastating effect, destroying the searchlights and setting the Japanese cruiser on fire. It sank in less than five minutes, and *Helena*'s gunners began firing on three different targets at once, one of them a much more powerful Japanese battleship.

According to radio officer Lt. C.G. Morris, "It was a picture too vast for the imagination, and even when it was over no man could quite put the flaming bits of the puzzle together or be sure of what he had seen." The *Helena*'s forward turrets were scarred by shrapnel and a shell went through the pyrotechnics locker but didn't explode. One of the *Helena*'s sailors was killed by flying shrapnel on the searchlight platform, and the cruiser was nearly struck by the badly damaged *USS Juneau*. Although *Helena* survived the battle with only one casualty and no serious damage, the rest of the American fleet was not so lucky.

As dawn broke over Guadalcanal, the sea was riddled with burning and sinking ships. Hundreds of wounded sailors were struggling to stay afloat in the shark-infested waters. Two American admirals were dead and Captain Hoover of the *Helena* found himself the senior surviving officer. He took command of the fleet and withdrew. *Helena* escorted two badly damaged cruisers, *San Francisco* and *Juneau*, away from the battle, but they were discovered by a Japanese submarine, and a torpedo slammed into *Juneau*. Aboard *Helena*, Lt. Morris described the explosion, "Suddenly without warning she leaped from the sea in a blinding burst of light." The ship exploded and sank within seconds, killing more than 600 sailors instantly. "All we saw of the ship herself was a 5-inch gun turret, completely intact, hurtling through the air high above the *Helena*'s stack.... Nothing was under it. Nothing at all. The *Juneau* had vanished as though she had been in a mirage."

Stunned watchers on the *Helena* were convinced that no one could have survived such an explosion. Captain Hoover, worried that more torpedoes might be on the way, ordered the rest of his ships to keep moving, despite the fact that the captain of the *Juneau* was Lyman K. Swenson, his close friend and former classmate. Because he made no effort to pick up the estimated 100 survivors of the *Juneau*, most of whom eventually drowned, Captain Hoover was relieved of his command and sent home. Although

Hoover was later exonerated by a board of inquiry and awarded his third Navy Cross for his part in the Battle of Guadalcanal, the incident devastated the morale of the *USS Helena*'s crew. According to Morris, "the ship said goodbye to him proudly. He had taken us almost unscathed through the Battle of Cape Esperance and the Battle of Guadalcanal, two of the most violent night engagements in history."

October 1942

· October 1. Thirty-five mile an hour speed limit goes into effect.
· October 4. St. Louis Cardinals win the World Series after defeating the New York Yankees four games to one.
· October 7. US Marines begin offensive at the mouth of Matanikau River on Guadalcanal.
· October 8. Gold mining in the state is halted in order to free up miners and materials for more vital mineral production.
· October 11 & 12. *USS Helena* plays a crucial part during the night sea battle of Cape Esperance.
· October 14. Five German divisions attack Soviets holed up in the Tractor Factory at Stalingrad.
· October 23. British begin offensive at El Alamein.
· October 31. Idaho Vandals defeat Montana Grizzlies 21-0 in football.

November 1942

· November 2. Arthur L. Higgins, fourth and last son of Missoula founder C.P. Higgins, dies at age 69.
· November 7. Montana Grizzly football team is defeated 33-0 against Oregon State.
· November 8. U.S. troops land in North Africa (Operation Torch).
· November 12. British troops retake Tobruk.
· November 13. *USS Helena* fires first in a sea battle off Guadalcanal which prevents Japanese from landing reinforcements.
· November 14. Butte theaters reopen after a three-week strike. Montana Grizzlies are defeated 13-0 by the California Golden Bears.
· November 18. Gas rationing books are issued.
· November 19. A massive Russian counter-offensive on the Don River surrounds German forces at Stalingrad.
· November 21. Five hundred soldiers arrive in Butte to work in the mines.

6

Montanans In The Jungle

In the South Pacific, the U.S. and Australian armies began to move against the Japanese invaders of New Guinea. The 32nd Division went to New Guinea first, followed in mid-December by the 41st (Sunset) Division, including some 1,200 Montanans serving with the 163rd Infantry Regiment. The Montana National Guardsmen had spent the last four months of 1942 training at Rockhampton, Australia. They celebrated Christmas while sweating in the tropical heat aboard a troopship sailing north from Australia. After a harrowing journey across the submarine-infested waters of the Coral Sea, the Guardsmen arrived at Port Moresby, New Guinea. Hudson transport planes ferried the soldiers over the Owen Stanley Mountains, the same mountains in which Vern Haugland had been lost some three months before. More than a year after the Japanese attack on Pearl Harbor, the men from Montana were about to see their first combat, in the malarial jungles of New Guinea.

The men of the 163rd were headed for Sanananda, on the northern coast of Papua, where the final stages of the bloody Buna-Gona campaign were being played out. The lumbering Australian planes carried them into Dobodura, a primitive airstrip carved into the jungle 10 miles from the front line. As soon as the soldiers of the 163rd exited the planes, the Hudsons were loaded with scores of sick, wounded and dispirited American and Australian soldiers. Under the leadership of Col. Jens Doe, the 163rd spent New Year's Day relieving Australian troops and the American 126th Infantry. The sight did little to buoy their confidence. Only 95 of the 126th's 1,100 men were still combat effective. Lt. Gen. Eichelberger, the former superintendent of the U.S. Military Academy at West Point, and the American commander on the scene thought, "They were so ragged and so pitiful that when I met them my eyes were wet."

The 163rd Combat Team dug into the jungle only a few yards from veteran Japanese soldiers along the Sanananda Trail. The soldiers from Montana endured constant sniper fire, short rations and tropical disease as they began to learn the art of jungle fighting. As much as 10 inches of rain fell in one night, and the soldiers often waded hip-deep in the water.

According to General MacArthur's staff in Australia, Sanananda was a mopping-up operation. General Eichelberger on the front lines thought differently. "Instead, it was a completely savage and expensive battle." The 163rd found itself facing the main Japanese force, several thousand men, and in the dense jungle of the Sanananda Trail the Japanese and American positions became mixed, a situation that worried Eichelberger. "Our supply lines ... ran through dense jungle, and these dangerous routes were necessarily under constant patrol."

A staff officer in Port Moresby didn't think Colonel Doe and the 163rd were moving fast enough, so Eichelberger went forward to check on them. "American soldiers were lying across the road and firing; there were also Americans and Japanese firing behind us. We were at the Fisk Perimeter--so called for Lieutenant Harold R. Fisk, the first officer of the 163rd to be hit in battle.... This was Doe's command post. It had a roof of sorts and revetments to protect it. I said. 'Where are the Japs?' Doe answered, 'Right over there. See that bunker?' I saw it and [General] Vasey saw it, and it was only fifty yards away. He gave us some hot tea and then went on with the attack. Vasey was satisfied with Doe's determination, and so was I."

In an engagement on January 5th, Company B of Poplar lost eight dead and three wounded, the first Montana casualties suffered by the 163rd. Capt. Duncan V. Dupree of Poplar was one of those killed at Sanananda. During the second week of January, Maj. W.R. Rankin of Bozeman led G Company and the rest of the Second Battalion of the 163rd through thick jungle 700 yards to the west of the main position, where he blocked the Japanese escape route along the Killerton Trail. This isolated the remaining Japanese forces into small pockets of starving men. Back home, state newspapers quickly figured out that the Montana National Guard was involved in the fighting at Sanananda. Interviewed about his friend W.R. Rankin, State Forester Rutledge Parker said, "Jungle fighting is second nature to the major. He has lived all his life in the mountains and is one

December 1942

- December 2. World's first nuclear reaction takes place at University of Chicago.
- December 5. Montana Grizzlies lose final game of the season, 38-0 against UCLA.
- December 9. First WASPs begin ferrying planes into Great Falls.
- December 18. Meat ration cut to 35 ounces per week.
- December 21. Two army officers die in crash of light plane near Helena.
- December 24. "Worlds Most Awful Battle," underway on the outskirts of Stalingrad. Ralph "Red" Morrison of Helena, a pioneer of Montana aviation and a former state legislator, dies in a plane crash at MacDill Field, Florida.
- December 27. 163rd Infantry Regiment, Montana National Guard, arrives at Port Moresby, New Guinea.
- December 28. Military Policemen from Great Falls Air Base are involved in a gunfight at a Black Eagle bar. Four civilians are wounded.
- December 30. B-17 crashes 11 miles south of Musselshell, killing all 12 aboard.

General Eichelberger discusses strategy at Sanananda with Col. Jens Doe, commander of the 163rd Infantry Regiment, formerly the Montana National Guard. The 163rd Infantry Historical Committee

Sanananda

- Staff Sgt. Paul Ziegele of Jordan won a Distinguished Service Cross after crawling up to a Japanese position and trying to pull the enemy machine gun out by the barrel. He was unsuccessful but eventually managed to shoot the three Japanese gunners.
- Staff Sgt. John L. Mohl of White Pine won his Distinguished Service Cross for singlehandedly taking out a pillbox at Sanananda, then he and another man silenced five more pillboxes. He then helped evacuate eight wounded men.
- Master Sgt. Herbert T. Warren of Suffolk was one of the first Montanans to be awarded a Legion of Merit medal for his actions at Sanananda.
- Capt. Mark D. Holcomb, a Whitefish doctor, was awarded the Legion of Merit by General MacArthur for providing medical service under fire at Sanananda.
- Lt. Byron Armstrong, of Glasgow, Co. G of the 163rd, won two Silver Stars and a Bronze Star. He eventually became a battalion commander of the 163rd.
- Sgt. Ronald Bretzke of Glasgow was posthumously awarded the Silver Star. Just before he was killed, he saved the life of his commander by shouting a warning.
- Sgt. James Boland was posthumously awarded the Silver Star for "extreme gallantry." Five hundred people, including Governor Ford, attended the medal ceremony at the Great Falls Civic Center.
- Montanans winning the Silver Star for bravery at Sanananda included Capt. John L. Hoffman, Capt. William C. Benson of Great Falls (his second), Col. C.R. Dawley of Great Falls, Staff Sgt. Harry Trodick of Great Falls, Sgt. Robert Mitchell of Poplar, Lt. Daniel G. Massing of Moulton, Capt. Conway T. Ellers of Shepherd, Pvt. Raymond A. Ackerman of Fraser, and Harold Pynter of Bozeman.

Scenes of the battle around Sanananda. Soldiers from Montana found rough going in the thick jungle and swamps of Papua-New Guinea. THE 163RD INFANTRY HISTORICAL COMMITTEE

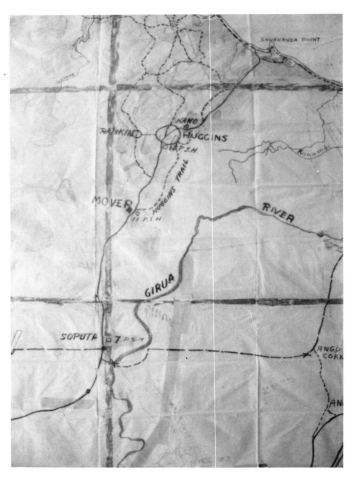

Original tissue paper map of the Sanananda area showing the location of the Huggins and Rankin perimeters. The men of the Montana National Guard defeated a large force of Japanese during this final battle of the Buna-Gona campaign. THE 163RD INFANTRY HISTORICAL COMMITTEE

Officers and men of the 163rd Infantry Regiment in New Guinea. THE 163RD INFANTRY HISTORICAL COMMITTEE

January 1943

· January 1. Point rationing system begins.
· January 4. Montana pioneer Andrew Garcia dies at Fish Creek at age 86. *USS Helena* bombards Japanese on Munda and is attacked by dive-bombers.
· January 14. President Roosevelt and Winston Churchill meet in Casablanca.
· January 15. WPB orders bakeries to stop slicing bread.
· January 16. Blizzard rages across the northern plains of Montana.
· January 17. The production of firearms, ammunition, and fishing tackle is completely halted. The sale of type-writers is also halted.
· January 21. Schools are closed and roads drifted in throughout much of northern Montana. Temperatures plummet to 30 degrees below zero.
· January 23. 163rd Regiment overcomes last Japanese resistance at Sanananda.
· January 28. One thousand people watch "E" ceremony at Anaconda smelter.
· January 29. Bobcat basketball team defeats Grizzlies 56-45.

of the best outdoorsmen I know."

According to General Eichelberger, "The 163rd had to do most of the nasty job of obliterating the enemy in a series of scattered skirmishes. The defeated Japanese would not give in." The men from Montana adapted to jungle fighting quickly and one after another the last Japanese strongholds were eliminated. As the Japanese began to evacuate, Australians and Americans hit them from all sides. On January 16, G Company of the 163rd received heavy machine gun fire from several Japanese huts which had been used as a field hospital, and some 50 armed Japanese soldiers were killed there. The notorious Japanese broadcaster "Tokyo Rose" called this incident a massacre, and thereafter referred to the 163rd as the "Butchers" of Sanananda. General MacArthur, on the other hand, cited the 163rd and the rest of the 41st Division for "extraordinary courage."

In three weeks of intense fighting the regiment had taken almost 25 percent casualties. Although most were victims of disease, the Montana Regimental Combat Team suffered 97 dead, 4 missing, and 215 wounded in actual combat. Out of the 3,820 men who had flown into Dobodura, 923 had been felled by disease or Japanese bullets. In turn, the Americans of the 163rd killed 1,200 Japanese, one quarter of the 5,000 lost at Sanananda. By the end of January 22, 1943, the fighting at Sanananda was over. Col. Charles Dawley of Great Falls, interviewed by a reporter, said, "tell our folks through their newspapers ... about the grand job these boys did today. Tell them that we are doing our very best to take care of their lads."

After the battle the 163rd spent several months building roads, draining swamps, and constructing huts. Distinguished Service Crosses were awarded to three members of the regiment, and 58 others (36 of them Montanans) won the Silver Star. General MacArthur personally awarded the Distinguished Service Cross to Col. W.R. Rankin of Whitehall and Cpl. Carlton O. Tidrick of Belton. Rankin, commanding one of the 163rd's battalions, singlehandedly crept to within 30 feet of Japanese positions and called in mortar and artillery fire on them. Tidrick won the DSC when his platoon was cut off by machine gun fire. Despite being wounded in three places, Tidrick continued to lead his men in an assault on a Japanese stronghold only 20 feet away, forcing the Japanese to withdraw.

While the men of the Montana National Guard were stuck in the steaming jungles of New Guinea, workmen were completing the new barracks going up at Fort Harrison, even though most of the hand-picked commandos of the First Special Service Force spent the winter living at camps in the mountains west of Helena. They learned winter survival skills and cross-country skiing. Each of the Forcemen spent six weeks at a camp near Blossburg on the Continental Divide, where they lived in railroad boxcars while enduring temperatures of 50 degrees below zero. Twelve Norwegian instructors taught them to ski, and at the end of the training each man could ski 30 miles a day carrying a loaded pack and a rifle. They also learned to drive the custom-made snowmobiles called Weasels that had been designed for their planned raid on Norway. The Forcemen didn't know that the Army had canceled Operation Plough, and that most of their specialized training would never be used.

Military plane crashes in December claimed the lives of two army officers from Fort Harrison and 12 airmen from Great Falls, where construction of the new air force base was completed ahead of schedule. The East Base project had been handled by a local contractor, the Birch-McLaughlin Company, who in one day moved as much as 104,925 cubic yards of dirt. Some of the airmen at Gore Field were sent into the nearby hills armed with axes and saws to obtain rough lumber for the base.

Across central Montana, satellite bases of the Great Falls facility were also being built at Glasgow, Lewistown, and Cut Bank. These facilities were used for the training of bomber crews. Gunnery and practice bombing ranges were established near each of the bases, as well as additional practice ranges at Fort Benton and 12 miles north of Winnett.

Large numbers of Soviets, including writers, journalists and diplomats, traveled the air route from Moscow to Great Falls, where they were allowed almost total freedom. Although the Soviets were a valued ally of the United States, they were also actively engaged in intelligence gathering in the United States. Lt. Col. Lewis J. Clarke said, "the Russians in Montana and Alaska spent much of their time trying to worm out secret information from Americans."

Soviet spies had no trouble entering the United States. According to Maj. George R. Jordan, Soviet planes landing at Great Falls often let passengers off at the far end of the runway, where they would hop over the airfield fence and run for waiting taxicabs

Salaries

Wages were frozen at no more than 15 percent above January 1, 1941 levels, and no more than $25,000 annually. Nevertheless, wages in many industries increased substantially during the war years. The average Montana worker made one hundred dollars more in 1942 than during the previous year. Part of this was due to the 48-hour work week required of most miners and lumber industry employees. Miners, lumbermen, and workers in other vital industries were not allowed to quit their jobs without permission. Throughout the war years, Montana suffered from a shortage of cowboys, sheepherders and farm laborers. In 1943 there were 3,593 state employees, 5,168 city and county employees, and 10,000 federal employees in Montana. Many businesses printed lists of their employees in the service as a form of advertising.

- ACM Miners & smelter workers - $7.25 to $8 per day.
- Civilian workers at Spokane air base - $1,260 per year for both men and women (48-hour work week).
- Defense plant welders - $62 to $72 per week.
- West coast aircraft factories - $14 per day.
- Shipyard welders - up to $1.20 per hour.
- Cooks and housekeepers - $25 to $30 per month.
- Sheepherders - $100 per month, plus room and board.
- city laborers in Great Falls - $6.75 per day.
- FBI agents - $1440 per year, starting salary.
- Radio technicians - $1440 to $2600 per year.
- Sugar Beet Workers - Minimum wage of $.40 per hour. They were paid $13 per acre for thinning, $4 per acre for the first hoeing, $3 per acre for the second hoeing, $1.25 for each ton harvested for the first 12 tons, and $1.15 per ton after that.
- Mayor of Great Falls - annual salary increased from $3,000 to $3,600 in 1943.
- University professors - Highest paid received $3,360 in 1941, raised to $4,800 by 1945.
- University presidents - The Presidents of MSC, UM, and the School of Mines each made $6,500 per year. The presidents of Eastern, Northern, and Western made $6,000 per year. Ernest Melby was paid $10,000 per year as Chancellor of Education.

Men At War

- 2nd Lt. Marshall C. Wells of Dodson was awarded the Silver Star for his actions in North Africa. On December 12, 1942, over Tripolitania, his cargo plane containing gasoline was set afire and the pilot was killed. Wells (the copilot) safely landed the plane despite being wounded, and then helped his wounded crew chief and radio operator to safety, despite an imminent explosion. They were taken prisoner by the Germans but Wells escaped after nine months in captivity.
- Sgt. Clarence Blend was awarded the Distinguished Flying Cross for his actions on October 9, 1942, when he shot down a German FW-190 from his B-17.
- Lt. Robert W. Sellos of Philipsburg was the pilot of a B-17 which carried radio correspondent Walter Cronkite on a bombing raid over Wilhelmshaven, Germany. According to Sellos it was a "damn good run."
- Skiing clubs in the state helped recruit 400 Montana skiers for the 87th Mountain Infantry Regiment, 10th Mountain Division.
- The 280th Ordnance unit at Flora, Mississippi, was comprised of 120 Montanans, plus a few out-of-state officers, and was commanded by Capt. Frank Winters of Butte.

without going through customs. Maj. Gen. Follette Bradley stated that, "I also personally know that scores of Russians were permitted to enter American territory in 1942 without visa. I believe that over the war years this number was augmented at least by hundreds."

No doubt the Soviets paid close attention to a weekly column running in the *Great Falls Tribune* called "Air Base Notes," which kept residents abreast of doings at the base, as did a base publication called the *34th Bomb Burst*. Even though there was a war on, not all was serious business at the base. In early December 1942, Tommy Dorsey and his orchestra performed at the Great Falls Civic Center in a show open only to soldiers. Many soldiers were disappointed when the world-famous Harlem Globetrotters canceled a planned game at the air base, but it wasn't long before Louis Armstrong and his band showed up in Great Falls to entertain the troops. Local citizens mounted drives to collect books, athletic equipment, and fleece wool jackets for the fliers, and soldiers of the 7th Ferrying Group were invited to the Dutt ranch outside of Great Falls, where they could ride horses, picnic, and relax. In an attempt to cut down on less wholesome forms of entertainment, the military declared all bars in the Great Falls suburb of Black Eagle off-limits to soldiers after a gunfight erupted between civilians and two military policemen. Four civilians (including two women) were wounded in the incident. The Black Eagle bars remained off-limits to servicemen until the spring of 1945.

The first women ferry pilots arrived at the air base in December. They were WASPs (Women Airforce Service Pilots). One of the new pilots was a celebrity, Katherine "Kitty" Rauls, who had won several national swimming titles and had been voted the country's top female athlete in 1937. It wasn't long before the air base began hiring women mechanics and electricians to service the planes. Many Montana women joined the new Women's Auxiliary organizations that each branch of the service was forming. Fifteen WACs were sworn into the Army at the state capitol in Helena, and 14 others joined the WASPs at the Great Falls Air Base. By early spring of 1943, more than 300 Montana women had joined the WACs. Recruiters in the state were also expected to sign up 18 Montana nurses each month, and hundreds of other women around the state were encouraged to become nursing students. The WAVES boosted recruiting with their slogan, "serve your country in your country-release a man to fight at sea."

Women moved into the work force in unprecedented numbers during the war years, and by the end of 1942 they held one of every 10 factory jobs. In Montana, women filled the vacancies created by the huge numbers of men who had enlisted in the past year. They became firefighters, mail carriers and "radioettes" (the term given to women radio operators working for Northwest Airlines) and were actively recruited as pilots by the Helena aeronautics school. Thousands of women across the state volunteered for the Red Cross and were kept busy drawing blood and preparing bandages. Others took over management of family farms and small businesses and many women left the state for high-paying jobs in defense industries. One newspaper reporter lamented that, "shaving appears to be the only male chore left to Montana men."

The first full year of war brought many other changes to the Treasure State. Seventy-five thousand people had left the state, 40,000 of them to the military, yet $61,000,000 in war-related contracts had been awarded in the state during the last six months of the year, creating many new jobs. Although Great Falls, Helena, Butte, and Anaconda all benefitted from the increased war activity, many businesses were forced to close and cities like Billings, Bozeman and Missoula suffered. Work on the Fort Peck Dam was stopped because of shortages of construction materials, and all but two WPA projects in the state were shut down, (the two remaining projects were the WPA nursery school program and the microfilming of state documents).

The loss of population resulted in a sharp drop in the collection of state and local taxes in 1942, even though the income of those who stayed had climbed. The $26,000,000 worth of war bonds that Montanans bought in December also took money out of the pockets of local merchants. On the other hand, Montana farmers enjoyed their best harvest in two decades, and the average worker in the state earned significantly more than in previous years.

Employees of the Anaconda Copper Mining Company received Christmas greetings from two prominent Army generals. Douglas MacArthur and Dwight Eisenhower sent letters thanking the miners and smelter workers for their valuable contributions to the war effort.

In January the state's largest employer, the Anaconda Copper Mining Company received an Army-

Guard at the Anaconda Copper Mining Co. smelter at Anaconda. MHS 8128

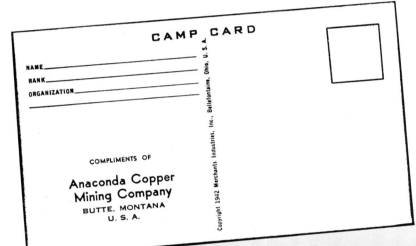

A sign outside the Anaconda Copper Mining Company in Butte, September 1942. Another attempt to curb absenteeism. LC-USW3-8231-D

Navy "E" award for producing record amounts of vitally needed metals. Governor Ford spoke before a crowd of almost 1,000 people at the ceremony in Anaconda. A large "E" banner was unfurled from the smokestack, and employees were awarded pins to wear. On the following day a similar ceremony was held at the ACM plants in Great Falls and East Helena (which together had 1,883 employees). The Great Falls smelter won five of the coveted "E" awards during the war, which was quite remarkable considering that by the time of the first award, 532 employees of the plant were serving with the military (13 had been killed in action and another five were listed as missing).

The ACM plants in Montana produced gold, silver, platinum, palladium, arsenic, bismuth, cadmium, lead, molybdenum, chrome, selenium, and vanadium, but copper was by far the most important mineral produced for the war effort. Montana mines produced 12 percent of the country's copper needs. An article in *Copper Commando*, a magazine produced by the company, revealed that 3,000 pounds of copper were needed for each B-17 bomber, and 1,000 tons of the precious metal were required for every battleship that went to sea.

ACM also helped the military develop a top-secret coil for magnetic mines, and detection gear for magnetic mines. The company also produced copper for the Soviet Union, but the quality of some of the company's products was questionable, and in 1944, ACM was fined $10,000 for deliberately producing defective telephone wire sold to the Army. Four former officials were sentenced to jail time and a $300,000 civil suit was filed against the company.

Although the mines at Butte were producing huge amounts of the red metal, recycling was also encouraged. A 200-year-old copper kettle was donated for scrap by a Plentywood woman, and theaters in Great Falls began giving free admission to children who brought in one pound of copper scrap.

Yellowstone Park officials also did their part to aid the war effort. They filled 30 rail cars with scrap metal unearthed from an old garbage dump. The heavy snow during the winter of 1942-43 caused severe problems in the world's first national park, where officials were forced to shoot nearly 4,000 elk in an effort to keep the rest of the herd from starving. Park rangers originally planned to use the meat to supply the Japanese-American relocation camp at Heart Mountain, Wyoming, but protests from Montanans forced the government to sell the unrationed elk meat on the open market.

The sale of firearms, ammunition, and fishing tackle was finally halted, but Rep. James O'Connor successfully lobbied on behalf of Montana ranchers who demanded ammunition for predator control. Even the U.S. Army was having a hard time finding some types of weapons and they began buying shotguns from Montana hunters in order to arm Military Policemen.

The American Legion and some department stores across the state accepted donations of large hunting knives to equip troops fighting in the jungles of the South Pacific. The Harlowton American Legion held a dinner in which the admission charged was a hunting or folding knife, and machinists at the Montana Power Company and the Anaconda Company volunteered to manufacture thousands of sturdy hunting knives for soldiers. Volunteers working in the shops of the Montana Power Company made 3,400 knives in Great Falls. They had plenty of good steel but did have trouble finding enough leather for scabbards. Many of these knives were sent to soldiers serving with the 163rd Infantry Regiment, which had priority at first, but eventually knives were sent to anyone who asked, and the extras were sent to the San Francisco port of embarkation.

Despite the omnipresent war, despite the fact that outdoor Christmas lights were discouraged by the War Production Board because they wasted energy, the holiday spirit was alive and well in Montana. Across the state, many drug stores and retail outlets advertised Christmas gifts for men overseas (money belts, wallets, shaving and sewing kits, towels, and stationery were recommended). Local women passed out Christmas gifts to soldiers passing through the state on troop trains. As Christmas approached, one witty Kalispell resident applied for enough gasoline and tire coupons for an upcoming tour of the nation. He signed the application, "S. Claus." For those looking for a quiet getaway, Boulder Hot Springs Resort offered a special Christmas rate of $25 per week.

As war raged around the world, the New Year brought a major winter storm which closed schools and drifted snow over highways and railroad tracks in western Montana. The city of Missoula turned off half of the street lights in town in an effort to conserve energy.

In the South Pacific the *USS Helena* had a new captain. Captain Charles P. Cecil, who had been awarded the Navy Cross for his actions at the Battle of Santa Cruz, was a 1916 graduate of the Naval Academy at Annapolis. The *Helena* left port as soon as he took the helm of his new command, but after a full year of war and 60,000 sea miles, the *Helena*'s engines were in bad shape and the ship's hull was covered with barnacles. Sailors who thought the *Helena* might return to the U.S. for an overhaul were disheartened when the ship returned to patrolling the dangerous waters of the Coral Sea. On January 4, 1943, the *Helena* endured an unsuccessful but harrowing attack by Japanese dive-bombers while steaming into Blanche Channel in the Solomon Islands.

Three weeks later the ship returned to the same area, an area that would become all too familiar to the *Helena*'s sailors. According to the ship's radio officer, Lt. C.G. Morris, "Kula Gulf is a sailor's nightmare, a blind alley, a dead end street. It was prowled by Jap subs and guarded by Jap planes operating from Kolombangara and Bougainville on the west, New Georgia on the east." The *Helena* moved cautiously into the gulf and began firing on Japanese troops stationed at Vila and Stanmore Plantation. Morris described the bombardment. "Every ship in the line is hurling its thunder and the night shudders as though made of jelly, warm jelly, pressing against a man's hands and face and body and trembling there in shocked surprise." The ship's guns set the airfield at Kolombangara afire, and *Helena* steamed out of Kula Gulf before Japanese planes could respond. In February the *Helena* docked in Australia for 20 days, and each sailor received a well-deserved 10 day leave.

On December 8, 1942, in a meticulously researched speech which she entered into the *Congressional Record*, Jeannette Rankin blasted President Roosevelt's actions during the months leading up to Pearl Harbor. In her final months in the U.S. House of Representatives, Rankin never wavered from her belief in peace. After relinquishing her seat in Congress, she returned to Montana in 1943 to look after her 90-year-old mother.

Freshman Mike Mansfield on the other hand, was on his way to Washington to take his seat in what would be the first term of his 10 years in the U.S. House. An acknowledged expert on Asia, the freshman representative was appointed to the prestigious House Foreign Affairs Committee. One of his first concerns was correcting the unequal draft regulations that resulted in Montana's married men being drafted before married men in most other states.

February 1943

- February 2. Last German troops at Stalingrad surrender.
- February 6. Track star Greg Rice of Missoula wins a record 57th race at Madison Square Garden.
- February 12. Foresters Ball held at University of Montana.
- February 14. Germans begin an offensive in Tunisia and defeat American troops at Kasserine Pass.
- February 15. Bobcat basketball team defeats Denver University 56-47.
- February 17. University of Montana celebrates 50th Anniversary.
- February 18. Sale of canned meat and fish is suspended. Grizzly basketball team defeats Denver University 66-61.
- February 20. Denver University defeats the Grizzlies, 49-47.
- February 22. Ration book #2 is issued.
- February 27. A massive explosion rocks the Smith Mine at Bearcreek, trapping 74 men inside. Bobcats over the Grizzlies 69-59 in Missoula.

Rep. Mike Mansfield, a former University of Montana history professor, took his seat in Congress early in 1943. He was elected to five terms in the U.S. House before moving to the Senate, where he served as Senate Majority Leader under four presidents. He later became U.S. ambassador to Japan. UM 85-217

Mansfield called for a national draft pool in order that each state share the draft burden equally.

Rep. James O'Connor, representing the eastern half of Montana, served as the chairman of the House Indian Affairs and was also on the Census and Flood Control committees. He was concerned that minimum prices be set in order to protect small farmers. Senator Murray was also interested in improving conditions for Montana farmers. He urged that the Federal employment service be overhauled to prevent labor shortages on farms and pressured the all-powerful War Production Board to allot more farm machinery to Montana. Senator Wheeler, the chairman of the Interstate Commerce and Judiciary committees, served on the Steering Committee, Public Lands Committee and the Senate Indian Affairs Committee. Frank C. Walker of Butte, formerly the U.S. Postmaster General, became the chairman of the Democratic National Committee.

Meeting for the first time in January, the 28th Montana Legislature voted to purchase a regimental flag for the 163rd Infantry Regiment. Gov. Sam Ford urged legislators, of whom there was but one woman (Democrat Margaret L. Peterson of Missoula) to begin planning for the postwar economy. The lawmakers also approved Governor Ford's plan to sell $10,000,000 in bonds to finance highway construction after the war. George O'Connor was elected speaker of the Montana House. Sen. John Campbell of Missoula proposed cutting the state income tax in half to relieve the burden on families hard hit by the military buildup and to head off a proposed elimination of the tax. Other items on the agenda included a stream protection bill and the Yellowstone River Compact, an interstate agreement recently approved by the North Dakota legislature. The Senate first asked for a two-year delay in implementing the agreement, then voted against ratification.

Legislators also passed a non-binding resolution that prohibited anyone of Japanese ancestry from becoming an American citizen, and asked the federal government to increase the mandated speed limit for buses and trucks from 35 to 45 miles per hour.

Despite a state budget surplus of $20,000,000, the legislators voted to slash $470,000 from the University system budget. They also ordered lumber and mine workers to increase their work week to 48-hours.

Something of a political crisis erupted in Helena when an Army officer became alarmed over an outbreak of venereal disease and demanded that

Air raid shelter on Highway 93 at the Stevensville turnoff. The Fort Owen Inn now occupies this site. LC-USF34-65332-D

Governor Ford close the brothels operating in Helena, Butte, and Great Falls. Although at least 100 prostitutes were known to have followed the Army to Helena, there was a notable reluctance on the part of Montana lawmen to crack down. Local sheriffs refused to intervene until they had received a complaint from a dissatisfied customer. The legislature initially balked at providing $26,000 to finance closing of the brothels, but under continuing pressure from the Army, the money was finally allocated. Also passed was a related bill allowing health departments to examine anyone suspected of having VD. The military requested, unsuccessfully, that the Senate pass a bill that would close all bars located within 25 miles of a military base at midnight.

In early 1944, with venereal disease again on the rise among the servicemen of Cascade County, a meeting of 50 local citizens was held in Great Falls to come up with a solution. Tex's Place and the Palm Garden bar were declared off-limits to air base personnel, and shortly thereafter 18 hotels and 14 bars in Great Falls and Black Eagle were added to the list because of the threat of venereal disease. Ten of the establishments were later dropped from the list, but the Great Falls City Council also halted beer sales after midnight and prohibited dancing in taverns and beer halls. Two Great Falls girls were arrested for being "pickup girls." They were given 90 day sentences with 60 days suspended if they left town. Cascade County Commissioners allocated $4,700 to open a detention hospital for VD cases, and applied for federal funds for a venereal disease control center. The measures proved effective, and the disease rate in Great Falls soon dropped. After the First Special Service Force left Helena, the venereal disease rate in that city also dropped dramatically.

On February 17, 1943, the 50th birthday of the University system was celebrated at the University of Montana. The keynote speaker at Charter Day was the Dean of Faculty, R.H. Jesse, who reviewed the history of the University and commended original faculty members William Aber and Frederick Scheuch for their part in planning the tree-lined Oval at the campus. University President Ernest Melby also gave a short speech, but the ceremony was kept low-key out of respect for the 550 students and faculty who were serving in the armed forces. One former student in the news was football great Eso Naranche. Only a year before he had worn the Grizzly uniform in the East-West Shrine game, but by the early spring of 1943, he was wearing a different uniform, and was reported to be in combat against the crack German Afrika Korps in Tunisia.

Four out of five of the 1,008 students registered at the University during winter quarter were women, but the ratio changed somewhat when 1,000 men of the Army Air Force began arriving in Missoula for pilot training. The men of the 317th College Training Corps, mostly from California, stepped off the train in late February and were greeted by a major blizzard. North Hall (now Brantly) and the Forestry Building were turned over to the aviation cadets, who studied math, physics, aeronautics and physical training. Most of the regular students moved to fraternities to make room in the dorms for the new soldiers. The trainees marched between classes and were not supposed to speak to coeds on campus, but according to Professor H.G. Merriam, "the trainees were not overserious in class or out, indeed were ebullient."

The 1942-43 University of Montana Grizzly basketball team won their opening games against the Utah Redskins and a team fielded by the Army Air Force base at Great Falls. The Montana Grizzlies split two games with the Idaho Vandals and beat Utah State for a 7-2 record early in the season, before being defeated by the Bobcats 45-56. Fill-in basketball coach Clyde Carpenter received orders to report to the Navy in early January and Missoula High coach Eddie Chinske took his place. On their last road trip of the season, the Grizzly basketball squad traveled to Washington state, where they won one of two games against Whitman College and suffered defeat at the hands of Pasco Naval Air Station and Gonzaga. At home they fared a little better, splitting a two-game series with Denver University and another with the Bobcats.

At the State College in Bozeman, John "Brick" Breeden's 65-man Bobcat athletic department was reduced to 19 players by the war. The Bobcats lost two games against Utah State but had better luck against the North Dakota Bisons and the Grizzlies. They won 15 consecutive games, including three of the season's four Cat-Griz games. In lieu of a state tournament, the Bobcats were declared the state champion.

Like the University, the College at Bozeman also hosted 500 Army Air Force trainees, who arrived in March. The students studied engineering and radio in conjunction with their military training. They stayed at Hamilton Hall and the women's

One of the highly unpopular fiber-board license plates that were issued in 1944. The oversized plates forced car owners to purchase larger license plate brackets for their vehicles.

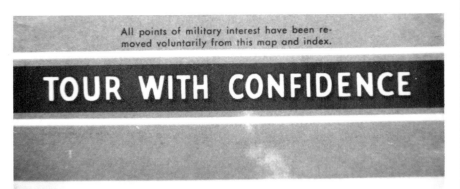

Wartime map of Montana. Note the disclosure on the front.

Sidney

The seat of Richland County had a population of approximately 2,000 during the early '40s. Located in the Yellowstone Valley near the North Dakota border, Sidney was primarily an agriculture and trade center. Harry Clark served as mayor during the latter years of the war. The town was served by the weekly *Sidney Herald* newspaper and by KGCX radio, one of the state's older stations. The Lower Yellowstone Irrigation project provided water for 60,000 acres of crops in the Sidney area; two thirds of this acreage was planted in sugar beets and most of the rest was in wheat. Sidney High School offered classes in war mechanics and postwar relations, and students from the school earned a total of $15,000 harvesting sugar beets in 1942. In the years prior to the war, homesteaders driven off their farms by drought had gradually replaced migrant Mexicans and Filipinos in the beet fields, but with the labor shortage brought on by the war, Mexicans and Japanese-American workers again returned to the Sidney area. Company A of the 163rd Infantry Regiment (Montana National Guard) was primarily made up of Sidney men.

sororities on the Quadrangle, while the co-eds in Bozeman moved out of their dorms and into unused fraternities to make way for the incoming aviation trainees. One hundred and twenty women lived in the SAE, Sigma Chi, Sigma Nu, and Phi Sigma Kappa fraternities, although all of them dined at the Sigma Chi house in two shifts.

Aviators also trained at Billings Polytechnic, while Navy, Marine, and Coast Guard officers studied at the School of Mines and Carroll College. Carroll College played host to 370 Navy men, while 90 percent of the resources of the School of Mines were devoted to training other Navy personnel. Seven buglers lent a military air to the School of Mines as the Naval reserve men were called to classes and meals. Approximately 1,750 officers and pilots were eventually trained at Montana colleges. In order to handle the huge numbers of men entering the military, the state enlistment center in Butte was enlarged to handle Army, Navy, Coast Guard, and Marine enlistments.

Restrictions were lifted on retread tires in February 1943, but a new regulation made monthly tire inspections mandatory. Quotas were also set on the number of new cars and bicycles that could be sold in the state. Montana's quota for March 1943 included 227 cars and 257 bicycles. In other news, shoe rationing went into effect without warning, limiting each person to the purchase of three pairs of shoes per year. Women were asked to donate their worn out stockings to offset a shortage of silk and nylon, and collection centers were set up in all women's clothing stores.

By late February 1943, melting snow and ice jams caused widespread flooding in eastern Montana. An ice jam along the Yellowstone River inundated parts of Dawson and Richland Counties, and the town of Ekalaka was completely cut off when two bridges washed out. Two hundred farm families were evacuated in the Jordan area because of fears the Big Dry Dam might break.

A different kind of tragedy occurred at mid-morning on February 27, 1943. Bearcreek, a bustling mining town, boasted 14 saloons and not a single church. Located seven miles southeast of Red Lodge, Bearcreek was home to Montana's largest underground coal mine, the Smith Mine, owned and operated by the Montana Coal and Iron Company, and had been in operation since the turn of the century. Seventy-seven miners were deep inside that morning when a tremendous explosion rocked the mine, knocking five-ton mine cars off their tracks and shredding huge ventilation fans. Those not killed outright by the explosion were rolled over and over by the force. Hoist operator Alex Hawthorne managed to get to a phone and reported, "Something's wrong down here. I'm coming out." Overcome by the poisonous methane gas that was filling the mine, Hawthorne collapsed next to the phone. In Bearcreek and nearby Washoe and Red Lodge, sirens summoned rescuers. Working without breathing masks or any other equipment, rescuers immediately entered the mine. Alex Hawthorne, Willard Reid, and Eli Houtonen were found near the entrance, unconscious but alive. The methane gas prevented rescuers from going further into mine. As anxious families gathered outside, a call went out to trained mine-rescue crews around the west.

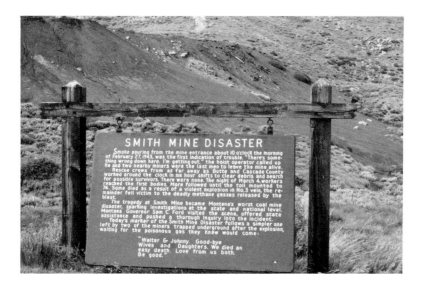

State highway sign marking the site of the Smith Mine Disaster at Bearcreek, where 74 miners died in Montana's worst coal mining tragedy.

7

Soviet Spies In The Big Sky

Specially-trained rescue crews rushed to the scene of the Smith Mine disaster from the Mouat and Benbow mines near Columbus, from Roundup and Klein, from as far as Butte and Salt Lake City. Their efforts were futile however. Eight days after the explosion, the bodies of the last of the miners trapped underground was found. Montana's worst coal mining disaster had claimed 74 men, and a memorial service was held in the Bearcreek High gymnasium.

An investigation called for by Governor Ford determined that a massive build-up of methane gas had been ignited by either an electrical fuse tripping or by one of the miner's carbide lamps. The coroners jury recommended 10 suggestions to increase mine safety, and these were later written into state law. Six months after the disaster, a mine rescue team was finally formed at Bearcreek.

March brought a major blizzard to the state and the subsequent spring flooding resulted in $1,000,000 in damages and caused three deaths, including that of a soldier from Fort Harrison who drowned in a coulee. A record 3.01 inches of rain fell in Missoula in April, and eight inches of snow fell in Great Falls on May 10. More than 100 basements on the west side of Butte were flooded and the rail bridge between the Anaconda Smelter and Butte washed out, closing the smelter. The waters of Black Coulee Creek flooded Malta and a broken water-main inundated downtown Great Falls. The Shields River overflowed and dynamite was used to break ice jams on the Milk River. Miles City was isolated after several major bridges over the Yellowstone washed out, forcing the Northern Pacific and the Milwaukee Road to share their tracks for a few days. The federal government eventually paid to replace the washed-out bridge at Fallon because it caused a 150 mile detour. The new bridge over the Yellowstone was completed in November 1944.

By the spring of 1943, the new air force base at Great Falls bustled with activity. More than 2,000 employees, many of them women, worked overtime to speed the flow of war materials bound for the Soviet Union. Not everything flown out of Great Falls qualified as essential war supplies, however. During the war years, $180,000,000 worth of women's apparel were airlifted to the U.S.S.R., and items as small as one tobacco pipe, $10 value, were listed on the manifests. Cigarette cases, American phonograph records, women's compacts, and 13,000 sets of false teeth were among the "vital" war supplies shipped to Moscow.

The Soviet officers stationed at Great Falls soon acquired a reputation for not paying their bar bills, preferring instead to plug their money into the slot machines at the officer's club. An enterprising bartender diplomatically ignored the ever-increasing bars tabs, and instead rigged the slot machines so that they paid out less frequently.

Since the Lend-Lease program was considered vital to the war effort, almost no restrictions were put on the Soviets at Great Falls, and the city became a hub of espionage activities. Soon after the undocumented Soviets began entering the United States large numbers of identical black patent leather suitcases, tied with cord and sealed with red wax, began arriving back in Great Falls, where they were placed under armed guard and flown to the U.S.S.R. without ever being examined by U.S. authorities. Maj. George Jordan, who suspected that the Soviets were stealing morphine ampules from first aid kits at the base, once took it upon himself to open some of these suitcases and found they were full of maps, industrial data, patent documents, blueprints of U.S. industrial plants, railroad tables, documents from Oak Ridge, Tennessee on nuclear physics, and U.S. government documents, including some from State Department official Alger Hiss, a man who would eventually be convicted as a spy. According to Col. Ponton D'Arce of the 7th Ferrying Group, the Soviets, "could have sent the Capitol Dome via Moscow without our knowing what was in the boxes."

A new material which most people had never heard of was also headed to the U.S.S.R. On March 23, 1943, 691 pounds of uranium nitrate and uranium oxide were shipped from a Denver company to Colonel Kotikov at East Base. Apparently, this uranium was given to the Soviets with the approval of the highest levels of the U.S. government. Harry Hopkins, one of President Roosevelt's top aides, ordered authorities in Great Falls to expedite this

RATIONING

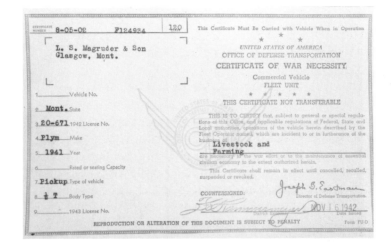

shipment. Although the Soviet officers stationed in Montana claimed they wanted the radioactive material for medical purposes, and to harden gun barrels, it was probably not a coincidence that the Soviet nuclear weapons program began as soon as the first shipment of uranium from Great Falls arrived in Moscow.

In June 1943, the Soviet Purchasing Commission in Great Falls received another 15 wooden boxes full of uranium ore from an Ontario mining company. Three-quarters of a ton of uranium salts were eventually shipped through Great Falls, and the Soviets wanted to buy more. The Soviets also received two-and-a-half pounds of refined uranium metal, half of the United State's stockpile at the time. Enough fissionable material was shipped out of Great Falls to enable the Soviets to build their first atomic bomb. The Soviet Purchasing Commission in Great Falls also acquired other materials useful in nuclear research, including 12 tons of thorium and quantities of cobalt, graphite, and cadmium.

Although the Russians stationed in Montana engaged in many questionable activities, it turned out that the uranium shipments had been cleared by the highest levels of the U.S. government. The War Production Board, the State Department, Lend-Lease officials, and representatives of the top-secret Manhattan Project had all given their approval. After the war the Joint Congressional Committee on Atomic Energy investigated the Soviet activities at Great Falls but found that, "refusal to ship might have been more informative to the Russians than any help they could derive from the small quantities of materials requested."

By the spring of 1943, the effects of World War II were felt in almost every aspect of daily life. A year before, the prospect of sugar rationing had seemed bad enough, but by March 1943 all canned and frozen food, dried fruits and vegetables, meat, butter, cheese, and fish, some 200 foods in all, were rationed. Shoppers faced a bewildering array of ration coupons and a point system that changed almost daily. Each person was allotted 48 ration points per month, enough to purchase 48 jars of baby food, three-and-a-half pounds of frozen vegetables, or two cans of scarce pineapple. Most fruits and vegetables were rated at eight to 13 points per pound, and price ceilings were set on tomatoes, beans, carrots, cabbage and peas. After Senator Wheeler intervened, exceptions in the point rationing system were made for sheepherders living a long distance from town.

A week before the new system went into effect, the sale of butter and fats was frozen for one week, causing a sudden run on grocery stores. Shortages of eggs caused a cancellation of the annual Easter egg hunt in Great Falls, and an uncertain supply of hard liquor led to impromptu rationing of customers at some stores. Cigarettes were one of the few items not restricted.

Some of the new regulations reached the point of absurdity, including a government-imposed ban on slicing bread, which was meant to save labor and energy, but instead caused extra work for bakeries. After a few weeks, sheepish officials dropped the ban and no one seemed to remember whose idea it had been in the first place.

Applicants for Ration Book #2 were required to fill out an application for every member of the family and declare what food they had on hand. Even the ration books were in short supply, and Yellowstone County, which was issued 43,000 books, nearly ran short after 1,000 books were sent to Anaconda to help with an anticipated shortfall there.

Ration card holders were only allowed to buy 35 ounces of meat per week at first, an amount that steadily decreased as the point values of beef began to climb. To the dismay of a few old-time Montana cowboys, unrationed horsemeat began appearing on the dining room table. There were an estimated 75,000 to 100,000 horses available for slaughter in the state, and although most were spared, during the summer of 1944, 500 wild horses were rounded up on the Rocky Boys Reservation and sold for meat. Nationwide food shortages caused many households and most restaurants to observe meatless Tuesdays, and as the weather warmed, gardening became a patriotic national pastime. Nearly every household and many businesses began preparing the ground for Victory Gardens. Some were communal efforts, like the four-acre garden in Livingston tended by 18 employees of the Montana Power Company. Even the University got in the act, and the Pharmacy School planted a Victory drug garden to produce pharmaceuticals, such as atropine, Egyptian henbane, and volatile oils. The Agriculture School at Montana State College provided expert advice and distributed publications on Victory Gardens. The Victory Garden program eventually supplied 40 percent of the nation's vegetable needs.

Fort Missoula internees (both Japanese and Italians) also raised huge Victory Gardens, including 30 acres of vegetables, 25 acres of potatoes and 60 acres of wheat. The wheat was used primarily to feed the 1,000 chickens the detainees produced each month for their own consumption and for sale. The Italians prepared the ground and were in charge of landscaping the gardens, while the Japanese proved considerably better at working with the plants. Victory Gardens also produced one half of the food consumed by state institutions in 1943. 4-H clubs in the Billings area raised 180,000 pounds of beans on 120 acres for the institutions, while 425 cases of tomatoes and 500 cases of string beans were provided by farms in the Bitterroot Valley.

In order to further boost food production, the federal government provided $30,000,000 to improve Montana's rural highways, and put conscientious objectors to work on farm improvement projects at a former CCC camp near Terry. The government also began paying for electrical hookups to remote ranches in the state. The amount the government paid was related to how much each rancher produced for the war effort.

Women in Montana recycled almost a ton of old stockings each month, and the state ranked fifth in the nation for collection of silk and nylon. Department stores not only coordinated the recycling of stockings, they also set up booths to sell war bonds and to promote recruiting into the women's auxiliary organizations like the WACs and WAVES. In order to better serve shoppers who were working overtime, many stores stayed open during the evening. The expiration of ration coupons caused a rush on shoe stores in Great Falls and the Paris Fligman department store in that city won the right to display a "T" banner after more than 90 percent of the employees purchased at least 10 percent of their income in war bonds.

In national news, *Mrs. Miniver* swept the Academy Awards, winning Oscars for best film of 1942, best direction, best screenplay, technical awards, and the best actress, Greer Garson. James Cagney won the best actor award for *Yankee Doodle Dandy*, while Clark Gable and Bette Davis were declared America's favorite screen stars in a national poll. Movies showing in Montana theaters included a Humphrey Bogart picture, *Across the Pacific*, and *Mr. Smith Goes to Washington*, starring Jimmy Stewart. Popular war movies included *Crash Dive*, *One of Our Planes is Missing*, *Wake Island*, *Remember Pearl Harbor* and *Flying Tigers*, starring John Wayne and Anna Lee.

During the summer of 1943, some scenes of a major Hollywood production, *Buffalo Bill*, were filmed near Crow Agency. An elderly Crow woman helped stagehands erect 17 tepees for the movie after the men of the tribe confessed their ignorance of the proper procedure. Indian extras who provided their own horses were paid $7 per day. The movie, starring Maureen O'Hara, Joel McCrea, and Anthony Quinn, was released in 1944.

Like almost every other segment of the population, Montana's Native Americans were wholeheartedly behind the war effort. Assiniboine and Yankton Sioux, Crows, Cheyennes, Blackfeet, and Gros Ventres all served with the 163rd Infantry Regiment in New Guinea. Nationwide, an estimated 15,000 Indians served in the armed forces, and another 4,000 women worked in defense plants. Nineteen Native Americans from Montana served with an engineer battalion stationed in Massachusetts.

The Blackfeet, the largest tribe in the state, were very supportive of the war effort. By the summer of 1943, 133 tribal members had enlisted in the Army and another 34 were in the Navy. Two Blackfeet women enlisted in the WACs, and Minnie Spotted Wolf of Heart Butte joined the Marine auxiliary. In an attempt to hasten victory, several dozen tribal members threw a barbecue and traditional powwow at the new Cut Bank Air Base.

Although the Blackfeet were some of the poorest residents of the state, much of the money they earned from cattle raising and oil leases from the Cut Bank field was spent to support their soldiers. The 13 members of the Blackfeet council sent $1,000 to the state war fund and another $1,750 to the reservation Red Cross chapter. The Browning War Mothers Club raised lambs to earn money, which they used to send a letter and one dollar to each Blackfeet soldier each month. The Blackfeet had an influential friend in Senator Wheeler, who met with them regularly, and who in 1943 introduced a bill to turn over to the tribe $150,000 held by the government since the treaty of 1885.

Forty percent of the able-bodied male Crows also served in the armed forces, including Barney Old Coyote Jr., who, on the day after Pearl Harbor, hitchhiked from the Crow Reservation to Billings in order to enlist. He won an Air Medal for being a gunner on a plane that sank a submarine in the Mediterranean. T.O. Coyote, a full-blooded Indian from Billings, was a waist gunner on a B-17. After one bombing raid over Italy, he was quoted as saying,

Scene from the movie "Buffalo Bill," which was partially filmed on the Crow Indian reservation during the summer of 1943.

U.S. Forest Service smokejumpers designed and built firefighting equipment in a room in the upper floors of the Park Hotel in Missoula. The equipment designed by smokejumpers in Missoula influenced the parachuting equipment adopted and used by the U.S. Army in World War II. USFS 431809

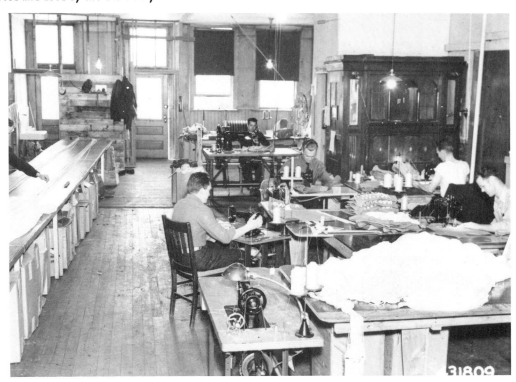

Men at War

- Sgt. Henry Buller of Billings (B-17 gunner) won the Distinguished Flying Cross and Silver Star with oak leaf cluster for two attacks on Rabaul in which several Japanese Zeros were shot down.
- Capt. James Murphy of Roundup (B-17 pilot) was awarded the Distinguished Flying Cross and the Silver Star with four clusters for his actions at Midway, Bismarck Sea, and New Guinea.
- Maj. Norvall Bonawitz of Missoula, a pilot, destroyed a Japanese train in Indochina.
- Cmdr. D.B. Overfield of Fort Benton commanded the naval reserve base at Anacostia, D.C.
- Maj. Gen. James L. Bradley, formerly commander of a battalion at Fort Missoula and a National Guard unit in Helena, was given command of the 96th Division at Camp Adair.
- Lt. Cmdr. Ben Hardin of Butte commanded a naval base in the Aleutians.
- Maj. Samuel R. Peterson of Plentywood was awarded the Legion of Merit for a reconnaissance flight over Attu.
- Lt. Luther S. Gustafson was posthumously awarded the Distinguished Service Cross for singlehandedly destroying a machine gun nest in Tunisia on April 28, 1943.
- Lt. Bill Burghardt, the former University of Montana ski coach and rodeo performer, fought from Oran to El Guettar in a tank destroyer battalion before he was captured in North Africa on March 25, 1943. He was held at Oflag 64 and spent his time in prison writing a winter sports text book.
- 2nd Lt. Cody G. Robinson of White Sulphur Springs was posthumously awarded the Silver Star by General Patton for leading a charge that broke a German attack in Tunisia.
- 1st Lt. Douglas Crichton of Deer Lodge was a P-38 pilot awarded the Distinguished Flying Cross for his actions in North Africa.

Miles City

In 1943, three out of every four residents of Custer County lived in the county seat of Miles City (7,175 population). L.S. Keye, mayor of Miles City, was re-elected in April 1945. Miles City was the center of agriculture and trade in southeastern Montana, and was served by the *Daily Star* newspaper, as well as a new radio station, KRJF. Although farming had been important in the 1920s, by the 1940s Miles City was once again primarily a livestock center. The town's major industries included a large stockyard, a packing plant, and a world-class saddlery employing as many as 18 skilled craftsmen. A U.S. Range and Livestock Experiment Station, established in 1926, was located at the site of historic Fort Keogh, on the outskirts of town. Miles City was also home to the Custer County Junior College, founded in 1939, and the State Industrial School, headed by Carl Horn. A Miles City landmark vanished when the George Wah laundry, which dated to the turn of the century and was the last Chinese laundry in the city, closed its doors. As the war drew to a close, Rep. Mike Mansfield proposed a new Veterans Administration Hospital at Miles City. On August 17, 1945, a fundraising campaign was started and $29,000 was raised in just 25 days, almost double the anticipated goal. Ground was broken for the new hospital in the fall of 1948, and the building, which served 1,100 vets each year, was dedicated August 19, 1951.

March 1943

- March 2. Battle of Bismarck Sea begins. Eight Japanese transports and four destroyers are sunk over three days.
- March 6. Major snowstorm closes highways and Great Falls air base.
- March 8. Charles Bair, pioneer rancher and financier dies in Billings, age 85.
- March 15. Income tax deadline.
- March 17. Downtown Great Falls is flooded when a 12-inch water main breaks.
- March 20. Two Japanese farm workers are killed near Miles City when a train hits their truck.
- March 25. One hundred basements are flooded in Butte. Black Coulee Creek floods Malta.
- March 28. Miles City is isolated when floods wash out highway and rail lines. Two troop trains are stranded on the tracks. Eso Naranche, all state football player, is killed in action in North Africa.
- March 30. High water washes out the rail line between Butte and the Anaconda smelter.

May 1943

- May 1. Ceiling on restaurant prices goes into effect.
- May 2. *Daily Missoulian* celebrates 70th year of operation, longest continuous publishing of any newspaper in the state.
- May 6. A nationwide radio program, "Victory Parade of Spotlight Bands" is broadcast from the Great Falls air base.
- May 11. American troops invade the Japanese-held island of Attu.
- May 13. Last of the Axis troops in North Africa surrender at Tunis. *USS Helena* bombards Kolombangara, Enogai, Bairoko Harbor, and is attacked by Japanese planes.
- May 20. Heavy fighting on Attu.
- May 16. Nazis crush last Jewish resistance in Warsaw ghetto.
- May 23. A B-17 from Lewistown crashes in Yellowstone National Park, only one of the 11 men on board survives.
- May 30. Memorial Day. Americans complete occupation of Attu. Four Havre businesses are destroyed by fire.

April 1943

- April 3. Prairie fire southwest of Miles City scorches 8,000 acres.
- April 6. First Special Service Force parades through Helena prior to their departure.
- April 10. Plane crash near Warm Springs kills a Johnson Flying Service flight instructor, his father, brother, and brother's girlfriend, all of Missoula.
- April 12. Second War Bond drive begins.
- April 15. Nelson Eddy gives a free concert for air base personnel at the Great Falls Civic Center. Butte Purples take first place in Missoula invitational track meet.
- April 18. Japanese Admiral Isoroku Yamamoto is killed by U.S. fighter planes.
- April 19. Warsaw ghetto uprising begins.
- April 20. Sixty conscientious objectors to the draft become U.S. Forest Service smokejumpers.
- April 24. Great Falls Victory Parade features a display of warplanes and vehicles from the air base.
- April 25. Easter.
- April 30. Representative Mike Mansfield gives a nationwide radio address on the situation in Asia.

"we really scalped them."

Nellie Warrior of Wolf Point was the first Native American to enter the WACs, while Private Charles Ball, an Assiniboine from the Fort Belknap reservation, was awarded the Distinguished Service Cross, the Army's second highest medal, for his part in the fighting on Bataan. Even the tiny Rocky Boys Reservation held a sun dance to promote victory, and like the Blackfeet, the 2,600 enrolled members of the Flathead, Salish and Kootenai tribes donated $1,000 to the state war fund.

The 1,600 members of the impoverished Northern Cheyenne tribe could only afford to donate $100 to the state war fund, but they contributed in other ways. The Cheyennes raised beef and planted a Victory Garden in Lame Deer that provided food for 400 people. The tribe also had their own coal mine for heating needs, plus a small sawmill to provide lumber for homes.

In Missoula 1,000 people attended a ceremony at the University campus when 78 students were mustered into the Army Reserve. Enrollment at the University during spring quarter dropped to 736 students, down 25 percent from the 1,008 registered winter quarter. Three hundred students attended summer session at the University, including 14 men in the military who were taking correspondence courses. The much-smaller Great Falls College of Education had an enrollment of 190 students during the summer session.

As at Missoula, Montana State College's celebration of the 50th anniversary of the state university system was fairly subdued. On April 17, Francis E. Thompson, the President of the School of Mines, gave a short speech and a student dance was held that night in Bozeman. Two hundred and nineteen students graduated from MSC during the spring of '43 while another 56 graduated from Northern Montana College.

The University presented its Grizzly cup award to Henry Dahmer of Havre, an athlete with an excellent academic standing who was serving in the Marine Corps at the time of the award. Although spring football and track at the University were canceled because of the war, the University ROTC rifle team attended the national finals. J.W. Stewart, the former head of University athletics from 1922-1932, died suddenly while visiting at the home of long-time University track coach Harry Adams in Missoula. Adams himself was serving with the military at the Seattle port of embarkation. Another former member of the University athletic department, skiing coach William Burghardt, was a prisoner of war in Italy.

George Ott Romney and Schubert Dyche of the Bobcat athletic department both worked for the Red Cross in London. They held a reunion attended by more than 20 Montanans serving in England. Max Worthington, a former Bobcat athlete and future administrator, left his position as the head of physical education at Helena High, and took a commission as a lieutenant (jg) in the Navy Reserve.

Although no state basketball tournament was held in 1943, coach Harry Dahlberg's Butte High team was declared the winner of the Big 16 season title after compiling a record of 11-4. Butte Central finished in second place with a 10-4 record, and the Anaconda Copperheads and Missoula Spartans tied for third. In May 1943, several high school track meets were held around the state. Seven teams attended the Missoula invitational track meet, which was won by the Butte Purples. The Ravalli All-Stars, a combined squad of Corvallis and Hamilton high schools took second place while the Great Falls Bisons captured third. In the Electric City, the Great Falls Bisons hosted Havre and Helena schools in a track meet won by the home team.

A pickup team of Great Falls high school students named the Gladiators beat the Air Force Ferrymen hockey team 20-3, and local boxers defeated the air base Ferrymen 5 matches to 1 in front of an enthusiastic audience of 1,800 soldiers. Local citizens were not allowed to watch the boxing matches hosted by the air base because the bouts violated state boxing regulations. Missoula distance runner Greg Rice competed in the Millrose Games at Madison Square Garden, where he won a record-breaking 57th straight victory. In a widely publicized race later in the summer, Rice suffered defeat at the hands of Swedish champion Gunder Haegg at the AAU 5,000 meter race in New York. At the end of the track season Rice took a job teaching physical education to 2,400 Merchant Marine cadets on Long Island, which left him little time to train. He did take time out from his busy schedule to tour Montana as part of the Third War Bond drive.

Tragically, Grizzly standout and all-state high school football star Eso Naranche, who had played in the East-West Shrine Game in 1942, was killed in action on March 28, 1943, while serving with the Army in North Africa. He was survived by his wife, who worked in a defense plant in California. A few

Greg Rice of Missoula won 57 straight races before falling to Gunder Haegg of Sweden during the spring of 1943. sc

weeks before his death, Naranche and his battalion had been surrounded at Djebel Essouda but managed to escape. Representative Mike Mansfield paid tribute to his former student, and read a *Butte Standard* article on him into the *Congressional Record*. "Eso came up the hard way. He worked in the Butte mines to finance his education and everything he received he earned himself." The Butte High athletic stadium was named after Naranche.

During the first week of April 1943, Governor Sam Ford and thousands of cheering bystanders watched as the 2,300 U.S. and Canadian soldiers of the First Special Service Force paraded through the streets of Helena prior to their departure from Montana. After nine months of training at Fort Harrison the unorthodox Forcemen had become experts in parachuting, skiing, demolition and hand-to-hand fighting. They had also become adopted residents of Montana's capital city, and more than 200 marriages occurred between Forcemen and local girls in the days before the commandos shipped out. The mission to Norway for which they had been trained had been canceled, and the soldiers were destined for an invasion of the Japanese-held island of Kiska, in the Aleutians.

They boarded a train bound for Norfolk, Virginia, where the Forcemen were scheduled for landing craft training. The swaggering Forcemen soon proved they could climb landing nets with full packs and rifles, and could do it significantly faster than the best Marine units. The natural enmity between Marines and Army troops led to dozens of brawls at Norfolk, and the local commanders were glad when the Forcemen pulled out of town.

Three-and-a-half years after the invasion of Poland had ignited the flames of World War II, thousands of Polish Jews armed with homemade weapons began a battle to the death with Nazi stormtroopers in Warsaw. Elsewhere in Poland, a mass grave containing the bodies of 4,000 Polish army officers murdered by the Soviet Red Army was discovered at Katyn. Closer to home, the news that three American fliers captured after Doolittle's raid on Tokyo the previous year had been executed by the Japanese caused a national outcry in April. The Japanese also began releasing the names of dozens of Montana men who had been captured in the Philippines a year before. In many cases, days after the men had been listed as prisoners, it was announced by the Japanese that they had died in captivity.

Local news in April included the publication of *Murders at Moon Dance*, the first book by Choteau writer A.B. Guthrie Jr. The Pulitzer Prize-winning author would later describe his first book as "trash." Shortly after the book's publication, Guthrie won a fellowship to Harvard University. His father on the other hand began serving a term as the Teton County Treasurer. April 1943, also saw a serious measles outbreak in Kalispell.

In Washington, Montana's senior senator, Burton K. Wheeler, successfully pressured the War Production Board to allow the manufacture of more farm machinery, and introduced a bill to regulate railroad rates, which he thought were too high. Wheeler opposed a state quota system for the draft, and urged the President to adopt a Japan-first war strategy, since the Soviets showed no willingness to help in the Pacific War. When asked if he supported a postwar international police force to keep the peace, Senator Wheeler was firmly opposed while Senator Murray was in favor of it. Murray also introduced a bill to provide land for homeless Indians.

Rep. James O'Connor worked to raise the state's tire quota, and sought federal funds for a wool scouring plant in Billings. He also argued against liberalization of the federal silver policy, and rebuked those of his fellow lawmakers who opposed President Roosevelt's war policies.

Rep. Mike Mansfield, an expert on Asia, gave a nationwide radio address on April 30, 1943, on the topic, "What Are We Going to do About the Pacific?" He advocated driving the Japanese off of Kiska and Attu because, "the Aleutians offer a war path to Japan's front door."

In the closing days of the 1943 State Legislature, lawmakers rejected a law to legalize slot machines and small stakes gambling, cracked down on prostitution, killed a bill to close bars near military bases after midnight and passed a law protecting a reporter from having to reveal his source. They also created the Montana War Council to advise the governor on defense policy affecting the state. The Council had sweeping powers in case an emergency arose. By the time the tax deadline rolled around on March 15, the Montana Department of Revenue had collected $8,497,852 since the first of the year.

Days after the legislature adjourned on March 8, the frozen body of a man was found by children in a vacant lot next to the state capital. The body had a Christmas card with $5 in it, and it was believed the man had been there since December without being noticed by the lawmakers who commonly walked through the area every day.

By the end of April 1943, state legislator's feared they might have to be called back into special session to deal with a funding crisis at the State Hospital at Warm Springs and the state school for the "feeble-minded" at Boulder. At the last minute private citizens donated $50,000 to care for the 1,900 patients at the state institutions. It was revealed later that some state legislators had even written personal checks in order to avoid a special session.

One of the year's biggest political scandals involved the Montana State Game Warden, Dr. J.S. McFarland, who was sued by the Montana Furriers Association for illegally selling 459 beaver pelts. He was exonerated of those charges but was then sued again, for slander this time, by the Furriers Association and a private furrier. He claimed it was an attempt to intimidate him because he was cracking down on the fur farmers. Governor Ford supported McFarland throughout the controversy, which lasted for many months. Although McFarland successfully weathered the crisis, he resigned his post in the summer of 1945 in order to operate a dude ranch in northwestern Montana, and A.A. O'Claire of Kalispell was named to replace him.

In other state news, Governor Ford declined an invitation to the opening of the original composition, "Montana" which was performed by the Cincinnati Symphony Orchestra on March 26. More than 125,000 Montanan's purchased war bonds in the second nationwide drive held between April 12 and the end of the month, and the state exceeded its quota of $35,582,000 by some $5,000,000. All Montana counties exceeded their quota, Cascade County by more than $1,000,000 after throwing a parade and Victory Ball to promote the War Bond Sales. Two thousand people attended the ball, held at the Great Falls Civic Center. The Victory Parade featured bombers flying overhead, military vehicles and a marching band provided by the Great Falls air base.

Although the state experienced a slight decrease in crime after the attack on Pearl Harbor, the number of murders jumped significantly in 1942, from an average of 12 murders per year to 16. Bearing out this trend were several sensational murders and assaults during the spring of 1943.

Early in the year, a Lewistown cab driver entertaining several friends was shot and killed by his wife. His wife was charged with first degree murder, and was found guilty of manslaughter. In mid-March, Arthur Wankle of Miles City was convicted of second degree murder for killing Amy Janssen, age 26, who died trying to flee a moving car. She was buried in a shallow grave. A week later, Wankle's accomplice Fred Moffat of Miles City was also convicted.

In April, an 11-year-old Ovando boy was charged with first degree murder after shooting his 12-year-old friend with a .22 rifle. They had looted a summer cabin with the intention of running away to Siberia, and were arguing over a sword one of them had found when a fight ensued.

Law enforcement officials also worried about a rise in crime among juveniles, especially girls, most of whom were arrested for prostitution and delinquency. Fifty-three women were arrested in Great Falls for prostitution, which carried a maximum sentence of 90 days in jail or a $300 fine. An 800 percent increase in venereal disease had been reported in Great Falls during the past year, but much of the rise was probably due to more efficient reporting. Juveniles were also responsible for the rash of car thefts that struck Great Falls, but all of the 21 cars stolen were later recovered. Vagrants in the Electric City were rounded up and given a choice of either finding a job or enlisting, and many judges commuted the prison sentences of convicts who enlisted.

A 20-year-old Japanese-American man from the internment camp at Heart Mountain, Wyoming was arrested in Butte after buying a camera. He was let go several days later when he claimed he didn't know it was illegal to possess a camera, since many of the Nisei internees at Heart Mountain already owned radios and cameras.

Like the year before, 1943 was an exceptionally good year for the state's fledgling oil industry. Much of the activity was centered around Cut Bank, were the best wells produced 35 barrels an hour. Union Oil Company bought out the Cut Bank properties of the Glacier Production Company, and the Northwest Refinery in Cut Bank was awarded an Army-Navy "E" award for their high production. The oil activity at Choteau created a housing shortage and a local boom. Oil was also struck in Musselshell, Pondera and Liberty Counties, but only the Musselshell site yielded much petroleum. The Continental Oil Company plant at Lewistown shut down permanently, while the Treasure State refinery reopened in Shelby. The Texas Company operated in the Butte area, while the Socony-Vacuum Oil Company was based near Great Falls. Other oil facilities

A small oil refinery typical of those existing in Montana during the pre-war years. Much of the oil activity in Montana was centered around Cut Bank. MHS 957-574

An aeronautics class from Cut Bank gathered around their surplus military trainer. The postwar availability of surplus airplanes tremendously boosted the number of aviators in the state. MHS 946-669

Lumber Industry

Montana's 16,000,000 acres of commercial timberland made the lumber industry the most important manufacturing business in the state in the 1940s. Prior to the war at least 2,600 people were employed in the state's lumber industry, a number that decreased considerably once war broke out. Many Montana loggers who enlisted in the military were assigned to the 796 Forestry Battalion, a unit that sought out woodsmen from Montana, Utah, Wyoming, Arizona, Nevada, Oregon, Washington, Idaho, Colorado, and Michigan. Company C of the 796th was deployed to New Guinea and the Philippines. They constructed a "million dollar road" in New Guinea made of pure mahogany logs. Small operators from the West Coast began moving into western Montana, where they competed with established firms like the Anaconda Company and the Great Northern Railroad's subsidiary, the Somers Lumber Company. Several small portable mills began operating in Western Montana. The state's largest mills were the ACM mill at Bonner and the J. Neils Company in Libby, which sold 95 percent of their planed lumber to the military or contractors working on military projects. Other important lumber centers included the Northern Pacific tie plant at Paradise, the Flodin lumber mill at Plains, and a new mill which was built at Thompson Falls to replace one destroyed by fire. In the spring of 1944, the Pack River Lumber Company, owner of the Thompson Falls mill, began negotiations to buy 60,000 acres of timber owned by the Northern Pacific Railroad. There were three mills at St. Regis, and towns like Missoula, Hamilton, Eureka, and Troy also boasted sawmills. Anaconda's Bonner mill was capable of handling 150,000,000 board feet per year, but only turned out 106,000,000 board feet in 1943, substantially less than in 1942. Most of the logs milled at Bonner were cut in the Blackfoot and Bitterroot drainages. In 1944, local sawmills experienced their best year since the turn of the century, and production during the first three months of 1944 was 12 percent greater than during the same quarter in 1943. The harvest of telephone poles became increasingly important in Montana during the war, as the industry turned from scarce red cedar to lodgepole pine. Christmas trees were also big business, especially in Lincoln and Flathead counties, but because of the severe labor shortage only 1,500,000 trees were shipped from western Montana in 1943, a 30 percent reduction from the year before. At Libby the reduction was closer to 50 percent (by 1944, the number of Christmas trees harvested in the state soared to 2,750,000).

The Bonner lumber mill, owned and operated by the Anaconda Copper Mining Co., sat at the confluence of the Clark Fork and Blackfoot rivers. It is now owned by the Stimson Lumber Co. USFS

An aerial view of the Bonner mill, one of the largest employers in Montana. SC

A certificate presented to the Kalispell Elks Lodge for their contribution to the national war fund drive held by the Elks fraternal organization. Montana consistently led the nation in donations to the national war bond campaigns, as well as state, local and private fund-raising efforts designed to support the war effort. BOB STEPHENS, KALISPELL, MONTANA

in the state included the Yale Refinery in Kalispell, and the Laurel refinery. Production in the state's oil fields rose from 660,000 barrels in May to more than double that by August, and by the end of 1943, almost 8,000,000 barrels of oil had been produced in the state. Record prices were bid for drilling rights on the Blackfeet Reservation, and late in the year Montana Dakota Utilities began construction on a 10-inch, 82-mile long pipeline from Elk Basin to the Billings refineries owned by Standard Oil and the Yale Oil Company. (In May of 1944 the Yale Oil Company merged with the Consumers Oil and Refining Company to form the Carter Oil Company).

In May 1943, the *Daily Missoulian* celebrated its 70th year of operation. The anniversary at the state's oldest newspaper was kept low-key because the paper was struggling with war-related shortages of newsprint, lead, and employees. Since many of the *Missoulian*'s veteran reporters were serving in the armed forces, much of the newsroom staff consisted of University journalism students who were filling in. At the *Great Falls Tribune*, managing editor R.D. Warden joined the Navy, and was replaced by city editor A.H. Raymond. Raymond left the *Tribune* in early 1944 to take over the helm of the *Montana Oil and Gas Journal*, also located in Great Falls, and was replaced by William Zadick. In other journalism news, Butte native Richard O'Malley, a University of Montana graduate who had previously worked for the *Great Falls Tribune*, was promoted to head the Helena office of the Associated Press. O'Malley was eventually transferred to Denver, and then was sent to cover the fighting in the Pacific. After the war O'Malley wrote the book *Mile High, Mile Deep* about his childhood in Butte. At least one source later credited Richard Kilroy O'Malley with creating the graffiti "Kilroy was Here," which American soldiers scrawled on walls across the globe.

Newspaper headlines in May reported that the last German troops in North Africa had surrendered at Tunis, and American soldiers had invaded the Japanese-held island of Attu. On May 25, Capt. Thomas P. O'Donnell, a prominent athlete, student, and 1941 graduate of the University, was killed on Attu. His widow was presented with his Distinguished Service Cross, awarded for his "extraordinary heroism." Elsewhere in the Pacific the light cruiser *USS Helena* shelled Japanese positions at Enogai Inlet and Bairoko Harbor in the Solomon Islands, and shot down two Japanese torpedo planes.

An incident that was quickly forgotten in 1943 became national news 45 years later. In 1988, after the massive North Fork forest fire swept Yellowstone National Park, the remains of a World War II bomber were re-discovered in the Park. In the early morning hours of May 23, 1943, a B-17 bomber based in Lewistown ran into trouble on a training flight over the Madison Plateau area of Yellowstone. Second Lt. William F. McDonald was asleep near the forward escape hatch when he heard the pilot order abandon ship. As the copilot screamed to "Get out now. Get out now," McDonald felt the plane shudder and bank to the left, then spin out of control. He rolled out of the hatch seconds before the plane hit the ground and exploded, killing the other 10 men aboard. McDonald's parachute snagged in some trees and a snowdrift cushioned his fall, but he wandered in the woods for two days before park ranger Tom Ela found him. Since military plane crashes were an almost everyday occurrence in 1943, this incident received little publicity and was nearly forgotten until the wreckage of the plane was exposed by the 1988 fire. The Park Service has since removed 25,000 pounds of debris from the site, including belts of live .50 caliber machine gun bullets, but portions of the B-17 still remain inside Yellowstone.

8

The *Helena* Goes Down Fighting

During the first week of June 1943, a blizzard dumped up to four feet of snow in the Great Falls area, cutting telephone, telegraph, and power lines. A week later, with the Missouri River already at flood stage, half an inch of rain fell in less than an hour and inundated streets in the Electric City. Flooding was also reported on the Sun and Marias rivers, making it the wettest June since records were first kept in 1895. Flooding and blizzards killed seven in 1943, and caused $3,500,000 damage.

As if nature's flooding wasn't bad enough, the Bonneville Power Administration announced plans to raise the level of Flathead Lake 17 feet to provide more water for hydroelectric dams downstream. The plan, which called for the flooding of 30,000 acres, 2,200 homes and 200 businesses, met with strong opposition at meetings in Kalispell and Missoula. Rep. Mike Mansfield joined with the Confederated Salish and Kootenai tribes in opposing the plan, and more than two dozen witnesses testified against it at a meeting in Missoula attended by Governor Ford and Senator Wheeler. Realizing the depth of the opposition, Bonneville officials backed down on the Flathead plan within a week, and instead proposed building a new dam at Hungry Horse, an idea which had the support of Montana's congressmen. A dam site on the Blackfoot River was also under consideration.

The development of water resources was a major issue facing Montanans during the war years. In particular, the debate over how to develop the Missouri River became a major political issue which took several years to resolve. Governor Ford blasted the Army Corps of Engineers for their Missouri River plan, which was intended to develop more of the Missouri's potential for irrigation and hydroelectric generation. In eastern Montana, the new reservoir behind Fort Peck Dam was nearly half full by the summer of 1943, and water was backed up for a distance of 150 miles. The first Fort Peck generator was already installed and it went on line on July 1, although work on the other generators was halted because of a lack of funds. Seven federal reclamation projects which had already been completed in Montana were given credit for the production of $7,000,000

worth of food crops and several million dollars worth of livestock, and a new organization was formed to promote further water projects. Wesley D'Ewart, who would eventually represent Montana in the U.S. House of Representatives, was elected as the first president of the Montana Reclamation Association.

With precipitation, snow pack, and runoff all well above normal, farmers and ranchers looked forward to a bumper crop, although they still worried about the chronic labor shortage. Thirteen thousand men in the state had agricultural deferments, which kept them out of the military, but there were still not enough laborers in Montana fields to ensure that the crops were harvested. Governor Ford urged the Federal government to send German prisoners of war (POWs) to Montana, and Senator Murray announced that some 2,000 POWs would be sent to the Treasure State, and would be housed in camps at Billings, Havre, and Sidney.

Although no POWs arrived until 1944, more than 1,000 Mexicans did arrive to work in the labor-intensive sugar beet fields. Bowing to pressure from local farmers, the Ravalli County Loyal Americans League dropped their opposition to migrant workers, and several hundred Mexicans passed through Missoula on their way to farms in the Bitterroot Valley. Another 125 Mexicans worked in the Townsend area. More than 300 worked farms near Sidney, while 135 went to Forsyth and Miles City. In all, some 1,200 Mexicans spent the summer in Montana.

In addition to the Mexicans, 450 Japanese-Americans (Nisei) found temporary employment with the Great Northern Railroad while waiting for the sugar beet crop to mature. Offices were opened in Havre, Billings, and Helena to aid farmers in obtaining Nisei farm laborers. Camps were set up in Stevensville and Corvallis, and some of the Japanese-Americans lived in an old hotel in Townsend.

Many high schools across the state closed early for summer break in order that students could help with the crops. A total of 11,000 students, known as Victory Farm Volunteers, worked on farms in 1943, including 181 boys and 84 girls from Great Falls High. The students spent an average of two months

June 1943

- June 1. Liquor rationing begins in Montana. 1,400 state coal miners go on strike.
- June 3. Blizzard dumps four feet of snow on the Great Falls area, cutting telephone, telegraph, and power lines.
- June 4. Coal mine strike is called off.
- June 6. Three boys drowned at Great Northern reservoir outside of Billings. Three Butte men drowned at Delmo Lake while fishing.
- June 12. Major air battle near Guadalcanal.
- June 13. 28 cars of a freight train derail near St. Regis.
- June 15. Flag Day.
- June 19. Bomber crashes just outside of Great Falls, killing six. Several members of the crew survive.
- June 20. Three Missoula men die when a 17-car log train derails and falls into the Bitterroot River.
- June 25. Violent hailstorm strikes Lewistown area.
- June 28. First generator goes on line at Fort Peck Dam.

Air War Europe

- J.R. Burton, a pilot from Billings who served in the Royal Air Force, was awarded the Distinguished Flying Medal by the King of England at Buckingham Palace.
- Sgt. Clarence Blend of Great Falls won the Distinguished Flying Cross and an Air Medal with nine oak leaf clusters after surviving 51 combat missions over Europe.
- Lt. Enoch Porter of Great Falls was killed in action August 1, 1943, during a bombing raid over the Rumanian oil facilities at Ploesti. He was posthumously awarded the Distinguished Flying Cross.
- Lt. Ralph Cummings of Great Falls was also awarded the Distinguished Flying Cross for the raid on Ploesti.
- Tech. Sgt. Cullen Lee of Sun River was in a bomber shot down in August 1943. Captured by the Germans, he was awarded the Distinguished Flying Cross and two oak leaf clusters to the Air Medal while in captivity.
- Lt. Paul Hartman, a B-17 pilot, and Lieutenant Charles A. Jacobson, a B-17 bombardier, were reunited in a German POW camp in August 1943. They had been classmates together at Great Falls High.

Pacific

- Marine PFC Patrick D. Fleming of Milltown was awarded the Silver Star for his actions on July 10, 1943, when he killed a Japanese machine gunner on New Georgia and evacuated two wounded Marines.
- Capt. Edwin W. Allard of Billings was awarded the Distinguished Flying Cross for unescorted photo reconnaissance work over Japanese-held islands in the Solomons.
- Lt. (jg) George Hopkins of Great Falls was a Catalina pilot who helped pick up survivors of the *USS Helena*. He had 700 flight hours and had seen action at Kula Gulf, Rendova, Bougainville, Rabaul, Wake, and the Ellice Islands.
- Marine Lt. Philip Leeds of Havre was a pilot shot down near Munda. He rejoined his outfit on Guadalcanal after being missing for eight days.
- Marine Lt. Thomas Tomlinson of Missoula was another pilot active in the dangerous skies above the Solomon Islands.
- Cpl. Byron D. Hurley of Wagner was posthumously awarded the Silver Star for his work as a medic at Tambu Bay, New Guinea on July 28, 1943.
- Technician 4th Class Eugene O. Durand of Hall was awarded the Silver Star for gallantry at Tambu Bay, New Guinea.
- Technician Richard H. Brookings, was a medic awarded the Silver Star for his actions at Tambu Bay, New Guinea on July 28, 1943.
- Staff Sgt. Robert S. Elliot of Great Falls was awarded the Silver Star for his actions on August 13, 1943 on Roosevelt Ridge, New Guinea. A member of the 41st Division, he was a medic who administered plasma to a wounded man under fire at great risk to his own life.

in the fields, and were paid a wage of $.90 an hour. In addition, 669 high school boys worked for the Forest Service and 455 more worked for the railroads. In the fall, several rural high schools in the Billings area closed so students could help harvest beets.

A warm and wet August brought a record yield of 70,000,000 bushels of winter wheat. Wheat farmers in Cascade County reaped yields of 35 to 40 bushels per acre, and the 16 flour mills around the state produced over 200,000 barrels of flour each month. Throughout the war years, Montana farmers harvested an average of 67,000,000 bushels of wheat. Although 90 custom combiners from Oklahoma arrived to help with the wheat harvest, the crop was so large that Governor Ford asked the Army if the 464th Quartermaster Regiment, stationed at Fort Harrison, could provide soldiers to help harvest crops, and 150 soldier-volunteers worked the fields in Daniels and Sheridan counties.

Other important crops in Montana included the 4,300 acres of potatoes growing along the Great Northern Railroad route near Havre, as well as a $500,000 pea crop harvested in the Flathead valley. Mustard growers along the Hi-Line harvested as much as 500 pounds per acre, and a new mustard cleaning facility was planned for the Sunburst area.

Montana livestock producers raised approximately 1,400,000 cattle, 2,660,000 chickens, and 2,300,000 lambs during the summer of 1943. Farmers and ranchers not only had to cope with gas rationing and severe shortages of farm equipment and labor, but they also had to deal with a loss of state support. By the summer of 1943, nine Montana extension service agents were serving in the armed forces, and resources at the Agricultural School at Montana State College were strained to the limit. The College was forced to cancel their annual livestock show.

The severe shortage of able-bodied workers prompted officials at the Immigration and Naturalization Service's detention camp at Fort Missoula to parole some of the 1,200 Italian civilians detained there. These Italian detainees had been behind bars for two years, and they were anxious to work. Many of these men were immediately hired by the Northern Pacific, the Milwaukee Road, and the Great Northern railroads. The Florence hotel in Missoula employed two Italian chefs and several busboys who had once been crewmen on a luxury ocean liner. Others worked at St. Patrick Hospital and as gardeners for local citizens. Sixteen of the Fort Missoula detainees found employment in Great Falls, at Columbus Hospital and the Coca-Cola bottling plant, while 360 others went to work for the Forest Service. By the end of July, two-thirds of the Italians at the Fort were on work release.

The Forest Service paid the Italians according to the Army pay scale ($50 per month). They fought fires, piled slash and built trails in the Kaniksu, Coeur d'Alene, Clearwater, and Kootenai National Forests. According to Axel Lindh, Assistant Regional Forester, "the Italians are doing their work well, with enthusiasm for outdoor life despite the different environment under which they are living in the woods." Foresters considered the Italians much better workers than the high school students who were also working in the woods. Sixty Region One employees returned from the guayule project in California, which was scaled back because of the promise of synthetic rubber, and many found that they were among the 150 Forest Service employees in the Region who had been released for more essential war jobs.

In a break with tradition the Forest Service also hired 10 local women as fire lookouts on the Kootenai National Forest, while 60 conscientious objectors to the draft began smokejumper training at the Seeley Lake Ranger Station. The Forest Service also trained Coast Guard rescue parachutists and army medical officers at Seeley Lake. Although only 10 fires were reported in Region One during June, the last week of July saw 207 fires burning in the Northern Rocky Mountains, prompting Rep. Mike Mansfield to ask for an increase in firefighting funds. Smokejumpers, (or "firechuters" as they were sometimes called) made 71 jumps on 31 different fires, and saved $75,000 by quickly suppressing 14 major fires during 1943. The firefighters had a new weapon in their arsenal, and for the first time began using army flamethrowers to light backfires. The army on the other hand, had learned something from the smokejumpers. Maj. Gen. William Lee, who had visited Missoula's parachute training facility in 1940 and had taken home a smokejumper parachute, gave credit to the Forest Service for greatly speeding up the development of U.S. Army parachuting.

The Forest Service shops in Missoula were kept busy during the summer of 1943 repairing heavy equipment used on the Alaska Highway project. More than 450 trucks and pieces of heavy equipment were eventually repaired in Missoula. The accounting and personnel departments of the Alaska Highway division of the Public Roads Administration (PRA) were also moved to Missoula, and employed 50 people.

The mining industry in Montana was booming in 1943, partly because the Forest Service had recently spent $900,000 building mine-access roads to 29 new mines in the state. In April alone, 6,000 ounces of placer gold and 687,560 ounces of silver were produced in the state. Montana ranked third in the nation in silver production.

The Benbow mine near Columbus shipped 250 tons of ore concentrate per day, and the total was expected to hit 800 tons once a new bridge was constructed and larger trucks could take the road. Electric locomotives brought ore to the mine mouth, and a two-and-one-half mile-long tramway took ore from the Benbow mine to the mill. The Benbow and the nearby Mouat had 11,000,000 tons of known reserves of chrome, or 64 percent of the total known to exist in the U.S. The two mines near Columbus supplied 80 percent of the country's chromite demand during the early part of the war. Unfortunately for the miners on the Stillwater, as time went on, high-grade chrome was shipped from Africa and the Mediterranean at a lower cost than the chrome produced in Montana, and both the Benbow and Mouat were eventually closed.

Reserves of tin, antimony, chrome and manganese were stockpiled in Butte and Philipsburg, and the U.S. Bureau of Mines tested clay deposits at Lewistown, molybdenum deposits at Neihart and tin deposits at Basin. The vermiculite plant at Libby was expanded, and the Jardine arsenic mine, just outside of Yellowstone Park, was reopened.

Although the WPB lifted restrictions on metal lids for canning jars, the collection of scrap metal continued in 1943 with another major scrap drive held from June 7th through the 13th. Each Montana farm was expected to find 1,000 pounds of scrap metal. Boy Scouts in Great Falls mounted a copper drive.

In early June, the United Mine Workers struck coal mines nationwide. Led by district president W.A. (Tony) Boyle from Billings (who would eventually lead the national United Mine Workers), 1,400 Montana coal miners joined strikers in Wyoming, Colorado, New Mexico, Washington and Utah. President Roosevelt ordered the striking miners back to work and the union complied within a few days. Over the objections of Montana Congressmen

O'Connor and Mansfield, an anti-striking bill was passed by the House of Representatives. Montana coal mines affected by the strike included those at Red Lodge, Great Falls, Bozeman, Stockett, Sand Coulee, Belt and Colstrip. Especially hard hit was the Roundup area, where coal mining represented the major industry. Mines in the Roundup area included the Roundup Coal Mining Company, the Bair Collins Coal Company of Roundup, which operated the Prescott Mine (employing 65 men and producing 700 tons of coal per day), the Jeffries Coal Company, the Cottonwood Coal Company of Giffen (117 employees), the Republic Coal Company of Klein, and the Brophy Coal Company. Like every other industry in the state, owners of coal mines were hard hit by the labor shortage. For example, by the fall of 1944, 66 employees of the Stockett coal mine were serving in the armed services.

The Anaconda Copper Mining Company, the state's largest firm produced 1.3 billion pounds of metal, mostly copper, per year (this figure did not include the chrome production from the Mouat and Benbow). ACM spent $77,000,000 annually on their Montana operations, and paid $3,527,000 in taxes. The ACM plant at Great Falls was awarded yet another Treasury "T" award during the summer of 1943 after employees spent 10 percent of their paychecks on war bonds. The Great Falls plant, as well as the ACM East Helena plant, was also awarded a second "E" award for production. Although highly paid by Montana standards (ACM miners made as much as $8.00 per day) 350 ACM miners at Columbus went on strike in July because of a wage dispute.

Senator Wheeler, Representative Mansfield, and Governor Ford joined small mine operators in calling for a higher meat ration for miners and laborers, and the meat ration of state miners was nearly doubled. The Butte miners seemed more worried about rumors that whiskey was in short supply.

In July, Allied troops under Generals Patton and Montgomery invaded Sicily. Among the invasion forces were two officers from Lewistown, Brig. Gen. Henry A. Cheadle, and Maj. Kenneth Dows, who went ashore with the 1st Infantry Division. Messina was captured with little opposition, and two weeks after the invasion, Italian dictator Mussolini was deposed and placed under arrest. His Fascist party was dissolved and a new Italian government was formed. On the eastern front, the Russian's counterattacked at Orel and heavy fighting was reported near Smolensk and in the Kuban bridgehead. Presi-

Smelter Hill in Great Falls. The ACM smelter in Great Falls was one of the three large smelters operated in Montana by the company.
UM 83-112

Great Falls

One of Montana's major cities, Great Falls underwent tremendous changes during the war years, more so than any other city in the state. The air base brought new housing, new jobs, and a new permanent industry to the city on the banks of the Missouri. Cascade County, with a population of 48,229 by the end of 1942, grew 15 percent in just two years, at a time when the rest of Montana lost population. Cascade County had 199 employees and a $31,000 monthly payroll in 1944. That same year, the Cascade County War Chest drive collected $69,653 for the war effort, $2,000 short of their goal. With a population of almost 29,000, the city of Great Falls was served by the best newspaper in the state, the *Great Falls Tribune*, and two radio stations, CBS affiliate KFBB and KXLK, which broadcast NBC's Z-net. The city boasted eleven hotels including the Rainbow, the Stevens Hotel (50 rooms), and the Falls Hotel (100 rooms). Clothing stores included the Paris Fligman Company, Strain Brothers, Penneys and Hughes. The Hub was a favorite mens store. Great Falls theaters included the Liberty, Rainbow, and the Civic Center, and admission prices ranged from $.11 to $.50. Great Fall's supermarkets included Newmacks Super Market, Bertsches Food Market, the White House Grocery and Market, and Murray Boy's Market. A hub of the Great Northern and Milwaukee Road railroads, Great Falls was also a banking, commercial, and agriculture center. On the north side of the river, the suburb of Black Eagle grew up near the ACM metal reduction works, which refined zinc and copper. In the mid-1930s, the Great Falls smelter and wire and cable mill employed 2,500 men, but that number declined at the end of the decade. Great Falls' industries were powered by electricity produced by the 70,000-horsepower Morony Dam. The Rex flour mill employed 90 while the Sapphire flour mill employed 35. The city also had an oil refinery and cracking plant. Volk Brewery of Great Falls called itself the "Nations Biggest Little Brewery." The Charles M. Russell Museum opened in 1930, and a one million gallon municipal swimming pool, built with WPA labor, opened in 1934. Great Falls boasted two hospitals, Columbus Hospital and Montana Deaconess. The College of Great Falls, founded in 1932, offered degrees in education, nursing and medical technology. The State School for the Deaf and Blind had an enrollment of more than 100 students. One of the largest high schools in the state, Great Falls High graduated 273 seniors in 1944. Republicans controlled the Great Falls City Council, and in April 1945, incumbent mayor E.L. Shields was defeated by alderman Fritz Norby, an insurance man, by 1,000 votes.

dent Roosevelt and British Prime Minister Winston Churchill met in Quebec to plan war strategy. One of those helping Americans wade through all of the confusing war news was 32-year-old Chet Huntley, a graduate of Whitehall High School, who was in charge of the CBS bureau of war information, and was also the director of special events and news analysis for CBS.

More and more Montanans, especially fliers, found themselves headed for the European theater. One of the more distinguished airmen from Montana was Col. Hubert Zemke, age 27. Zemke was a former Montana middleweight boxing champion from Missoula who had been nicknamed the "Hub" by sportswriter Ray Rocene after winning 56 of his 59 fights. He worked as a forest fire lookout on the Lolo National Forest until enlisting in 1936. Before America's entry into the war, he trained British, Russian, and Chinese pilots in the art of flying American planes. Zemke commanded the 56th Fighter Group, based in England, which soon became famous as "Zemke's Wolfpack." After 30 combat missions over Europe, Zemke was awarded the Silver Star and Distinguished Flying Cross for "brilliant leadership."

By June 1943, 92 percent of the U.S. budget was being spent on the war, and more than 150,000 American lives had been lost. Tens of thousands of others had been wounded or were missing. In the Pacific, U.S. Marines fought their way north up the Solomon Islands, striving to cut supply lines to the Japanese base at Rabaul.

The men of the 163rd Infantry Regiment were still on New Guinea, primarily because it was considered too dangerous to return them to Australia as long as Japanese submarines and planes controlled the Coral Sea. The men spent their time improving military facilities near Sanananda. After seven months on the tropical island, Harlowton resident Hugh Reynolds wrote home that, "Our eats are pretty good, and we live in as nice a place as there is on this island. We have a swimming hole carved out of solid rock. The jungle is something like they picture it, only not as pleasant." In July and August the Montanans of the 163rd Infantry finally boarded ships for the dangerous journey across the Coral Sea. The veterans of Sanananda were headed back to Rockhampton, Australia, for six months of retraining and refitting. Once there, 21 Montana men of the 163rd were commissioned as officers.

The *USS Helena* was in the midst of the fighting

Ernest Melby, the controversial president of the University of Montana. Melby served a short-lived stint as Montana's first chancellor of higher education. UM 81-4

July 1943

- July 1. Ernest Melby becomes Chancellor of the Montana University system. Newsprint production slashed.
- July 2. Four die in a tanker truck fire at Cut Bank.
- July 4. Frank O'Neill of Great Falls, who was a cook during the Civil War, celebrates his 104th birthday.
- July 6. Light cruiser *USS Helena* is sunk by three Japanese torpedoes during the Battle of Kula Gulf.
- July 10. British and American soldiers begin landing on Sicily. Louis Armstrong and his Orchestra give a concert for servicemen at Great Falls Civic Center.
- July 17. 500 delegates attend 25th annual American Legion convention in Bozeman. Ceremony to honor *USS Helena* is held in Helena.
- July 22. Palermo falls to American forces.
- July 23. Two men are killed in crash of light bomber at Great Falls.
- July 25. Three miners are killed in a cave-in at the Leonard Mine. Philip Coleman is arrested for murder of Carl and Roslyn Pearson.
- July 28. Military plane makes a forced landing five miles northwest of Reedpoint. Japanese successfully evacuate Kiska without being spotted.
- July 31. Temperature of 106 degrees is recorded in Roundup.

in the Solomons when U.S. forces began landing on New Georgia at the end of June. Once the sun set on the Fourth of July, the *Helena* and a number of other American ships steamed into treacherous Kula Gulf. Covering the landing of U.S. troops at Rice Anchorage, the Helena's six-inch guns opened fire on now-familiar targets, the Japanese positions at Enogai Inlet and Bairoko. The destroyer *USS Strong* struck a mine and sank, but the *Helena* was untouched.

On the following day, Adm. Warden L. Ainsworth's task force was steaming down the Slot when they received word to turn back to Kula Gulf to meet a Japanese force of 10 destroyers. They went to battle stations at 10 p.m. Like the *Helena*'s two previous sea battles, the night was pitch-black with gusty rain squalls. The 10 Japanese ships were already in Kula and were steaming north when the three American cruisers and four destroyers entered the Gulf. The crack gun crews of the *Helena* opened fire at 1:58 a.m., firing as never before. Two thousand six-inch rounds and 400 smaller shells poured from the smoking muzzles of the light cruiser, leading the Japanese to believe that the U.S. Navy had developed "six-inch machine guns."

Under the constant pounding, a Japanese destroyer sank beneath the waves. Another was badly damaged and sunk by planes the following day. The speed of the gunners made the *Helena* an awesome sight in battle, but the constant muzzle flashes also made the cruiser a well-lit target. Nine minutes after opening fire a Japanese "long lance" torpedo slammed into the bow of the ship, killing everyone in the forward engine room. Radio officer C.G. Morris picked himself off the deck, "in total bewilderment, unable to believe we had been hit." After a few seconds *Helena*'s guns ceased firing because the ship was trembling. Two more torpedoes knocked out all lights and communications, and everyone aboard knew the *Helena* was doomed. She was listing badly, her back broken and with water pouring over the quarterdeck and midships. Crewmen hurriedly burned papers and threw sensitive equipment overboard while signalmen blinkered a distress signal. Men in the after engine room were forced to climb a high ladder in the absolute darkness because their regular escape route was flooded. At 12:20 the captain ordered abandon ship.

Seaman Bill Hunter of Harlowton went over the side of the ship and tried but failed to make it to a life raft. He watched as the *Helena* folded in two and sank. After sinking, a section of *Helena*'s bow broke

Hubert Zemke, a Missoulian of German descent. "Hub" Zemke became one of America's top-scoring aces in the skies over Europe. "Hub" Zemke

Sicily

· Tech. Sgt. Leslie Steilmon of Camas was awarded the Silver Star for his actions on July 11, 1943, when his C-47 was hit while dropping paratroopers on Sicily, then crashed and burned. He re-entered the burning plane under enemy fire and made sure the pilot and copilot had gotten out safely.
· 1st Lt. Robert L. Watts of Great Falls was posthumously awarded the Distinguished Service Cross for "extraordinary heroism above and beyond the call of duty" during fighting at Troina, Sicily.
· Technician 5th Class John F. Breitmeier of Harlem was awarded the Bronze Star for his skill as a radio operator during the Sicilian campaign, July 10, to August 17, 1943.
· Chief Quartermaster Darwin L. Dilno of Great Falls was one of the few survivors of the *USS Maddox*, sunk off Sicily during the landing of Allied troops.

free and floated back up, made buoyant by a water-tight compartment. Many of the men returned to the floating section of ship and watched the end of the battle, while others floated in the water.

After *Helena* failed to answer roll call, destroyers *Radford* and *Nicholas* returned to the Gulf to search for survivors. One destroyer spotted the floating bow in the darkness and, thinking it was a Japanese ship, opened fire. The men on the bow thought the destroyer might be Japanese, but they were desperate and flashed the *Helena*'s bow number through the night. Japanese ships were in fact still in the area, and torpedoes sliced through the water as the American destroyers came up, but they did no damage. The two destroyers lowered boats and began picking up survivors, including Bill Hunter. Lieutenant Morris was being pulled up a line to the *Radford* when the destroyer spotted a Japanese ship and began firing. "The ship reared in the water like a kicking mule, and I swung there against her throbbing plates, helpless, battered, hanging on with God knows what." He was soon pulled aboard.

The two destroyers rescued 750 *Helena* survivors, but dawn forced them to retire to the south, out of range of Japanese planes. They left their boats however, which plied back and forth picking up survivors in the water, including Captain Cecil. Cecil ordered the boats to make for New Georgia, where they landed at dusk. They crossed a coral reef and spent the night at the edge of the jungle, where they were found and rescued by the destroyer *USS Gwin* on the following day.

Some of the men still on the floating bow decided to abandon the sinking wreck and make for the nearby island of Kolombangara, but the current carried them past. More survivors were found in the water as they floated. They drifted into two groups and about 60 men landed on the Japanese-held island of Vella Lavella before dawn on the 7th, where friendly natives hid the sailors from Japanese patrols. A second group of more than 100 survivors were about to float past Vella Lavella at noon on the 8th when the strongest swimmers decided to make for shore. They also found friendly natives who helped pull the men on the rafts to safety. Japanese landing barges nearly discovered this group, but a strafing run by American planes drove them off. That night gunnery officer Warren Boles swam back out to sea, and signaled two of the six American destroyers that had returned to search the waters of Kula Gulf. Four landing craft swung close to the beach and picked up the survivors from Vella Lavella. More than 1,000 of the 1,200 *Helena* crewmen were eventually rescued and reunited at Tulagi. One hundred and sixty-eight died.

According to Bill Hunter, there were eight Montanans aboard *USS Helena* when she sank, and all survived. Besides Hunter, they included Bill Sundermeyer of Darby, Charles Dekolas of Barber, N.E. Lane of Augusta, a man named Hanson from Hardin, and one Butte man. By the time it went down, the *Helena*'s guns had fired more shots in anger than any other ship in the U.S. Navy, and the crew earned the Navy's first Unit Commendation. According to the citation, "Her brave record of combat achievement is evidence of the *Helena*'s intrepidity and the heroic fighting spirit of her officer's and men."

At home the sinking of the *Helena* was announced while some of the survivors were still in the water of the Kula Gulf. Military personnel and civilians from around the state attended a memorial for the ship in Helena, where Governor Ford said, "We have been brought here not only to pay tribute to our brave men but by the urge to register our outrageous protest against the sinking of one of the fightingest fighters in Uncle Sam's great navy."

The sinking of the *Helena* provided an effective theme for the third war bond drive in Montana. "Avenge Montana's Glorious *Helena*-Back the Attack by Sacrifice," was the slogan adopted as 15,000 volunteers canvassed the state in an effort to raise $35,000,000. The money was earmarked for a replacement for the *Helena*, and in a letter to Governor Ford, Secretary of the Navy Knox promised to name the next available cruiser *Helena*. The state's Naval recruiter called for 1,000 "*Helena* Avengers" to man the new ship.

In July the men of the First Special Service Force boarded two Liberty ships for the Japanese held Aleutian island of Kiska. On the voyage to Kiska, the men heard that the ship named after their adopted hometown, the *USS Helena* had been sunk in the Pacific. From out of their pockets and money belts, from the ship's safe and the pots of the floating crap games, the elite soldiers chipped in $5,418 to send to Mayor J.J. Haytin of Helena for a memorial.

By the end of the month the FSSF set up camp on Amchitka Island and began preparing to land on Kiska. On August 15, while the Second Regiment waited at Amchitka to make a planned parachute drop, the rest of the Force, augmented by 20 Alaska

Scouts, paddled ashore at Gertrude Cove and fanned out across the island, five hours before the main landing force. They found the Japanese gone, and the Second Regiment parachute drop was called off. Three days after the invasion, the Force was ordered to return immediately to San Francisco. General Eisenhower had requested their presence in Europe.

After the First Special Service Force pulled out of Fort Harrison, the Fort was occupied by the 464th Quartermaster Truck Regiment. Comprised of 600 trucks and some 2,000 men, one of the first duties of the new unit was to tour the state picking up the massive piles of scrap metal filling the streets in most Montana towns. The Bitterroot Valley alone yielded 100 truckloads of scrap metal.

Actor Robert Young also toured the state as part of the war bond drive. He threw out the first pitch in a baseball game held at Fort Harrison between the Army and a team from East Helena. After riding a dog sled at Camp Rimini, he threw out the first pitch of a baseball game between the Bombers and the Hilltoppers in Great Falls, in front of a crowd of 2,000.

A $3,000,000 dollar contract to expand the Great Falls air base was awarded to the Birch and McLaughlin Company, which had worked on the previous contract. There were other changes at the base as well. Col. Ponton D'Arce was transferred to Michigan and Col. Eugene Stevens took command of the 7th Ferrying Group. Stevens himself was soon replaced by Col. Harry B. Johansen. Col. Raphael Baez succeeded Col. Eaton as commander of the air base, and Capt. Harold F. Watson, one of Doolittle's Raiders, was also transferred to the air base. The base had brought so many people to the area that a severe housing shortage developed, and the government allocated $1,000,000 dollars to construct new housing for servicemen and their families. Fifty buildings were renovated to provide housing for 375 families and 30 individual air force base workers.

Segregation reared its ugly head at the air base when officers approved separate and unequal United Service Organization (USO) clubs for black and white soldiers. The USO for white soldiers was built on First Avenue North in Great Falls. The facilities included a library, showers, mending room, day care, a dark room and a selection of games. Several hundred women volunteers served the soldiers at a snack bar. In the first six months of operation some 119,522 soldiers used the USO facilities in Great Falls.

A separate USO club for black soldiers was built on Central Avenue at a cost of $4,000. It was staffed by Negro Red Cross women. Great Falls also had a chapter of the National Association for the Advancement of Colored People (NAACP), headed by Leo LaMar. During the spring of 1945, the organization charged that three black children in Great Falls were victims of racial discrimination after they were refused permission to appear in the annual Civic Center Ice Carnival. The director of the carnival claimed it was not discrimination, but lack of talent, that kept the children out of the show. He offered to find a place for them, but their parents refused because there was not enough time to make costumes. Race relations also played a part in a criminal trial in Great Falls, when two women (age 19 and 20) were charged with vagrancy and being dissolute persons because they frequented with blacks at the Ozark Club. The judge suspended 60 days of their 90-day sentence on the condition they not associate with blacks again. He erased their court record because he did not want this "blemish" on it.

Wartime shortages and restrictions severely curtailed traditional summer entertainment in Montana, and Cascade and Yellowstone County both canceled their summer fairs. Glacier Park hotels and buses did not operate in the 1943 season but limited services (meals, gas, and some lodging) were still available in both Glacier and Yellowstone Parks. Although few tourists made it to Montana in 1943, thousands of soldiers were passing through the state on troop trains. Deer Lodge residents donated enough ration coupons so that local women could serve coffee and homemade donuts to soldiers on the troop trains. Red Cross volunteers in Havre spent their summer wrapping surgical dressings for the military. They turned out 15,000 dressings in June alone.

Fireworks had been banned by the 1943 legislature for the duration of the war, but whiskey drinkers were allowed to buy an extra pint during the week of July Fourth.

August brought the circus to the Treasure State. Six thousand people attended a matinee of the Cole Brothers Circus in Great Falls, and 8,000 saw the night show. A few days later three circus elephants were struck by lightning in Dillon. Two survived, but "Pitt," an elephant believed to be 80 years old, was killed. Pitt was the last survivor of a noted elephant troupe that had performed a military skit during

World War I. The circus later erected a granite memorial to Pitt at the Dillon Fairgrounds. In 1993, the King-Royal Circus laid a wreath on Pitt's grave. The ceremony was attended by 100 Dillon residents, 20 of whom had been at the circus the day Pitt died. Two circus elephants who had been comrades of Pitt in 1943 also attended the ceremony.

In April, the State Board of Education had appointed University President Ernest Melby as the first Chancellor of the university system, setting the stage for a long-running feud between Melby and the state legislature. Melby took over his new post on July 1, 1943, while Law School Dean Charles Leaphart replaced him as president of the University. Since his arrival at the University in 1941, Melby had worked for more funding for the school. As one of his last acts as president, he reported to the legislature that, "Montana State University has suffered so severely in the past that its present morale and spirit seem quite remarkable. I know of no university which has carried on in the last decade under as serious difficulty...it has rendered a type of service which is far more significant than would be expected in view of the support the State has given the institution."

Sporting events were curtailed by the war, but not eliminated altogether. Eddie Chinske won the 1943 state golf championship at Whitefish, and a 10-day drive brought in 1,000 items of sports equipment, which were donated to the air base at Great Falls. The base, which had already supported hockey, basketball, and boxing teams, fielded two different baseball teams. The "Bombers" represented the Great Falls air base while the 7th Ferrying Group sponsored the "Hilltoppers." The 474th Quartermaster Regiment from Fort Harrison fielded a team that went undefeated after 21 games. Other prominent teams across the state included the Great Falls city champions, the "Selects," and the runner-up "City Barmen." In one of the highest scoring games of the season, the Missoula American Legion team beat Anaconda 30-5. The Great Falls Legion Juniors defeated a team from Miles City 8-6 to take the state championship, but they were soon vanquished by a team from San Francisco in the regional semifinals, held in Billings. In late August the American Legion World Series, involving the regional winners from California, Washington, Oregon, Montana, Idaho, North Dakota, South Dakota, Minnesota, and Iowa, was held at Miles City.

The crime rate in Montana seemed to soar with the advent of warm weather, and law enforcement targeted juveniles of all ages. In June, the Great Falls police confiscated 24 bicycles because local children were riding in the downtown area. In early August five drunk teenagers shot up Harlowton with a high-powered rifle. Two were sentenced to 90 days in jail and fined $200, while the others received lesser sentences. In Choteau, an intoxicated Ernest Swayze was wounded in a shootout with the county sheriff after Swayze shot up a local restaurant, wounding one man and taking a woman hostage. Swayze was charged with assault with a deadly weapon. Four Great Falls teenagers were charged with burglarizing 30 cars, while in Bozeman a woman chiropractor was charged with second degree murder after performing a botched abortion. Three inmates in the Helena jail knocked out a guard and escaped, but they were soon recaptured in Anaconda after a stolen car was found in the area.

A brutal murder outside of Missoula in July resulted in the arrest of a serial killer. Montanans were shocked when the bodies of railroad foreman Carl Pearson and his wife Roslyn were found at their Lothrop home, 30 miles west of Missoula. Two men who had been employed by Pearson the day of the murder were soon arrested. According to court testimony, Philip Coleman, age 29, and Lewis Brown were camped near the Pearson house after a day's work on the railroad. With the help of Brown, Coleman faked an illness and lured Mr. Pearson outside. Coleman hit Pearson from behind hard enough to kill him, then entered the house and murdered Mrs. Pearson in her bed. After stealing Mrs. Pearson's purse, Coleman fled in the Pearson family car, but was soon arrested in Drummond. Charged with the murder of Mrs. Pearson, Coleman had to be removed from the Missoula County jail because of the threat of mob violence. Two dozen lawmen were on hand to protect Coleman when he was charged with a second murder count in Missoula. Brown was sentenced to life for his part in the murder of Mr. Pearson, and 10 days after the murder, Philip Coleman, who like the other defendant was black, was sentenced to die by hanging on September 10, 1943.

August 1943

- August 2. American bombers attack Ploesti.
- August 4. Billings Polytechnic celebrates 35th Anniversary.
- August 5. A 7th Ferrying Group pilot dies in a plane crash six miles from Great Falls.
- August 6. "Pitt" the elephant dies after being struck by lightning in Dillon.
- August 8. Great Falls Legion Juniors beat a Miles City team 8-7 to take the state championship. Eighteen-month-old Chinook boy is found alive but weak after spending three days lost on a ranch.
- August 9. Consolidated Freightways warehouse and 25,000 pounds of freight burns in Shelby.
- August 12. Fighter plane from 7th Ferrying Group crashes near Belt, pilot killed.
- August 14. Soviets advance toward Kharkov and Smolensk.
- August 15. 34,000 U.S. and Canadian soldiers land on Kiska.
- August 17. Montana Flour Mills Co. and 100,000 bushels of wheat is destroyed by fire in Great Falls.
- August 23. Soviets celebrate the recapture of Kharkov.
- August 25. Eleven die when a B-17 crashes north of Winnett.
- August 29. Nazis proclaim martial law in Denmark.

Montana State Prison

During the 1940s, the Montana State Prison, located in downtown Deer Lodge, was administered by Warden John Henry. The cellblock buildings, which had been constructed in 1896 and 1912, were badly outdated by the war years. An investigation by state officials in 1931 called the prison "an eyesore to the state.... crying out in its filth and sanitary condition." An administration building was constructed in 1932, but nothing was done to improve the lot of the prisoners. The prison population at Deer Lodge declined significantly during the war years, and averaged about 350 inmates at any one time, down from a pre-war average of 500. The prisoners manufactured license plates and worked in a garment factory in the hospital-industrial complex at the prison. In 1942, the state legislature authorized $8,000 for a tannery at the prison, but it was never built. In June 1943, the prisoners at Deer Lodge were employed re-icing railroad cars containing 20,000 tons of beef, because the beef was in danger of spoiling. Other than that, most prisoners had little to occupy their time and were expected to observe a strict code of silence at all times. They lived in cells which measured eight feet by six feet and were seven feet tall. Prisoners were required to take a shower twice a week. Escapes were not uncommon at the prison, and one of the more notable escapes of the war years occurred in May 1945, when an inmate stole a blue sedan belonging to the State Motor Vehicle Registrar. The escapee was caught in Helena four days later. The 30,000-acre prison ranch provided all food for state institutions, but the Montana State Federation of Labor regularly condemned the "starvation menus" at the state institutions.

A guard tower at the former Montana State Prison in downtown Deer Lodge. The old prison now houses a museum and the Towe antique car collection.

Montana Ships

While the *USS Helena* was certainly the most famous ship with a Montana connection, it was by no means the only one. The *USS Montana* (BB67) was under construction in early 1942 when the Navy decided the design of the 58,000 ton battleship was already obsolete, and it was scrapped. As part of the war effort, the presidential yacht *Mayflower* was rechristened the *USS Butte*. Built in Scotland in 1896, she displaced 1,780 tons and had blockaded Havana during the Spanish-American war. The *Butte* was refitted with guns and depth charge racks and served as a Coast Guard convoy escort ship. The *USS Micka*, a destroyer escort named for Lt. Edward Micka of Baker was launched at New York. Micka had won the Navy Cross and Defense Medal for assisting in the destruction of 17 enemy planes and three machine gun nests. He was killed when his plane was shot down on a strafing mission during the invasion of North Africa in November, 1942. The destroyer *USS Brough* was named after Lt. (jg) David Brough, killed in the Aleutians. His sister lived in Butte. The Jaycees in Great Falls sponsored a Landing Ship Tank (LST), and took donations of goods for the ship's commissary. The combat transport *USS Missoula* gained fame because the original American flag raised over Iwo Jima was from the ship. *USS Pondera*, a transport, was launched at Vancouver, Wa. It was named for Pondera County after the county led the nation in the fifth war bond drive. A destroyer escort was named after Lt. (jg) William M. Holt of Great Falls, who was killed in action on August 7, 1942, and who was posthumously awarded the Distinguished Flying Cross for "Heroism and extraordinary achievement" near Guadalcanal. The *USS Shelton*, named after Ensign James A. Shelton of Denton, who had been killed attacking the Japanese fleet at Midway, was also a destroyer escort. The *USS Shelton* was commissioned in May 1944 and was sunk on November 20, 1944.

The *USS Missoula*, an attack transport that played a crucial role in the assault on Iwo Jima, one of the toughest battles of the Pacific war. SC

9

Montana Buys A Warship

As the summer of 1943 turned to fall, volunteers finished preparations for the third war bond drive, which officially opened on the ninth of September. In the Treasure State, the official theme of the drive involved buying a replacement for the USS Helena. A lithograph of the *USS Helena*, drawn by artist Branson Stevenson of Great Falls, was given to purchasers of war bonds, and the 17th of the month was declared "Avenge *Helena* Day." Lt. Cmdr. Charles O. Cook, one of the surviving officers of the *USS Helena*, toured the state speaking at war bond rallies, ($200,250 was pledged at one such rally in the Great Falls Civic Center), and sports celebrities like Missoula track star Greg Rice also toured the state. The U.S. Navy sent their 22-ton "cruiser on wheels" to help with the drive, and the Coast Guard sent Lt. Cmdr. Jack Dempsey, former heavyweight boxing champion, to referee boxing matches across the state. Those seeking admission to the boxing matches were required to make a pledge to buy war bonds, and 3,500 boxing fans in Helena pledged almost $100,000.

A Jaycee rally in Great Falls brought in $263,583, while the Blackfeet tribal council pledged to buy $75,000 worth of war bonds. Montana railroads contributed $2,530,000 toward the third war bond drive, and every Montana county exceeded the quota. The average Montanan bought war bonds worth $38.13, more than $14 above the national average. On a per capita basis, Montanans bought more war bonds than the residents of any other state during the third drive. The state as a whole topped the $35,000,000 quota by more than $6,000,000, and the fund-raising effort was so successful that the Secretary of the Navy promised to name the next available cruiser *USS Helena*. (The third U.S. Navy warship to bear the name *Helena* was launched in April 1945 and saw action during the Korean war.)

September also brought a return to the classroom for Montana's 60,000 school children. Enrollment during the 1943-1944 school year was down five percent from the year before, reflecting the large number of residents who had left the state to work in high paying defense industries on the west coast. Many of those who had left were teachers, 500 in the past two years. State Superintendent of Schools Elizabeth Ireland reported that 146 former teachers had enlisted in the service while another 214 teachers were employed in defense plants. Ireland issued more than 700 emergency teaching certificates to volunteers willing to help keep the schools open. Although the number of teachers was down, in 1943 the state school fund provided each district with $8.00 per student, the highest amount ever.

College students also returned to the classroom, and Montana's new chancellor of the university system continued his criticism of the state legislature. Dr. Ernest Melby condemned low teacher salaries and the lack of funding for higher education, warning that, "the University system is either worth spending money on or it is not worth having." Registration at the University of Montana during fall quarter fell to 664 students, a 30 percent drop in one year, and women students outnumbered the men by two to one.

Registration at Montana State College in Bozeman also fell 35 percent during the same period and would have been lower except for the popularity of their new nursing school. Eastern Montana Normal School (Billings) lost 60 percent of its students while Western Montana Normal (Dillon) and Northern Montana College (Havre) were at 50 percent of their prewar enrollment. The enrollment figures were somewhat misleading however, because they didn't count the hundreds of military men training at Montana institutions. Nearly the entire student body at the Montana School of Mines was comprised of Navy engineering students, while hundreds of Army aviation cadets learned to fly on the campuses at Bozeman and Missoula.

With hundreds of new pilots taking to the skies over Montana, it came as no surprise when the number of air-related fatalities soared. In September, two planes collided over Missoula, killing two instructors from the Johnson Flying Service and two student pilots of the 317th College Training Detachment stationed at the University. It was the first fatal accident for the Johnson Flying Service. In the eastern half of the state, 10 fliers were killed in a B-17 crash near Fort Benton, and a 7th Ferrying Group pilot was killed when his fighter plane crashed at the Great Falls air base.

The Montana Grizzly football team scheduled a game with Idaho during the fall of 1943, but were forced to cancel because the team had few players and no coaches. Head football coach Doug Fessenden was a major stationed at the Amarillo Air Base, while assistant football coach George "Jiggs" Dahlberg served as a first lieutenant in charge of physical education at Camp Lawton, Washington. The Pacific Coast Conference was subsequently notified that the University of Montana was dropping their football program for the duration of the war. Nationwide, more than 300 other colleges also dropped their football programs due to the war.

On a related note, Maj. Gen. Frank Milburn, the Grizzly football coach from 1926 to 1930, was featured in a September 1943 issue of *Look* Magazine after an embarrassing incident in North Africa. An over-exuberant Australian soldier mistook the major-general for an Italian prisoner of war, and kicked him in the rear end. Milburn took the incident in stride, at least in front of the photographer, although the fate of the Australian remains a mystery.

Back home, 7,000 football fans watched as the Missoula Spartans played the Anaconda Copperheads, one of the toughest teams in the state. The Copperheads had already shut out half the teams in the state, including a big win over the Miles City Cowboys, but the Spartans were just too tough for the team from Anaconda. Coached by Ed Chinske, the team from Missoula High defeated Anaconda 13-7, guaranteeing themselves a berth in the state championships against the Billings Broncs, leaders of the Big 5 Conference. The Helena Bengals also had a successful season, shutting out the Bisons (34-0), Butte (6-0) and Bozeman (30-0) before falling to the Billings Broncs in a battle for the title game.

As a major blizzard swept across the state, the Spartans and the Broncs met on an icy Naranche Memorial Field in Butte, where the Missoula team battled to a 7-6 victory, their first state championship in 22 years, (the Spartans would retain their title for the next three seasons).

As students returned to school and volunteers sold war bonds, one of the state's most notorious criminals spent his last days pacing the floor of his cell. Held in the Missoula County Jail for the murder of Mr. and Mrs. Carl Pearson at their home near Superior, transient Philip Coleman admitted to authorities that he had committed his first murder at the age of 14 and had killed 22 people since then. He blamed his problems on alcohol but added, "I guess I just went nuts." In his last hours Coleman provided details of eight of the murders, including the previously unsolved killing of an elderly Helena man two months before. Early on the morning of September 10, 1943, Philip Coleman died by hanging in the basement of the Missoula County Jail. His was the last execution carried out in Montana.

Several other violent crimes occurred during the fall. Dora Williams of Hardin was accused of stabbing railroad section hand Fred Robinson to death on November 19. She pled guilty to second degree murder, and one week after the murder was sentenced to 40 years in prison.

Pete Buchak of Fergus admitted crushing the skull of Mrs. Roy McDonald with a rock during an argument but was found innocent of murder by a jury. Abe Racine of Conrad was sentenced to life at hard labor for the murder of his wife. Most crimes were not so violent, however. In October 1943, Great Falls police made 86 arrests for four major thefts, seven car thefts, 46 bike thefts, seven burglaries, two forgeries, 17 petty larceny cases, one robbery, and two incidents of shoplifting.

Although the crime rate had dropped sharply since 1941, Great Falls experienced a rash of burglaries and in mid-winter, 10 members of a juvenile crime club were arrested for shoplifting and purse-snatching. As a result, a strict 10 p.m. curfew was imposed on those age 16 and under in Great Falls, the first such curfew in the state.

At the same time, local law enforcement authorities learned that untaxed liquor flowing from the midwest to the pacific northwest was passing through Montana. Two arrests were made after 500 cases of untaxed whiskey were seized from a truck in Malta. The two suspects eventually pled guilty to interstate shipment of liquor without proper labeling. Even though the country's retailers reported large stocks of liquor on hand, Montana liquor stores sometimes had a difficult time obtaining enough beer and liquor to meet demand, and one liquor store in Helena was mobbed when a new shipment arrived. The sale of liquor was a $7,000,000 business in the state in 1943, and also figured in a controversial state supreme court decision involving a plan proposed by the State Liquor Control Board. The board wanted to purchase stock issued by two Kentucky distillers. Governor Ford opposed the plan and the Court agreed with him, although two justices dissented publicly with the majority opinion. State liquor store owners, who felt the plan would have helped ease the liquor shortage, were furious at the governor, and two members of the Liquor Control Board, Chairman Frank J. Ward of White Sulphur Springs and A.E. McFatridge, resigned in protest. Administrator T.H. MacDonald was later ousted with the tentative approval of the Board.

By the fall of 1943, more and more Americans were being sent overseas. Allied forces on Sicily crossed the Strait of Messina and landed on mainland Italy on September 3, 1944. In southern Italy, American and British troops met strong opposition from German infantry dug in along the Gustav Line. Cpl. Warren B. Williams of Boyd was awarded the Silver Star for his actions during October 1943, when he moved his machine gun squad to within 50 yards of German positions in Italy, killing five and wounding two. Williams was killed in action on May 24, 1944.

After their abortive trip to Kiska, the men of the First Special Service Force returned to San Francisco, where half the command was given 10 days leave. The rest boarded trains for the East Coast. In mid-October 1943, General Frederick and two of his officers flew to Europe, then on to Casablanca. The majority of the Forcemen traveled by train to Hampton Roads, Virginia, where they boarded the troopship *Empress Of Scotland*. In early November they arrived in Casablanca, then traveled by train to Oran, Algeria, and boarded yet another ship, this time bound for Italy. On November 19, they arrived in Naples and soon moved to the former Italian artillery school barracks at Santa Maria, where they underwent training in mine warfare while waiting for their equipment to be unloaded.

Although most of Italy was firmly under German control, the Italian government signed a formal armistice with the Allies and declared war against Germany in mid-October. The news from Italy was of particular interest to the 1,000 Italian internees at Fort Missoula. The Italians, most of whom had been released from the detention camp on work details, hoped to immediately return home. Rumors circulated that the Italians might even be returned to their impounded ships, but the men were disappointed to learn they would have to remain in Montana until the situation in Italy stabilized. Since they were no longer considered enemy aliens the Italians were required to register for the draft, and several volunteered to serve in the U.S. armed forces.

The Immigration and Naturalization Service also held a number of Japanese-born community leaders from Hawaii and the West Coast at Fort Missoula. Late in the year, 258 more Japanese were transferred to the Fort, where they remained until March 1944. Some of these men were residents of South American countries like Peru and Bolivia, and had been interned while traveling in the United States. They were allowed a degree of self-rule at Fort Missoula, where they lived in dormitories of 40 men. The Japanese were responsible for their own cooking and cleaning. They were allowed to fish in the Bitterroot River, fielded baseball teams and constructed a nine-hole golf course. During the fall many of the Japanese were trucked to the Bitterroot Valley to help pick the apple crop. Some of the Japanese internees served as volunteers with the Missoula rural fire district, and in October 1943 six of them successfully extinguished a house fire in the Orchard Homes area.

The Japanese were often allowed to leave the Fort and spend the day in Missoula, and some of these men discovered the graves of 50 Japanese railroad workers who had been buried in Missoula cemeteries between 1900 and 1909. The Japanese internees expressed gratitude that the graves had been well tended, even in the midst of a bitter war against Japan, and 24 Japanese priests were allowed to hold a Buddhist service to honor their ancestors.

Only 300 Nisei farm workers made it to Montana in 1943, compared with 1,000 the year before. The sugar beet harvest was slowed by snow and rain but farmers worried more about the chronic lack of available labor. A mechanical sugar beet thinner was tried out in Malta, and two mechanical sugar beet harvesters were used near Billings, but these machines were of little help to the average farmer. Thousands of human laborers were needed to save the precious sugar crop from rotting.

Fortunately, help was on the way. Hundreds of migrant workers from Mexico arrived by train. More than 600 Mexicans helped harvest the sugar crop in the Bitterroot Valley, while 400 worked in the Sidney area. These beet pickers were guaranteed a minimum wage of $.40 an hour, up a dime from the previous year, although their actual wages were determined by the number of tons picked. According to Albert H. Kruse, State Commissioner of Agriculture, "The Mexicans are good workers and we are glad to have their help."

Even with 4,000 people working on the sugar

September 1943

· September 2. Ten men die in a B-17 crash five miles east of Ft. Benton.
· September 3. British forces invade southern Italy. Thousands view pet and doll parade in Great Falls.
· September 8. Italian surrender announced.
· September 9. U.S. Fifth Army lands at Salerno, Italy. Third war bond drive starts.
· September 10. Convicted murderer Philip Coleman dies by hanging, Missoula County Jail. Two aviation instructors and two students are killed in collision of their planes near the Missoula airport.
· September 12. Australian troops capture Salamaua, New Guinea. Mussolini is freed by Nazi commandos.
· September 13. Gen. Chiang Kai-shek becomes president of China.
· September 16. Australian troops on New Guinea capture Lae.
· September 24. 7th Ferrying Group pilot dies in air crash at Great Falls. Germans begin to evacuate Smolensk. Welder-caused fire causes $60,000 damages to the American Crystal Sugar Co. in Missoula.
· September 25. Duck season opens.
· September 26. O.F. Goddard, ex-chief justice of Montana Supreme Court, dies in Billings at age 90.
· September 27. Residents of Naples revolt against German occupiers.
· September 30. British troops near the outskirts of Naples. Silk recycling is halted because it has been so successful.

Montana State College

A. L. Strand became president of Montana State College in 1937. He presided over numerous changes on the Bozeman campus in the years before the war. An enlarged engineering library opened in October 1939 and the Student Union building opened just a year later, the same month that the College began a program for training civilian pilots. Initially, 20 students studied navigation and meteorology. As tensions mounted around the world, the College developed a defense-related curriculum which emphasized math, engineering, drawing, machine design, welding, auto mechanics, and metalwork. A radio operators course was eventually added to the catalog. The College's engineering students were highly sought after for defense work, and were paid a $75 per month stipend. Once war broke out, President Strand urged students to stay in school until called to the military. In 1942, spring break was canceled so that students heading to the military could graduate two weeks early. Strand left Bozeman on October 5, 1942, and was escorted away with full military honors. Dean of Engineering William Cobleigh filled in as temporary president for the next school year. In the fall of 1942 Cobleigh threw the entire quarter off-schedule when he released all male students and faculty for three weeks so they could work in the sugar beet fields. Football was cut for the duration of the war, but the College did participate in basketball and other sports, even though the athletic budget was greatly reduced. The war also caused dramatic fluctuations in enrollment. When the war began in 1941, enrollment at the College in Bozeman was at an all-time high of 1,801, and for the first time the College had a larger enrollment than the University in Missoula. Over the next two years the College lost 900 students. Enrollment rebounded in 1944 and 2,000 students registered in 1945. By the fall of 1946, the College was overflowing with 3,591 students. Roland R. Renne, head of the Agricultural Economics Department, became acting president September 1, 1943, and was inaugurated as president on April 10, 1945. After a year of negotiations with the military, the College set up a pilot training program, and 500 men of the Army Air Forces arrived on campus on March 31, 1943. They were split into groups of 100 men each for five months of training. The trainees stayed in Hamilton Hall and in the women's sororities at the Quadrangle (for the next 18 months most of the women on campus lived in the men's fraternities, which were vacant because the men had all enlisted). A total of 2,905 military students trained in this program before it was terminated June 30, 1944.

harvest, farmers needed another 1,000 laborers. Although 131 enlisted men from Fort Harrison had helped with the grain harvest in August, the needs of the sugar farmers far exceeded any help the military could provide, and officials appealed for volunteers. Fortunately, more Mexicans, as well as migrant workers from Arkansas, arrived to help with the beet harvest.

The 1943 sugar crop was somewhat smaller than the record 915,000 tons produced in 1942, but it was more profitable for the farmers. The Utah-Idaho Sugar Company reported that the average yield at Chinook was down from 11.5 tons per acre in 1942 to a little over nine tons per acre. Even so, the Chinook district produced 15 percent of the Montana crop. The government paid beet growers a subsidy to grow sugar, boosting the price farmers received to more than $11.50 per ton, almost $2.00 more than was paid the previous year.

In 1943, agriculture generated one of every two dollars in the Montana economy, and farmers enjoyed their most profitable year on record, with estimates of the year's farm production ranging from $188,000,000 to $235,000,000. The average farmer made just over $6,000 from his 1943 crop, and the value of his land had jumped 25 percent in just three years. The wheat crop was estimated at 71,000,000 bushels, down somewhat from the 73,782,000 bushels harvested in 1942, but was worth an estimated $83,000,000. The largest potato crop in 22 years yielded 2,760,000 bushels from 24,000 acres, and brought Montana farmers $4,000,000. Corn and bean production also hit record levels, as did the Flathead pea crop, valued at $1,000,000. Montana ranked first in the nation in mustard production, second in alfalfa seed, third in the production of wheat and seed peas, fourth in the production of sugar beets and flax seed (a record $12,000,000 worth of flax was harvested in 1943), as well as fourth in the number of irrigated farms, the size of farms, and the value of farm machinery. Honey production was particularly important in the Harlowton area, and 374,000 pounds of honey were produced statewide in 1943. Many rural areas of the state were not yet connected to the power grid in 1943, and only one quarter of Montana's farms had electricity. Despite their own severe problems, Montana farmers donated $2,870 and 15,000 pounds of seed to the Soviet Union for use in areas ravaged by the Nazis.

Cattle shipments from the state in 1943 were 14 percent higher than during the previous year, and estimates of total livestock production ranged from $85,000,000 to $134,000,000. Two Great Falls men purchased 100,000 deeded and leased acres of the Phillips ranch near Malta. The state ranked sixth in the nation in hay production and seventh in feeder cattle. In 1943, the state boasted 165,000 dairy cows and 698,000 pigs, substantially more than the 480,000 pigs raised just a year before. Nevertheless, Montana pig farmers suffered from government-imposed price ceilings, and were particularly hard-hit by an epidemic of ergot poisoning, which killed off several thousand young pigs during 1943. Montana's sheep industry ranked third in the nation in 1943, and investors in the Malta area planned to open a new Angora woolen mill. The 1943 wool crop was worth an estimated $13,300,000, but a lack of labor and grain forced sheepmen to sell off lambs.

Ration Book #4, which contained hundreds of ration coupons and was intended to last for several years, was issued in November 1943, and new blue and red ration tokens were issued to provide change for the ration coupons. Harried shoppers found that the point values of canned fruits and vegetables changed almost daily. Meat and cheese points were raised and supplies were further reduced, despite the shipment of 2,250,000 pounds of cheese from small factories located in Corvallis, Charlo, and Ronan. The cheese was destined for the Lend-Lease program instead of domestic consumption.

There was a severe orange juice shortage in Montana, and disposable diapers appeared on grocers shelves for the first time, their invention spurred by the war-time shortage of cloth diapers. Rationing became such a part of everyday life that a burglar who stole meat from a refrigerator in Great Falls left ration coupons worth 60 points on the kitchen table.

Virtually all types of food were rationed by the fall of 1943, and the 14 community canning centers located in Missoula and in smaller communities from Charlo to Sidney operated at full capacity. Montana had the nation's largest community canning program, and canning facilities were available at many schools. The program was under the supervision of local school boards and was capable of putting up 1,000,000 cans of locally grown fruits and vegetables per year, much of it grown in Victory Gardens. The state of Montana canned much of the food consumed by state institutions, but by the summer of 1944 institutional food canning was dropped by the state because of the increasing availability of commercial canned food. Even some of the commer-

Sugar beets for the sugar factory at U&I Sugar Co., Chinook, Montana. MHS 940-926

Beginning in 1942, cultivation of the lowly sugar beet became a vital part of the nation's war effort. The American Crystal Sugar Co. in Missoula was typical of the several large sugar refineries in Montana. MHS 949-995

Italian detainees from Fort Missoula harvest sugar beets in the Bitterroot Valley. The labor shortage proved troublesome for farmers throughout the war years. Montana's beets were picked by high school and college students, Italian and Japanese-American detainees, migrant workers from Mexico and Jamaica, as well as German and Italian prisoners of war. MHS PAC 84-34

cial canned food came from Montana, specifically Hamilton, where the Parker Canning Company employed 70 people dehydrating fruits and vegetables.

Most people had a hard time putting meat on the table. The situation was eased somewhat when 90 bison were slaughtered at the National Bison Range at Moiese and the meat was sold in Missoula. Another 400 buffalo were killed in Yellowstone National Park. The Blackfeet were given almost one-third of that meat, and tens of thousands of pounds of bison meat were sent to other Indian reservations in Montana, Wyoming, Kansas, and North and South Dakota. Meat rationing made hunting a necessity for many families, but the big game harvest was hindered by a lack of snow in the mountains and a critical shortage of ammunition. Shotgun shells were unavailable at any price and big game hunters were only allowed to buy 20 cartridges apiece. There was also an acute shortage of fishing gear.

New government regulations required hunters to pre-register for ammunition and to recycle hides and fat for defense purposes. Hunters throughout the state mobbed sporting goods stores on October 1, the day that ammunition was supposed to go on sale, but the little ammo that was available was quickly bought up by scalpers who sold it at greatly inflated prices. The situation eased somewhat in mid-December, when 67,000 rounds of centerfire ammunition were sent to the state for predator control. Predators killed in 1943 included one wolf, 48 bears, 62 bobcats, and 1,400 coyotes.

Warm weather was blamed for the light harvest of game animals. Only 535 antelope were killed in the 1943 season, which ran from October 15 to January 15th, and the deer harvest was also down. Early in 1944 a special elk hunt was held at Gardiner, but only 125 animals were killed, compared with 7,200 elk killed during the same time period the year before. In March 1944, local residents accused soldiers at Gore Field of killing a local antelope herd in violation of state law, but the Army denied the slaughter and no charges were brought. At least 163 grizzly bears were known to exist in Montana, and limited bear hunting was allowed. In the fall of 1943 a 1,000-pound grizzly was killed in Sun River Canyon and a 900-pound bear was shot near the mouth of Dearborn Canyon after it slaughtered 32 sheep.

On November 2, 1943 President Roosevelt seized the nation's coal mines after 500,000 union coal miners walked out for the second time in six months.

Led by Tony Boyle, the district president of the United Mine Workers, Montana's 2,500 union coal miners joined the strike on the second day. The laborers quickly won a daily wage increase of $1.50 (boosting their daily wage to $8.50 per day) in exchange for adopting a nine hour work day, up from seven hours. Tony Boyle eventually became national president of the UMW.

Gov. Sam Ford called on more Montana women to join the Women's Army Corps (WAC) as well as the related organizations of the Navy and Air Force (WAVE and WASP). Most department stores featured recruiting booths for the organizations and a statewide campaign enrolled more than 40 women, many of whom were sworn in on the steps of the state Capitol in Helena. The women were presented with the state flag carried by the 2nd Infantry (Montana volunteers) in Mexico and World War I.

Almost 400 Montana women were already in uniform by the fall of 1943, including Ensign Billye Wyatt, the first woman from Montana to enlist in the WAVEs. Wyatt returned to the state to help in the recruiting drive.

Many of the WACs were nurses, and others served as drivers, clerks and typists, while the WASPs were responsible for ferrying aircraft from factories to wherever they were needed. In a recent *Missoulian* interview, WASP pilot Martha L. Volkomener of Glasgow said, "My experience was one I absolutely would never give up, I think that was the most interesting flying I've ever done." She added, "We flew every airplane the military had at that time including the B-29 and the jets."

The WACs, WAVEs, and WASPS were not the only Montana women who played a part in the war effort. Hundreds of women enrolled in nursing programs while many others served as Red Cross volunteers. Baxter General Hospital in Spokane, where

---

Women's Army Corps (WAC)

- Maj. Betty Clague, WAC, was the former head of women's physical education at the University of Montana. She was awarded the Bronze Star for the China-Burma-India theater.
- Pvt. Norma E. Rasmussen of Lodge Grass was the first air WAC to earn flying status. She did flight tests on electrical equipment in B-24 bombers.
- Nurse Mina Larson of Libby was stationed on Guadalcanal during the spring of 1944.

October 1943

- October 1. Statewide scrap drive begins. Nine men are killed when their bomber crashes east of Big Sandy.
- October 2. Australian troops in New Guinea capture Finschhafen.
- October 7. A pilot is killed when his fighter plane crashes east of Stockett.
- October 8. Billings Broncs defeat Great Falls Bisons 6-0.
- October 9. Antelope season closes after 657 antelope have been killed statewide.
- October 11. New York Yankees win the World Series by defeating the St. Louis Cardinals 2-0 in the fifth game of the series. Three Gore Field fliers are killed in a B-24 crash at Colorado Springs.
- October 13. Italy declares war on Germany.
- October 14. U.S. Air Force bombs German ball-bearing plant at Schweinfurt, 60 bombers lost. Fifty-eight are hurt after Milwaukee Road eastbound *Olympian* derails near Miles City after the tracks washed out. Most of the passengers were servicemen and WACs. One passenger later died of his injuries.
- October 15. Last day to send Christmas gifts to men overseas. Big game season starts.
- October 16. Missoula Spartan football team defeats Helena Bengals 33-20. A fire in Billings causes $170,000 damage to the Stockman's Bar, the Elks Club, and the Midland Bank Building.
- October 20. Two dead, two injured in Billings house fire. Montana Education Association meets in Miles City.
- October 23. Fighter pilot dies in a crash near Lewistown. A hit-and-run driver kills a Billings woman.
- October 25. Soviets launch major offensive across the Dnieper River.
- October 27. Navy Day.
- October 28. Four hundred Farm Union delegates meet in Havre.
- October 30. Marines land at Choiseul in the Solomon Islands.

Dillon

Dillon replaced Bannack as the seat of Beaverhead County in 1881. The town was named for Sidney Dillon, a railroad man who oversaw construction of the Utah and Northern line from Utah to Butte. This was the first railroad built in Montana and it reached Dillon in 1880. Dillon had a population of 2,993 in 1940, but lost more than 500 people during the next three years. During the war years, Dillon served as headquarters of the Beaverhead National Forest and was also a center of mining and agriculture. Gold mining was a major industry, and commercial deposits of graphite, talc, and phosphate were also found in the area. In the 1940s Dillon was the largest wool shipping point in Montana and boasted a warehouse capable of storing 3,000,000 pounds of wool. The town had two newspapers, the *Daily Tribune* and the weekly *Dillon Examiner*.

Western Montana Normal College in Dillon specialized in training teachers. The school had 72 students enrolled during the fall of 1942; a year later that number had dropped to 41 students, even though the state desperately needed more teachers. Dr. Sheldon E. Davis served as president of the institution from 1919 to 1946. Ernest Melby, Chancellor of Higher Education, proposed a plan to turn Western Montana into a vocational school, but the legislature refused to go along. Dillon suffered its worst fire in 15 years when a vacant building was destroyed in May 1944. A month later two-and-a-half inches of rain sent both the Beaverhead and Red Rock rivers over their banks, causing major flooding in the Dillon area.

many of the sick and wounded of the 163rd Infantry Regiment were sent, hired 15 Montana women in an effort to make the soldiers feel at home. In 1943, Missoula Red Cross workers prepared 282,000 surgical dressings, collected blood, provided services for wounded men and the families of soldiers, and put together the Red Cross parcels that were essen-

tial for the survival of prisoners being held in Germany and Japan. The Cascade County Red Cross shipped 63,000 surgical dressings in just two months. The Red Cross halted the volunteer effort to manufacture surgical dressings early in 1945 because of a huge surplus. Roundup Red Cross workers made kit bags for soldiers, and the Navy Mothers of Roundup published a monthly four-page newsletter for their sons. The workload of the Red Cross in Great Falls was eased somewhat when the new United Service Organization (USO) took over some of the duties previously performed by the Red Cross.

In cities across Montana, women made a concerted effort to meet the troop trains that passed through every day, and a special effort was made during the Christmas holiday season. Volunteers in Butte estimated that 500,000 servicemen passed through the Mining City in 1943, and four volunteers (drawn from a pool of 400) met each train and passed out cigarettes, candy bars, fruit, playing cards, postcards, magazines, and books. A serviceman's canteen was opened near the Whitefish railroad station, and similar programs were mounted in nearly every Montana town with a railroad depot.

Along with all of the other shortages, Great Falls suffered through a severe housing shortage. A wartime government survey found that only one percent of available rentals in Great Falls were in adequate shape. During the 1930s, only 20 houses per year had been constructed in the Electric City. That number increased 10-fold in 1940 and 1941, but the war put an end to the building boom, and only 12 residences were constructed in Great Falls during 1942. By late 1943 the civilian population of Great Falls had increased 5,128 (from 29,990 to 35,118) since 1940, while only 350 residential building permits had been issued during the same period. A survey of housing found that the city of Great Falls had 8,815 residences on January 1, 1944. In response to the shortage, the Federal Housing Authority announced the importation of 100 trailers to the Great Falls area, and construction began on hundreds of apartment units. The trailers came from the Block P mine at Hughesville, which had been shut down by the government in order to transfer workers to more important mines. Renting for $6.00 a week, the trailers at the Victory Trailer Court were 7.5 feet wide, 22 feet long, and housed four. A number of existing buildings in Great Falls were converted into apartments, including the Oasis Building in Black Eagle, the Imperial Grocery, the Lincoln School, the Lowell School, and the Roslyn Apartments. By the end of 1944, 2,376 new housing units had been provided in the state, most of them in Great Falls.

Because of the influx of people, Mayor Shields of Great Falls also asked the federal government to provide more water storage tanks in the city, even though military guards already protected the Great Falls water supply from sabotage. The city announced plans to build the largest concrete water tank in the world, at a cost of nearly $300,000, and the government agreed to pick up two thirds of the cost of the tank. When it was completed in 1945, the tank measured 160 feet in diameter and had a capacity of 4,750,000 gallons.

Late in 1943, J.K. Howard's *Montana: High, Wide, and Handsome* was published by Yale University Press. It quickly became a best seller and was chosen by the Book of the Month Club. *Winter Wheat*, the sixth book by Montana novelist Mrs. R.F. Schemm, was published by Harcourt Brace and Company, and chosen as a selection of the Literary Guild.

November saw the merging of two of the oldest newspapers in the state. The Montana Record Publishing Company bought the Independent Publishing Company (both newspapers were founded in 1866) and announced plans to produce one paper, the *Helena Independent-Record*.

Much to Gov. Sam Ford's chagrin, reporters from the new paper were on the scene to witness him chasing an escaped pig around the grounds of the state Capitol. (The pig was sent by the governor of Nebraska, who had lost a bet that citizens of his state would buy more war bonds than Montanans.) The pig escaped from the governor and caused quite a stir until a bystander finally captured it. (After embarrassing the governor, the hapless pig wound up as Sunday dinner for the children housed in state institutions.)

Four hundred people attended a nine-state Republican conference which took place in Missoula in mid-October. Predictably, the banquet speakers praised Governor Ford's leadership while blasting the Roosevelt administration. Although Senator Wheeler was a Democrat, he too opposed the administration, especially President Roosevelt's plan to draft nearly all adults. Wheeler introduced a bill to defer drafting of fathers, some of whom were drafted while some single men had either not yet been called or had been released for work in war industries. The situation also caught the attention of Rep. Mike Mansfield, who accused the selective service of "bungling shiftless methods." Mansfield also urged Secretary of State Cordell Hull to expedite relief packages to American prisoners being held in Japan and the Philippines.

In other political news, senators Wheeler and Murray and representatives Mansfield and O'Connor introduced identical bills calling for the construction of Hungry Horse Dam. This was perhaps the only issue on which all four members of Montana's congressional delegation agreed. President Roosevelt and British Prime Minister Winston Churchill met in Cairo with Chinese President Chiang Kai-shek and then traveled to Teheran where they met with Soviet leader Joseph Stalin. They discussed the upcoming invasion of Europe and Stalin pledged that the Soviet Union would join the fight against Japan as soon as the European war was over.

In the Pacific, American forces in the Solomon Islands moved steadily northward, landing at Bougainville in November, where 60,000 Japanese awaited them. Among those wading ashore on Bougainville was Marine Pvt. Lee Shaw of Roundup a veteran of the Japanese attack on Pearl Harbor and the initial landing on Guadalcanal. PFC Roscoe R. Downs of Glendive won a Bronze Star for his actions on Bougainville, where he and two other men volunteered to rescue a patrol trapped in a gully. They deliberately drew fire and forced the Japanese back with machine gun fire while the patrol made it to safety.

The war against the Japanese entered a new phase when American forces invaded the Gilbert Islands. On November 20, 1943, landings were made on Tarawa Atoll and Makin Island. Although the tiny islands were quickly captured, the fighting was intense and very bloody for those involved.

Killed in the initial landing on Tarawa was Marine PFC Douglas K. Campbell, son of state senator John Campbell of Missoula. Doug Campbell had been captain of his high school football and basketball teams and played for three years in the Montana state legion baseball league. Campbell field, Missoula's former baseball park, was originally named after his father (who had been instrumental in its construction in 1934) but also honored PFC Campbell.

Other Montanans killed on Tarawa included Marine Lt. Hugh D. Fricks of Helena, who was awarded a posthumous Navy Cross for directing machine gun fire until he was mortally wounded, and Marine Sgt. James R. Atkins of Lonepine, posthumously awarded a Silver Star for supervising the unloading of tanks on the beachhead. Among the Montanans who survived the hellish battle in the Gilberts was Cpl. William O. Hutchinson of Great Falls and the Second Marines, a veteran of

---

November 1943

· November 1. American Marines land on Bougainville in the Solomon Islands.
· November 5. American carrier planes and heavy bombers attack Japanese warships at Rabaul.
· November 7. Natural gas explosion in Anaconda levels a block long federal housing project, injuring two.
· November 10. Marine Corps Day.
· November 11. Henry L. Myers, former U.S. senator from Montana (1911-1923) and associate justice of the Montana Supreme Court (1927-1929), dies in Billings.
· November 12. Soviet offensive at the Pripet Marshes.
· November 17. Two Great Northern "speeder" cars carrying members of a track repair crew crash 35 miles east of Libby, killing two and injuring 13, one of whom died later.
· November 20. U.S. Marines land on Tarawa Atoll and Makin Island.
· November 22. Roosevelt, Churchill, and Chiang Kai-shek meet in Cairo.
· November 23. Albemarle Apartment building in Butte burns, $11,000 damages. Tarawa taken.
· November 25. Missoula Spartans defeat Billings Broncs for state football title.
· November 28. Teheran conference begins in Iran. Churchill, Stalin, and Roosevelt agree on the planned invasion of Europe and Stalin pledges to join fight against Japan when the European war ends.

Guadalcanal, and Pvt. George J. Webster of Homestead, who was awarded the Silver Star for destroying two pillboxes on Makin.

One of the largest U.S. Navy fleets assembled up to that time, including 11 aircraft carriers, supported the Marine landings in the Gilberts. Although the sailors aboard the ships were safely out of range of the machine gun bullets and shells that raked Tarawa and Makin, they too faced mortal danger. Four days after the initial landings on Tarawa and Makin, a

Japanese submarine fired a torpedo at the *USS Liscome Bay*, a brand-new escort carrier. The torpedo set off aircraft bombs and aviation fuel stored aboard the ship, and the *Liscome Bay* exploded into a raging inferno and sank within 20 minutes, carrying 650 members of her crew down with her, including Seaman George Bellusci of Missoula. Bellusci's family has extensively researched the sinking of the *Liscome Bay* and in 1992 they attended a reunion of the survivors held at Astoria, Oregon.

Air War Over Europe

Kalispell residents Ed Fuller and Jack Paliga were prisoners together at Stalag XVII-B in Austria during the war, although they didn't know each other until they lived in the same neighborhood in Kalispell in the 1950s. Fuller was a upper turret gunner in a B-17 shot down June 22, 1943. He parachuted to safety, but was captured and held at Stalag XVII-B, near Krems, Austria. Some months later, he was joined in captivity by Jack Paliga of Stockett, whose B-24 had been shot down October 1, 1943. Seven weeks after his capture, Paliga was awarded the Distinguished Flying Cross. Besides Paliga and Fuller, at least two dozen other Montana men were held at Stalag XVII-B.

· Lt. Arthur Jacobson and Lt. Paul Hartman, both of Great Falls, were interned at Stalag Luft III, near Sagan, Germany.

· Tech. Sgt. Robert Steele, a former guard on the Great Falls Bison football team, was a crewman on a B-17 hit by flak on a bombing raid near Athens. After crash landing the crew managed to contact the Greek underground. All 10 crew members made it safely back to Italy four months later. Steele was a veteran of 30 missions.

· The 390th Bomb Squadron, which had trained at the Great Falls air base, took part in a bloody raid on Schweinfurt, Germany on October 14, 1943. The squadron lost one plane and had 14 others damaged. They were awarded a Presidential Unit Citation.

U.S.S. "Helena"   3rd WAR LOAN

WE BOUGHT A SHARE IN HER

10

The Long Winter Of 1943

As November of 1943 turned into December, Montana newspapers were filled with news of the Allied offensive in the Monte Camino region of Italy. This was of particular interest to the several hundred Montana women who had married members of the American-Canadian unit known as the First Special Service Force. Just a year before, the Forcemen had been learning winter survival skills, skiing, and rock-climbing in the mountains near Helena. Now the highly trained commandos were about to use their hard-earned skills in the icy mountains of Italy. Attached to the 36th Division (II Corps), the First Special Service Force was assigned to the formidable task of taking Monte La Difensa. The 3,000 yard front on Difensa was heavily fortified with pillboxes and machine guns, manned by crack German troops. The area had already been the scene of an unsuccessful 12-day battle in November.

On the night of December 1, 1943, the Forcemen hiked 10 miles up the mountain in pouring rain, reaching a sharp ravine where they concealed themselves until darkness fell on the second of December. Using the rock-climbing skills they had learned in Montana, 600 Forcemen of the Second Regiment began moving up the sheer, icy cliffs in the darkness, fixing ropes as they went. The exhausted Forcemen who reached the top hoped to wait until dawn to attack, but falling rocks alerted the Germans and flares revealed the presence of the Forcemen. A wild and bloody fight broke out on top of the fog-shrouded mountain, and artillery fire from both sides made the mountain appear as if it were on fire. By dawn, the mountain that had held up the American advance for weeks was firmly in the hands of the First Special Service Force. Seventy-five Germans lay dead, another 43 were prisoners, and the remainder fled to nearby Monte La Remetanea.

The Force's victory had come at a terrible price however, and casualties had been heavy. Canadian Lt. Col. Tommy MacWilliam, commander of the First Regiment, was killed by mortar fire, as were many of his men. The wounded went down the same way they had come up, by rope. It took 10 men eight hours to bring each casualty down the mountain. Those Forcemen not in front lines were pressed into

duty as pack mules, and for seven days the men made two trips a day (six hours per trip) up the frozen cliffs of Difensa, carrying ammunition, food and water.

On the 6th of December, the Forcemen took Monte La Remetanea, and on the following day they tied in with British troops on their left. In six days of fighting, the First Special Service Force sustained 511 casualties, including 73 dead, 9 missing, 313 wounded, and 116 exhaustion cases. They returned to the Santa Maria barracks and held a memorial service for their dead.

Just before Christmas, they were again sent to battle, this time at Venafro, which the BBC called "the hottest spot on earth." Their winter training at Helena proved invaluable, as the Forcemen attacked one German stronghold after another in the steep mountains of Italy. At dawn on Christmas Day they attacked Hill 720 (Monte Sammucro) in the middle of an artillery duel, where they flushed out snipers and machine gunners at an additional cost of 77 dead and wounded.

The First Special Service Force kept fighting through the early weeks of January. They excelled at the hand-to-hand combat in the frozen mountains, and many prominent war correspondents (including Ernie Pyle, Clark Lee, and photographer Robert Capa) covered the colorful Forcemen. In the first week of January they seized Monte Radicosa, Monte Vischiataro and surrounding peaks, then attacked Hill 702 with light casualties. They took several hills without resistance and brought up supplies for the main attack, but most of the Germans had pulled back. One lost Forceman, however, stumbled into a cave and captured 20 Germans. On January 6, the First Special Service Force captured Mt. Majo and other peaks in heavy fighting. They beat back 27 separate German counterattacks using captured German machine guns and ammunition, and suffered the loss of 22 additional Forcemen. By the time they were pulled out of the line on January 17, only one quarter of the men were combat ready, and over 1,400 of the Force's 1,800 combatants were casualties. Even the supposedly non-combatant Service Battalion was down to 50 percent strength due to wounds and exhaustion. They were given 10 days to

General Frederick meets with Gen. Mark Clark, commander of the American Fifth Army in Italy. Bob Durkee, Helena

Forcemen Hill and Wright preparing to defuse a mine at Radicosa. Bob Durkee, Helena

Soon after the invasion of Kiska, the First Special Service Force was ordered to Italy at the request of Dwight Eisenhower. Gen. Robert Frederick leaving a staff meeting at Radicosa, Italy. Bob Durkee, Helena

Col. Edwin Walker presides over a First Special Service Force awards ceremony at Santa Maria barracks, Italy.

Bob Durkee, Helena

Memorial service held at Santa Maria barracks for the 73 Forcemen killed on Monte Difensa.

December 1943

· December 1. Teheran Conference ends.
· December 3. Statewide paper salvage drive begins. Duck season ends.
· December 5. Montana actor George Montgomery marries Dinah Shore.
· December 6. A University student with the 317th Training Detachment dies from exposure at the base of a cliff in Pattee Canyon near Missoula.
· December 7. More than 1,100 civilian employees at Great Falls Air Base and 34th Subdepot are honored with an "emblem of civilian service." Twenty-three new WACs are sworn in at Butte.
· December 9. Deaconess Hospital in Great Falls records birth of 12,000th baby.
· December 16. A bomber based at Great Falls crashes at Kearney, Neb., killing one crewman.
· December 17. Eighty-six student nurses complete training at Montana State College.
· December 20. Butte Safeway warehouse burns, causing "tremendous" loss.
· December 24. Two men are arrested after a dynamite explosion at the Silver City nightclub in Butte injures 15 people.
· December 26. Chicago Bears defeat Washington Redskins 41-21 for national football title. German cruiser *Scharnhorst* sunk off Norway.
· December 27. The U.S. Army takes over the country's railroads to avert a threatened walkout.
· December 29. Gavin Theater in Stevensville is destroyed by a fire which also damages nearby buildings.
· December 30. Havre schools reopen after scarlet fever outbreak. U.S. Marines capture Cape Gloucester airfield on New Britain.

January 1944

- January 1. Gordon Tupper, aged 96 and a Civil War veteran, dies in Missoula.
- January 6. A musical entitled "Memories on Parade" is put on by the University and Army trainees in Missoula.
- January 7. Fifth Army captures Mt. Majo in Italy.
- January 8. Montana Aviation Committee meets in Missoula.
- January 9. A fire in Helena destroys the historic five-story Montana National Bank, built by C.A. Broadwater, injuring eight and killing two elderly women who lived on the fourth floor. A 10-year-old boy who tried to rescue the two women was critically burned but survived. He was released from the hospital in April.
- January 19. High winds spread 300 prairie fires across Blaine, Hill, and Cascade counties.
- January 21. Four students at Missoula High are injured, two seriously, when their chemistry experiment explodes. Soviets take Novgorod.
- January 22. British and American troops begin landing at Anzio.
- January 24. Three die in a house fire six miles from Glasgow. Two miners are killed by a dynamite blast at the Brittania Mine in Butte.
- January 27. Soviet Red Army breaks 900-day siege of Leningrad. Robert Alexan Der Thornburg of Hamilton celebrates his 96th birthday in Hamilton. He fought with General Lee at Gettysburg and was believed to be the last Civil War veteran in Montana. Cold Wind (age 100) a Crow Scout who had ridden with General Nelson Miles at the Canyon Creek Battle with the Nez Perce, is buried at Custer Battlefield.
- January 28. *USS Missouri* launched.
- January 31. American forces land on Kwajalein atoll.

Navy

- A very high number of Montana men (at least 10,000) served with the Navy during World War II. By early 1943, 777 men from Cascade County had enlisted in the Navy.
- Capt. Archibald E. Uehlinger of Kalispell was awarded the Silver Star by Navy Secretary Knox for his actions aboard a battleship in the Solomons that shot down 32 planes.
- Cmdr. George C. Towner was the executive officer on a heavy cruiser in the Pacific. He visited his wife in Great Falls during the fall of 1943 for the first time in one and a half years. Not long afterwards he was promoted to a full captain.
- Rear Adm. John H. Hoover, formerly of Great Falls, who had won the Navy Cross in 1918, was awarded the Distinguished Service Medal for driving German submarines out of the Caribbean. He was then transferred to the Central Pacific where he commanded aircraft based in the Gilbert Islands during the Marshall Islands campaign.
- Radioman 1st Class Aleck G. Alexander of Superior was a crewman on a flying boat that rescued 15 airmen from Kavieng harbor on February 15, 1944. His pilot was awarded the Medal of Honor and he was awarded the Silver Star.
- Radioman 1st Class George W. Harrison of Butte was awarded the Distinguished Flying Cross and Presidential Unit Citation for his actions with the "Black Cat" squadron during the fall of 1943 and the winter of 1944. He was a University of Montana graduate who served aboard a Catalina flying boat in the Southwest Pacific theater. He flew over the Celebes and New Guinea and once helped rescue 200 Australian commandos surrounded near Wewak.
- Cmdr. Wreford "Moon" Chapple of Billings was awarded two Navy Crosses and two Silver Stars for "conspicuous gallantry". He was a 1930 Annapolis graduate who commanded the submarine *S-36* at Lingayen Gulf in December of 1941, where he had little success against the Japanese invasion fleet because of faulty torpedoes. He was then given command of the submarine *USS Permit* one of the first American subs to penetrate the Sea of Japan. Chapple took *Permit* to the western coast of Hokkaido, where on July 7, 1943 he sank two small freighters. He ended the war as an admiral.
- Capt. Leo B. Schulten of Helena was awarded the French Croix de Guerre with gold star for his actions along the French coast.
- Capt. Louis Dent Sharp from Fort Benton was a destroyer captain during the war. After the war he was promoted to admiral and eventually commanded the Pacific fleet.

recuperate.

Although it had been an open secret in Great Falls for some time, the government finally disclosed the route of the Lend-Lease planes being turned over to Soviet pilots at Fairbanks, and *Life* Magazine printed a map of the air route which revealed Great Falls as the southern hub of the route.

The Soviet Union had already received 2,000 A-20 attack aircraft along the Great Falls-Alaska-USSR pipeline, and by the end of April, 1944, the United States had delivered more than 6,000 planes to the Soviet Union, most of them via Great Falls. Three hundred and sixty planes left Gore Field each month, and each plane carried a full load of cargo. Much of the cargo was destined for the Soviet military, but the planes also carried wheat seed, tractor parts, and farm implements donated by Montana farmers. Nine of the ferry pilots stationed at Great Falls were awarded Distinguished Flying Crosses for their "extraordinary and meritorious achievements" while flying the dangerous ALSIB route.

Not all of the air traffic flowed from the U.S. to the Soviet Union, however. Major General A.I. Belyaev of the Soviet Purchasing Commission flew from Moscow to Great Falls to inspect the facilities there, and many Soviet diplomats passed through Montana on the way to Washington, D.C. The wife of Maxim Litvinov, former Soviet ambassador to the U.S., spent some time in Great Falls on her way from New York City to Moscow. Vice President Henry Wallace also flew through Great Falls on his way to Moscow.

The Russians stationed in Great Falls reportedly were fond of American clothing, jewelry, and milk shakes. Not all of their activities were quite so innocuous, and Maj. George Jordan became increasingly concerned about the rampant Soviet espionage at Great Falls. In January 1944, Jordan traveled to Washington to discuss the material being shipped to the U.S.S.R. This resulted in investigations by the Customs Department, the FBI, the Immigration and Naturalization Service, and the Censorship Department. The Soviet activities were so blatant that even some Russians were bothered by them. In April 1944, Victor A. Kravchenko of the Soviet Purchasing Commission resigned because he did not agree with some of the Soviet activities directed against the U.S. and Britain. Still, little was done to stop Soviet espionage at Great Falls, and U.S. Army officers at the base were never given

authority to halt suspicious shipments. Security was tightened at the base however, and the armed guards, two of them women, guarded against sabotage. At least one U.S. soldier was accidently shot by sentries at the air base.

Many other changes occurred at the air base during early 1944. On New Years Day, 1944, the Air Transport Command took over jurisdiction of the air base from the Air Service Command. Col. R.L. Meredith replaced Col. Raphael Baez as commander of the 34th subdepot, Great Falls Army Air Base, while Col. Henry B. Johanson became commander of the 7th Ferrying Group. Cascade County commissioners voted to rename Gore Field after Col. Earl T. Vance, a pioneer aviator killed in a plane crash in Colorado in February 1944, but Colonel Johanson requested that the name change be postponed until the military left Gore Field, and the city revoked the change.

The 34th Subdepot vacated the Great Falls fairgrounds in mid-February, after having improved the fairgrounds by pouring concrete floors in many of the buildings. Training of bomber crews was halted as the Second Air Force prepared to move out completely. Local contractor Dudley-Anderson received an additional $111,375 contract for work at Gore Field, which included the construction of a dental clinic, a surgeon's building, a finance building, three motor repair buildings, a crash truck shed, and smaller buildings.

The Montana Reclamation Association, an organization destined to play an important part in one of the most divisive political issues in the state during the mid-40s, was formed in December 1943. At the initial meeting in Bozeman, Governor Ford spoke before the new group and urged the development of a comprehensive plan for development of the Missouri River. The new organization put forth numerous projects, including a plan to irrigate 162,000 acres of western Montana and 170,000 acres in the Missouri Basin. In a related matter, the $40,000,000 Hungry Horse Dam bill made its way through Congress, and several Montanans, including Representative O'Connor, testified in favor of the bill before the House Reclamation subcommittee hearings in February.

The New Year brought predictions that rockets, jet airplanes and helicopters would revolutionize transportation after the war, but few people believed that television would soon become a billion dollar industry. Of more immediate interest, blackouts and air raid drills were canceled in Montana, and the ban on the sale of typewriters was lifted. New models of a few household appliances were put back into production, although shortages remained until the end of the war. By the spring of 1944, the state was allotted 45 new passenger cars per month, but the gasoline ration was cut to two and a half gallons per week for those working in non-essential professions. Tire rationing remained a major headache for drivers, and a firm in Butte was forbidden to sell tires for 10 months because of blatant violations of the rationing regulations.

The shortage of gasoline and tires (it was estimated that the state needed an additional 30,000 passenger car tires) during the previous year resulted in a 40 percent decline in highway traffic across the state. The number of valid drivers licenses dropped by 12 percent, and traffic deaths in 1943 dropped 16 percent (92 compared with 110 fatalities in 1943). State employees traveled 56 percent less miles in 1943 than in 1941, partly because the Montana Highway Patrol, which had 100 officers just before the war, lost more than 25 percent of its personnel to the military. Because steel was in such short supply, Montana license plates issued in 1944 were made of green and white fiberboard. The new license plates were larger and thinner than their metal counterparts, prompting many complaints from indignant motorists who were forced to buy new license plate brackets. The despised fiberboard plates are now collector's items.

Despite the massive influx of workers, the demand for military material had outstripped the manufacturing capacity of the West Coast factories, leading the Pacific Car and Foundry Company to relocate their assembly line for M-26 tank recovery vehicles to Billings, in order to free up their Renton, Washington plant for the production of aircraft parts. Known as "dragon wagons," the tank recovery vehicles were similar to tractor-trailer units but featured an armored cab which could pull a trailer containing a Sherman tank at 30 miles an hour.

The company leased the Midland Empire fairgrounds, where cranes and hoists were installed in the main auditorium building. The tank recovery vehicles were assembled on two assembly lines. Each vehicle had a 400 horsepower engine and two transmissions, one for pulling the 30-ton tanks aboard, and one for highway driving. The tanks sat on a standard 40-foot-long heavy-equipment trailer, which was manufactured by the Pointer-Willamette Company at the old Williams Motor Company building in Billings. The M-26s carried a variety of tools and spare parts, enabling the crews to make on-the-spot repairs. In the summer of 1944, after the vehicles were re-designed, the Army ordered a 25 percent increase in production at the Billings plants, and extended the contract for one more year. The Pacific Car and Foundry Company was awarded an "E" award for high production.

Proud workers installed a metal plaque in the first vehicle which read, "This retriever is the first off the new assembly line at Billings, Mont. U.S.A. May its stout heart and brawn be a reminder that these same qualities along with unyielding devotion to the cause of our country prevail among the workers and the community, who are helping to speed along many more for delivery on time. Dec. 22, 1943." In the spring of 1945 this plaque was found in the belongings of a soldier killed in Europe. The fate of the first tank retriever is unknown.

Other Montana companies involved in defense contracting included the A.N. Metal Products Company of Billings, which turned out 15 pontoons for the Navy every day, and the Sullivan Valve and Engineering Company of Butte, which in 1943 won a contract for work on a top-secret government project underway at Hanford, Washington.

After two years of fighting, 117 Montana men had been killed in World War II, (83 soldiers and 34 sailors and Marines). An additional 45 soldiers were missing in action and 69 had been wounded (71 Montana sailors and Marines were missing in action and 16 had been wounded). Dozens more were known to be prisoners of war in territory held by Germany and Japan, and the casualty lists printed in every newspaper grew longer each week.

According to the number of rationing books issued in the state, 88,237 people had left Montana in just two-and-a-half years. Missoula County alone had lost 13 percent of its population since the 1940 census. Although most of the loss represented people who had enlisted in the military, more than 20,000 Montanans were employed in the airplane factories and shipyards on the West Coast. Although the labor shortage in the state eased somewhat, the unemployment rate remained at nearly zero. On the other hand, the rate of both marriages and divorces soared during the war.

With the exception of the construction, mining, and travel industries, Montana businesses enjoyed a record year in 1943. Businessmen and politicians

Entrance to the Midland Empire Fairgrounds in Billings. During the war the fairgrounds was converted into an assembly line for the production of M-26 tank recovery vehicles. MHS 941-102

Kwajalein

American forces landed on Kwajalein Atoll on January 31, 1944, after the most intense naval and aerial bombardment of the Pacific war. Five days later, after wiping out the 8,500- man Japanese garrison, American forces were in complete possession of the atoll.

· Lt. Mark P. Mowry of Havre was posthumously awarded the Distinguished Flying Cross for strafing Japanese ships, artillery positions, and planes over Kwajalein.

· Capt. Bruce C. Babbitt of Missoula was awarded the Silver Star at Kwajalein. He led a counter-attack that stopped a threatened Japanese breakthrough on February 3, 1944.

· Capt. Robert J. Kretzer of Missoula was awarded the Silver Star. Under heavy fire he managed to keep his company intact while moving them to the start line for a successful attack on February 3, 1944.

· PFC Harold R. Rediske of Ryegate, (Fourth Marine Division) was awarded the Silver Star for helping rescue wounded while under fire at Kwajalein. Rediske moved to Livingston after the war.

· Gunners Mate 1st Class Henry L. Green (USN) of Havre was in the first wave on Kwajalein and helped blow up pillboxes. He had previously served in Burma, and was in Shanghai in 1937 when the Japanese bombed that city.

February 1944

· February 1. First Special Service Force arrives at Anzio.

· February 4. U.S. forces capture Kwajalein Atoll.

· February 7. A broken track causes a Great Northern train derailment 15 miles east of Great Falls. Great Falls air base hospital treats 22 soldiers and a porter.

· February 14. A dance in East Helena turns into a brawl between juveniles, which then continues at the police station. A 50-year-old barn at the State Hospital at Warm Springs burns to the ground, killing four horses.

· February 15. Abbey at Monte Cassino is destroyed by American bombers. Temperatures drop below zero as a blizzard roars across the state.

· February 17. U.S. Navy planes and ships begin a two day raid on Japanese base at Truk.

· February 19. U.S. forces land on Eniwetok.

· February 22. The ACM clubhouse and bowling alley on Smelter Hill in Great Falls is destroyed by fire, causing $50,000 damage.

· February 23. Japanese resistance on Eniwetok ends. U.S. Navy aircraft attack Japanese positions on Saipan and Tinian.

· February 28. U.S. Third Division beats off German attack at Anzio.

· February 29. U.S. Fifth Cavalry lands on Admiralty Islands.

began planning for the postwar economy. Governor Ford announced that his postwar plans emphasized highway construction ($40,000,000), reclamation projects ($100,000,000), rural electrification ($3,400,000) and building projects ($8,000,000). Governor Ford, along with O.S. Warden, were the keynote speakers at a meeting of Montana Inc. in June 1944. Two hundred business and community leaders met at the Placer Hotel in Helena to discuss the postwar economy. Senator Murray, chairman of the Senate Small Business Committee, also turned his attention towards the problems of converting industry back to a peacetime economy. Senator Murray also expressed concern about postwar relations between the United States and the Soviet Union.

In the U.S. House, Rep. James O'Connor wanted to limit the amount spent on rebuilding Axis countries after the war. O'Connor was booed by House Republicans after he chastised them for voting against Roosevelt's plan to raise taxes by $10 billion. Rep. Mike Mansfield wrote a bill to finance the college education of returning veterans. In February 1944, Wendell Wilkie, President Roosevelt's opponent in the 1940 election, made campaign stops in Billings and Great Falls. Wilkie was again seeking the GOP Presidential nomination, and in Great Falls he spoke in front of 2,000 people at the Civic Center. Along with colonels Johanson and Meredith of the air base, he was adopted into the Blackfeet tribe. Sen. Everett Dirkson, another GOP candidate for president, also toured the state and spoke in Helena and Billings (neither Wilkie or Dirkson won their party's nomination in 1944). State supreme court justice Leif Erickson announced his plans to run for governor, while Montana's attorney general, John W. Bonner, a lieutenant colonel serving with the U.S. Army in London, announced he would not run for re-election. In 1948 Bonner was elected governor of Montana.

In statewide business news, tax delinquency hit an all-time low, while retail activity in 1943 jumped 44 percent. W.E. Rice purchased the Rainbow Hotel in Great Falls for an estimated $220,000, and turned over management to L.W. Carter, who already managed the Northern and Grand Hotels in Billings. In Butte a new $600,000 addition to St. James Hospital in Butte was completed, and one of the longest telephone lines in the world (3,000 miles) was completed early in 1944, connecting remote Alaska with Helena and the rest of the world (by 1944 there were

84,000 telephones in the state). On the downside, some Montana businesses ran afoul of the new government regulations, particularly the price controls set by the Office of Price Administration. Two landlords in Great Falls were indicted for rent regulations, while three laundries in that city threatened to close unless OPA raised their price ceilings (the laundries backed down when OPA held firm).

The production of gold, silver, lead, and zinc dropped during the war years, but the production of copper, oil, coal, and gas went up. Montana mines pumped $53,600,000 into the state's economy in 1943, an 11 percent decrease from the year before, primarily due to the restrictions on gold mining. Although gold was being found in conjunction with other mining activities, most operations that strictly produced gold had been shut down. One exception was the Perry-Schroeder gold dredge near Helena, which was allowed to continue operating because it produced significant numbers of industrial sapphires. Even though large-scale gold mining was prohibited, a small gold rush developed near Helmville when dozens of prospectors staked claims.

The Mineral Reserves Board closed the Block P mine at Hughesville (in the Little Belt Mountains), and ordered ACM to close the Benbow and Mouat mines at Columbus in order to shift miners to copper mines and smelters at Butte and Anaconda.

Although copper was the most vital mineral extracted from the honeycombed hills of Butte, the Anaconda Copper Mining Company operations at Great Falls and Anaconda also produced 40,000,000 pounds of zinc per month, and the Silver Butte Mining Company announced plans to build a 50-ton zinc mill at Libby. Manganese, vital in the manufacture of dry-cell batteries used by the military, was also highly sought after. The Philipsburg area and the Emma Mine in Butte produced a high proportion of the U.S. supply of manganese, and a 400-ton mill was opened in Butte to process the metal. Not all mines benefitted from the wartime economy however, and major stockholders of the Philipsburg Mining Corporation met in St. Louis and decided to liquidate the company.

Even though 600 ex-soldiers continued to work in the Butte mines, the labor shortage remained, and miners statewide were ordered to work 48 hours per week. On the other hand, the metal shortage had eased enough that after two years of nonstop activity, Butte mines began closing on Sunday for the first time since Pearl Harbor. During the fall of 1943, a labor dispute threatened to close the Butte mines, and ACM and four labor unions took their differences to the national war labor board. Demanding a $2.00 per day raise and two weeks paid vacation instead of one, the miners voted to hold a strike vote on December 21 if their demands weren't met. Senator Wheeler intervened, and requested a $1.00 per day pay hike for the miners, and the strike was called off. Miners were also upset when the price of a pasty, one of the staples of life in the Mining City, went up to 40 cents apiece because of government price regulations.

A flurry of new mineral exploration promised to increase Montana's contribution to the war effort. The Bureau of Mines planned a talc mine near Ennis, while copper ore was discovered near Dixon. Iron deposits found near Stanford, Choteau, and White Sulphur Springs were tested using magnetometers. The Choteau deposits looked particularly promising, and in 1945 ore from Choteau was smelted at a Helena firm and an iron ingot was poured. The end of the war however, eliminated the need for additional supplies of iron, and the deposits were never developed.

A phosphate plant was built near Hall, in the Drummond area, and phosphate was also mined at nearby Garrison. Vermiculite was produced at the Universal Zenolite Insulation Company at Libby and a new vermiculite mine was contemplated in the Bearpaw Mountains. A bentonite mill opened at Aberdeen, while the Jardine Mining Company near Yellowstone Park produced tungsten. The corundum deposits in Gallatin County were called the world's best and were developed beginning in 1944. Radio quality quartz crystals were discovered near Hot Springs, while deposits of optical calcite, used in the production of scientific instruments and military gunsights, were explored near Big Timber and Clyde Park. Development of the Clyde Park deposit brought in a flood of workers, and government trailers were transferred from Great Falls to the Shields River area in order to house them all.

The ongoing scrap drives proved to be another important source of metal. PFC Floyd A. Durfey of Richey, who won a Silver Star at Guadalcanal and was discharged because of his wounds, was made the honorary chairman of the state scrap metal drive. More than 400 rail cars containing 39,500 tons of scrap metal were shipped out of state during the last six months of 1943. During the first six months of 1944, the Federal government called on Montana to

collect 16,800 tons of scrap, but the quota was exceeded by 313 percent when Montanan's brought in 52,686 tons of scrap. With the vast amount of metal being turned in, the recycling of toothpaste and shaving cream tubes was dropped as the metal shortage grew less acute.

The Treasure State typically led the nation in the collection of scrap metal, as well as the collection of wastepaper and household fats. Rag collection began in May 1944, and by the end of the year more than 200 tons had been collected in the state. Montana housewives turned in 76,691 pounds of fat in January. This was double the quota and tops in the nation. Collection of household fat was enhanced by the awarding of two ration points for every pound of fat turned in. Throughout the spring of 1944, Montana and Idaho housewives led the nation in fat collection, often collecting more than double the quota, and almost 350 tons of household fats were collected in the state in 1944.

That same year, paper was added to list of items in short supply, and mills had a hard time turning enough out paper shopping bags and cardboard boxes. The state was asked to collect 47,500 tons of waste paper in 1944, and paper drives were mounted in many cities. Every family was asked to donate 10 pounds of paper, and organizations like the Jaycees and the Veterans of Foreign Wars managed to collect more than 100 tons of paper during several drives. Madison County shipped 72 tons of waste paper in one month, the highest per capita total in the nation. During another month, Meagher County collected 32 pounds of wastepaper for every resident of the county, the highest average in the country, and the state as a whole was usually ranked very high in paper collection. More than 9,000 tons of paper were donated in 1944, or 36.8 pounds for every man, woman, and child in the state.

Despite the curfew, Great Falls officials continued to have problems with juvenile delinquency and police officers in the Electric City began issuing arrest warrants for curfew violators. Four Great Falls boys, aged 14 to 17, managed to avoid the curfew restrictions by leaving town. They were eventually arrested by police in Colorado Springs after a three-state crime spree involving 13 stolen cars and 22 burglaries.

In other criminal news, a brazen army trainee at Montana State College became the most unpopular man in Bozeman after he was arrested for stealing $1,200 from the wallets of 200 of his fellow soldiers while they slept. In late January 1944, the half-naked body of Mrs. Luzeen Turk was found murdered in Butte. Three days later her husband, Joseph Turk was arrested and charged with manslaughter in the death of his wife. A month later, two Missoula men, Folger Leroy White and Lewis W. Hemmert, were arrested by the FBI for an $8,070 bank robbery in Spokane. One man was believed responsible for two robberies of the same bank and the other was his accomplice.

Missoula residents closely followed the murder trial of Sylvester "Ole" Ward, who went on trial for the 1940 shooting of University of Montana student Robert Rooney. Ward was found not guilty by reason of insanity and was sent back to the State Hospital at Warm Springs, where he had spent the past three years.

The weather in early 1944 was so balmy that the Plentywood golf course opened to serve January duffers. The mayor of Great Falls went so far as to invite the Brooklyn Dodgers for spring training in his city. Even though the temperature in northern Montana was warmer than in the southern United States, the Dodgers declined. The warm weather and dry conditions had a down side though, and high winds spread more than 300 prairie fires across northern Montana in early 1944.

The winter months also brought a serious flu epidemic, which swept the state in January, making thousands seriously ill and killing at least 27. A number of communicable diseases which have been nearly eradicated today were common during the war years. Fifteen polio cases were reported statewide during 1943, Dawson County suffered an outbreak of whooping cough, and a scarlet fever outbreak closed schools in Havre and Great Falls. The state suffered nine more deaths from tuberculosis in 1943 than in 1942, but by 1944 the TB death rate had sunk to its lowest level since record-keeping began.

The 1944 high school basketball season was dominated by the Great Falls Bisons, who played 16 conference games and lost only one, a double-over-time thriller against Livingston. The Bisons clinched the Big 16 regular season by defeating Anaconda 33-23, then defeated Butte Central 44-42 for the Class A championship. The Wolf Point Indians won the Class B title after defeating Dillon, but fell to the Bisons in the state championship game, 69-52.

Gasoline rationing and the enlistment of many players and coaches decimated both high school and college athletics during World War II, but an in-creased military presence brought a number of new teams to the state. Boasting names like the "Flyers," the "Bombers," and the "Medics," the air force base at Great Falls sponsored at least eight basketball teams, including two women's teams, the Gore Field WACs and the "Bomba Dears." Other teams at Great Falls were fielded by the enlisted men, the officers, the 18th Service Squadron, the 25th Squadron and flight control. The Air Force teams scheduled games with the state's colleges and high schools (including the Missoula High Spartans) as well as with the Army "Truckers" stationed at Fort Harrison and the Navy V-12 trainees at Carroll College in Helena and the School of Mines in Butte.

The military aviation students at the University of Montana and Montana State College were not allowed to participate in sports, and this severely limited the basketball prospects for both the Bobcats and the Grizzlies. Because so many men had enlisted during the past year, the Montana Grizzlies had no players or coaches returning from the previous season and they won only two of their 12 games, perhaps their worst season ever.

In their sole game of the season, Brick Breeden's Bobcats defeated the Butte Boosters. The Carroll College Saints won two games over the Great Falls Bombers.

As a part of the fourth war bond campaign, Capt. John S. Young, co-pilot of the lead plane on the Ploesti raid, spoke at a war bond rally held at the Great Falls Civic center in early January. The Great Falls air base band went on tour to promote war bond sales, and 1,000 people attended the concert held in Malta. As in previous campaigns, Montana led the nation in war bond sales. The state's quota in the 4th war bond drive was $31,000,000, but the final tally of $41,762,978 topped the quota by 135 percent.

In January 1944, the Soviet army broke the 900-day siege of Leningrad and a massive Allied air campaign began against military, industrial and civilian targets in Germany. During late February 1944, massive air raids were launched against the German aircraft industry.

Katrin Gibney lived in Berlin at the time and worked as a censor of movies for the Nazi Minister of Propaganda. She recorded the air raids in her diary, which she kept carefully hidden from the Gestapo. Her diary chronicled the hardships of living in a nation that was being pounded from the air day and night. One entry read "Once more sirens are yelling through my sleep! Wake up with a start. Full

Italy

- Sgt. Harold W. Piper of Malta, paratrooper, was posthumously awarded the Silver Star for saving the life of his platoon leader under fire in Italy on January 1, 1944.
- 1st Sgt. John R. Lyman of the 504th Parachute Regiment (82nd Airborne), was awarded the Bronze Star for his actions on December 16, 1943 at Hill 730, San Pietro, Italy. He scouted out a battalion command post, laid telephone line from his company to the command post, then carried water back to his wounded men while under fire.
- Lt. William Galt of Great Falls was awarded the Silver Star and Purple Heart on his 24th birthday after leading his men through a minefield in Italy in December. A former student at Montana State College, he served with the 168th Infantry Regiment of the 34th "Red Bulls" Division.
- Capt. Burleigh T. Packwood of Whitefish was awarded the Silver Star for his actions on January 26, 1944 when he and his men drove Germans out of four positions while under heavy machine gun and artillery fire.
- 1st Lt. William A. Rogers of Edgar was posthumously awarded the Silver Star for his actions with a four-man reconnaissance patrol under fire on January 28, 1944. He led his battalion in an attack through the area he had scouted, but was killed the next day.
- Lt. Donald Bonawitz of Hardin destroyed two German Mark IV tanks with his light tank at Campolean, then led a successful tank attack against German infantry.

Air Offensive Against Germany

- Gay Rieder of Kalispell was awarded the Distinguished Service Cross, signed by General Doolittle, for a bombing mission over Germany in February 1944.
- 1st Lt. Frederick C. Wagner of Kalispell was awarded the Silver Star at a B-24 base in Italy for a February 23, 1944 bombing raid. He managed to hit his target despite having two gun turrets shot out and nine passes by German pursuit planes.
- Col. Hubert Zemke of Missoula was awarded the Distinguished Service Cross for missions on February 11 and March 6, 1944. He already held the Silver Star, Distinguished Flying Cross with three clusters, the air medal with three clusters, and the British DFC. By January Zemke was listed as among America's top 20 aces with 14 enemy planes to his credit. His fighter group had downed more than 100 victims. Zemke and two of his subordinates, Francis Gabreski and David Schilling, were known to the Luftwaffe as the "terrible three."
- A B-17 named "Northern Queen," bought with war bonds from six northern states, dropped bombs on Wilhelmshaven, Germany, in early February 1944. The bombs had the names of 10 Montana cities written on them.

Glasgow

Glasgow, the seat of Valley County, had a population of 3,798 in 1940, after a boom in which the population nearly doubled between 1933 and 1937 during the construction of Fort Peck Dam. President Roosevelt visited Glasgow during a 1934 inspection of Fort Peck Dam. The city's mayor during the war years was E.J. Kjelstrup. He was re-elected in 1945. Glasgow, on the Great Northern Railroad line, was a center of agriculture, construction, trade and services. Early in 1945 the Glasgow flour mill operated 24 hours a day in order to fill a large military contract. During the summer of 1945 Glasgow celebrated the 140th anniversary of the Lewis & Clark expedition.

Company G of the 163rd Infantry Regiment was made up primarily of Glasgow men. Capt. J. L. Hoffman, formerly a grocer, served with the 163rd in the southwest Pacific. He received a Silver Star for his actions at Sanananda, and mailed home a Japanese sword that had been nicked by bullets. Lt. Col. Carl E. Hammerness, the former commander of the Glasgow National Guard, was a battalion commander with the 41st Division. At least 30 Valley County men were killed in the war.

The Glasgow Air Force Base was constructed as a satellite base of the Great Falls facility for the training of bomber crews. A room key from a Glasgow hotel was carried as a good luck charm by a B-17 gunner through 25 missions, then returned to the hotel. The Glasgow Air Base was turned over to Valley County after the Air Force pulled out, and was temporarily converted to house German prisoners of war sent to work in the sugar beet fields. After renting it to the Boeing aircraft company for 10 years as a test facility, the base was sold to Boeing in 1991 for $3,000,000. Fifty years after the B-17 crews left Glasgow, the base was still being used to test Boeing's new 777 airliners.

alarm?...

Down to the cellar I fly: three flights of stairs—out into the courtyard—next door back in again—another half flight down and into the neighbor's cellar. An iron door slams shut behind me, and I am in a cobweb underworld of sorts. Also a world of anxious listeners-the accumulated apprehension of the past months hovering over us all." After the war she married an American and moved to Ovando, where she lived for many years before moving to Missoula.

Early in 1944, the attention of the world's news media was firmly riveted on Italy, where in mid-February American bombers ignited a controversy when they destroyed the historic Italian abbey at Monte Cassino. An attempt to break the stalemate in the Italian mountains led to the landing of British and American troops at Anzio, south of Rome, but the plan backfired, leaving thousands of soldiers trapped in a small beachhead while crack German units tried to push them back into the sea.

Shortly after the initial landing south of Rome, the First Special Service Force received orders to land at Anzio. They hit the beaches of Anzio on February 1, a week after the initial landings. They were assigned to hold 13 kilometers along the extreme right flank of the beachhead, despite the fact that only one of the Force's regiments, (the Third) was at full strength. Stationed along the Mussolini Canal to the sea, the 68 officers and 1165 enlisted men of the First Special Service Force held nearly one quarter of the perimeter at Anzio. They dug into the banks of the canal itself and began fighting their own private war against the Germans. In the flat plains of Anzio, each house became a potential sniper nest or forward artillery post. With darkened faces, the Forcemen spent their nights in aggressive patrolling behind enemy lines, and the Germans soon learned to fear the "Black Devils of Anzio."

Bill Mauldin, a cartoonist who depicted the life of front-line soldiers, reported that "My favorite outfit at Anzio was called the 1st Special Force....This swashbuckling unit ended up at Anzio because after the Norway operation was called off nobody could figure out what to do with them....They occupied the extreme southern rim of the Anzio perimeter. It was the only quiet place on the entire beachhead. They had the German's terrorized. Every night or so they would form up monster "patrols." Upwards of 300 men would set forth toward enemy lines to see what fun they could have." The commandos had leaflets printed up with their insignia on it, then made a habit of leaving their calling cards on the bodies of dead German sentries. Soon after the Force arrived on the scene, the Germans began pulling further back in their sector. The German's were bewildered by the Black Devils, and thought there must be at least a division of them.

The Forcemen took control of several farmhouses and small villages along the front and began collecting livestock, including milk cows, chickens, and pigs. The deserted village of Borgo Sabotino was taken over by a company of the First Special Service Force, who dubbed it "Gusville" after Lt. Gus Heilman. According to Mauldin, who used the Forcemen as inspiration for several of his popular Willie and Joe cartoons, "the 1st Special Force, as a result, was able to live comparatively well....Using the survival techniques they had been taught they did some fishing with hand grenades and found buried wine casks by locating the steel hoops with mine detectors. Unfortunately, I wasn't able to use all of the material I got while hanging around that outfit. It was so wild it defied caricature."

Anzio

· Lt. Robert Bangert of Great Falls led 27 engineers ashore at Anzio in a mission to destroy bridges before the Germans could counterattack over them.
· Lt. John Walker of Helena lost a leg at Anzio while serving with the First Special Service Force.
· Lt. Taylor Radcliffe of Helena, a member of the First Special Service Force, was captured by the Germans at Anzio in March. He was beaten in the throat with a rubber hose but he knocked out a guard and managed to escape from his captors when an artillery barrage distracted them. He freed two other prisoners and they hid throughout the following day. They were discovered the following night and Radcliffe was shot in the foot. He managed to crawl to a village where a patrol of Forcemen found him. Radcliffe recovered from his wounds in time to lead the Allied advance into Rome.

11

☞ Taking The War To The Enemy ☜

On March 6, 1944, "Black Monday" to the bomber crews, 660 American bombers set off for the first heavy bomber raid on Berlin. One of the heavy bombers contained a crew of Montana men who had named their B-24 "Hellgate," although on this day they were flying a different aircraft. (The men believed that the "Hellgate" survived the war.) Three of the officers on board, 2nd Lt. Guy Rogers (pilot), 2nd Lt. John S. Hightower (navigator), and Warrant Officer Joseph S. Root Jr. (bombardier) were from Missoula, while 2nd Lt. Oliver Proteau (copilot) was from Great Falls. Rogers and Root both attended Willard School, and all three attended Missoula County High School, where they played football and basketball. Root and Rogers also attended the University of Montana.

The crew trained in Tonopah, Nevada, before flying to England via Palm Beach, South America, Africa, and on to Norwich, where they were stationed with the 754th Squadron, 458th Bomb Group, 8th Air Force. On March 6, the fliers dropped their load of bombs on the Berlin rail yards and were flying at 21,000 feet when an anti-aircraft shell exploded in the cockpit and started a fire, burning Rogers in the face. Rogers later described the explosion. "[It] blew out the oxygen set-up, the internal communications set-up, and set me on fire immediately." As the copilot took over the controls, Rogers ran for the fire extinguisher in the rear. The plane was again hit by anti-aircraft fire and exploded, shattering Rogers' leg, and knocking him unconscious. The next thing he knew, he was falling to Earth in a flaming piece of wreckage. "My clothes were all burned off and I couldn't raise my head and I finally realized that the spot of red on my underwear was the ripcord to my parachute."

He pulled the ripcord on his seat parachute, which jerked him free of the spinning wreckage, but he was very near the ground when the parachute opened. He hit hard and his parachute dragged him across a field. A furious German farmer on a horse galloped across the field and urged his horse to trample the enemy airman, but Rogers managed to evade the horse's hooves and was finally rescued by two German soldiers, who carried him away on a

stretcher. He was taken to the Berlin jail, which was full of American airmen from the 69 bombers that had been shot down on the raid. In the jail Rogers was reunited with Proteau, who he later learned was the only other survivor of the plane. After 12 hours in the jail, he was taken to a hospital, where he was given minimal treatment for his fractured leg. Gangrene set in and after three-and-a-half months, his leg was amputated at the hip. He spent another three-and-one-half months in a Berlin hospital, while British and American bombers pounded the city night and day.

Rogers was selected for repatriation in October 1944, and on January 15, 1945 he was transferred to Switzerland along with 1,200 other wounded POWs. He returned home on the Red Cross ship *SS Gripsholm*. After the war, he was fitted with an artificial leg, and he eventually learned to walk without crutches. He worked at a service station in Missoula, served a term in the state legislature, and managed car dealerships in Deer Lodge and Philipsburg. He then returned to Missoula and served as postmaster for 18 years before retiring in 1972. Shortly after the war Francis Proteau was killed in a crop-dusting accident near Great Falls.

After six months in Australia, the Montanan's of the 163rd Infantry Regiment returned to Finschhafen, New Guinea in February 1944. In April they boarded transports which carried them to the Admiralty Islands, far to the north of New Guinea, as a diversion for the planned landings at Aitape and Hollandia. Operating independently under the command of newly promoted Brig. Gen. Jens Doe, the 163rd landed at Aitape on the northern coast of New Guinea on April 22, 1944. The Japanese were taken by surprise and the initial landing was made against light resistance. Completely surprised, the 1,000-man Japanese garrison fled from the combined firepower of the destroyers and carriers just offshore. Rice was found still cooking in Aitape village as the troopers from Montana moved in. The 163rd easily seized the airstrip and had it back in operation within three days.

The fiercest fighting of the Aitape operation came on April 27, 1944 when the 38 men of the

Wakde

- Maj. Leonard Wing of Bozeman commanded the Wakde operation.
- 1st Lt. Kenneth Leibach of Plentywood, E Co. of the 163rd, was killed in action May 18, 1944 on Wakde.
- Staff Sgt. Walter Buckles of Poplar (part-Sioux) killed three Japanese at Toem in a patrol led by Capt. Edward Reams of Billings.
- John M. Adams of Dodson was killed in action after he and another man killed 17 Japanese entrenched in a bunker.
- Jimmie Eder of Wolf Point (Sioux) mowed down 15 Japanese setting up a machine gun and mortar.
- PFC Robert D. Teela of Havre was awarded the Silver Star by General Doe. Teela, armed only with a knife, swam after three Japanese trying to flee the island in a canoe. They lobbed grenades at him but he ducked underwater, then killed one man with a knife after the Japanese ran out of grenades. The other two men in the boat were captured by a patrol boat.

Kalispell

Throughout the war D.S. Cameron served as mayor of Kalispell, a city of 6,094. The seat of Flathead County was a center of tourism and trade, and some of the important industries included dude ranching, fishing and boating, and lumber production. The city was on the Great Northern Railroad line and served as headquarters for the Flathead National Forest. Logging, Christmas tree production, and the state's fledgling cherry industry employed many of the residents of Kalispell. Flathead Lake and Glacier Park drew many tourists to the area, but tourism dropped significantly due to the war. Many of those who did come stayed at the Kalispell Hotel. Before the war a WPA project landscaped 40 acres of parks in Kalispell. KGEZ radio station (1340 on the radio dial) had operated in Kalispell since 1927. E Company of the 163rd Infantry Regiment was originally comprised of men from Kalispell, and at least 81 men from Flathead County lost their lives during the war.

March 1944

- March 1. Huge snowfall blocks many rural roads. Red Cross fund-raising drive begins.
- March 3. One man is killed and two injured in an explosion in the Northern Pacific Railroad tunnel under construction east of Bozeman.
- March 4. Doolittle Raider Dave Thatcher is featured on a radio program on the Blue Radio network. The show also features messages by President Roosevelt and Eisenhower.
- March 6. Two civilians flying an Aeronca trainer are injured in a crash at Apgar after striking a power line. Minus 16 degrees recorded in Glasgow.
- March 13. J. Russell Sweet, age 39, a former UM football star from Miles City, dies of a heart attack in California. In the 1924 East West Shrine game he caught a touchdown pass thrown by fellow UM player "Wild" Bill Kelly, then kicked the winning point. The following year he ranked second in the nation in points scored. He was also a star track performer and was unofficially credited with tieing the world 100 yard dash record. Before his death he had been a coach at a San Francisco junior college. He has since been inducted into both the University's Track Hall of Fame and the Football Hall of Fame.
- March 14. Five-year-old Billings boy is run over by a train and loses leg.
- March 15. Massive bombardment at Cassino precedes Allied attack.
- March 19. German troops move into Hungary to shore up their Eastern front. A 7th Ferrying Group pilot is killed in the crash of his light bomber at Stockett.
- March 22. Japanese troops cross into India from Burma.
- March 24. British General Orde Wingate, leader of the "Chindit" commandos, killed in a plane crash in Burma. Gasoline explosion in a Baker garage destroys eight cars and causes $40,000 damage.
- March 30. Montana Hotel in Helena is damaged by fire. All 19 guests are evacuated safely.
- March 31. Palau Island is attacked by 11 U.S. aircraft carriers. Old grandstand at Anaconda is destroyed by fire.

Second platoon of Company L, originally a National Guard company from Billings, blocked the Japanese escape at Kamti and repulsed a bayonet charge by 200 Japanese coming in from three sides. The soldiers killed 42 of the Japanese while suffering only two dead and one wounded. They remained in position for 36 hours with the aid of air-dropped supplies, pulled back for reinforcements, then reoccupied the roadblock. The men from Company L won a unit citation for extraordinary heroism.

The Aitape landing, in which 525 Japanese were killed, had been carried out at a loss to the 163rd of 14 killed and 23 wounded. Eighty-six Allied prisoners were liberated at Aitape. Hundreds of Japanese remained in the area, but the 163rd was needed elsewhere, and they were relieved by the 32nd Division on May 3. After the 163rd pulled out, the Japanese tried to retake the airstrip at Aitape, and a vicious two-month-long battle occurred.

Two weeks after leaving Aitape, the soldiers of the 163rd stormed Wakde Island, 450 miles west of Aitape. Although Wakde was only two miles long and a mile wide, it contained 100 Japanese pillboxes and bunkers, as well as 12 fortified caves which were invisible from the air. The 163rd first captured the village of Toem, on the mainland two miles from Wakde, where little resistance was met. On the following day Wakde was bombarded by ships, planes, and artillery. The reinforced First Battalion (Companies A, B, C, and F) of the 163rd landed by barge on May 18. They met a withering fire on the beach, but the former National Guardsmen pressed inland, aided by two tanks. Hampered by intense heat and a tangle of blasted coconut trees, it took the 163rd two days of fierce fighting to clear the island. More than 800 Japanese Marine Tigers were killed, and only one, a Hawaiian-born Japanese who spoke English, was captured. Twenty Americans were killed and 36 were wounded before the island was turned over to the U.S. Air Force.

Once Wakde was taken, the rest of the 163rd began aggressive patrolling in the jungle near Toem, where a strong Japanese presence was suspected. On the night of May 27, 1944, a surprise attack by 200 Japanese caught the men of the 163rd in their camp. Nine Americans were killed and eight others wounded before the Japanese were repulsed. The 163rd suffered a total of 40 dead and 107 wounded during the Toem and Wakde campaigns. Two thousand ill-equipped Japanese remained in this area until the end of the war.

Although thick smoke from fires in Canada caused closure of Gore Field for a day or so, 10 C-47 cargo planes loaded with U.S. Treasury Department engraving plates, ink, paper, and other materials were flown from Great Falls to the U.S.S.R. in May 1944. The purpose of these flights was to allow the Soviets to print the same German occupation money that was printed by the U.S. This is believed to be the only occasion in history when the Treasury Department turned printing plates over to anyone. The Soviets apparently printed $250,000,000 in occupation money, which they used to pay the Red Army for more than a year after the war. All of this money eventually came out of the pockets of the U.S. taxpayers.

Bert Fraser, commander of the Fort Missoula Detention Center, announced that the camp would be formally closed and the last of the prisoners transferred by May 1, 1944. This did not affect the hundreds of Italians who were on work release, but most of the 310 Italians still interned left town by train on April 3, 1944, although a few remained to help close the camp. One hundred recently arrived German prisoners were sent to work for the Forest Service, while most of the remaining Japanese prisoners were sent to camps in the South. Two hundred and ninety-three Japanese-Americans were relocated to jobs in Montana cities.

Community leaders worried that the loss of jobs from the detention camp would hurt the local economy, but Rep. Mike Mansfield managed to pull some strings and soon notified the local Chamber of Commerce that Fort Missoula would be turned over to the Army to be used as a detention camp for medium-security prisoners.

After a year of record precipitation, parts of northwest Montana suffered through the driest winter in 45 years. This changed when a March snowstorm blanketed the Hi-line. A couple from Fort Benton died of exposure after their car stalled only 200 yards from their house, and Governor Ford himself had to be dug out by state workers after his car got stuck in a snowdrift near the capitol.

The snow caused even more problems once it melted, and ice jams on the Yellowstone sent that river over its banks. By March 20, 300 Miles City residents were homeless after three feet of water inundated 150 homes and one square mile of that city's business district, causing at least $100,000 damage. A B-17 bomber based at Peterson Field in Colorado Springs dropped 16 bombs which relieved

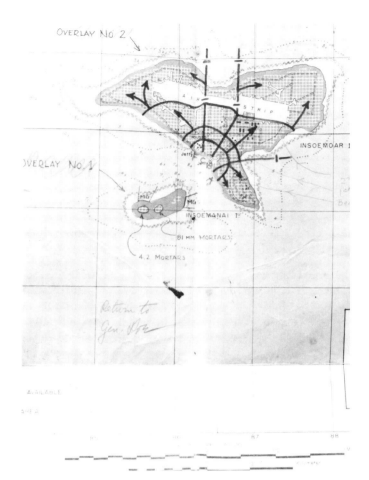

General Eichelberger with officers of the 163rd Infantry Regiment. THE 163RD INFANTRY HISTORICAL COMMITTEE

Topographic map of Wakde, which was comprised of the islands of Insoemoar and Insoemanai. U.S. Army troops invariably pronounced Wakde as **WAD**ke. The 163rd Infantry Regiment landed on Wakde on May 18, 1944. THE 163RD INFANTRY HISTORICAL COMMITTEE

A B-17 bomber named the *Spirit of Montana*. Bombers were also named after cities, counties and individuals from Montana. MHS 940-211

the pressure from the Yellowstone ice jam. Eight thousand acres were also under water in the Glendive area, and another ice jam, this one on the Tongue, sent that river to 12 feet above flood stage, again threatening Miles City.

The water subsided for a few months, but by late spring was on the rise again. High water struck the Glendive area particularly hard, and flash floods in June claimed the life of a six-year-old boy and tore two infants from their helpless parent's arms. The violent rainstorm uprooted trees, washed out the highway, and tore the roofs off of the Glendive post office and several houses. Lewistown recorded eight inches of rain in June, and at Roundup a cloudburst damaged a railroad bridge, cut the highway, and closed a coal mine.

On the other side of the state, the tiny community of Lima was isolated when the Union Pacific tracks and the only highway washed out. Severe flooding was also experienced in the Dillon area.

Floods on the Missouri in 1943 and 1944, as well as the need for cheap hydroelectric power, spurred government plans for flood control. U.S. Representative Whittington of Mississippi introduced a post-war flood control bill which provided $334,000 for projects on the Milk River and $200,000,000 for projects in the Missouri basin. In March 1944, Governor Ford met with seven other governors in Omaha to discuss a unified Missouri River plan, but they decided further study was needed. The Montana Taxpayers Association needed no further study to know that they "strongly objected" to the proposed Missouri River plan. This did not dissuade Senator Murray however, who in August introduced his Missouri Valley Authority (MVA) bill, claiming that, "Development of this region would add materially to the national strength and prosperity." Murray's MVA bill, which would affect some 350,000 square miles in the Missouri basin, had the backing of the Roosevelt administration. Governor Ford, on the other hand, made three trips to Washington, D.C. to testify against the MVA plan. The MVA remained a hot political issue for several years.

Other water developments were also under consideration. Governor Ford appointed a 10-man commission to study the proposed Yellowstone River compact, and at the urging of Senator Murray, the Senate approved funds for irrigation projects in the Bitterroot Valley. The Crow tribe went on record opposing a national river-and-harbor bill because it did not safeguard their upstream irrigation rights.

The dam project proposed for the Hungry Horse area of northwestern Montana kept gaining momentum, despite Acting Interior Secretary Abe Fortas threat that his department would support the Hungry Horse plan only if it was postponed until after the war. In June, President Roosevelt signed the Hungry Horse bill, and a month later Governor Ford attended a conference on the proposed Hungry Horse project in Kalispell.

Despite the 2,000,000 acres of irrigated farmland in the state, water remained a big concern for most Montana farmers. Farmers became alarmed when only 50 percent of the normal precipitation had fallen by early spring, and although heavy rains in May eased their worries a little, agricultural experts predicted that the production of sugar beets, peas, flax, and potatoes would likely fall short of expectations because of dry weather.

The labor shortage continued to be another major problem for farmers, but things promised to be better in 1944 than during the past few years. Senator Wheeler informed Governor Ford that 7,000 prisoners of war would be sent to the state to provide farm labor. Five thousand POWs were expected to work in the sugar beet fields, while 2,000 were allocated to wheat farmers. Farm experts estimated that an additional 4,185 beet workers were needed, but arrangements had already been made to bring in thousands of Mexican nationals. Camps for the Mexicans were established at Billings, Hardin, Missoula, Chinook, and Sidney. Some of the Mexicans arrived in early spring of 1944 to help with the lambing season, and by mid-May close to 4,000 Mexicans were either in the state or on their way.

In early May ration points were removed on all beef except steak and roasts. Meatless Tuesdays were discontinued because of a surplus. (Points on beef, lamb and some canned vegetables were temporarily re-imposed a few weeks later.) Ranchers had 1,700,000 cattle on state ranges by the end of 1944, and the beef industry continued to boom. The Great Falls livestock yard did double the business in 1944 than they had during the previous year. Wellington Rankin, the richest man in Montana and the owner of at least three other ranches, purchased the 66,000 acre Ringling Ranch, while the 100,000 acre Flying D ranch, south of Bozeman (which would eventually belong to Ted Turner and Jane Fonda), was sold to the Irvine Company for $1,500,000. South of Two Dot, the 9,000 acre American Fork ranch, owned by Wallis Huidekoper, was bought by the Army Quar-

April 1944

- April 1. U.S. Navy planes bomb Japanese forces based on the Caroline islands. Long-time Kalispell police chief Levi Gaustad resigns.
- April 2. Soviets enter Rumania.
- April 3. German Battleship *Tirpitz* is damaged by British bombers. Three fliers from the 7th Ferrying Group are killed in a crash in Mississippi.
- April 4. A sheepherder is killed by lightning near Great Falls. He was found to have $10,000 in the bank.
- April 9. Easter.
- April 10. Odessa falls to Soviets. Fire destroys several buildings at the Montana State Game Farm at Ft. Peck, $15,000 damage.
- April 12. Butte deputy sheriff John Moore shoots a masked man three times during an armed robbery of a private citizen. The gunman survived.
- April 15. Great Falls Independents win city YMCA-military basketball league by defeating Gore Field Enlisted Men 63-53. A 7th Ferrying Group pilot is killed in a crash in Illinois.
- April 18. Four small children burn to death at Hays on the Fort Belknap Reservation.
- April 19. Soviets approach outskirts of Sevastopol.
- April 20. Hungry Horse project is passed unanimously by the U.S. House of Representatives.
- April 21. Rep. Mike Mansfield speech entitled "China: A Key to Victory" broadcast on NBC radio. He said the war in China would be won "by the bayonet and the rifle."
- April 22. Gore Field boxers defeat the Air Base Maulers 8-4.
- April 23. U.S. forces land at Hollandia and Aitape. Heavy flooding in Kansas and Missouri.
- April 28. Natural gas explosion destroys house in Great Falls.
- April 29. Two-year-old Zurich boy drowns in Milk River.

European Air War

- Lt. Duke Dunkerly of Glendive flew on the same raid over Berlin in which Guy Rogers was shot down. He was awarded the Distinguished Flying Cross and Air Medal with 3 clusters for his 25 missions over Europe.
- Maj. Ivan W. Eveland, a squadron leader and native Montanan who trained at Great Falls and Glasgow, was shot down over Europe but evaded capture for three months and made it safely back to England.
- 1st Lt. Paul H. Wilkins of Billings, a P-38 pilot based in Italy, was awarded the Distinguished Flying Cross on his second tour of duty for attacking five German fighters ganging up on another P-38. He shot down two and damaged another.
- Capt. Sherman Strate of Darby, stationed at a B-17 base near London, was a member of an American cricket team that lost a match by 93 runs but thoroughly amused their British audience with their baseball chatter.
- Staff Sgt. Oliver J. Russell of Dupuyer was awarded the Silver Star for a B-24 raid over Austria on May 24, 1944, in which his plane was badly shot up.

Aitape and Humboldt Bay

- Technician 5th Class William Reynolds of Norris was an artilleryman awarded the Bronze Star for his actions at Humboldt Bay, New Guinea. On April 23, 1944 he spent three hours in a burning ammunition dump helping the wounded to safety.
- Paul Hollister of Harlowton was a 1924 graduate of Harlowton High who worked as a cashier for the Milwaukee Road before entering the service with Company D of the 163rd. He led the assault unit into Humboldt Bay, New Guinea, then was promoted to major and awarded the Silver Star.
- Cpl. Harold G. Halverson of Great Falls was cited for gallantry for his actions on May 2, 1944 at Humboldt Bay. He was awarded the Silver Star.

termaster Corps. Cattle, sheep, and hogs added $93,000,000 to the state's economy in 1944.

By the fall of 1944 the Montana livestock industry was said to be in its best shape in history, despite a ring of cattle rustlers operating near Malta and Glasgow. The Phillips County sheriff publicly warned the rustlers that he knew who they were, and the cattle thefts quickly ended. Grazing fees on Federal land cost ranchers five cents per cow per month in 1944. Sheep ranchers paid only one cent per animal per month, but even that was too much for some sheepmen, who had been hit hard by the chronic labor shortage. The sheep industry as a whole was in trouble, and the number of sheep on Montana ranges dropped to 3,131,000. Less than 28,000,000 pounds of wool were produced in 1944, the fifth straight decline. Wool growers in other states were faced with the same problems however, and Montana still ranked second in the nation in wool production, behind Texas and ahead of Wyoming.

Prompted by the wartime demand for petroleum products, the oil industry in Montana produced an average of 8,500,000 barrels of oil annually. In early 1944 a gusher (the highest producing oil well of the decade) was struck at the Kevin-Sunburst field. The development of the Gage Dome oil-field northeast of Roundup, where the Northern Ordnance Company planned to drill four new wells, prompted so much activity that 100 government trailers were sent to Roundup to house all of the new oil-field workers. The Texas Company leased oil land in Liberty County, while the Carter Oil Company, which intended to become a major player in the Montana oil industry, purchased the Northwest refinery in Cut Bank, the Santa Rita Oil Company, and the 420-acre Yale refinery on the Yellowstone River at Lockwood. The Yale refinery was expanded in 1949, was sold to Humble Oil in 1960, and is now owned by Exxon. Before the war, the Conoco Company planned to build a refinery in the Billings area, but then postponed construction until after the war. The Conoco refinery first began production in 1949. The Laurel refinery, originally built in 1929 by the Laurel Oil and Refining Company, was closed for several years during the Depression, and then was bought by the Independent Refining Company. It was producing 5,000 barrels a day and had 50 employees when the Farmers Union bought the refinery for $750,000 on March 1, 1943.

During the war, the Home Oil and Refining Company built a $500,000 pipeline from Cut Bank to Great Falls. Other oil companies contemplated building an 1,100 mile pipeline from central Montana to Seattle, at an estimated cost of $15,000,000. To guard against sabotage and leaks, the oil-fields and pipelines were patrolled by troubleshooters on horseback who rode an average of 20 miles a day.

In mid-May 1944, Senator Wheeler visited the White House for the first time since 1940 in order to enlist President Roosevelt's support for the 100th anniversary of Samuel Morse's invention of the telegraph. Wheeler talked with the President for 45 minutes, throwing the President's schedule off for the rest of the day and raising speculation that Roosevelt might ask Wheeler to be his vice-president in the fall elections. Wheeler was shocked by Roosevelt's physical condition and rambling speech. He was doubly shocked when the President revealed to Wheeler the date of the proposed D-Day invasion, one of the most closely guarded secrets in the world. Wheeler later expressed "great concern about his [FDR's] alarming physical decline. To me he seemed a very sick man who was in no condition to carry on as President."

Wheeler also worried about the state of the world after the war, and he urged that a United States of Europe be formed. He correctly foresaw the dangers of dividing Europe into zones held by occupying armies, and predicted Soviet domination of Europe after the war. Senator Wheeler also sponsored legislation to reorganize the Federal Communications Commission, and to ban commercial sponsorship of news broadcasts, analysts, and commentators. The America First party wanted Wheeler to run as their candidate for president, but he refused.

In March of 1944, President Roosevelt sent Rep. Mike Mansfield to Burma to visit the troops. After his tour, Mansfield called British generals Wavell and Auchinleck "old and defeated," and urged that a caravan route be opened from Turkestan to Sinkiang, to provide war supplies to China.

State Democratic and Republican political conventions were held in Montana in mid-May 1944. The Democrats favored a fourth term for President Roosevelt while the GOP threw their support behind Thomas Dewey. Judge Leif Erickson and Austin B. Middleton, former warden of the Montana State Prison and the chairman of the Railroad and Public Service Commission, announced plans to run for the Democratic nomination for governor. Charles R. Miller of the Montana Drys (a party pushing the renewed prohibition of alcohol) also campaigned for the governor's office. State Sen. Dan Maddox of Hardin sought the Republican nomination for Congress, while Howard K. Hazelbaker of Missoula, a former state legislator, secretary of the Montana Press Association and a University journalism professor, ran for the office of secretary of state.

Fifty-two percent of the registered voters cast ballots in the primary election in July 1944, and Governor Ford won the Republican nomination for another term, while Leif Erickson defeated former governor Roy E. Ayers for the Democratic gubernatorial nomination.

State officials worried that because of a technicality in the state soldier ballot law, which allowed counting of absentee votes filed after November 7, Montana's vote in the 1944 presidential election might not count unless the Supreme Court acted, or a special session of the state legislature was called to change the law. Fortunately for Montana voters, the U.S. Supreme Court invalidated a portion of the law in order that Montana votes would count in the Presidential election.

March 15, 1944 was the deadline to file tax returns, and for the first time Montanans began to feel the pinch of the federal income tax. Because of a sharp increase in taxes, the federal government collected nearly $50,000,000 from Montanan's in 1944, compared with only $4,800,000 just three years before. The state of Montana collected a total of $19,000,000 in state, local, and school taxes in 1944, a drop of $2,000,000 over the past year. The decline in state tax revenue was due to the large number of people who had left Montana, as well as reduced sales of liquor and gasoline due to rationing.

Despite the tax increases, Montana businesses experienced a boom in 1944. Department stores enjoyed a steady rise in income, and the Great Falls and East Helena smelters owned by ACM were awarded their third "E" award for production. A 48-hour work week was urged for all workers in Great Falls by the local manpower commission, but manpower may have been a misnomer, since one quarter of the Great Falls labor force was comprised of servicemen's wives. Despite the shortage of workers in Montana, in April, 1944, Montanan's were urged to apply for high-paying jobs at Pasco, Washington. Although it was not revealed at the time, the workers were needed for the top-secret Hanford Works atomic facility.

Although the crime rate had dropped throughout most of the state, the presence of thousands of soldiers in Montana partially offset the severe reduction in population. Two drunk officers stationed at Gore Field beat the owner of a Great Falls hotel when he asked them to leave, and a Military Policeman at Fort Harrison was charged with rape. He was the last MP stationed at Fort Harrison; earlier in the year a Military Police unit formed at Butte was given jurisdiction over the entire state.

Great Falls police nabbed a soldier at Gore Field after he smashed a jewelry store window and grabbed $600 worth of jewelry, and Cpl. Charles Snyder was eventually court-martialed and sentenced to five years in jail. Alice Walker, a 57-year-old Great Falls woman was arrested by the FBI for harboring two Gore Field deserters. She was fined $100 and given a three month sentence.

Law enforcement officials were also on the lookout for con men pulling the "Mexican nylon scam." Door-to-door salesman preyed on unsuspecting housewives desperate to obtain new silk or nylon stockings. The con men sold rayon stockings for $10.00 a pair, but told housewives they would look just like nylon stockings if they were left in the refrigerator for two weeks.

There were also a number of more serious crimes during the spring of 1944. In April, Dan Morgan of Missoula was sentenced to life for the second degree murder of an Oregon man he met in Missoula. Although Missoula Police Chief Harry M. Smith thought that juvenile crime was actually on the decrease, other authorities around the state were not so sure. A 15-year-old White Sulphur Springs boy was shot in the arm by police during a robbery, and in Great Falls a police officer and deputy sheriff were assigned full time to check up on juveniles. In May, Yellowstone County officers were overwhelmed when a street fight erupted in Laurel between 50 boys from Billings and Laurel. Numerous law enforcement officers responded to the disturbance call, but the fight resumed at the Laurel jailhouse. In late May, Billings police arrested a 17-year-old Albuquerque man who stole a cab at gunpoint and then fired a shot at the cabbie as he fled. Besides being frequent victims of crime, cabdrivers were also the subject of a federal investigation. U.S. Marshals arrested two Great Falls cabdrivers for selling black market whiskey in May, and on the following day four Billings cabdrivers were also arrested in the whiskey probe.

In the world of books, Great Falls writer Norman Fox's sixth novel, *Thundering Trail*, was published by

Pacific

· Cpl. Philip J. Murphy of Columbia Falls, a radio operator on a B-17, was awarded the Distinguished Service Cross. On February 1, 1944 he was on a bombing mission from Guadalcanal when he was wounded in the leg while shooting at Japanese Zeros. He lay on his back and passed ammunition to the other waist gunner until he was wounded again. He was promoted to staff sergeant.

· Marine Cpl. Malvin McLinden of Trout Creek served with the First Marine Division at Cape Gloucester on New Britain. He was awarded the Silver Star after burying a Japanese pillbox with his bulldozer.

· Tech. Sgt. Neil MacPherson of Great Falls was awarded the Bronze Star for his actions with the 20th Bomber Command in India during the first five months of 1944. He was among the first contingent of his unit to arrive in India, and displayed great initiative in helping set up the first B-29 base in India with very limited supplies to work with.

· Cmdr. Joseph W. Callahan of Butte was a destroyer captain awarded a Silver Star for action off Rendova.

· Lt. Col. Maurice F. Taber of Lewistown was awarded the Silver Star and Distinguished Flying Cross for his actions while stationed in the China-India-Burma theater with the 14th Air Force. He was a West Point graduate who commanded a bomber squadron under General Chennault, and was featured in a *Saturday Evening Post* article called "Hong Kong Homecoming" by Ernest O. Hauser. His B-25 was shot down April 8, 1944 and he was declared Missing in Action.

· Capt. William D. Barnes of Craig was a P-38 pilot downed off Rabaul. He was shot at for two hours until he paddled out of range of Japanese guns, where a Catalina flying boat picked him up.

· Lt. Col. Norval Bonawitz of Missoula commanded a P-40 group in China. He was a University of Montana forestry school graduate who had been shot down in a Chinese river after downing two bombers, but managed to return safely to his base.

Italy

· Sgt. Floyd M. Boyer of Lame Deer served with the Third Division in Italy. He cleared a house containing more than 20 Germans, killing several of them, but he was killed in a subsequent operation and was posthumously awarded the Silver Star.

· 2nd Lt. Jack W. Lindeberg of Miles City commanded two tank destroyers that took out two German Mark VI tanks and one Mark IV in Italy.

· PFC Everette Thornton of Simms was awarded the Silver Star for his actions on May 25, 1944 at Carano, Italy. Under heavy artillery fire he drove an ambulance up to a bridge and evacuated the wounded despite three salvos of artillery fire that fell all around him.

· 1st Lt. Donald A. Bonawitz of Hardin was with the 1st Armored Division in Italy. He was awarded the Silver Star after he left his tank to remove 40 mines, then continued to lead his platoon despite being wounded.

· Joe Kuchinski of Bridger and four others of his paratrooper artillery battery (Fifth Army) were awarded the Silver Star for rescuing wounded men in a burning ammunition dump.

· PFC Aaron F. Welch of Oilmont won the Bronze Star for his actions during June and July 1944 at Ponte d'Istia Italy. For two days and two nights Welch and two other men strung six miles of telephone wire under constant fire.

· At least 22 Montanans served with the 361st Infantry Regiment, 91st (Powder River) Division in Italy.

· PFC Ralph E. Carrier of Choteau, 135th Infantry Regiment, 34th Division, was awarded the Bronze Star after he exposed himself to fire in order to locate a machine gun nest, which was subsequently knocked out by a nearby tank.

· Tech. Sgt. Jean D. Hanley of Ismay was posthumously awarded the Silver Star. He was fatally wounded in Italy after leading a patrol to within 100 yards of enemy lines, knocking out a machine gun nest and forcing a Mark IV tank to withdraw after he killed a gunner.

Dodd, Mead and Company. Western writer Frederick Faust, who under the pen-name Max Brand had written 85 books, was killed in Italy while serving as a war correspondent.

Harry Johnson, owner of a general store in Conner, wrote a song called "Goodnight Soldier" and sent it to his cousin, who was a housemother at Montana State College in Bozeman. The sorority girls didn't like the song and sent it back, but Johnson persevered and sent it to a Hollywood music producer who recognized its potential. To Johnson's surprise, the song became a smash hit, and a record-breaking 80,000 copies of the sheet music sold in one week.

In May 1944, as his newspaper approached 71 years of continuous operation, *Daily Missoulian* editor French Ferguson reported that 35 of his newspaper's employees were serving in the armed services. During the war years, the number of newspapers in the state decreased by 22 percent, and 33 of the state's 149 papers ceased publication. This number included the *Helena Independent* (which merged with the afternoon *Record*), the *Lewistown Telegram*, and the *Daily Record* of Roundup. By the summer of 1944 at least 11 weekly papers boasted women editors, including the *Augusta News*, the *Big Timber Pioneer*, the *Ronan Pioneer*, the *Camas Hot Springs Exchange*, and the *Dillon Tribune*. The *Montana Kaimin*, the newspaper of the University of Montana, reduced publication to just one issue per week. LeClaire Flint, the president of the Montana Press Association and the former editor of the *Livingston Enterprise*, took a leave of absence in order to work for a west coast defense plant. He was put in charge of official tours at the Boeing aircraft factory in Seattle.

In sporting news, boxing remained popular in the state and teams from Lewistown, Billings, Butte, the Army air base at Great Falls, and the Catholic Youth Center in the Electric City, competed at matches held in the Heisey Gym in Great Falls and the Civic Centers in Butte and Great Falls. Tickets to the AAU boxing match at Heisey gym cost $1.50; $1.20 for children and enlisted men. As the weather improved, Helena residents looked forward to the new 18-hole golf course under construction in that city, and in the Garden City, the Missoula Spartans swept the annual Missoula Invitational Track meet. Butte High took second place.

Spring brought the 1944 graduation ceremonies on Montana campuses. Montana State College graduated 112 seniors, while the University of Montana graduated 131. Both Northern Montana College and Billings Poly boasted 25 graduates. The Great Falls Victory Corps, sponsored by the American Legion, graduated 73 high school students trained in drilling and military procedure.

After parading through the streets of Great Falls to the Civic Center, 257 students nurses from Columbus and Deaconess Hospitals were inducted into the army on May 13, 1944. Governor Ford proclaimed the day as Cadet Nurse Corps Day and all 11 nurses training centers across the state held ceremonies.

As spring turned into summer, the stalemate that had gripped Allied forces in Italy showed signs of breaking. After more than three months in the Anzio beachhead, the men of the First Special Service Force prepared to leave their positions on the Mussolini Canal. After a 12-day rest, the Force was paired with the Third Division during a major Allied offensive that finally broke the German line at Anzio. The First Special Service Force spearheaded the right flank of the attack, advancing three miles the first day and cutting Route 7 to the right of the German-held town of Cisterna. They took heavy casualties, and the First Regiment alone suffered 39 killed and many wounded. The Forcemen dug in along Route 7, but were driven back by 17 Tiger tanks after the division that was supposed to be supporting their left flank failed to advance as swiftly as the fast-moving Forcemen.

Gen. Mark Clark presented General Frederick with the Distinguished Service Cross just before the Force attacked due north towards Monte Arrestino (May 25, 1944) and Rocca Massima (May 27, 1944). The tough commandos regrouped at Artena, where a heavy German counterattack took a heavy toll on the First and Third Regiments. They were pinned down in the ruined town under extremely heavy fire for several days as the Germans fired all of their ammunition preparatory to pulling out, and Artena turned into one of the Forcemen's toughest battles.

While the Forcemen and the rest of the Fifth Army battled their way towards Rome, halfway around the globe, the men of the 163rd Infantry Regiment also faced their toughest battle of the war. On May 31, 1944 two battalions of the 163rd were pulled out of the Wakde area and rushed to the island of Biak, where the other two regiments of the 41st Division, the 162nd and 186th Infantry Regiments, had landed four days before. The two regi-

The 317th Training Detachment parades in front of Main Hall at the University of Montana. Almost 1,000 aviators were trained at the University during the war. Hundreds of aviation students were also trained at Montana State College and Carroll College. sc

May 1944

· May 2. Fire at the Carston Packing Company in Billings causes $7,000 damage.
· May 3-5. Gore Field personnel present "Desert Fever", a six act play, at the Rainbow Theater in Great Falls.
· May 4. A dynamite blast destroys Butte apartment building, severely injuring one man. An unknown man who rented an apartment just minutes before the blast was suspected.
· May 6. Pensive wins Kentucky Derby.
· May 9. Soviets liberate Sevastopol.
· May 13. Six die and five are rescued when a bomber from Casper, Wyoming crashes two miles northwest of Miles City. Five thousand barrel a day oil well comes in at Gage Dome.
· May 18. Wakde is seized by the 163rd Infantry. Abbey at Monte Cassino taken by U.S. forces.
· May 19. Two hundred Butte miners from the St. Lawrence Mine walk off the job because they don't like the foreman. After a three-day strike the foreman is removed and miners return to work.
· May 21. "I Am An American Day." Two Great Falls men drown at Martinsdale Reservoir.
· May 25. Montana Stockgrower's Association meets in Miles City. One hundred oil truck drivers in Laurel and Billings go on strike, which ends after two days.
· May 26. U.S. Senate passes measure providing postwar construction funds for Hungry Horse dam.
· May 27. 41st Division lands on Biak Island.
· May 28. Browning Fair begins.
· May 29. University of Montana commencement.
· May 30. Memorial Day.

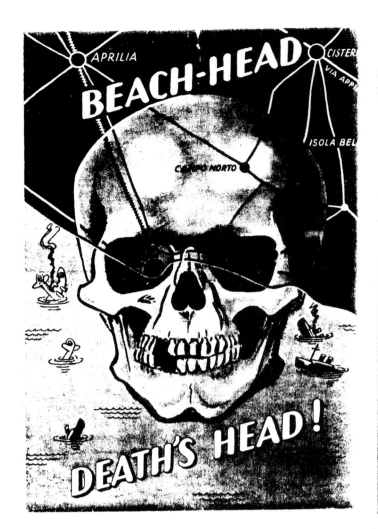

THE BEACH-HEAD

is going to be the big blow against the Germans.

Wasn't that the slogan when the Allied troops landed at Nettuno on January 21st?

TODAY

exactly three months of hard fighting have passed and you can now celebrate this event.

But it is still merely a beach-head, paved with the skulls of thousands of British and American soldiers!

The Beach-Head has become a Death's Head!

It is welcoming **You** with a grin, and also those who are coming after you across the sea for an appointment with death.

Do they know what they are in for?

Yes, they feel that they are landing on a

DEATH'S HEAD

A I · 065·4·44

A propaganda leaflet dropped by the Germans at Anzio. The Black Devils of Anzio printed up their own leaflets, which were left on the bodies of dead Germans. John Marshall

First Special Service Forcemen crossing the Mussolini Canal. Bob Durkee, Helena

ments had run into serious trouble while trying to capture the Mokmer Airdrome, one of three airfields on the island. General MacArthur wanted the Biak airfields because they were the only airstrips in the area capable of handling the heavy bombers of the U.S. Army Air Force. Unfortunately for the former members of the Montana National Guard, the 948 square miles of Biak housed more than 11,000 veteran Japanese soldiers of the 22nd Infantry and Japanese Marines, commanded by the able Col. Naoyuki Kuzumi.

Men At War

· Lt. John Doyle of Missoula (USN) was a veteran of the attack on Pearl Harbor. He commanded *LST 515* during a training exercise for the Normandy invasion in the English Channel. During "Exercise Tiger" two flotilla's of German torpedo boats attacked eight LST's at 2 a.m. on April 28, 1944. Three LST's (Landing Ship-Tank) were hit and set on fire, and two of them sank, killing at least 749 soldiers of the 4th Division. Disobeying orders to return to shore, Doyle rescued 90 survivors. "I just could not leave all those men out there in that cold water." Despite Doyle's heroism, the ocean was covered with bodies. Most drowned or were burned by gasoline pouring over the water. The dead were buried in mass graves and Eisenhower ordered the incident be covered up. Doyle was later interviewed for a 20-20 broadcast on ABC television. He received the Bronze Star for his actions at Normandy. Two years after Doyle's death in 1989, a stone monument honoring his heroism was placed in Missoula's Rose Park.

· Maj. Worthington C. Smith of Missoula, stationed in the Persian Gulf Command, was awarded the Soviet Order of the Fatherlands War, Second Class.

· Tech. Sgt. Henry Connell of Great Falls was an airplane mechanic who stole a P-40 and took it for a joy ride. His hand-written flying instructions blew away when he opened the cockpit and he crashed on landing, destroying the plane.

· Master Sgt. John Carlson of Missoula was a 23 year army veteran who held the world record with the .30 rifle, with a score of 99 out of 100. He was responsible for teaching marksmanship to fliers at Colorado Springs.

· Brig. Gen. Jay W. MacKelvie of Anaconda was promoted to major general in June 1944.

William Galt—Medal of Honor Winner

Capt. William Galt lived in Geyser and Great Falls before attending Montana State College, where he served as a cadet captain of the Reserve Officer Training Corps (ROTC) until his enlistment in 1942. While serving with the 34th Division ("Red Bulls") in Italy in December 1943 he won two Purple Hearts and the Silver Star for leading his men through a minefield on his hands and knees. On May 29, 1944, during the breakout from the Anzio beachhead, he scouted out German positions near Villa Crocetta, then led his battalion in an attack. When the attack faltered he commandeered the unit's only remaining tank destroyer. Standing exposed in the turret, he fired the machine gun constantly and threw grenades into German positions despite a flurry of gunfire. He killed 40 Germans who refused to surrender, but seconds later a shell from a German 88 gun hit the tank and he fell mortally wounded at age 24. His Medal of Honor was awarded to his wife, Mrs. Patricia Galt on February 19, 1945, at the Great Falls Air Base by Brig. Gen. Dave V. Gaffney. Soviet Maj. Gen. I.A. Abraskov and Col. A.N. Kotikov attended the ceremony, as did Galt's parents, Mr. and Mrs. Errol Galt. The Great Falls National Guard Armory was named in Galt's honor.

Leo J. Powers—Medal of Honor Winner

PFC Leo J. "Pop" Powers of Alder, one of 13 children, was a ranch hand who joined the 133rd Infantry Regiment, 34th Division ("Red Bulls") in North Africa, just before they landed at Salerno, Italy. "I don't know how I ended up overseas. I was about the oldest guy over there. They were kind of fouled up." On February 3, 1944, on Hill 175 near the town of Cassino, Powers became angry with an American major and with his own comrades who didn't want to move. His company of 200 men had been reduced to 35. "Eight of my buddies were killed that morning, and two others were wounded. The company commander was looking for volunteers to clean out the pillboxes, but I was so damned mad I decided to knock them over myself." He grabbed a rifle and grenades and singlehandedly attacked three German pillboxes. He crawled to within a few yards of one and tossed in a grenade, killing two Germans. Several others fled out the rear. He did the same to the second and third pillboxes. He was credited with killing five Germans, wounding 20, and his actions led to the capture of 12 more. Powers later commented that, "I was pretty uncomfortable there, with the machine gun and rifle bullets whistling by." According to his Medal of Honor citation "Private First Class Powers had worked his way over the entire company front, and against tremendous odds had single-handedly broken the backbone of this heavily defended and strategic enemy position, and enabled his regiment to advance into the city of Cassino." Six days later, in an abandoned building near the Abbey, a shell destroyed the building and killed 12 men of Power's platoon. He was buried but was dug out. Just a week after that he was badly wounded, and was eventually sent to Fort Lawton, Washington, where he served as an instructor. His Medal of Honor was announced in September 1944, and Representative Mike Mansfield read his exploits into the *Congressional Record*. Alder residents turned out en masse to welcome him home. On January 15, 1945 President Roosevelt handed the Medal of Honor to Mrs. Powers, who hung it around her husband's neck. Powers returned to Montana after the war, and in 1954 went to work for the Anaconda Copper Mining Co. at Anaconda. In 1958 he was an honorary pallbearer during the burial of unknown soldiers of WWII and Korea at Arlington Cemetery. He retired near Anaconda, died of a heart attack July 14, 1967, and is buried in Holy Cross Cemetery in Butte. His medal was stolen in Billings while it was on display in a traveling army recruiting van.

Henry Schauer—Medal of Honor Winner

PFC Henry Schauer of Scobey enlisted February 17, 1941, and trained at Fort Lewis, Washington, where he learned to shoot a Browning Automatic Rifle (BAR). He landed in Morocco with the Third Division, fought in Sicily, where he was wounded twice and spent 151 days in the hospital. He was awarded the Bronze Star as well as the Purple Heart with cluster. He told one interviewer that, "I get nervous as hell until I fire that first shot for the day. After that I don't worry much." He was with his unit at Anzio on May 23, 1944, when he stood up and advanced in the face of snipers, coolly shooting down four, then a fifth. Schauer's patrol was then pinned down by machine gun and artillery fire until Schauer ran within 60 yards of one machine gun emplacement and gunned down the crew. He then killed the Germans manning a second machine gun. His patrol reached the town of Cisterna that night and on the following day they came under fire from a German Mark IV tank and another machine gun. Schauer stood up and blasted the machine gun crew, forcing the tank to withdraw. Schauer was credited with killing 17 Germans in 17 hours with his BAR, and later claimed that coyote hunting in Montana had honed his shooting skills. His commanding officer called him "the best BAR man in the army." In October 1944, Lt. Gen. Alexander Patch pinned the Medal of Honor on Schauer and promoted him to technical sergeant. Schauer then returned to the U.S. to help with the sixth war bond drive. In December 1944, he appeared in a bond rally in Butte. Residents of Daniels County chose to name a new B-29 bomber the "Henry Schauer". He was honorably discharged June 9, 1945, and farmed in Montana until 1958. He entered the Miles City VA hospital for a time, then moved to Salem Oregon. On May 2, 1963 he attended a special Medal of Honor reception hosted by President John F. Kennedy.

William W. Galt was awarded the Medal of Honor for his actions during the breakout from Anzio. MHS 942-329

Leo J. Powers won his Medal of Honor at Cassino. MHS 945-680

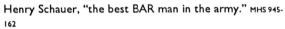

Henry Schauer, "the best BAR man in the army." MHS 945-162

Rep. Mike Mansfield on the Ledo Road, Burma. At the request of President Roosevelt, Mansfield made two trips to inspect American troops in the China-Burma-India theater. UM 85-207

Please Wait For Me

Words and Music by Helen Harstead

Published by Helen Harstead, 303 W. Park St. Butte, Mont.

12

☞ Rome, Normandy And Biak ☜

By the time the men from Montana landed on Biak, the 162nd Infantry had been turned back short of Mokmer airdrome after fierce fighting which included the first tank-to-tank battle of the Pacific war (five Sherman tanks destroyed seven Japanese tanks). Major Paul G. Hollister of Harlowton, who had been awarded his first Silver Star for Sanananda and a second for Humboldt Bay, was awarded a third for Biak, where he extricated his battalion of the 41st Division, and then led a successful attack. Hollister called in naval gunfire, artillery, and mortars to support his battalion, which fought off four separate Japanese tank attacks on Biak. Hollister, who also had an Air Medal, a Bronze Star, and a Presidential Unit Citation, was promoted to lieutenant colonel.

There were other promotions as well. Col. William Moroney replaced Jens Doe as commander of the 163rd. According to General Eichelberger, "Doe was a great fighter, he was also a stubborn, opinionated man, and our disagreements were spirited. Subsequently Doe became, with my recommendation, the 41st's commanding general."

The Second Battalion of the 163rd arrived from Toem on June 12 and replaced part of the badly mauled 162nd Infantry Regiment. Three days later the men of the Second Battalion were heavily shelled, but they silenced the Japanese guns with their 37mm antitank weapons.

For the men of the 163rd, Biak was perhaps their fiercest battle of the war, and the former National Guardsmen were met by heavy fire from Japanese airplanes, artillery, machine guns, and mortars. Fortunately, several Japanese efforts to land reinforcements failed, but the "Jungleers" of the 41st Division had all the trouble they could handle. The 163rd took several coral ridges around the Bosnek beachhead and tried repeatedly to take Lone Tree Hill. The fighting was often hand-to-hand. Although the jungle was not as thick as they had encountered at Sanananda, the terrain was just as inhospitable. Most of the supplies which reached the front-line soldiers had to be packed up the steep ridges on the backs of weary soldiers. Foul-tasting and barely drinkable water proved to be another major hardship.

The 163rd held the Mokmer airdrome, captured June 6, but was still being harassed by enemy artillery fire when General Eichelberger and his corps headquarters arrived on Biak to take charge in mid-June. General Byers, of Eichelberger's staff, soon visited the front lines of the 163rd to observe, not knowing that Japanese infiltrators had tapped an American phone wire and had heard he was coming. Although Byers escaped, a jeep was ambushed and several engineers were killed. Eight Japanese were eventually killed at the scene of the ambush. Two days of artillery and air bombing finally enabled the 163rd to take Lone Tree Hill, but as the Americans captured the high coral ridges, the Japanese retreated to three underground strong points.

The island of Biak was honeycombed with caves which the Japanese had thoroughly explored and improved upon. According to Eichelberger, "There were the East Caves directly above Mokmer Village, and there were the caves, farther down the coast, at the Ibdi Pocket." Colonel Kuzumi's headquarters and center of the Japanese resistance were the West Caves, otherwise known as "the Sump." The Americans began dynamiting the caves, and on June 22, 1944, Colonel Kuzumi passed out hand grenades, burned his documents, and ceremoniously disemboweled himself. Some survivors made a banzai charge against a squad of the 186th Infantry and over 100 Japanese were killed. A-20s and P-40s attacked the Mokmer caves, while B-24s and B-25s practiced skip-bombing at the Ibdi caves. On June 23, a massive three-day artillery barrage began hitting the Ibdi Pocket. After the planes and artillery had done their work, infantrymen moved in with flamethrowers and explosives. The 163rd's A and B companies attacked one side of the Ibdi Pocket on June 26, while F and G companies moved in from another direction. All met heavy fire from Japanese guns in the Pocket and by the Fourth of July General Doe decided to besiege the Pocket rather than take it by storm. Three more days of artillery fire rocked the Pocket before the Americans moved in again. The infantrymen eventually poured hundreds of gallons of gasoline down crevices in order to clear the caves, and after almost two months of vicious fighting, they overran the final 1,000 Japanese holding the Ibdi Pocket. The 163rd Regiment lost 67 dead and 408 wounded on Biak. The bloody and drawn-out defense of Biak, where the Japanese garrison had retreated into caves instead of wasting their strength in futile banzai charges, was studied closely by leaders on both sides, and led to a change of Japanese tactics in future battles.

The 163rd Infantry was nearly worn out after several months of almost continuous fighting without replacements. Governor Ford and Senator Wheeler asked that the Regiment be rotated back to the United States, but unfortunately for the Guardsmen from Montana, General MacArthur regarded the 163rd as one of his best units. The men from Montana were part of the most decorated Army division in the Pacific, and were needed for the planned invasion of the Philippines. Instead of being sent back to the United States, they were destined to spend the next six months recuperating on Biak, although a few individual members of the 163rd were allowed leave.

While the Montana Guardsmen fought their way through the jungles of Biak, world events moved at a rapid pace. In England the last-minute preparations for the invasion of Europe were underway, while in Italy the Allied armies pushed towards Rome.

In Italy, the First Special Service Force finally broke out of the carnage of Artena, then were strafed by German planes while traveling by truck past Colle Ferro on June 2, 1944. Supported by tanks from the 1st Armored Division, the Force attacked along Tor Sapienza into Rome. They reached the outskirts of Rome before midnight on June 3, 1944 and were shortly ordered to secure the Tiber River bridges.

Capt. Taylor Radcliffe, who had married a Helena girl, was credited with leading the first Allied patrol into Rome. Radcliffe had skipped out of a hospital on June 1 to return to the Force. He was chosen to lead a patrol composed of 60 men from each battalion of the Force, as well as several correspondents. They entered Rome early on the 4th of June but were pinned down for most of the day. Radcliffe was awarded the Distinguished Service Cross. After the war Radcliffe returned to Helena and served as deputy director of the Federal Housing Administration in that city. He later became the head of the First Special Service Force veteran's organization and still lives in Helena.

Maj. Gerry McFadden led a battalion of 380 Forcemen on the final assault on Rome. He had 80 men and 10 tanks left by the time they entered the ancient Roman gate of Porta San Paolo to seize the first Nazi held capital. "We were pushing too hard. We were under enormous pressure to take the first enemy capital—a mission accomplished when we seized 10 bridges of the Tiber." McFadden had but 23 men left standing when the fight for Rome ended. By the evening of the 4th the Forcemen had reached St. Peter's Square and each platoon held a Tiber bridge, although the Force had been so reduced in size that one of the vital bridges was held only by General Frederick and seven infantrymen. Frederick was in the thick of the fighting for Rome and was wounded three more times during the ensuing battle, bringing his total to nine wounds. The rest of the Force was in equally bad shape. A doctor (Capt. Sheldon Sommers) on the scene stated that, "Compared to the Rangers I thought the FSSF in the last four days into Rome looked more tired, worn down, and ragged than any infantry I had worked with. They moved under fire very well, like experienced infantry, and operated beautifully with tanks.... On the other hand there was a Canadian Indian in that action who was the drunkest combatant I ever saw."

On the 40th anniversary of the Force's entry into Rome (June 4, 1984), a marble placque was unveiled on the wall of the U.S. consulate in the Italian capital, honoring the Force's part in liberating Rome. Nearly 300 Forcemen attended the ceremony, including former battalion commander Maj. Gerry McFadden of Thunder Bay, Ontario. Also attending was General Frederick's daughter Anne Frederick-Hicks, and Sen. Robert Dole.

On the morning of June 6, 1944, a massive Allied invasion force appeared off the Normandy coast and began landing at five beaches. Thousands of paratroopers were already ashore by the time the first landing craft scraped on the beach. Allied planes circled the beaches looking for targets, while the largest fleet ever assembled pounded German positions. Thousands of Montanans participated in the D-Day invasion and the massive preparations for the landing.

At home, the news of the invasion was one of the most-eagerly awaited events of the war. Kathryn Wright was a reporter for the *Billings Gazette*. When the news came over the wire, her editors reset the banner headline in huge 72-point type, and printed it in red ink. Wright and other staffers each grabbed an armload of newspapers and headed for downtown

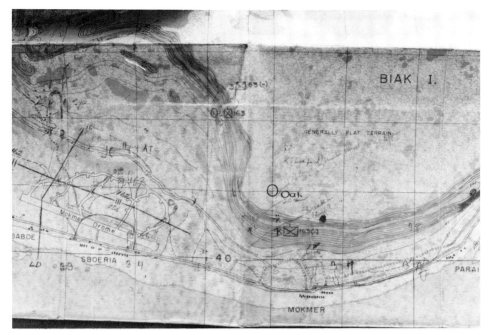

Topographic map, used by the officers of the 163rd, shows the Mokmer Aerodrome on Biak. THE 163RD INFANTRY HISTORICAL COMMITTEE

Col. Naoyuki Kuzumi, commander of the Japanese forces on Biak. THE 163RD INFANTRY HISTORICAL COMMITTEE

Japanese forces on Biak had to be dynamited from their caves. Aerial bombardment, naval gunfire and the considerable firepower of the 41st Division smashed much of the strategic island of Biak. THE 163RD INFANTRY HISTORICAL COMMITTEE

General Frederick and Col. Edwin Walker, the two commanders of the First Special Service Force. Bob Durkee, Helena

Forcemen on parade. Bob Durkee, Helena

Billings. Wright made for the train station. "I ran up and down the platform, shoving papers through the windows [of a troop train], making change....

"This went on until almost 7 a.m., when the last of my 200 papers was gone and real newsboys were on the job.

"I started back to the *Gazette*.

"Then all of a sudden, things blurred. I tried to rub the mistiness out of my eyes. No use. I stood

there on the corner, tears streaming down my face as the train moved out.

"Silhouetted in each window of each car was a soldier, maybe bound for the place he was reading about in the red-bannered *Billings Gazette*."

Although it seemed to be a complete disaster to the men on Omaha Beach, the long-awaited invasion was successful, and by nightfall on D-Day, the Allied Armies were moving inland.

In retaliation for the Normandy invasion, the Germans fired the first of their secret V-1 missiles on southern England. By the end of July, as the Soviets on the Eastern Front drove for Warsaw, Allied forces broke out of the Normandy beachhead and began racing through France. A week after the breakout, the U.S. Third Army, commanded by Gen. George Patton, was born at Avranches. The Third Army was a part of the Twelfth Army Group, the largest American fighting force ever assembled, and was commanded by Gen. Omar Bradley. During World War I Bradley had served as a captain with the 14th Infantry, and had been stationed in Butte from January to September of 1918.

June and July of 1944 were also busy months in the Pacific theater. Bombing raids launched from the carriers of the Central Pacific Fleet hit Saipan and the Japanese mainland. Two weeks after D-Day, Admiral Spruance's fleet sank two Japanese carriers and destroyed over 400 enemy planes at the Battle of the Philippine Sea. And by the end of July Guam was the scene of furious fighting.

As the pace of the war accelerated, many changes occurred at the bustling air base outside of Great Falls. In mid-June, Lt. Col. Johansen, the commanding officer of the 7th Ferrying Group was transferred to Long Beach, and his place was taken by Lt. Col. Reesor M. Lawrence, who had been the deputy commander at Great Falls earlier in the year. Lawrence was transferred little more than two months later, and Lt. Col. Kermit R. Hatt took command of the 7th Ferrying Group. Col. N.S. Vasin commanded the Soviet contingent in Montana, replacing Colonel Kotikov.

In June 1944, the 27th Transport Squadron of the 7th Ferrying Group was formed at Gore Field. The duties of the new squadron included transportation of air crews and cargo around the country, as well as the transfer of wounded soldiers. By the end of the summer a Military Air Transport (MAT) unit was activated at Great Falls in order to speed the transfer of vital supplies between Seattle and Dayton, Ohio. In August 1944, 80 civil air patrol cadets arrived for a week of training, and a new enlisted mens club opened at the base.

On the education front, the last air cadets left the University at Missoula. The aviation training program lasted from March 1943 to June 1944. Despite the absence of the aviators, the military training at the University continued, and a number of 17-year-old boys from throughout the West arrived in Missoula for a 12-week training course known as the Army Specialized Training Program (ASTRP). This program, which began in July 1944, was transferred to Stanford University at the end of the year because not enough recruits had signed up.

Although most of the University of Montana athletic department served in the military during the war years, the former coaches managed to keep in touch. Former football coach Maj. Doug Fessenden, stationed with the Air Force in Texas, traveled to Camp Polk, Louisiana to visit with Maj. Gen. Frank Milburn (the Grizzly football coach from 1926-1930)

and Maj. Harry Adams (former track coach and assistant football coach for 22 years).

Summer weather brought baseball fever to the Treasure State. In Great Falls alone there were 40 baseball games on the City-Air Force league schedule during the 1944 season. New teams in the league included the Gore Field Flyers and the Army Air Base Gunners. The dog trainers at Camp Rimini also fielded a baseball team named the Huskies. In late July the Independents defeated the Gunners (7-2) and the Officers (16-4), while the Bombers and Flyers played a three game exhibition series in Billings. The Montana School of Mines "Miners" won the 1944 state softball championship in Livingston after defeating the Bombers 5-4 in late August. A month later the Bombers defeated the Butte Navy "Engineers" 7-6 and 11-0 in the last two baseball games of the season.

The perennially tough Miles City American Legion Juniors defeated the Missoula Legion Juniors 11-2 to take the state Legion championship, but the

Wartime advertisements of the Milwaukee Road, one of several major railroads that serviced Montana communities. In Montana, the Milwaukee tracks ran through Miles City, Forsyth, Roundup, Harlowton, Three Forks, Butte, Missoula and St. Regis. SC

Biak

- Lt. Fritz F. Roll Jr. of Great Falls was awarded the Silver Star for his actions on Biak. On June 22, 1944 he and his isolated company calmly repulsed a 250-man Japanese banzai attack in which 119 Japanese were killed to the loss of one American. After 33 months overseas, Roll was finally given leave and returned to Great Falls in January of 1945.
- Capt. Arthur Merrick of Great Falls, a former University of Montana basketball star, was awarded the Silver Star and Purple Heart by General Doe. He was wounded in the hip on June 26, 1944 while leading his company in a reconnaissance under heavy fire which led to a successful attack against a Japanese strongpoint.
- Herman Zier of Agawam (near Choteau) was awarded the Bronze Star for exposing himself to gunfire in order to blast out a Japanese position on Biak.
- Capt. Earl S. Hooker of Great Falls (Co. L of the 163rd) was awarded the Bronze Star by General Doe. His company was one of three guarding a vital two-mile-long supply route on Biak.
- Capt. Harry B. Johnson Jr. of Great Falls won the Bronze Star for his work as the 41st Division's evacuation officer at Biak.
- Capt. Richard Satran of Whitefish was awarded the Silver Star for his actions on June 26, 1944, when he led an attack that regained lost positions. Satran called in mortar fire so closely to his own position that he was sprayed with shrapnel.
- Staff Sgt. William C. Bequette of Thompson Falls was awarded the Bronze Star by General Doe for conducting a four man reconnaissance patrol under fire during the landing.
- Staff Sgt. William Butts of Great Falls was awarded a Bronze Star for establishing a telephone line under fire.
- Staff Sgt. Lionel Sandon of Sunburst was awarded the Bronze Star. He was wounded after his squad flanked a Japanese pillbox to draw fire off a pinned-down company.
- Cpl. Everett Charlson of Great Falls won a Bronze Star for his actions with the 41st Division's mechanized cavalry reconnaissance troop. On July 1, 1944, near Mokmer airdrome, he singlehandedly fought off a Japanese ambush with a submachine gun until his men had safely withdrawn.

41st Division

- Col. Clarence H. Olson of Great Falls was awarded the Bronze Star for supply operations at Hollandia, Wakde, and Biak. He was a former Montana Commander of the American Legion.
- Col. Francis Mason praised those Indians from Montana who served with the 41st Division.
- Col. Charles Dawley, formerly of the 163rd Infantry, was transferred to the 641 Tank Destroyer Battalion, 41st Division, during the fall of 1943. A former Great Falls police chief and district manager of the John Leslie Paper Company, after three years overseas he was allowed home on leave in February 1945.

Air War, Italy

- Lt. Jack Larkin of Great Falls, a B-26 pilot, was awarded the Distinguished Flying Cross and Air Medal with two clusters. Stationed in Italy, he was interviewed on the Columbia radio network on March 12, 1944.
- Master Sgt. Aldon R. Nichols of Plentywood was the crew chief of a 15th Air Force B-17. From May 4, 1944 to Aug. 10, 1944, his aircraft flew 44 missions without breakdown despite suffering serious battle damage. He was awarded the Bronze Star.
- Tech. Sgt. Glenn D. Anderson of Ronan was a gunner and engineer on a 15th Air Force B-17. He was awarded a Distinguished Flying Cross for an August 17, 1944 raid on Ploesti.

June 1944

- June 4. Several local people and the mayor of Great Falls were interviewed for a KFBB radio program which was broadcast in Britain.
- June 5. Rome captured. High school air cadet trainees arrive at Montana State College for two quarters of training. Laurel fire destroys oil truck loading facility, $30,000 damage.
- June 6. D-Day Invasion of France begins on Normandy beaches.
- June 7. Mokmer airfield on Biak captured.
- June 9. Paris Fligmans department store in Great Falls is sold to a subsidiary of Allied Stores for $1,750,000.
- June 12. Fifth war bond drive starts.
- June 13. First V-1 rocket lands on England.
- June 14. Flag Day.
- June 15. Central Pacific Fleet lands Marines on Saipan and a strategic bombing campaign begins against Japanese mainland.
- June 17. "Go Western" parade in Billings.
- June 19. Battle of the Philippine Sea is won by Admiral Spruance after his fleet sinks two Japanese carriers and destroys over 400 planes.
- June 20. Five-year-old boy drowns at Helena after riding his tricycle into Ten Mile Creek.
- June 22. Great Falls Air Base Gunners baseball team defeats Flyers 12-4.
- June 23. Pilot is killed after his P-39 crashes near Pompey's Pillar.
- June 24. Five tons of waste paper is destroyed by arsonists in Great Falls. Compulsory 48 hour work week goes into effect for major industries.
- June 25. Augusta rodeo.
- June 27. U.S. Army captures Cherbourg.
- June 28. Truck accident near Boulder destroys 180 cases of liquor.

Air War Over Europe

- Maj. Joseph J. May of Havre, a squadron commander with the 409th Bombardment Group, Ninth Air Force, was awarded the Distinguished Flying Cross after he led a group of A-20s through heavy fog to an ammunition dump near Paris in August 1944. Flak badly damaged 13 of the 18 planes, but May found the target and all of his bombs fell within the dump.
- 1st Lt. Gordon F. Demers of Coffee Creek won the Distinguished Flying Cross for his actions on August 22, 1944 after his plane was attacked over Vienna by 25 fighters. His crew shot down three fighters but the bomber's #4 engine was destroyed by a direct hit. He kept the plane in formation and dropped bombs on the target before limping the plane home.
- Staff Sgt. Bob Nicholson of Stockett was awarded the Distinguished Flying Cross and Air Medal with three clusters while serving as a B-17 ball turret gunner in Europe during the Normandy campaign.
- A B-17 group which trained at Great Falls and was led by Col. Harold Bowman was rated the most accurate Eighth Air Force group in June, 1944. Bowman was awarded the Silver Star for a B-17 raid over Germany on February 20, 1944 that met heavy opposition.
- Col. Hubert Zemke's squadron shot down 17 Germans on July 4, 1944. His group boasted 38 aces claiming 508 total victories, the highest number of kills and the best ratio of victories (8 to 1) of any American fighter group in Europe. At the end of July, 1944, Francis Gabreski, one of the group's most skilled pilots was shot down over Germany. Zemke and Gabreski would eventually be reunited in a German POW camp. In August Zemke left the 56th Pursuit Group and took command of the 479th Fighter Group.
- Lt. Clarence Councell of Creston was an Eighth Air Force bombardier who dropped his bombs on target despite being seriously hurt by flak. He was awarded the Silver Star.

Miles City team lost the regional title to a team from Portland.

Tourist expenditures in the state hit the lowest level in many years during 1944. In Glacier National Park the Great Northern hotels and chalets remained closed throughout the year. Although a few tourist cabins were available in Yellowstone, most hotels and cafes in were closed, and the bus service ceased operation.

Governor Ford proclaimed July 3, which was a legal holiday, as Victory Garden Day, then traveled to Stevensville to watch the annual Independence Day rodeo. Residents of Butte honored servicemen on the Fourth of July by hosting a "Parade of the Colors." Fourth of July rodeos were held in communities across the state, including Drummond, Livingston, Roundup, Hinsdale, and Shelby, where 5,000 people attended the rodeo final. Five thousand people also attended the Augusta rodeo, where Montana rodeo legend Oral Zumwalt took first in calf roping and bulldogging.

Brig. Gen. D.V. Gaffney of the Alaska Wing of the Air Transport Command opened the Northern Montana Fair (Great Falls) on August 7. The fair included a landing craft exhibition, a Japanese Zero captured at Guadalcanal, and a fireworks display. A few weeks later a massive traffic jam developed as 10,000 people attended the Army War Show in Great Falls. The show featured a bazooka gunner destroying a small tank, a display of Very lights (flares), and a fire fighting demonstration. A 100-pound bomb was detonated by tracer fire, and the B-25s and P-39s on display fired their machine guns. After the show, a soldier from the air base was accidentally wounded by machine gun fire while helping clean up. The show was such a success that both Billings and Miles City requested that it be put on in their respective cities.

Helena residents were treated to a show of a different kind when a statewide convention of Boy Scouts was held in that city during the summer of 1944. Six hundred Scouts pitched tents on the grounds of Carroll College, and then took over the reins of state government for a day.

Temperature and streamflow levels were normal during the summer of 1944, but severe hailstorms in August did substantial damage to crops and buildings in eastern Montana. In the first week of August a storm pelted the Billings area with egg-sized hailstones and caused more than $1,000,000 in damage across eight counties. A week later a hailstorm accompanied by high winds cut a 20-mile-wide swath through wheatfields at Glendive and Sidney, destroying crops which had already been hard hit during the floods in June. Thousands of windows were broken, including 700 in the Sidney sugar factory alone. Glasgow was swept by hail later in the month, and 18,000 acres of wheat and sugar beets were damaged. Hail damage in 1944 reached its greatest level in 25 years.

Farmers in the Billings area received a break when 250 Italian prisoners of war arrived on June 8 for a six-week stay. They were housed at Kenney Hall on the grounds of Billings Polytechnic (Rocky Mountain College) at night, and spent their days on nearby farms thinning, blocking, and hoeing some 800 acres of sugar beets. There was also talk of housing other Italian POWs at a former CCC camp near Glasgow, but this plan was temporarily shelved.

The U.S. Forest Service hired 600 high school students for slash burning, blister rust prevention, and trail work during the summer of 1944. High school fire guards were trained at a former CCC camp near the Belt Creek Ranger Station, but even more lookouts and fire fighters were needed, and the Forest Service was forced to halt their tree planting projects due to the labor shortage. Several crews of Italian internees remained on the job for the Forest Service during the summer of 1944, and 16 German merchant marines were put to work building two forest bridges in the Choteau area.

The Lolo National Forest not only rehired 13 of the women who had served as fire lookouts during the previous year, they hired several additional female lookouts. The Forest Service even allowed the women to take their children and friends along for company, but the lookouts found that they were much busier in 1944 than they had been in 1943.

Region One reported 1,023 forest fires by August 20th, compared to only 484 fires during the same period of the previous year. Although more than three times the acreage burned in 1944 than in 1943, smokejumpers made approximately 250 fire jumps on 70 fires in 1944 with only one minor injury. The largest fire of the season was a 3,500 acre fire near Plains at the end of July. It was fought by 350 men and women, including Forest Service truck drivers, Northern Pacific employees, farmers, ranchers, loggers, and millworkers.

The Forest Service continued to work on military projects as well. Thirty mechanics employed at the Forest Service shops in Missoula finished repair-

Normandy

- Lt. Col. Herbert F. Batcheller was a 1928 graduate of Great Falls High who commanded a parachute regiment that landed in Normandy (he had also jumped in Sicily). He was killed in action on June 12. He had been awarded the British Distinguished Service Order for his actions in Italy.
- Staff Sgt. A. "Bud" Olson landed in Normandy via airborne glider. He was awarded the Bronze Star after he located enemy gun positions during a patrol on June 21, 1944.
- Sgt. Jim V. Groom of Missoula was captured by the Germans shortly after he parachuted into Normandy on June 6. He was eventually released from a German POW camp by the Soviet Army.
- Col. Walter M. Johnson was a West Point graduate stationed at Fort Missoula during the 1930s, where he married a Missoula girl. At Normandy, he commanded the 117th Infantry Regiment of the 30th Division. His unit landed in France six days after D-Day. The 30th Division was in the forefront of the fighting from Normandy through France and Germany. Interviewed by the *Missoulian* in 1987, he had this to say of war, "No, it's not glamorous at all. It's uncomfortable and cold, or hot, and muddy, and bloody." He was awarded the Silver Star with three clusters, the Bronze Star with five clusters, the Legion of Merit, plus awards from Britain, France, and the Soviet Union. He was eventually promoted to brigadier general and moved back to Missoula after his retirement from the army in 1957.
- Staff Sgt. Rex Duncan of the Fourth Division won two Bronze Stars for saving lives and equipment after twice entering burning vehicles loaded with ammunition (on June 7, 1944 and July 10, 1944).
- Cpl. John O. Stout of Chinook, a medic with the Second Armored Division, was awarded the Bronze Star for his actions on August 8, 1944 at Mortain, Normandy, when he went forward to provide first aid and evacuate several wounded men.
- John R. Greene of Lewistown was posthumously awarded the Distinguished Service Cross for extraordinary heroism. He was killed in action in August 1944, while leading his platoon in an attack on German positions in the Normandy hedgerows.
- Capt. Dennis M. Keating of Glasgow, a chaplain, was awarded the Silver star. Despite severe shrapnel wounds, on Aug. 7, 1944 he continued to give last rites and administer first aid to wounded under fire in France.
- PFC Thomas L. O'Connor of Butte was awarded the Silver Star by Gen. Omar Bradley after destroying several German gun emplacements and saving two tank destroyers.
- Seven Montanans parachuted into France on June 6, 1944 with just one regiment of the 82nd Airborne.

Pacific

- 1st Lt. John D. Shytle Jr. of Shelby was with the 14th Air Force in China. He was a B-24 bombardier credited with sinking a Japanese cruiser.
- Lt. Norman V. Laurich of Kalispell was awarded the Distinguished Flying Cross and a commendation from Rear Admiral H.W. Hill for ground support while serving with the Seventh Air Force over Tinian.
- Aviation Chief Ordnanceman Don Vonada of Helena was a veteran of 17 engagements from Pearl Harbor to Saipan. He was a bombardier on raids against Wake and Marcus islands, was on the *USS Saratoga* when it was hit early in 1942 by a torpedo, was on the *USS Yorktown* when it was sunk, then on the *USS Hornet*. He held a Presidential Unit citation and a Bronze Star.
- Lt. Robert Nelson, a 1936 Great Falls High graduate and MIT student, was a flier on an aircraft carrier. On Feb. 17, 1944 he led a section of torpedo bombers on a night carrier mission, and scored a direct hit on a large Japanese ship, for which he was awarded the Distinguished Flying Cross. He was one of 35 fliers downed during an April raid on Truk lagoon. A float plane towed Nelson and 11 other fliers (from five downed planes) to the submarine *Tang*, which took all of the rescued airmen and the float plane pilot aboard. Later in the year, Nelson was the first pilot to spot the Japanese fleet in the Philippine Sea on June 20, 1944. The fleet was immediately attacked and the Japanese aircraft carrier *Hiyo* was sunk. Two Japanese carriers, a battleship, and a cruiser were damaged. Nelson was awarded a Silver Star for contacting the Japanese fleet. He also had a Presidential Unit Citation. After 18 months of combat and 11 campaign stars, Nelson was discharged in June 1945 and took a job with the Monarch Lumber Company in Great Falls.

ing the heavy equipment used to construct the Alaska Highway just in time to receive a shipment of military trucks and tractors damaged in the Southwest Pacific theater. In July 1944, a battalion of Air Force combat engineers built Horse Heaven airfield for the Forest Service in 14 days as part of a training exercise.

At the end of the summer, Regional Forester Evan W. Kelley announced his retirement. He had worked his way up from a forest guard in 1906, and had served as Regional Forester for the past 15 years. He had also served as director of the guayule rubber project in Salinas, California from February 1942 to July 1943. The Missoula Chamber of Commerce held a retirement luncheon in the Florence Hotel for Kelley, and presented him with a mule named "Queenie." P.D. Hanson, the former Region Five forester, replaced Kelley.

Lumber remained in critically short supply despite the fact that by June 1944, 278,000,000 board feet of timber had been cut on Region One land in the previous year, an 80 percent increase from 1943. Although the largest Region One timber sales in 1944 were in Idaho and Washington forests, the Beaverhead National Forest had sold 4,000,000 board feet of timber during the past year, while the Bitterroot National Forest planned a 4,000,000 board foot timber sale at Laird Creek. One of the largest trees cut out of the Bitterroot during the summer, or any other summer for that matter, was a 600-year-old Ponderosa pine with a stump diameter of 64 inches. In 1942, a 38,000,000 board feet timber sale of white pine was put up for sale on the Clearwater forest in Idaho, but in Montana one of the largest national forest timber sales during the war was the 7,000,000 board feet purchased by the Flathead Pulp and Paper Company of Polson. The Montana and Idaho Lumber Company bought more than 1,000,000 board feet from the Gallatin National Forest near Bozeman. This timber sold for $2.00 per thousand board feet (the company was also responsible for a $1.00 per thousand slash disposal fee). Region One forests brought in $500,000 worth of timber sale receipts in 1943, up $184,000 from 1942. The Forest Service turned over $142,934 of their receipts to state schools in lieu of property tax payments. They also returned $9,200 to Montana counties in 1943. By 1944 the harvest was again on the rise, and 320,057,000 board feet of timber were cut in the Region One forests.

In late May 1944, 175 union members (including 50 women) at the White Pine Sash mill in Missoula joined 35,000 lumber workers throughout the Northwest in a wildcat strike. Within a day this strike shut down several mills in the Bitterroot Valley, but the strike was called off on June 1. The U.S. Labor Department settled 64 other labor disputes in the state during the first six months of 1944.

The state of Montana took an early lead in the fifth war bond drive, and never looked back. Two Medal of Honor winners, Charles "Commando" Kelly and Lt. Ernest Childers, toured the state to promote bond sales. Gore Field workers donated $113,275 for war bonds, and the Cole Brothers Circus gave away free circus passes to war bond buyers. Montana became the first state in the nation to reach the fifth war bond quota of $41,000,000, then exceeded that amount by $478,317.

By early 1944 the war was costing U.S. taxpayers $250,000,000 per day. There were 7,700,000 Americans serving in the army and 3,600,000 in the Navy. Thirty thousand Montanans had entered the armed forces since the attack on Pearl Harbor, and this number included 567 women, 350 of whom had joined the WAVES during the past two years. On the other hand some 3,800 Montanans had been released from service, many because of wounds or disabilities. By May 1944, seven Glendive men were known to have died (six in domestic plane crashes) while serving with the military. A survey of ration card applications allowed a fairly accurate count of Montana's population. Petroleum County (Winnett) remained the smallest county in terms of population (880 in 1944), while both Deer Lodge and Cascade Counties had gained population. Overall, the state had lost 13 percent of its population since the 1940 census, and an estimated 75,000 people had left the state in the past four years.

Many of them had moved to the west coast, where 600 former Montanans worked at Boeing's B-29 plant at Renton. Another 6,000 worked in the Kaiser shipyards in Oregon. These former residents of the Treasure State held a Montana picnic and beauty contest in a Portland park on June 12, 1944.

In August, French and American troops, including the First Special Service Force, landed in Southern France. The Forcemen had spent the month of June recuperating from combat at Lake Albano Italy, where the Pope had his summer residence. Before the Forcemen left the idyllic resort, a shakedown inspection retrieved many of the Catholic Church's priceless relics, which the Canadian-American unit had "liberated." The Forcemen also lost the

Saipan And Guam

- Pharmacists Mate 1st Class Walter E. Dodd of Missoula was awarded the Bronze Star for helping the wounded on Saipan. He served with the Fourth Marine Division.
- Lt. John Case Younglove, Fourth Marine Division, was wounded by a bomb on Saipan and died on a hospital ship. He was awarded a Bronze Star (posthumous).
- Marine Sgt. Junior L. Mulcahy of Great Falls was awarded the Silver Star for his actions of June 26, 1944 on Saipan. A group of Marines was ambushed on the beach and pinned down for several hours by Japanese only 30 yards away. Mulcahy volunteered to go for help but was wounded in the head. He managed to worm past Japanese positions and finally reached a parked jeep, then drove to an airfield. He passed out soon after sending out a rescue party and was evacuated to Seattle with a bullet in the base of his brain.
- Pvt. John Sangray of Augusta was awarded the Silver Star for his actions on July 4, 1944 on Saipan. A veteran of 17 battles, including those for the Gilbert and Marshall Islands, he shot a Japanese but this gave away his position and two grenades fell in his hole. He batted one away and held his helmet over the other, saving his life and that of another man.
- Marine Gunnery Sgt. Bert R. Nave of Carbon County was awarded the Silver Star on Saipan. He also had the Presidential Unit Citation and was a veteran of Tinian and the Marshalls. On Saipan he was wounded and his tank disabled. He switched tanks, was wounded again, and switched to a third tank, then pressed home the attack.
- Cpl. Harold Rediske of Ryegate was awarded the Bronze Star for rescuing a wounded man on the edge of an 80-foot cliff at Saipan while under heavy machine gun fire.
- Marine Col. John A. Bemis of Belt was awarded the Legion of Merit by Major General Roy Geiger for his work as artillery commander of the 3rd Marine Amphibious Corps at Guam.
- 2nd Lt. William Lazetich of Anaconda and 2nd Lt. Paul M. Szakash of Missoula waded ashore with the first waves of Marines who landed on Guam. Both had played football for the University of Montana and had gone on to professional football careers. Lazetich played for the Cleveland Rams before taking a job as the coach of Havre High School. Szakash played for the Detroit Lions.
- Col. Charles I. Murray of Billings was a Marine veteran of World War I who held the Navy Cross and Distinguished Service Cross. He was awarded the Bronze Star on Guam.

July 1944

- July 1. Fire at Butte manganese plant causes $3,000 damage. State Capitol bond paid off after 46 years. A woman in Wilsall receives a card mailed by her father in White Sulphur Springs (50 miles from Wilsall) on May 14, 1914.
- July 3. Soviets capture Minsk. Air Base Bombers sweep three-game baseball series over Miles City.
- July 4. Murrill's Cocktail Lounge in Great Falls has entire liquor stock seized for allegedly giving a false report of stock on hand.
- July 5. An Augusta bar owner kills a drunk cowboy in self defense.
- July 9. Japanese resistance on Saipan ends.
- July 12. A Hesper woman murders her husband and infant son, then sets fire to the house and kills herself.
- July 13. Dinah Shore sprains ankle playing softball at Lincoln while honeymooning with actor George Montgomery.
- July 17. Hundreds are injured and more than 300 die in the explosion of two ammunition ships in San Francisco.
- July 18. Primary election. Japanese Prime Minister Tojo resigns.
- July 20. A bomb planted by a German officer explodes in Hitler's bunker but does not kill him.
- July 21. Marines land on Guam.
- July 23. Missoula Legion Juniors defeat Great Falls Legion baseball team 5-4.
- July 24. Marines land on Tinian. Gore Field Flyers baseball team defeats Bombers 12-3.
- July 25. Normandy breakout begins.
- July 26. Great Falls Air Base Bombers over Officers 6-5.
- July 31. Adm. Charles P. Cecil, formerly the captain of the *USS Helena*, is killed in a plane crash in Pacific. U.S. Fourth Armored Division takes Avranches.

University of Montana

The tree-lined campus in Missoula, (known as Montana State University at the time), was the scene of marching columns of military trainees during World War II. In the early spring of 1943 the first of 1,000 Army Air Force trainees of the 317th College Training Corps arrived in Missoula. These men were housed in the dormitories, which only had a capacity of 500 students. During the summer of 1944 the aviation cadets began leaving the University, but a new military program brought 17-year-olds enrolled in the ASTRP program to the campus.

The University's enrollment during the first year of the war was 1,618. The following year enrollment dropped 25 percent to 1,118. By the fall of 1943 the school had only 1,028 students (not counting the military trainees), 650 of whom were women. During the 1943-44 school year, 25 percent of the school's 109 faculty members were on leave, and 40 others were occupied in teaching aviation students. During the war years, Dean Stone, who had founded the University's Journalism School 30 years before, died at his home in Missoula. T.C. Spaulding, Dean of the forestry school, oversaw a ten-acre nursery for shelter belt trees on the north end of campus (where the Harry Adams Fieldhouse and River Bowl now sit). Two of Montana's more successful writers, J.K. Howard and Mildred Schemm taught writing during summer sessions, and the Masquers theater group produced "The Phoenix" an original play written by associate English professor Grant Redford. The University Library was designated an official War Information Center, and the 143 bells of the carillon housed in the bell tower of Main Hall commemorate the University students who gave their lives in defense of their country.

In April of 1944 Dr. Ernest Melby gave up trying to reform the University system and resigned as Chancellor of Higher Education. He did resume the UM presidency, however, and was also appointed executive officer of the state board of education, although the legislature passes a law prohibiting University presidents from serving in this position. Melby drew up a plan to revise the University system, but the legislature rejected his plan. He also co-authored a book entitled, *New Schools for A New Culture*. Even after he gave up his chancellor's position, Melby kept criticizing the legislature for not merging the six units of the University system. He told a Kiwanis Club in Great Falls that, "education seems to have more enemies in Montana than any other state."

Lewistown

Located in the geographic center of the state, the seat of Fergus County had a population of 5,358 in 1940. The county lost some 2,000 people during the first years of the war. E.R. Roehl served as mayor and was re-elected in 1945. Served by the Great Northern and the Milwaukee Road, Lewistown was a railroad and trading center. Agriculture and construction were also important industries, as was the state fish hatchery. Small oil deposits were found at the Cat Creek oil field east of Lewistown. Travelers found accommodation at the Calvert Hotel and the Fergus Hotel and Cafe. In March 1944 the Shing Hie Chinese restaurant was sold, and the longtime owner left the area. The *Lewistown Telegram* ceased publication during the war, as did many other small newspapers around the state. Lewistown recorded 8 inches of rain in June 1944. In 1945, the state's first Hutterite colony was established near Lewistown.

The Lewistown air base was established in 1943 as a satellite of the Great Falls air base. The military spent $5,220 to provide recreation facilities at the Lewistown Civic auditorium for men stationed there. Planes based in Lewistown were part of the 145th Squadron, 385th Bomb Group of the Second Air Force. Local officials estimated that at least 1,600 men of Fergus County served in the armed forces. One of the best known was Lt. Robert Welden, a P-51 pilot with 76 missions and six enemy planes to his credit. Lewistown resident Maynard Stapleton painted a blue stripe on his house every time Lieutenant Welden downed another Nazi plane. Stapleton's unusual method of recording the pilot's success made him the subject of an interview on the radio program "We The People" on May 27, 1944 in New York City. Another prominent flier from Lewistown was Lt. Col. Maurice Taber, a West Point graduate who piloted a B-25 in the China-Burma-India theater, where Taber was killed. Company K of the 163rd Infantry Regiment was comprised of Lewistown men when the Montana National Guard was activated in 1940. Of the Lewistown men in the company, three were killed in action, one died of illness, one died in an accident, nine were wounded, and all but two were discharged by September 1945. At least 41 Fergus County men lost their lives in the war, as did one woman, 2nd Lt. Evelyn M. Gerdrum.

man who had singlehandedly formed and trained the unit. General Frederick, who had led the Force since the early days at Helena, was promoted and assigned to command an airborne unit. In little more than a year, Frederick had been awarded eight Purple Hearts, the Distinguished Service Medal, the Legion of Merit with cluster, the Silver Star, the Bronze Star, the French Legion of Merit, the French Croix de Guerre, the Order of St. Charles of Monaco, and the Italian Victory Medal. One tough non-com said that "It was here that all Forcemen cried like babies, when we said goodbye to General Frederick."

Col. Edwin Walker took over as commander of the Force. Although he was an able military commander, after the war Walker became an outspoken supporter of extreme right-wing political causes. Walker gained a degree of notoriety after Lee Harvey Oswald fired a shot at him with the same rifle that was later used to assassinate President John F. Kennedy.

During the invasion of Southern France on August 15, 1944, the Forcemen assaulted two small islands, the Iles d'Hyeres, where the German garrison was holed up in Napoleonic forts. Although the Force took many casualties while capturing the forts, by the following day the islands were firmly under Allied control. According to local papers, the "Helena Trained, Worldwide Super Troopers Strike Fear Into Nazi's Hearts." A week after the initial landing in Southern France, the French Resistance revolted in Paris and General Leclerc's 2nd French Armored Division raced to liberate the French capital.

The Forcemen were transferred to the mainland, where they occupied the extreme right flank of the Seventh Army's advance along the French Riviera. The filthy, ragged Forcemen liberated the mansions of the rich and famous at Nice, Cannes, and Grasse. By the end of the month they were at Villeneuve-Loubet. This became known as the Champagne Campaign, and more than a dozen Forcemen went AWOL at this time and took up permanent residence along the Riviera. Still, the Force retained the character forged into it at Helena. A Canadian journalist traveling with them marveled, "I have seen them start marching with full packs under a broiling sun, trudge all afternoon along a dirty, dusty road, or throughout the forests of Southern France, in order to reach the starting line at nightfall so they could fight. I have seen them fight for 60 hours straight to capture a town, then still have enough energy left to help the townspeople celebrate their liberation in an all-day party before they moved forward again at night."

August 1944

- August 1. Helena rodeo starts. Resistance on Tinian ends.
- August 2. Miners field day in Butte.
- August 5. Miles City baseball team defeats Missoula Legion 6-0.
- August 7. 13th annual Northern Montana Fair opens to record attendance in Great Falls. U.S. Third Army races across Central France. Pilot dies when his A-20 crashes 14 miles from Great Falls.
- August 8. Woman taxi driver is beaten and robbed of $33 in Great Falls.
- August 10. Japanese resistance on Guam ends.
- August 13. Midland Empire Fair opens in Billings. Strike closes Pierce Packing Co. in Billings after the company hires a non-union carpenter. Pierce Packing sues union for $150,000 damages.
- August 14. Cole Brothers Circus puts on two shows in Great Falls.
- August 15. Three drown in Thompson River. Allied forces land in Southern France.
- August 18. Five year old Charlie Crocker of Great Falls is flown to St. Louis for emergency surgery to remove a tooth stuck in his bronchial passages.
- August 20. Bombers defeat Selects 10-2 to win the Great Falls-Air Force baseball league title.
- August 22. Thomas E. Carey, state treasurer, is found dead of an apparent heart attack in a Spokane hotel room.
- August 23. French resistance (FFI) takes control of Paris after a bitter fight with the Germans. Week-long Pierce Packing strike ends in Billings after the company fires the non-union carpenter whose hiring led to strike. Rumania accepts Soviet armistice terms.
- August 25. General Leclerc's 2nd French Armored Division enters Paris.
- August 29. Soviet and Polish authorities reveal the atrocities committed by the Nazis at Majdanek concentration camp, where 1.5 million people were murdered.
- August 31. Soviets capture Bucharest.

Cargo Ships

American shipyards turned out hundreds of Liberty ships, identical mass-produced cargo vessels intended to carry war supplies to American forces overseas. One of the Liberty ships was the *Robert E. Clarkson*, launched August 31, 1944, at Houston and named for a longtime Teton County extension agent who had lived in Chinook and Choteau. His name was submitted by 4-H clubs and staff members at Montana State College for his contribution to Montana agriculture. Liberty ships were also named after these prominent Montanans:

· *Marcus Daly*	· *Thomas J. Walsh*
· *James M. Clements*	· *Charles A. Broadwater*
· *Sidney Edgerton*	· *Charles M. Russell*
· *Anton M. Holter*	· *Granville Stuart*
· *James Fergus*	· *Conrad Kohrs*
· *Luther S. Kelly*	· *Thomas C. Power*
· *Joseph K. Toole*	· *Frederick Billings*
· *W.W. McCrackin*	· *Chief Joseph*
· *Chief Charlo*	· *Howard Gibson* (Union Mt.)

· *Sam V. Stewart*, named for former Governor and state supreme court justice, was launched January 3, 1944 in Portland. Forty Montanan's attended the ceremony.

· *Wesley E. Barrett*, named for a merchant marine from Great Falls killed June 23, 1942 when the oil tanker *USS Raleigh* was torpedoed in the Gulf of Mexico. It was launched February 18, 1945 in Panama City, Florida.

As time went on, the Liberty ships were replaced by a new design, called Victory ships, which were faster and capable of carrying more cargo. The *SS Great Falls Victory* was launched at Richmond, California, in July 1945. The *SS Billings Victory* was launched a month later. The *SS Loma Victory* was launched at Portland, as was the *SS Bozeman Victory*, which on December 10, 1944 was christened by Mrs. Earl Dahl, a gold star mother with two sons and a daughter still in the service. Many Montanans working in Portland attended the launching. Thirteen other transport and cargo ships were named for Montana counties, including Beaverhead, Broadwater, Custer, Dawson, Fallon, Fergus, Gallatin, Glacier, Missoula, Pondera, Richland, Sheridan, and Wheatland. The *USS Dawson*, a combat transport, was named for Dawson counties in Montana and three other states.

Southern France

· Staff Sgt. Milton Brown of Plentywood was a veteran of North Africa, Sicily, and Anzio, where he led every reconnaissance patrol of his unit. He located German positions and artillery and accurately plotted their positions, once staying two nights behind enemy lines. During the invasion of Southern France on August 15, 1944, near St. Tropez he charged five machine gun emplacements with a rifle and grenades. He killed one German and captured 11 others, demolished a radio and four machine guns. He was killed in action in Southern France on October 22, 1944, and was posthumously awarded the Distinguished Service Cross and Legion of Merit.

13

☞ Back To School ☜

Nearly 1,000 students registered at the University of Montana during the Fall of 1944, up 113 from the previous year. The registration figures did not count the 190 17-year-old ASTRP students training at the University of Montana. The University also offered 16-week war training courses in drafting and machine design. Five thousand trainees took these courses from 1939 to 1944.

In other education news during the fall of 1944, 90 additional V-12 candidates reported to Carroll College for training. These men were the fifth class of Navy men trained at Carroll. Navy training at the Montana School of Mines was being curtailed, and the school announced plans to resume course work for non-military students in November.

Montana athletics received a boost when 1st Lt. George Dahlberg returned to his prewar position as basketball coach at the University of Montana. For the past two years he had been in charge of the physical education program at Camp Lawton, Washington. Assistant Professor Charles F. Hertler, who had headed the air cadet physical education program on the campus, replaced W.E. "Doc" Schreiber as head of the University's Athletic Department. Schreiber, who had headed the department since 1918 and had been an instructor for 42 years, took a leave of absence for a quarter, then returned to teaching part-time.

The 1944 high school football season was again dominated by the Missoula Spartans. Coached by ninth-year coach Eddie Chinske, the reigning state champion Spartans scheduled several regular season games, but Anaconda and Butte Central both canceled. In their only regular season game, the Spartans defeated the Billings Broncs 20-0. During the state championships in October, Missoula crushed the Helena Bengals 49-0, then took on Billings again on a snow-covered field in the Garden City, where the Spartans defeated the Broncs 27-6 and took home their second consecutive state championship. Anaconda won the Class A championship by defeating Glasgow 11-0.

The annual meeting of the Montana Education Association emphasized postwar planning for schools. The state had 91,000 public school students in 1944, 3,200 of whom were Native Americans. Great Falls teachers won a pay hike of $150 per year, but many schools still faced a severe shortage of teachers. The state was still short 1,000 certified teachers by the opening of schools in September 1944. Schools in Choteau opened two weeks late so that students could help with the sugar beet harvest.

By mid-October 1944, 5,964 foreign laborers were picking beets in Montana. The 150,000 tons of beets harvested in the Chinook district were brought in by 110 Jamaicans, 500 prisoners of war, and 680 Mexicans. Besides the Jamaicans working in the Chinook area, there were 164 more who worked in Sidney, Glasgow, and Hardin. Indians from the Rocky Boys Reservation also helped with the beet harvest, as did 30 farmers from Oklahoma who were employed in Valley County. In general, the labor situation in the state's fields was the best it had been since the war began, in part because 2,400 prisoners of war helped with the harvest. Most were Germans, although 750 Italian prisoners worked in the Billings area. Four hundred German POWs were also sent to the Billings area, where the Italian prisoners were held at Billings Polytechnic (Rocky Mountain College) and German prisoners were held at the Great Western Sugar factory. Hardin received 375 German POWs, 350 went to Ballantine, 325 to Sidney, and 250 each were sent to Chinook, Glasgow, Forsyth, and Miles City. The prisoners of war were held at local fairgrounds and abandoned CCC camps. They were under armed guard at all times and only army personnel were allowed to communicate with them. Two American officers and 30 enlisted men were assigned to guard each contingent of 250 German prisoners. The sugar companies were responsible for erecting barbed wire fences, two guard posts, and six searchlights at each camp. Additional camps were planned for Malta, Harlem, and Conrad in 1945, even though most of the prisoners spent only a month working in the fields of Montana.

The 700 Mexicans employed in the Sidney area left the state in August for work in the Dakotas, but returned in time for the start of the beet harvest.

Approximately 700,000 tons of beets were harvested in 1944, up from 1943, but less than the

Me, Sammy Wong, Say:

Please No Put
Victoly Parade
Before Victoly!
War No Won Yet!

Must Continue Buy
War Bonds —
More War Bonds!

This Mandarin Cafe ad ran in the *Great Falls Tribune* during 1944. While calling for "victoly" over Japan, it also reinforced racial stereotypes of Asians.

And
Especially
BUY BONDS
NOW!

Sure thing Amelicans get enmy on run in Europe and enmy maybe give up any tam. But that one only half the war.

In Pacific ocean bigger war still must be fight and many more lives lost. What you doing for helping win final victoly in Pacific?

You must continue help support war by buy war stamps, also war bonds. Evely week, evely month, evely chance you get and evely cent you can spare.

Thisee idee not for get more business— just for get folks buy MORE BONDS!

ME—SAMMY WONG

MANDARIN CAFE

122 Central Avenue   Phone 8078

harvest in 1942, when sugar mania had gripped the country. In order to spur sugar production, the government promised farmers a $1.50 per ton increase in the price paid for sugar beets. For western Montana farmers in the American Crystal district, this meant a total price of $13.72 per ton. Sugar beet growers were also allowed an additional 25 pounds of unrationed sugar for their own use.

The government had imposed a production goal of 7,700,000 acres of cultivated farmland in Montana, and to help meet this, the supply of new farm machinery was doubled from the previous year. Although production of many crops was slightly lower than the record 1943 levels, the average Montana farmer in 1944 made almost $800 more than he had the previous year.

Only 200,000 acres of flax were harvested in 1944, substantially less than during the two previous years. The yield was only one-third of the record 1943 crop, and because of this shortfall the government quota for 1945 was doubled. A mill to process flax and mustard was planned for Great Falls, at an estimated cost of $100,000, and a new vegetable oil plant was planned for the Conrad area.

Flathead growers enjoyed a record cherry crop in 1944, and 30 tons of cherries were canned each day in Hamilton. The largest cherry crop in years brought in $250,000 to orchard owners, who sent gift boxes of Montana cherries to President Roosevelt and his running mate, Sen. Harry Truman. Montana also produced 400,000 bushels of apples, compared to 258,000 bushels the previous year. The Eddy's bakery in Helena, employing 70 people, turned out canned fruitcakes. An unusual crop, wild arnica, was harvested in the Stanford area in 1944. The arnica flowers were picked and shipped to Eastern pharmaceutical firms for use in arnicin, a medicine used to treat bruises.

Montana's farms yielded 297,000 bags of beans in 1944, down considerably from the previous year. The corn harvest was double the average, and 25,800,000 bushels of winter wheat, 43,000,000 bushels of spring wheat, and 15,800,000 bushels of oats were harvested in 1944.

A new cheese factory opened at Fairfield, which boosted the statewide production of cheese to almost 4,000,000 pounds (80 railcars) per year, most of which went directly to the military and into Lend-Lease shipments.

The Fort Missoula Detention Center, which had been transferred from the jurisdiction of the Immigration and Naturalization Service to the Army earlier in the year, became home to 2,000 medium-security disciplinary prisoners during the late summer of 1944. The prisoners were shipped to Missoula from Leavenworth, Kansas. Under the command of Alexander Weyand, the Army Detention Center had 535 Military Policemen and service personnel, compared to 62 civilian and border patrol guards at the previous camp.

The larger number of guards were obviously needed, since the army prisoners presented authorities in Missoula with far more problems than the Italian and Japanese prisoners who had been housed at Fort Missoula during previous years. Although the foreign internees had made few escape attempts, the American prisoners quickly demonstrated that the Fort Missoula facility was not totally secure. During the first week of October eight prisoners being held for desertion and for being absent without leave (AWOL) escaped from the camp, including one who was described as particularly dangerous. One of these escapees burglarized the nearby house of rancher David Maclay and got away with a considerable amount of cash. He was apprehended in Iowa six weeks later and given a six-year sentence for the escape and theft. On October 16, 1944, four more prisoners escaped in a hail of gunfire, although one was later recaptured at Dixon. Three days later a prisoner was killed, another wounded, and a third recaptured during an escape attempt. Ten prisoners escaped from Fort Missoula on November 27, although three were recaptured near Noxon on the Idaho border, and six were caught near Polson after a 90-mile-an-hour car chase in which police fired repeatedly at the fleeing car. The last escapee was captured in Missoula a few days later. At the request of irate citizens, a siren was installed at Fort Missoula to warn residents when an escape attempt was underway.

The siren didn't stop the escapes however, and three more men got away during the first week of December. They scaled the fence while guards fired at them. Two of these men were captured near Lolo, and the other one, who had escaped once before, was apprehended near St. Ignatius. Eight of the recaptured prisoners were sentenced to an average of 17 years behind bars.

Juvenile crime remained a big headache for law enforcement authorities. An explosion in Great Falls at 11:15 p.m. on September 8, 1944, rattled the entire city. Police soon arrested a 13-year-old ringleader

September 1944

- September 3. British troops enter Brussels, Dillon rodeo begins.
- September 4. Labor Day (not widely celebrated because of the war). Bombers defeat City Bar 7-4 to win the Great Falls-Army League playoff title.
- September 5. Great Falls schools open. Richey schoolhouse damaged by hail, forcing children to use the jail as a classroom.
- September 11. Joseph T. McGreever, former Bobcat football star, killed in action in France at age 26.
- September 14. Six hundred state firemen meet in Polson.
- September 15. U.S. forces land on Peleliu.
- September 17. Operation Market Garden begins as airborne troops are dropped on five bridges in Holland.
- September 18. First hard frost of season.
- September 20. Duck season begins. The William Clark Chalet in Butte, built in 1885 as the copper king's summer home, is destroyed by an electrical fire.
- September 22. One airman dies in crash of his light plane on Mt. Wright, near the Bob Marshall Wilderness.
- September 23. Surrounded British paratroopers fight desperately at Arnhem. Fire destroys several historic buildings in Zortman. Great Falls Bisons football team defeats Conrad 66-0.
- September 25. Surviving British paratroopers are evacuated from Arnhem.

Hardin

The city of Hardin is named for Texas cattleman S.H. Hardin. During the war years, Carl Rankin served as mayor, and he won re-election in 1945. Hardin (population 1,169 in 1940) is the seat of Big Horn County (population 10,384 in 1940), which is home to the two-and-a-half million acre Crow Reservation, inhabited by 2,100 Indians. The Crow Fair was held every August. Although coal and bentonite are found in the area, agriculture was by far the largest industry in the 1940s, especially the production of alfalfa, wheat, oats, and barley. The region also produced sugar beets, and the Holly Sugar Company opened a plant in Hardin in 1936. A number of men from Hardin distinguished themselves during the war, and at least 22 Big Horn County residents were killed in World War II.

The county was home to Thomas D. Campbell of the Campbell Farming Corporation, the largest wheat farmer in the world. Campbell, who had started out with the backing of J.P. Morgan, leased as much as 150,000 acres of the Crow reservation, and at one time operated 500 plows, 600 drills, and 32 combines. Campbell originally proposed to the War Department that the hundreds of thousands of Japanese on the West Coast be relocated to the interior in order to ensure cheap farm labor. He served as a colonel in the Air Force, and was stationed in Washington, D.C. He was instrumental in the invention of the incendiary bomb, for which he was awarded the Legion of Merit. In early 1944 he was sent to Italy to begin investigating Nazi atrocities. As late as the 1950s Campbell was considered the largest wheat farmer in the world, and at one time he taught Russian farmers his techniques of dry land farming.

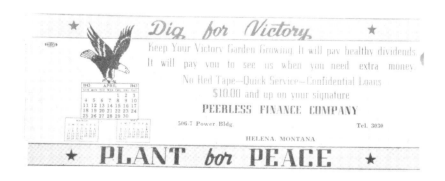

★ Dig for Victory ★

Keep Your Victory Garden Growing. It will pay healthy dividends.
It will pay you to see us when you need extra money.
No Red Tape—Quick Service—Confidential Loans
$10.00 and up on your signature

PEERLESS FINANCE COMPANY

506-7 Power Bldg.   Tel. 3030

HELENA, MONTANA

★ PLANT for PEACE ★

Europe, Ground War

- Lt. Col. G.D. Ellerson was awarded the Croix de Guerre with Gold Star by French General Juin. Ellerson was a 1935 graduate of West Point and the commander of a field artillery battalion in France.
- Capt. Russell C. Rockwell of Great Falls was awarded the Bronze Star for his actions as a traffic MP with the Third Army. He was responsible for keeping supplies moving to the front.
- 1st Lt. Dewey J. Sandell Jr. of Oilmont was awarded the Silver Star for his actions with the 117th Infantry Regiment in Germany. On October 8, 1944 he placed himself in an exposed position and directed artillery fire which broke up a German counterattack.
- Cpl. L.C. Briggs was awarded the Bronze Star for his actions in France on September 8, 1944. He zeroed in his field artillery battalion's guns while under heavy fire.
- Lt. Charles S. Baldwin Jr. was posthumously awarded the Bronze Star for his actions on October 13, 1944 while leading a 200-man patrol behind German lines at Aachen. Baldwin and all but two of his men were killed, but before his death Baldwin managed to radio the position of German artillery emplacements, which were knocked out by American guns. In July 1945 his parents were awarded his medal at a ceremony at the University of Montana attended by Dr. Ernest Melby and the rest of the faculty.
- Lt. Col. Horace N. Robbins of Chinook was awarded the Bronze Star for his command of the 126th Antiaircraft Battalion in England. His unit shot down 65 percent of the V-1 and V-2 weapons that passed overhead. By the time his unit relocated to Antwerp they were shooting down 97 percent of the V-weapons.
- Capt. C. Edgar Schenck of Great Falls was a paratrooper with the 82nd Airborne who was awarded the Presidential Unit Citation and a Bronze star for his actions during Operation Market Garden in Holland. He had previously jumped into Sicily, Salerno, and Normandy, and had been one of the first soldiers into Naples.
- Staff Sgt. George A. Boutilier of Great Falls was awarded the Bronze Star while serving with the Third Army. He was a tank crewman who was wounded in the stomach.
- Sgt. Wilmer Mahugh of Glasgow served with the 36th Infantry Division in France. He ran through a minefield under shellfire to help a wounded medic, then used the medic's supplies to aid five wounded men despite suffering from his own wounds. He was awarded the Silver Star.

October 1944

- October 2. Uprising in Warsaw ends after 68 days, 200,000 Poles are dead and much of the city is ruined. A staff sergeant of the 7th Ferrying Group is stabbed to death near Ft. Benton, suicide suspected.
- October 6. Butte High football team defeats Helena High 14-7.
- October 9. The St. Louis Cardinals defeat the St. Louis Browns 3-1 to win the World Series. Six charged with the murder of Frederick Kembel, a Billings man.
- October 11. Two German POWs escape from a farm near Hathaway.
- October 12. Carrier planes bomb Formosa.
- October 14. Billings Broncs defeat Great Falls Bisons 14-13.
- October 15. Soviets capture Riga.
- October 20. Senator and vice-presidential candidate Harry Truman speaks in Butte. U.S. troops land on the Philippine island of Leyte. Missoula Spartans defeat Billings Broncs 27-6.
- October 21. American troops capture Aachen.
- October 22. Battle of Leyte Gulf begins. The Japanese fleet is decisively defeated in the battle, which lasts for several days. Mt. School of Mines Navy football team defeats Great Falls Bombers 19-6.
- October 23. Two German POWs escape from the Sidney camp, one is believed to be wearing women's clothing after starring in a play.
- October 25. Soviet troops enter Norway.
- October 26. Montana Education Association meets in Helena.
- October 27. Navy Day.
- October 28. Prison inmates and Warm Spring patients help Forest Service put out a 90-acre fire near the Deer Lodge racetrack. Helena Bengals defeat Great Falls Bisons 27-7.
- October 29. Pheasant season opens. Marine "Devildogs" from Pocatello defeat East Base Bombers 19-6 in Great Falls.

and two 16-year-old boys who had set off 54 pounds of dynamite stolen from a hardware store and a highway construction site. The boys, who said they just wanted, "to hear the noise," were charged with violating the Federal Explosives Act. They received three years probation for the blast.

In another incident, three boys sentenced to the Miles City Industrial School overpowered their parole officer 28 miles east of Great Falls. The officer was shackled and thrown in the back seat, but he managed to pull his gun. He wounded one teenager in the chest and fired several times at another. The third boy escaped but later gave himself up.

Not all crimes were linked to juveniles, however. In September 1944, a soldier from the Great Falls Air Base pleaded not guilty in the armed robbery of a Belt tavern. In October two disgruntled employees at the Capitol Commission Company in Helena were arrested for trying to steal a company truck loaded with sugar. This led to the roundup of a black-market sugar ring and more arrests. The thieves were sentenced to two years in prison. A Butte man, Dominick Bracco, admitted killing his wife with an axe and was committed to the State Hospital at Warm Springs. Another Butte man, tavern owner James Lonzo Booth was arrested for the murder of James E. Clem on October 8, 1944. Booth claimed he acted in self-defense.

The United States manufactured 230,000 planes between 1940 and 1944. In the wide open spaces of Montana, the potential of postwar aviation was widely discussed, particularly among the 1,028 licensed pilots in the state, many of whom met at the Missoula meeting of the Montana Aviation Committee during the fall of 1944. During the war years, the state boasted 75 airports, 19 of which were suitable for large planes. A new airport was built at Livingston, and Great Falls was predicted to be a postwar air hub. Northwest Airlines, which already made stops in Billings and Great Falls, filed an application for an air route from Milwaukee to Seattle, with stops in Great Falls and Spokane. Northwest, which wanted to expand their Montana service to two flights per day, expressed interest in providing service to smaller communities like Havre, Cut Bank, Shelby and Kalispell, and also wanted to initiate a direct flight from Butte to Portland. A new charter airline, Arrow Aviation, opened for business in Great Falls, and on September 1, 1944, Western Airlines began flights to Alaska and Canada through Great Falls. The Air Force arctic training camp was moved from Colo-

rado to East Base, and the Air Transport Command began flying the new Douglas C-54 cargo planes into Great Falls.

Although the number of plane crashes had fallen sharply once most of the aviation trainees left the state, planes kept disappearing in the state's rugged terrain. In late September 1944, one airman was killed in a crash on Mt. Wright, northwest of Bynum. Another airman, A.E. Perkins, parachuted to safety on September 23, 1944, after his plane went down in the Little Belt Mountains. He spent five days walking before being rescued near Neihart. The body of his pilot was recovered in the wreckage of the plane a month later.

In October, two planes collided in the air over East Base. Both pilots were pulled from the flaming wreckage. One was a Chinese-American WASP, Hazel Ying Lee, who died from her injuries more than a month later. Just days after Lee's death, a WAC at Gore Field was seriously injured when she walked into the spinning propeller of a bomber.

Aircraft production reached such a peak that for the first time during the war, the military began disposing of surplus trainers. Sixty-five light airplanes, including Taylorcrafts, Aeroncas, and Fairchilds, went on sale at the Morrison Flying Service in Helena, with prices ranging from $1,800 to $8,000. The military also sold war planes to schools for educational purposes, as long as the school paid the freight and promised not to fly the planes. The Air Force asked $350 for B-17 bombers and $100 for P-40s.

Although rarely seen in the air, helicopters were much in the news. Less than a year after an experimental helicopter was demonstrated for the public in Washington, D.C., the Air Force opened its first school to train helicopter pilots. Intrigued by the possibilities of vertical air travel, Billings trucker Fred Cloud filed an application to use a helicopter to transport freight and passengers. His application was shelved when state agencies could not decide who had jurisdiction over helicopters.

At about the same time that the Army began selling surplus airplanes, the first surplus (and well-used) army jeeps showed up in Montana car dealerships. Many of the other items which had been in short supply for the past few years also reappeared in Montana stores. Rationing restrictions on inner tubes, canned vegetables and baby food were dropped, but there remained a severe shortage of children's clothes, work clothes, cigarettes and cigars.

Although food was becoming more plentiful in the stores, hunting remained an important source of meat for many Montanans. The 1944 state hunting season ran from October 15 to November 15. Hunters were required to show a valid hunting license before they could buy ammunition, although by the end of the year the government announced plans to lift restrictions on the sale of ammunition and civilian firearms. In the past year, 39 federal hunters had killed 65 bears, 226 bobcats, and more than 7,000 coyotes. A small bear was killed in a residential district of Butte and a wolf was shot near Helmville at the end of the year. The Montana fish and game department began planning the state's first ever official moose hunt, to be held in the Beartooths.

During the fall of 1944, a number of politicians toured the state seeking votes. F.F. Haynes of Forsyth ran against Congressman O'Connor, while Max Gallaso of Butte sought the congressional seat held by Mike Mansfield. President Roosevelt picked a new running mate during his campaign for an unprecedented fourth term. On October 20, 1944, vice-presidential candidate and Sen. Harry Truman spoke in the Democratic stronghold of Butte, where he publicly questioned the character of Republican presidential candidate Thomas Dewey. Truman also denounced isolationists. Senator Wheeler, who was vacationing at Lake McDonald, was insulted because he was not invited to the rally and because he took Truman's comments about isolationists personally. Wheeler held a grudge against Truman until the vice-president apologized to him for the speech he had given in Butte.

Thomas Dewey and his running mate, Gov. John Bricker of Ohio, also visited the Treasure State during the 1944 election. Dewey was in Billings on September 16, and Bricker made a five-city tour of the state on October 9.

The most interesting contest in Montana was the governor's race between incumbent Sam Ford and Leif Erickson. Erickson enjoyed the support of many influential Democrats, such as Great Falls mayor Ed Shields and Lester Loble, the recently appointed chairman of the state Democratic party. Erickson ran an aggressive campaign, blasting Ford for the actions of the state Liquor Board, and charging the governor with bungling a 1943 highway bill that was later declared unconstitutional by the state supreme court. George R. Niewoehner, a White Sulphur Springs lawyer, entered the fray when he charged

that records showed Erickson had attended Supreme Court hearings when he was actually in Chicago refereeing a railroad labor hearing. Niewoehner was eventually charged with contempt for trying to use the records of the Supreme Court for political purposes. Although he pled not guilty, he was found guilty of contempt by the Supreme Court and fined $250. He asked for an appeal and that his fine be repealed, but both requests were ultimately denied.

The Missouri Valley Authority was another hot issue during the 1944 gubernatorial campaign. Ford and the conservatives opposed the MVA bill, which Senator Murray had introduced. Senator Murray ran against Wellington Rankin, Montana's richest citizen. Murray urged reform of the nation's health care system, as well as the expansion of Social Security. He also supported more aid for the Yugoslavian partisan forces led by Marshal Tito. Montana's junior senator also co-sponsored the Murray-Truman-Kilgore bill to increase benefits for veterans. Although Murray easily won re-election, he thought the 1944 campaign was "the worst I have ever seen here." He charged the state Republican party with wrong-doing and demanded an investigation of their finances. He also accused the state's newspapers, particularly those owned by the Anaconda Copper Mining Company, with waging a "fascist campaign to confuse and deceive Montana's voters."

Feelings still ran high after the election, and a Wilsall man was charged with killing his brother over a $300 election bet. Voter turnout during the election was extremely high, with 83 percent of Montana's registered voters casting ballots, including 9,478 Montana servicemen. The election in Montana turned'out to be a ringing endorsement of the incumbent candidates. Mansfield, O'Connor, and Murray all retained their seats in Congress. President Roosevelt easily carried Montana, and Governor Ford had a margin of 25,000 votes over his challenger, Leif Erickson. Erickson applied for a Navy commission soon after losing the election, and in July 1945 he was elected President of a 10-state organization pushing for passage of the MVA bill.

Representative O'Connor, who served on the Indian Affairs Committee, spent a considerable amount of time working to improve the plight of Montana's Indians, including sponsoring legislation to give Indians the right to vote. Although most were not allowed to vote, approximately 18,000 Indians lived in Montana in the early 1940s. Most lived on

November 1944

- November 3. Snow closes Yellowstone Park. Two children die in a fire at the old hotel in Turner. Billings Broncs defeat Helena Bengals 35-6. Missoula Spartans take Big 5 title by defeating Butte 20-9.
- November 4. Wellington Rankin speaks on campaign issues during a radio speech on KFBB. Great Falls Bisons defeat Miles City Cowboys 81-0.
- November 5. Three children die and one is seriously burned in a Kalispell fire.
- November 7. Election day.
- November 11. Armistice day.
- November 12. German battleship Tirpitz sunk in Norwegian fiord.
- November 13. Snowstorm blankets the state. Armed robber takes $150 from a jewelry store in Billings.
- November 14. Transport plane from Great Falls crashes at Casper, Wyoming, killing 11. Fifty cases of smallpox are reported in Hamilton.
- November 16. Two elderly Butte women are killed after being struck by a car.
- November 17. A major allied offensive begins in Europe. Billings Broncs defeat Anaconda 22-20 in overtime. In their seventh straight victory, the Missoula Spartans defeat Lewiston, Idaho 31-0.
- November 18. U.S. troops enter Metz.
- November 20. Sixth war bond campaign opens.
- November 22. B-29s raid Nagasaki and Omura.
- November 23. Thanksgiving Day. A 7th Ferrying Group pilot dies in a crash near Miles City. Two planes collide over East Base, seriously injuring both pilots. One was a WASP who later died of her burns.
- November 24. U.S. Third Army captures bridges over Saar River.
- November 29. Home defense troops in British Columbia and Quebec are rumored to be mutinying over a government plan to draft them. B-29s raid Tokyo. Two freight trains collide at Roundup.

Italy

- Staff Sgt. John Whittle of New Deal, with the Third Division in Italy, was awarded the Bronze Star after he shoveled dirt on burning 105mm ammunition and prevented it from exploding.
- PFC Ivan E. Benick of Miles City was awarded the Bronze Star for keeping front-line troops supplied with ammunition in Italy.
- Pvt. Yoke Sagami, a Nisei who had relocated from the West Coast and worked in the Chinook beet fields, was killed in action while serving in Italy. (The Nisei units in Italy suffered very heavy casualties and won more decorations than any other comparable unit in the U.S. Army.)
- PFCs Hugh W. and Howard Neill, twin brothers from Windham, served as litter bearers with Fifth army in Italy. Hugh W. Neill was awarded the Bronze Star for his actions in September 1944 with the 91st Division. He led a squad of stretcher bearers under fire to evacuate wounded.
- Staff Sgt. Orris I. Galland of Outlook was a medic with the 788th Ordnance Company, 86th Division, Fifth Army, who was awarded the Bronze Star after caring for six wounded men during an air attack by six German planes at Fondi, Italy early in 1945.
- PFC Felix Necklace of Fort Kipp was a soldier with the 133rd Infantry Regiment in Italy who was awarded the Bronze Star for his actions on March 7, 1945, when he inspected 800 yards of telephone wire under heavy mortar and machine gun fire.

the state's seven reservations, although at least 2,200, mostly Chippewa and Cree, were landless Indians. Many of these Indians lived on Hill 57 in Great Falls while they sought a permanent home near Landusky. O'Connor's House committee investigated the Bureau of Indian Affairs and, not surprisingly, found that Indians had been badly treated. O'Connor urged better education for Native Americans, the reorganization of government Indian programs, and a speedier resolution of disputes. His committee traveled throughout Montana and two other states and held hearings on the many problems affecting Indian reservations. The committee met in Billings, Great Falls, Browning, Hardin, and Wolf Point. Representative Mansfield attended the meeting in Great Falls, where the major topic was the alleged discrimination against Indian children at Great Falls' Franklin school, where 42 Chippewa-Cree and mixed blood "landless" Indians were taught in the "Indian Room," the only segregated schoolroom in the state. Residents of the Rocky Boys and Fort Belknap reservations also complained of discrimination, as well as lack of medical care. The 1943 death rate on Indian reservations was more than three times the national average, and tuberculosis, alcoholism, and peyote use were all common on the reservations.

The previous summer had been a busy one for Montana's Indians. A three-day fast that included prayers for victory had been held at the Rocky Boys Reservation at the end of June 1944. The Blackfeet also held an encampment at Cut Bank just before the Fourth of July. At the same time, a four-day Sun Dance was held at the Crow Reservation near Hardin, and Indians from five of Montana's seven reservations were invited. The guests of honor included Sergeants Henry Old Coyote and Barney Old Coyote, both veterans of 50 combat missions with the Army Air Force. All seven of Montana's reservations sent representatives to a meeting at Blue Bay on Flathead Lake in 1945, where they formed an intertribal council called the American Indians of the State of Montana. They later held a two-day meeting in Great Falls, where they heard a talk on tuberculosis and discussed the rehabilitation of returning veterans. At the meeting, Indian tribal leaders again asked that the discriminatory liquor laws be repealed.

Some members of the Blackfeet tribe were particularly anxious to change the Wheeler-Howard Bill (also known as the Collier Act), sponsored by Senator Wheeler in the 1930s. Even Senator Wheeler admitted he didn't like the bill, and controversy over the bill led to a division on the Blackfeet Reservation between the tribal council and elders of the tribe. Five Blackfeet elders demanded that the tribal council be disbanded, and they traveled to Chicago to ask that a number of changes be made in the Wheeler-Howard law. They wanted the repeal of the discriminating Indian liquor laws, tribal handling of oil leases, more control over fish and game, establishment of a livestock association, establishment of a scholarship fund, and changes to tribal elections. They also wanted to remain wards of the government and to limit the tribal benefits to those who were at least one-sixteenth Indian.

In October, 500 volunteers canvassed the streets of Great Falls collecting money for that city's war chest drive, and by the end of the month the $91,000 goal was exceeded by more than $10,000. The sixth war bond drive was also underway, and by the third anniversary of Pearl Harbor, Montana became the first state in the nation to meet the quota. Missoula elementary school children alone bought $45,321 in war bonds during the 1944-45 school year. The Boeing Company presented the state with a model of a B-29 bomber for exceptional performance in the sixth war bond drive. Admiral Nimitz sent a letter to Cascade County thanking them for war bond sales. The first six counties (Prairie, Daniels, Judith Basin, Treasure, Teton, and Phillips) to exceed their war bond quotas were honored by the military and were allowed to name a B-29 Superfortress. Phillips county named their B-29 after Lt. Cmdr. Lee S. Pancake of Malta, who was the staff commander of destroyer squadrons in the Pacific and who was killed in action October 26, 1942 at the Battle of Santa Cruz. He was posthumously awarded the Navy Cross. Daniels County named their B-29 after Don Collins, a B-17 gunner who had been killed in action over the North Sea on February 3, 1944. Twenty-four Montana counties were eventually honored in this fashion, and one bomber was named for the "Cascade County Bisons."

On September 15, the First Marine Division landed on Peleliu in the Palau Islands, and soon encountered fierce Japanese resistance. A week after the initial landing U.S. Army soldiers were brought in to replace some of the Marines, who had taken very heavy casualties. More than a month passed before Peleliu and the nearby island of Angaur were secured.

By October, American soldiers had returned to

Native Americans

- The Cheyenne Reservation. 1,700 members of the Northern Cheyenne tribe lived on their reservation near Lame Deer during the 1940s. In December 1943, Frank Redcherries, a great grandson of tribal chief Little Wolf, became the first Cheyenne to be sent overseas. Tribal elders danced and chanted before he left.
- The Crow Reservation. Robert Yellowtail served as superintendent of Crow Agency from 1934 until his resignation in the mid-1940s. Barney Old Coyote, who enlisted immediately after Pearl Harbor and flew 50 combat missions in North Africa and Europe, had his story entered into the Congressional Record by Representative O'Connor.
- The Blackfeet Reservation. In terms of population, the Blackfeet were the most numerous of Montana's tribes, with nearly 5,000 members in 1940. They started a Remember Pearl Harbor Society to provide support for soldiers at the Cut Bank Air Base. In May 1945 the Interior Department provided $600,000 for construction of a tuberculosis hospital on the Reservation. In September 1944, a war memorial for 500 Blackfeet servicemen was unveiled in Browning by Governor Ford and Mrs. Robert Salois. At that time, four Blackfeet servicemen had been killed in the war.
- The Fort Belknap Reservation was populated by Assiniboine Sioux and Gros Ventre. A number of Fort Belknap men served with the 163rd Infantry Regiment. Other Fort Belknap servicemen included Pious Wing, killed in action at Normandy, and Daley Carrywater, killed in action in Italy.
- The Fort Peck Reservation. During the summer of 1942, many of the Assiniboine Sioux from Fort Peck and Fort Belknap traveled to a Sun Dance held at Pine Ridge, South Dakota to pray for the safe return of 2,000 Sioux in the armed forces. Approximately 400 members of the tribe served in the armed forces, and at least one, Alexander Dumarce, was killed in action.
- The Flathead Reservation. As early as the summer of 1942, 125 Salish, Kootenais, and Pend d' Oreille were serving in the armed forces, including PFC Louis Charlo, who helped raise the flag over Iwo Jima and who was killed on that island.
- The Rocky Boys Reservation was the smallest of Montana's reservations, and was home to less than a thousand Chippewa and Cree. In the summer of 1944 they held a three-day fast on the reservation to pray for victory in the war.

Air War, Europe

- Staff Sgt. Scott Warden of Great Falls was a ball-turret gunner in a heavy bomber. He was awarded the Distinguished Flying Cross, an Air Medal with 3 clusters and a Presidential Citation for the England-Russia shuttle bombing raid and 30 missions over Europe.
- Tech. Sgt. Henry Meyer of Geraldine was a flight engineer on a B-24. He was awarded the Distinguished Flying Cross for helping his pilot and co-pilot bring home a crippled bomber after a raid on Munich. Seven other crew members safely parachuted over Allied lines in Italy.
- Capt. Louis H. Norley of Conrad, who had served with the American Eagle Squadron of the Royal Air Force before American entry into the war, was a P-51 pilot who shot down a German ME 262 jet fighter over Europe.
- 1st Lt. Louis F. Jurgens of Great Falls was a 15th Air Force B-17 pilot. He was awarded the Distinguished Flying Cross for his actions on an October 25, 1944, raid on Pilsen, Czechoslovakia. His plane took two direct hits from flak, which knocked out one engine, the stabilizer, oxygen supply, and communications. Despite the damage, he flew the aircraft for four hours and landed with 10 minutes of fuel left.
- Maj. Charles H. Burton of Great Falls was an 8th Air Force B-17 pilot who was shot down and captured on September 27, 1944. He was held at Stalag Luft I for seven months before his release in May 1945.

the Philippines, and on the 26th of October, the Japanese fleet was decisively defeated in the three-day Battle of Leyte Gulf.

In England, Col. Hub Zemke's score in the air over Europe continued to rise. In the fall of 1944 he traded in his P-47 Thunderbolt for a new P-51 and soon was credited with 17 victories in the air and seven on the ground. He had also accumulated a Distinguished Service Cross, Silver Star, Distinguished Flying Cross with seven clusters and an Air Medal with three clusters. By mid-October, when another ace was reported missing, Zemke became the leading ace in Europe (his score was surpassed by Major George Preddy in late October). After 450 hours of combat and 154 missions, Zemke was due to become the Chief of Staff of the 65th Fighter Wing, but he managed to get in one last mission, on October 30, 1944. He was flying his last mission over Germany when his P-51 ran into turbulence and spun out of control. The right wing tore off and the plane disintegrated. Zemke was badly bruised but parachuted to safety. On the following day he was captured by German farmers. After being interrogated for several days, he was sent to a transit camp aboard a train. The man who was credited with destroying 50 locomotives found himself the victim of a strafing by American P-47s. Cannon shells ripped open the passenger car he was riding in, and a little German girl was killed and fell across his legs. Zemke helped rescue passengers until they realized he was an American, when they turned on him. A German lieutenant rescued him from the passengers, but as they were leaving the scene, the car he was in crashed. He was taken to a luxurious German hunting lodge where several German officers tried to convince him to lead a squadron against the Soviets. After he refused, he was put back on a train. At Hanover station he survived a raid by heavy American bombers. He was then sent to Stalag Luft I at Barth, Germany, where he was the highest ranking Allied officer.

While Zemke was cooling his heels behind barbed wire, his old outfit, the 56th Pursuit Group, toasted their former leader during their second anniversary celebration. In 400 missions the group had shot down 800 enemy planes and boasted 51 aces. One of Zemke's former subordinates was Captain Verne Hooker, of Great Falls, a P-38 and P-51 pilot with the Distinguished Flying Cross and 65 missions over Europe. The Missoula Jaycees awarded Zemke their distinguished service award,

and his wife and parents attended the ceremony, where a color film of his flying was shown.

Mrs. Sam Ford, wife of Montana's governor, helps out during a Red Cross fund-raising drive. MHS PAC 80-87

Peleliu

- Hospital Apprentice 2nd Class Russel Anson Maxfield of Fairfield was posthumously awarded the Navy Cross for his actions with the First Marine Division on Peleliu, where he aided many wounded under intense fire, before being killed in action on October 3, 1944.
- PFC Clarence O. Kelley of McAllister, First Marine Division, was a crew chief on an amphibious tractor who was awarded the Navy Cross for his actions at Peleliu.
- Cpl. Clifford C. Longacre of the First Marine Division was posthumously awarded the Silver Star for his actions on Peleliu, where he covered a night withdrawal by half tracks, then drove forward and engaged the Japanese in a firefight until he was killed.

Pacific

- .At least 20 Montanans served with the 7th Bombardment Group in the China-Burma-India theater.
- Cmdr. Justin A. Miller of Missoula piloted a Navy B-24 that was hit by anti-aircraft fire after it bombed and strafed a Japanese-held island on October 18, 1944. Three men were killed when the plane crashed 10 miles out to sea. Eight members of the crew made it back to the island safely, but on the following day another B-24 shot down a Japanese bomber, which crashed into their camp, killing one and injuring two. After scavenging food from the Japanese bomber, Miller and his co-pilot set out on a homemade raft on October 27, and made contact with Philippine guerrillas on November 2. They were eventually rescued by American forces after two months in Japanese held territory.
- Lt. Miller Hansen of Great Falls was awarded the Bronze Star after volunteering for underwater demolition and reconnaissance on Leyte. Under heavy fire, he spent two days before the invasion mapping many of the obstacles placed on Leyte beaches by the Japanese.
- Pvt. William Mooney of Butte was awarded the Silver Star for his actions in the South Pacific, where he rescued a wounded man under fire and destroyed radio equipment to keep it out of the hands of the Japanese.
- Lt. (j.g.) Arthur F. Doherty of Great Falls was a Helldiver pilot who was awarded the Distinguished Flying Cross for attacking a Japanese carrier and assisting in its destruction. Low on fuel, he ditched in the water.
- Capt. Harrington Harlow of Roundup flew the first reconnaissance mission over Waleai Island using 1828 navigation charts. He was awarded a second Distinguished Flying Cross.
- Cmdr. Peter H. Alexander of Butte won the Merchant Marine Medal of Honor for assisting an infantry division at Halmahera and Mroriki Islands.
- Lt. Stanley Johnson, who had been missing in action near New Britain for the past year, was posthumously awarded a Silver Star. His wife accepted his medal at a ceremony at Gore Field. Johnson also had been awarded the Distinguished Flying Cross and Air Medal.

Display windows at Fligelman's department store in Helena supported military recruiting drives and the seventh war bond campaign. MHS PAC 76-84

14

☞ Fire From The Sky ☜

On December 11, 1944, two western Montana loggers were cutting timber at Truman Creek, southwest of Kalispell, when they made an unusual discovery. They found the wreckage of a huge, cream-colored paper balloon, painted with a green rising sun and Japanese characters.

An alert newspaperman in Libby heard of their discovery and printed the news. Within days *Time* and *Newsweek* picked up on the story of this latest Japanese invasion threat, and the secret was out. The F.B.I. investigated the balloon found in western Montana, and revealed that similar balloons, which had been designed to carry incendiary bombs, had been found in California and Hawaii as early as November 1944. A news blackout was soon imposed and it wasn't until the end of the war when most Americans learned of the extent of the Japanese balloon bomb campaign. The balloons were made by Japanese schoolgirls, of either rice paper coated with paraffin or tightly laminated mulberry tissue paper, glued together with potato paste. The balloons were more than 30 feet in diameter, 70 feet high, and had a capacity of 18,000 cubic feet. They were capable of carrying 800 pounds of cargo, which normally consisted of ballast plus four small incendiary and one high explosive bombs. In the case of the Kalispell balloon, the bombs had already been dropped.

The balloons, designed to start devastating forest fires throughout the West, represented a desperate attempt by Japan to damage the U.S. economy. Six thousand of the balloons were launched from ships, submarines, and Japanese-held territory. Carried by the high-altitude jet stream, the balloons traveled as far as Michigan, Mexico, Canada, and Alaska, but only 342 were found in the U.S. Although the balloons were very ineffective in starting forest fires, they were not harmless. On May 5, 1945, a pregnant woman and five children were killed by a balloon bomb while they were on a fishing trip near Bly, Oregon. Other than this incident, the balloons caused only a few small fires and a minor power outage in Washington State. No damage was recorded by any of the balloons found in Montana. At least 35 balloons are known to have landed in Mon-

tana, but it is possible that many more balloons landed in remote areas of the state without being found. Balloon bombs were found near Lame Deer, Lodgegrass, Hardin, Riverdale, Cascade, Eden, Flathead Lake, Deer Lodge, Hays, Boyd, Laurel, Bernice, Hammond, Whitehall, Legg, Divide, Benchland, Harlowton, Broadus, Hammond, Coram, Nyack, Sula, Glen, Laurel, Bozeman, Dillon, Turner, Philipsburg, Loring, Dodson, Pryor, Boulder, Monida, and Babb. Five balloon bombs were found in Phillips County, and another balloon came down 18 miles from Great Falls. One enterprising Montana sheriff shot a Japanese balloon out of the sky with a rifle.

While the first balloon bombs were falling on Montana soil, the First Special Service Force, which had suffered a 600 percent turnover in personnel since its formation in Helena, was disbanded in December. The few remaining Canadians returned to their own army, and Brig. Gen. Edwin Walker took many of the Forcemen with him to his new command, the 474th Infantry Regiment, where, ironically, they were destined to be sent to Norway to take the surrender of German troops stationed there. Although some of the Forcemen finally made it to the place they had been trained to attack, and although they had distinguished themselves in every battle they fought in, the unit had never been used to its full potential. Canadian journalist Sholto Watt declared that, "It is no less than tragic that this North American corps d'elite could not have been employed in the lightning, staggering blow for which it had been trained." On December 5th, 1944, at Villeneuve-Loubet, France, the Force paraded in honor of their dead before their flags were furled and cased for the last time.

Just a few days later, the German Army launched their last great counteroffensive, the Battle of the Bulge. One of the many Montanans involved was 1st Lt. John Toole of Missoula, who served with the 15th Infantry Regiment of the Third Division. During the war the Third Division suffered 4,922 men killed in action, the highest death rate of any division in Europe. Forty men of the Third Division were awarded the Congressional Medal of Honor, includ-

Men of the 474th Infantry Regiment (Sep) unloading gold bullion and art treasures from 24 10-ton trucks, into the Reich Bank of Frankfurt, Germany. The horde, found a few days before in a Merkers salt mine, totaled one third of the entire German gold reserve, April 12, 1945. BOB DURKEE, HELENA

Col. Edwin A. Walker awarding the Bronze Star Medal for heroism to Master Sgt. Robert Durkee in Oslo, Norway. BOB DURKEE, HELENA

474th Infantry members in Nuremburg, Germany. The Infantry was composed of former FSSF members. BOB DURKEE, HELENA

HE SHARES
You can, too!

U. S. Navy Official Photo

MONTANA WAR FUND, INC.
Representing NATIONAL WAR FUND

NATIONAL WAR FUND
★ ★ ★
FOR OUR OWN – FOR OUR ALLIES

In the Strength of the Lord...

MONTANA WAR FUND

1945 Campaign Opens October 1

War Fund Sunday — September 30

Japanese fire balloons. FDR

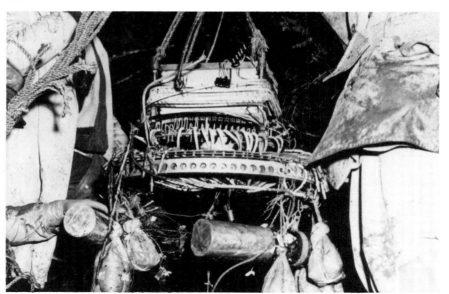

The Triple Nickels

Individual African-Americans had a hard time winning acceptance in the segregated Army of the 1940s, and black units had an even harder time. The 555th Parachute Infantry Regiment, better known as the "Triple Nickels," was one black unit that faced numerous hardships unknown to white regiments. Organized at Camp Mackall, North Carolina, late in 1944, the 555th immediately ran into trouble while trying to fill the ranks with qualified black officers and enlisted men. The 555th met resistance from Army brass at all levels, and the unit was never able to find enough qualified recruits. Therefore, it was considered unfit for combat and was never provided the equipment that was given to other Army airborne units. Had it not been for the discovery of Japanese balloon bombs in the American West, the 555th probably would have been disbanded without ever seeing action of any kind.

After the widely publicized discovery of a Japanese balloon bomb near Kalispell, Army officials sought out units that could be spared to fight fires. The 555th Parachute Infantry was chosen for the job, and the "Triple Nickels" was first sent to Oregon, where the Forest Service intensively trained the black soldiers. Besides fire-fighting, map-reading, and survival skills, the soldiers were taught to cordon off and disarm the balloon bombs. According to Lt. Col. Bradley Briggs of the 555th, "We blew up only those bombs that represented a danger. The bomb disposal unit would retrieve others for delivery to intelligence personnel."

The fire-fighting operation was dubbed "Operation Firefly," and during the summer of 1945 the 555th Parachute Infantry jumped 95 soldiers on three big fires in Montana. These fires were in the Bitterroot Mountains, Cabinet Mountains, and the Meadow Lake area. The "Triple Nickels" also fought fires in Oregon, Washington and California.

Other black soldiers served in Montana, including 600 African-Americans who were sent to Butte to work in the mines in 1942. Numerous blacks also served with the 464th Quartermaster Regiment at Fort Harrison and at the Great Falls Air Base.

Troopers line up for a practice jump. JESSIE MAYS VIA SMOKEJUMPER ARCHIVES

Top: Jumping on a fire. JESSIE MAYS VIA SMOKEJUMPER ARCHIVES

Bottom left: Loading supplies into a C-47 cargo plane to drop with the jumpers. JESSIE MAYS VIA SMOKEJUMPER ARCHIVES

Bottom right: Getting set to jump. JESSIE MAYS VIA SMOKEJUMPER ARCHIVES

December 1944

- December 2. Montana Grizzlies lose basketball game to Gore Field Flyers 49-43.
- December 3. Civil war erupts in Greece as royalists fight leftists.
- December 7. Montana Grizzly basketball team loses to Gonzaga 42-33.
- December 8. Montana Grizzly basketball team loses to a team from Ft. Wright (near Spokane), 43-38. School of Mines Navy trainees defeat Montana Bobcats 51-38.
- December 5. The Army Corps of Engineers takes control of Glasgow, Lewistown, and Cut Bank airfields, which have been declared surplus.
- December 9. Carroll College Navy trainees defeat East Base Bombers 63-32. School of Mines Navy trainees defeat Montana BobCats 56-41.
- December 15. U.S. Sixth Army invades Mindoro. East Base Bombers defeat Gore Field Flyers 61-42. A train wreck at Gold Creek kills one man and burns up a freight car full of cigarettes.
- December 16. German offensive begins in the Ardennes forest.
- December 17. Gore Field Flyers (hockey) team defeats Butte Copper Kings 6-4.
- December 21. Great Falls Bisons defeat Choteau High 44-22.
- December 22. 101st Airborne holds Bastogne against repeated German attacks.
- December 23. McBee Motor Company garage in Billings is destroyed by fire, $100,000-$150,000 damage. A man dies of a heart attack while helping move belongings from an apartment adjacent to the fire.
- December 24. Charlo butter and cheese factory is destroyed by fire, $25,000 damage.
- December 25. East Base Bombers defeat Gore Field Flyers 6-1 in hockey.
- December 26. Fourth Armored Division relieves 101st Airborne at Bastogne.
- December 27. Governor Ford is sworn into his second term.
- December 28. Bachelor Officers Quarters at Gore Field gutted by fire. Gore Field Flyers defeat Montana Bobcats 49-36.
- December 31. Organized Japanese opposition on Leyte ends. Longtime Missoula mailman Louis Brutto retires after 40 years on the job. Since 1918 he had walked an estimated 100,000 miles delivering the mail.

Third Division

- Lt. John Toole, wounded on Christmas Day, returned to duty with the Third Division on March 12. By April 18, 1945, his unit had reached Nürnberg, where Toole was hit in the arm but continued to lead his men throughout the day, at one point running 100 yards under fire along a railroad embankment. By nightfall his men occupied strong positions in the city, but Toole was badly wounded and the battalion surgeon sent him to the rear, then on to Rheims. He was awarded a second Silver Star. Of the 12 officers with Toole when he joined the Third Division, five were killed in action, six wounded, one taken prisoner. After the war the Third Division occupied Austria. Toole later published his wartime experiences under the title *"Battle Diary"*.
- Staff Sgt. Albert "Spud" Valacich of Black Eagle served 31 months in actual combat with the Third Division without suffering a scratch. He fought at Casablanca, Sicily, Salerno, Anzio, Cassino, Naples, Rome, and Southern France. He was awarded the Bronze Star, the French Croix de Guerre, and a Presidential Unit Citation.
- Sgt. Charles A. Pagenkopf of Hamilton also served with the 15th Infantry Regiment, Third Division. He was awarded the Bronze Star for his actions on December 26, 1944, when he delivered ammunition in a jeep over a mined road that was being shelled by point blank artillery fire.
- Capt. Robert L. Bangert of Great Falls also served with the Third Division, where he was awarded the Silver Star after directing an armored bulldozer to fill in an antitank ditch on the Siegfried Line while under heavy artillery, mortar, and machine gun fire for 45 minutes.

ing Toole's fellow company commander, Audie Murphy, the most decorated American soldier of the war. The Third Division made six amphibious landings and fought from Casablanca to Berchtesgaden, Germany. Toole landed at Utah Beach in September 1944, and in violation of orders, began keeping a diary of his experiences on V-mail forms. Eventually published as *Battle Diary*, Toole's account of the European war was written from the point of view of a man in the front lines of combat.

On Christmas Day 1944, near Benniwihr, France, Toole was wounded by a mortar. "All of a sudden something knocks me flat like I'd been hit with a baseball bat. A fraction of a second later I hear a mortar shell explode close to my rear. I know I'm hit and I am instantly jubilant. I run back about forty feet and fall in a hole." A medic and another man carried him to an aid station. "They put me down in a litter in a church, medic gives me a shot of morphine. I start to feel fine. I'm lying in a comfortable pool of warm blood. The roof of the church is burning and flaming pieces of wood crash down. I don't mind. I'm very happy." He was awarded the Silver Star, Bronze Star, and two Purple Hearts. Toole was also instrumental in the awarding of a Congressional Medal of Honor to Staff Sgt. Gus Kefurt, who had been killed in action at Benniwihr on the same day Toole was wounded. The Medal of Honor was awarded to Kefurt's widow in 1948.

Before being shipped overseas, John Toole was stationed at Fort Benning, Georgia where he had gone through officer's training school. After Toole's graduation, he was allowed to return to Missoula on leave. As he was leaving Fort Benning, Col. Walter M. Johnson gave Toole $5.00 to place flowers on his mother's grave at St. Mary's cemetery in Missoula. In Europe, Colonel Johnson commanded the 117th Regiment of the 30th Division in Belgium. His unit landed in France in June 1944 and then captured Maastricht on the Belgium-German border. They participated in nine other battles, including breaching the Siegfried Line along the German border. Johnson was awarded two Silver Stars and the Bronze Star. His first Silver Star was awarded for Mortain, where he was trapped in a French farmhouse for two weeks during fierce fighting. By the end of April 1945, Colonel Johnson was given complete administrative control over the 400,000 residents of Magdeburg, Germany. He joked that he was mayor, city council and police chief rolled into one.

As the fighting continued in the snow of the Ardennes Forest, an emergency call went out for trained sled dogs and search dogs. The Army shipped 109 dogs and 27 men, all of whom had trained at Rimini, to aid the American soldiers bogged down in the cold and snow at the Battle of the Bulge. The dogs were particularly useful in rescuing wounded men from the deep snow.

While Montana infantrymen pushed closer to the German border, at home, it was the holiday season. Lincoln County shipped 283 rail cars full of Christmas trees. The Billings women's auxiliary of the American Legion collected Christmas gifts for veterans at the VA hospital at Fort Harrison, while Glendive women provided 400 boxes of cookies and other gifts for servicemen aboard troop trains passing through town. Children benefitted from the better quality of toys available in 1945. The holiday itself was extremely cold over much of the state, with Butte recording a temperature of minus 34 degrees.

The holiday season had little effect on crime, however. In December, a Billings woman who had been married just one day was charged with stabbing her husband to death. Just before Christmas the partially nude and frozen body of 14-year-old Mary Jane Bird Rattler was found at a gravel pit near Browning. Seventeen-year-old Michael Weasel Head was arrested and pled guilty to voluntary manslaughter in the case. Since alcohol was deemed to be a contributing factor, the boy's uncle was convicted of providing alcohol to minors. One of the more spectacular murder trials of the winter took place in Billings in February 1945. Wyoming rancher Henry Goodman and several of his relatives were tried for the murder of Frederick Kembel, who had been killed in October 1944 at a sugar beet dump near Billings. According to Kembel's mother, she found her son beaten almost unconscious. As he stumbled to his feet Goodman shot him with a rifle. Goodman claimed he had acted in self-defense. At one point the courtroom had to be cleared of all spectators because the crush of people was cracking ceilings in the room downstairs. Judge Harwood eventually dropped most of the murder charges against Goodman and his relatives because of evidence that Kembel's 14-year-old brother may have fired the fatal shot.

In late February 1945, Forest Service law enforcement agents aided by pilot Dick Johnson of Missoula captured a 44-year-old man wanted for selective-service violations and for pilfering dozens of Forest Service lookouts, cabins and private homes.

Europe

- Cpl. John C. Haschke of Choteau was awarded the Bronze Star for his actions from November 29, 1944 to December 2, 1944. A member of the 102nd Division, Haschke repeatedly exposed himself to danger in order to maintain contact between two units.
- Tech. 5th Class Charles A. Belinak of Klein was awarded the Silver Star for his actions with the 143rd Infantry Regiment in France. Along with his company commander, he crossed a river into German-held territory. His superior was killed but Belinak remained and guided over other troops under fire until he was ordered to the rear. On the way to the rear he repaired a broken pontoon bridge and then carried two wounded men across the bridge to safety.
- PFC Hugh Butler of Helena was under fire in Europe when word came that he had received a Congressional appointment to the U.S. Military Academy at West Point.
- Lt. Raymond J. Albano of Heron killed 82 Germans and captured 31 others while serving with the 95th Division in Europe.
- 2nd Lt. James H. Dickson of Bozeman was a former student at Montana State College who continued to lead his platoon of the 94th Division in the capture of an assigned objective despite being wounded. He was awarded the French Croix de Guerre.
- Maj. Gen. Frank Milburn, the former coach of the University of Montana football team, commanded the U.S. 21st Corps in the battle of the Colmar pocket.
- Pvt. Charles Bartlett of Belton knocked out a German self-propelled gun by running in front of it and tossing a grenade into a open hatch. He then captured 43 Germans with an empty gun.
- Lt. Col. LeRoy Anderson of Conrad was awarded the Silver Star for commanding a tank battalion in Europe. He had already won a Bronze Star for his actions in France and Belgium. After the war Anderson remained in the Army Reserve and was promoted to general. He served in the state legislature for 10 years, then served two terms as congressman from the Eastern District of Montana. In May 1990 the building housing the headquarters and museum of the 81st Tank Battalion at Fort Knox, Kentucky was named Anderson Hall in his honor. Anderson passed away in 1991 at age 85.

Battle of the Bulge

- Catholic chaplain John Sheehan of Butte was awarded the Silver Star for saving the lives of two men when they were cut off at Bastogne.
- Sgt. Jack Galt of Great Falls was awarded the Bronze Star for heroic achievement during the siege of Bastogne. He was in the medical detachment with the 101st Airborne. He drove a jeep through heavy mortar, machine gun and artillery fire which killed his companion and damaged his jeep, but he managed to evacuate a number of wounded, repeatedly exposing himself to danger.
- Lt. Col. R.V. Bottomly Jr. of Great Falls, the son of Montana's attorney general, was awarded the Silver Star and the Bronze Star for his actions on January 3, 1945 at Bastogne with the 101st Airborne. He was a veteran of Normandy and Arnhem.
- Capt. Marvin H. Adams, a chaplain from Valier, was awarded the Bronze Star for his actions from December 24, 1944 to February 23, 1945 in France and Belgium during the Battle of the Bulge. "His efforts and tireless work contributed immeasurably towards the successes of his battalion and merits commendation of a high order."
- Staff Sgt. G. Roger Lund of Sunburst was awarded the Bronze Star for his actions during the Battle of the Bulge, where as a member of the 194th Glider Infantry, 17th Airborne Division, he hopped on an abandoned jeep and drove supplies to the front under heavy fire, then evacuated several wounded men. He was killed in action in Germany on March 28, 1945.
- Maj. Thomas J. Brennan of Havre, a former trainmaster for the Great Northern, commanded the 732nd Railway Operating Battalion, which contained several other Montana railroad men. They were commended for their work with the Third Army during the siege of Bastogne.
- Col. James H. O'Neill was the former vice president of Carroll College. He served as the chaplain of the Third Army. In December 1944, Gen. George Patton told O'Neill he was sick of seeing his soldiers fighting mud and floods as well as Germans. Patton asked O'Neill to write a prayer asking for good weather. O'Neill replied, "It isn't the customary thing among men of my profession to pray for clear weather to kill our fellow man." Patton insisted however, and O'Neill wrote a prayer, which was copied and distributed to 300,000 soldiers. On December 23, the weather cleared for six days, and a grateful General Patton awarded O'Neill the Bronze Star.

Before his capture, the man, who had been eluding authorities along the Idaho-Montana border for years, had pulled all of his teeth with a wire because of severe decay.

Pilot Dick Johnson was the brother of legendary mountain pilot Bob Johnson. Dick Johnson graduated from the University of Montana in 1917, and had spent 20 months overseas during World War I. He learned to fly from his brother Bob and obtained his commercial license in 1930. In 1935 he landed between sheer canyon walls to rescue a sick Forest Service employee stranded on a sand bar in the Salmon River. Just a few days after helping the Forest Service capture the fugitive, fifty-five-year-old Dick Johnson was piloting two other men engaged in an aerial census of elk in the Teton Mountains of Wyoming when his plane crashed, killing Johnson and one other man. The man who survived the crash tried to walk out, but passed out in the snow, where he was found by two rescuers.

In December 1944, the University of Montana lost a former president, Dr. Clyde Duniway, who died in California at age 78. He was an author of a biography on Daniel Webster, and served as the University's president from 1908-1913. Duniway Hall on the east end of the campus honors the former President.

The Montana Grizzlies played 20 basketball games during the 1944-45 season, including games against the Gore Field Flyers and the Carroll College Navy trainees (which the Grizzlies lost 57-43). By January, three of coach George "Jiggs" Dahlberg's players had enlisted and another had been injured. Dahlberg was forced to fill out his squad using University students who were enrolled in Physical Education. Dahlberg announced that 90 percent (133 of 147) University athletes who had participated in football, basketball, and track between 1937 and 1943 were serving in the armed forces. The team received another blow when long-time trainer Naseby Rhinehart left the University to work in a war plant in Seattle. Rhinehart was a 1935 graduate of the University who had won the Grizzly cup plus nine letters (the maximum possible) in football, basketball, and track. After the war Rhinehart returned to the University and continued to train generations of Grizzly athletes until his retirement in 1982.

At Montana State College in Bozeman, John "Brick" Breeden encountered the same sort of problems that his rival coach experienced in Missoula. Breeden started the season with 26 men, but 11 either enlisted or were drafted by the end of the season, and his team got off to a rocky start, losing their first four games. By early March the Bobcats had a record of nine wins and 13 losses.

In other basketball news, Billings Polytechnic resumed the sport after a one year hiatus, and a plan was proposed to reorganize the state's athletic conferences. The 31st annual state high school basketball championship was held in Billings, where the Helena Bengals defeated Dillon High 53-23 and took the state Class A championship, while Columbus won the Class B title. The Bengals then defeated Columbus 43-33 and were crowned the state champions.

Eleven thousand farms in the state, one in every four, had central electricity by early 1945. Residents of Toole County received public electricity for the first time in mid-February, thanks to the Rural Electrification Administration (REA). In the spring of 1945 the Federal Power Commission ordered the Montana Power Company to make accounting changes that cost the Anaconda subsidiary an estimated $51,000,000.

In other business news the Grand Hotel in Great Falls was sold to a Minneapolis firm, and the all-powerful War Production Board (WPB) approved the construction of the top two stories of the Northern Hotel in Billings. Upon completion, the Northern became the largest hotel between Seattle and Minneapolis. Gas tax receipts in the state were up 11.12 percent from the year before but still down 8.8 percent from 1942 levels. Canned goods and meat were once again put on the list of rationed goods, and the WPB ordered the size of bath towels shortened to save fabrics. Montana stores had a hard time stocking candy and cigarettes, and Senator Wheeler promised to investigate the shortages.

Rep. Mike Mansfield embarked on another six-week visit to Burma and Chungking, China as a special emissary of the President. He paused in Missoula long enough to tell University students that the Pacific war was, "not half over." Upon his return, Mansfield prepared a full report for President Roosevelt, portions of which were revealed in his January 23, 1945 address before the Montana House. Mansfield thought the situation in China had improved since his last visit, and he praised the appointments of Maj. Gen. Albert Wedemeyer, commander of all American forces in China, and Patrick Hurley, the new ambassador to China, as "excellent choices."

The Western Front

- Staff Sgt. Melvin R. Blatter of Chinook was awarded the Bronze Star for his actions on February 3, 1944 when he covered his company withdrawal under fire in France. He was killed in action on April 5, 1945 in Germany.
- Sgt. Harry Carpenter of Great Falls was awarded the Silver Star for his actions in France. In January 1945 he destroyed a German machine gun nest and killed five SS stormtroopers. On February 9, while attempting to rescued a friend who had stepped on a mine, Carpenter also stepped on a mine, which blew off his right leg below the knee and killed the wounded man.
- Col. Norman C. Caum was awarded the Legion of Merit after leading his regiment (242nd Regiment, 42nd Division, Seventh Army) against German resistance in Alsace, January 1945. He also saw combat on the Siegfried Line and east of the Rhine. He was awarded the Bronze Star with cluster for his actions between the 15th and 19th of April, 1945 in an attack on Furth, Germany.
- Capt. Marvin A. Adams of Valier was the chaplain of the 290th Infantry Regiment, 75th Division. He had already been awarded the Bronze Star when he won the Silver Star for his actions on January 18, 1945 in Belgium. He led a litter squad through enemy lines and supervised the evacuation of 25 wounded men under fire.
- Bert Armstrong of Glasgow was 50 yards ahead of his platoon when he killed one German and captured 16 more in Belgium in January 1945. He then led his platoon to their objective. He was promoted to sergeant and awarded the Silver Star. His brother, Maj. Byron Armstrong served with the 163rd Infantry in New Guinea.
- Maj. John Harrison of Harlowton served with the 7th Corps at Normandy, and was awarded the French Croix de Guerre and the Bronze Star for his part in the battle of Aachen.
- Capt. Harry Turney-High of Missoula, a former anthropology professor at the University of Montana, commanded the British-American bodyguard that protected Dutch Queen Wilhelmina on her nine-day tour of liberated Holland. Queen Wilhelmina had left the country in May 1940 as German tanks swept across Holland. She praised Turney-High for his cooperation during her tour.
- Sgt. Steve Fischer of Great Falls was an Army chauffeur who drove Dutch Queen Wilhelmina on her nine-day tour of liberated Holland. He had previously served as driver for British Prime Minister Winston Churchill, and generals Eisenhower and Marshall.

January 1945

- January 1. Two new state supreme court justices are sworn into office. Great Falls Selects defeat Gore Field Flyers (hockey) 12-6.
- January 3. U.S. Navy carrier aircraft bomb Formosa and the Ryukyu Islands. Bobcats defeat Utah Agriculture College 42-41.
- January 4. Congress authorizes $42,000,000 for the construction of Hungry Horse dam.
- January 5. Two Nisei working at Essex for the Great Northern Railroad are arrested in Kalispell for impersonating FBI agents.
- January 6. A prisoner escapes from Fort Missoula. Great Falls Bisons defeat Billings Broncs 55-29. Missoula Spartans defeat Bozeman High 76-35.
- January 8. Margaret Park in Great Falls is renamed Charles M. Russell Park.
- January 9. U.S. Army begins landing at Lingayen Gulf on Luzon. A Gore Field pilot dies in crash in Yukon.
- January 10. Another Fort Missoula prisoner escapes.
- January 12. Major Soviet offensive begins on the Eastern front. Civilian ammunition sales are again halted. Havre High defeats Great Falls Bisons 42-26.
- January 14. Rep. James O'Connor dies in Washington D.C. of a sudden heart attack at age 66.
- January 16. Vandals break 100 windows at Lowell School in Great Falls.
- January 18. Meatless Tuesdays are again reinstated, as is butter rationing. Great Falls Bisons defeat Butte 50-38.
- January 20. Rep. James O'Connor is buried in Livingston. Gore Field Flyers over Navy Miners 46-41.
- January 21. Hungary declares war on Germany.
- January 22. Chinese forces clear the Ledo road, opening a land route to China.
- January 25. U.S. troops take Clark Field in the Philippines. FBI agents arrest three Butte men suspected of operating a major auto-theft ring. Contraband tires, tubes and tools are also seized.
- January 30. The Eager Company store in Winnett, the largest business in Petroleum County, is destroyed by fire.

Mansfield's trip to the Far East was, at least temporarily, his last venture into foreign affairs. Upon his return to the United States he learned of the death of his colleague in the House, Rep. James O'Connor of Livingston, who at age 66 had suffered a fatal heart attack in Washington, D.C. A friend and ally of Sen. Burton K. Wheeler, O'Connor had served in the U.S. House since 1937. The death of O'Connor left openings in several House committees vital to Montana (flood, irrigation, Indian affairs, public lands, and territories) and Representative Mansfield resigned from the House Foreign Affairs Committee in order to take over O'Connor's five committee assignments.

In quick succession, several other Montana politicians also passed away. Perhaps the most shocking was the death of Howard K. Hazelbaker, a former state senator who had run for Secretary of State in 1944 and for Congress against Mike Mansfield in 1942. Age 37 at the time of his death in January 1945, he was a University journalism professor and secretary of the Montana Press Association. He had been ill for several weeks before passing away in Missoula. In February, state Sen. Thomas E. Gilbert of Dillon died of a heart attack, and in March, former Montana governor Elmer W. Holt, a Miles City native, died in Seattle. As Senate President, Holt had succeeded to the governor's office in 1935 after Gov. Frank H. Cooney died, and he served out the remainder of Cooney's term.

As the 29th State Legislature convened in Helena, Republicans controlled both houses by wide margins, and George W. O'Connor was elected Speaker of the Montana House.

One of the legislature's chief concerns was the condition of state institutions, particularly the State Hospital at Warm Springs. Besides the criminally insane, the nearly 2,000 patients at Warm Springs included those suffering from cancer, (40 to 50 cancer cases who received no treatment), tuberculosis (12 to 15 patients who were usually segregated from the others), and epilepsy (150 patients). Jack Toole, a state legislator who visited the hospital, found it to be overcrowded, filthy, and a fire trap. He reported to the legislature that, "In the room... where the food is brought from the kitchen and hence dispensed to the eating tables, the odor of sewage and dampness was so obnoxious as to be nauseating to me, who was just walking through the place." Guards at Warm Springs were paid from $65 to $85 per month and according to Toole, "one of the problems of the institution is to prevent as much as they can the guards from physically abusing the patients."

One of the proposals before the 1945 legislature was to move the State Hospital from Warm Springs to a location with more room for agricultural land. Another bill proposed to close the Western Montana Normal College at Dillon and transfer some of the patients from Warm Springs there. This bill was killed in the House. Republicans voted down a proposal by Governor Ford to appoint two committees to investigate conditions at the state institutions and the University system.

The Senate passed a bill to put the state back on standard time but it was vetoed by Governor Ford. The legislature finally ratified the Yellowstone River Compact with North Dakota and Wyoming. They also increased the University system budget by $600,000 per year, approved $4,500,000 for postwar construction, passed a bill calling for Alaska statehood, and killed measures to legalize gambling and impose a tax moratorium. Governor Ford won a victory when the state Supreme Court overturned a decision by Attorney General Bottomly and ruled that the legislature could spend the state's $5,000,000 in surplus funds for postwar work.

The Montana legislature also voted to oppose Senator Murray's MVA bill. The MVA bill was the major topic at a meeting of the State Reclamation Association in Helena, where publisher O.S. Warden and Wesley D'Ewart pushed through a resolution opposing the Missouri Valley Authority. They also called for a continuation of the policy where Montana water projects came under the control of the Army Corps of Engineers and the Reclamation Bureau. Despite this setback, a group of supporters of the MVA bill also met in Helena and formed an organization to promote Senator Murray's bill. Senator Murray called the opponents of his bill, "seekers of special privilege," and contended the Missouri Valley Authority would eliminate squabbles between the Army Corps of Engineers and the Bureau of Reclamation. The MVA controversy continued for more than another year, and a number of hearings were held in the 10 states affected by the bill. Several organizations were formed to lobby in support of or against the MVA bill, which was eventually defeated, despite the support of President Truman.

The Republican-controlled Montana Senate passed a bill to elect Congressman O'Connor's successor by a convention of city delegates rather than

Rimini

The Army's War Dog Reception Training Center was established in the CCC camp at Camp Rimini, near the Continental Divide west of Helena, in October 1942. Run by the Army Quartermaster Corps, the camp was at first intended to train dogs for the First Special Service Force, stationed at nearby Fort Harrison, and for their planned mission to Norway (Project Plough). The buildings at the camp were remodeled, and new ones were built. The camp eventually had four barracks, a messhall, headquarters, veterinary office, and a slaughterhouse where broken-down horses were killed to feed the dogs. At first the dogs were quartered in wooden crates which had contained space heaters sent to Fort Harrison. Better dog kennels were later built.

The camp was commanded by Maj. E.J. Purfield of the Quartermaster Corps, and was usually staffed by seven to nine officers and 120 men, many of whom were novices being trained to handle sled dogs. Some of the dog trainers were veterans of Admiral Byrd's expeditions to the Antarctic. The man responsible for purchasing many of the dogs was Eddie Barbeau, a Minnesota trapper of Ojibway descent, who stayed in Helena after the war and was considered a leader of Helena's Native American community when he passed away in 1994. Although some of the dogs at Rimini came from the Dogs for Defense program, Barbeau actively sought out trained sled and pack dogs and bought them from their owners. Siberian Huskies, Alaska Malamutes, and Eskimo dogs made the best sled dogs, while St. Bernards and other large breeds were used as pack animals. The experiments with pack animals were unsatisfactory, as most of the dogs had trouble carrying anything more than an adequate supply of dog food, and this part of the program was phased out after 150 dogs had been trained. None of these dogs was actually used in combat. Once Project Plough was canceled, emphasis at the camp shifted to providing sled and rescue dogs to the Arctic Search Rescue Units of the Air Transport Command. The sled teams were stationed at intermediate points along the air route from Great Falls to Alaska in order to cut the rescue time if a pilot went down in the inhospitable terrain. Dogs trained at Rimini were used in Alaska, Canada, Maine, Labrador, Greenland, and Newfoundland. At least 1,000 dogs were trained at Rimini. Workers at Rimini also researched, designed and built a number of new types of dog sleds. The camp was closed in March 1944, and 250 dogs were sent to Fort Robinson, Nebraska. The remaining dogs were returned to their owners or sold. The buildings at Camp Rimini were sold in early 1945 and few remain. A Boy Scout camp now occupies the site.

Navy

· Lt. Samuel G. Parsons of Great Falls was awarded the Distinguished Flying Cross by the Commander in Chief of Atlantic Forces for a rocket and depth charge attack he made on a submarine despite anti-aircraft fire that damaged his plane.

· Rear Adm. Donald B. Beary of Helena, commander of the Atlantic Fleet Operational Training Command, was awarded the Distinguished Service Medal.

· Adm. John H. Hoover of Great Falls was awarded his second Distinguished Service Medal from Admiral Nimitz for his service from November 1943 to August 1944, during which time he commanded naval aircraft in the Central Pacific during the Gilberts, Marshalls and Marianas campaigns. On March 4, 1945 Admiral Hoover was the guest of honor at a Montana party held in the Marianas islands.

· Petty Officer 1st Class Walter Johnson of Malta was the engineering officer on board submarine *USS Guardfish*, which spent three weeks lying under Tokyo Bay.

· Navy Coxswain Robert Trodick, the first Montana boy to enlist at age 17, had survived the sinking of the *USS Porter* at the Battle of Santa Cruz. He was awarded the Navy and Marine Corps medal for his actions on February 11, 1945 when he dove off a destroyer to save the life of a downed aviator.

· In May 1984, 150 U.S. submarine veterans of World War II met in Missoula for a regional meeting. Among those attending were Paul Snyder, Missoula (*USS Sunfish*), Roy Bulger, Helena (*USS Pollach*), and Ray Karr of Missoula who was on the *USS Parche* from 1942 to 1946.

· In 1991, crewmen of the *USS Ellet* held a reunion in Missoula, organized by Frank R. Lewis of Missoula and attended by Jack Morris of Troy.

Philippines

- Cpl. Ralph E. Nebel of Belt was awarded the Silver Star for his actions on Luzon. He was a pathfinder with the 11th Airborne Division, and jumped several days before the February 3, 1945, assault on Tagaytay ridge. Accompanied by several others, he rode a motorbike through 1,000 yards of Japanese territory under fire to help safeguard paratroopers as they landed.
- 2nd Lt. James C. Lindholm of Great Falls was awarded the Silver Star for his actions at Villa Verde Trail on northern Luzon. He replaced a wounded forward observer, and for eight days in a row he crawled into a forward position in order to better direct artillery fire.
- Lt. Jerome E. Patton of Portage was awarded the Silver Star for his actions with the 61st Field Artillery Battalion on Luzon. A forward observer, he was seriously wounded but remained at his post and called down fire until the attack was repulsed. He was killed in action February 28, 1945.
- Lt. Paul E. Timm of Lindsay was awarded two Bronze Stars. The first was for his actions on December 1944 on Leyte when he rescued a wounded man while under machine gun fire. In March 1945 on Luzon he rescued several wounded men under fire.

Iwo Jima

- Marine Sgt. James J. Powers of Butte was awarded the Navy Cross for his actions on Iwo Jima. He was lowered by rope 100 feet down a sulphur quarry where Japanese soldiers were known to be hiding. He set off explosives to seal the opening of the cave, but badly hurt his hands as he swiftly climbed the rope. He was later wounded in the chest by a sniper.
- Pharmacists Mate 2nd Class John W. Van Landingham of Missoula, was awarded the Silver Star for treating four wounded men under fire at Iwo Jima.
- Pharmacists Mate 3rd Class Arnold T. Cole of Billings was awarded a Bronze Star after he was wounded on Iwo Jima while crossing an open field to help a wounded Marine.
- Lt. Arthur W. Zimmerman of Fairfield was a veteran of Saipan and Tinian. Out of the eight officers of his company, five were wounded in the first six hours on Iwo Jima. He was awarded the Silver Star for assuming command of his company of the 4th Marine Division after his commander was killed. He ran back to the beach and found a tank, then directed it against Japanese emplacements until his men could lob explosives in.
- Gunnery Sgt. Ruben Fuhrman of Opheta was awarded the Bronze Star for leading a rifle platoon after his platoon leader was killed. He crossed open ground to obtain a rocket launcher but was wounded before he could return.
- Marine Staff Sgt. Gerald Storms of Miles City was awarded the Bronze Star for risking his life to receive a critical radio message on Iwo. He ran 100 yards through shelling to listen to the radio message in a vehicle after his radio was destroyed.
- Marine PFC Richard S. Schiltz, captain of the 1938 state champion Billings Broncs football team, was killed in action on Iwo Jima March 4, 1945.

"Our Flag is Still There"

TODAY the knowledge that "our flag is still there" brings hope an courage to all men who fight for Freedom . . . everywh re.

We salu te the flag, we salute the members of our Great Falls di ision who have left us for the service.

We s te every man and woman who is helping their count to defeat the Axis.

* * * * * HONOR ROLL * * * * *

DAVID H. MIKKELSON	TED RAGATZ	GEORGE H. ROBINSON
ADELBERT ZANDER	E. K. CHEADLE JR.	FORREST E. PULLIAM
MILO SANDS	ELI P. JOHNSON	HARRY COOK
DONALD W. EDWARDS		GILVRAY F. MATHEWS

Montana-Dakota Utilities Co.

Eighth Street and Central Avenue   **Phone 3281**

This Montana-Dakota Utilities advertisement, which appeared in the *Great Falls Tribune*, was typical of the war-related ads run by many businesses, large and small.

Anaconda

Anaconda served as the seat of Deer Lodge County, the only county in the state to have a significant population increase during the war years. By 1944 the county had 14 percent more people than it had just four years before. In 1943, Patrick T. O'Brien defeated incumbent Ralph Thorson for the mayor's position, but two years later, democrat Barney McGreevey took over the reins of city government. The three-story Montana Hotel provided accommodations for visitors to the city, and other attractions included the zoo, playground, and picnic area located near the smelter, as well as nearby Georgetown Lake and the Deerlodge National Forest. Anaconda's dominant industry, however, was the manufacturing of metals. The Anaconda Copper Mining Company dominated most facets of life in Anaconda. Copper and zinc ore from the Butte mines was crushed and sorted, then roasted in furnaces and separated at the Washoe Smelter, which employed 3,500 men at the height of the war.

The *Anaconda Standard* was one of many newspapers across the state controlled by ACM. Prominent Anacondans who served overseas included a former professional football player, 2nd Lt. William Lazetich, who fought with the Marines in the Pacific. At least 41 men from Deer Lodge County died in the war.

Europe

· PFC Kenneth Moore of Great Falls was awarded the Bronze Star for his actions on December 12, 1944, in Germany. He was a radio operator who moved to an exposed position on the shattered second floor of a house in order to call in fire missions.
· Pvt. Edward A. Warner of Winnett was posthumously awarded the Silver Star for carrying messages to pinned down troops under fire in the Ardennes Forest. He was killed in action on December 7, 1944, after having been overseas just one month.
· PFC George F. Taylor of Big Sandy was awarded the Bronze Star for his actions on November 29, 1944, near Barr, France. He crawled 50 yards through shell fire to administer first aid to a wounded medic, then dragged him back. On December 14, 1944, he repeatedly exposed himself to danger as he carried wounded men to safety in France.
· PFC Henry Jacobson and his twin, Cpl. Alvin Jacobson were both captured in Belgium on December 7, 1944, and both wound up in the same German prison camp. They were released from prison in May 1945.
· Capt. J. Stanley Kimmitt of Great Falls was awarded a Bronze Star for his actions from December 13, 1944, to March 8, 1945, in Germany, where he exhibited aggressive leadership and frequently went forward under enemy fire to observe the results of his field artillery battalion.
· PFC Benijiro "Boon" Ochitani of Malta, former captain of the Malta Mustangs football team, was awarded the Silver Star for his actions with the 442nd (Nisei) Regimental Combat Team in France. "The courage and determination displayed by Ochitani was the key factor in the battalion's successful attack."
· Sgt. Robert A. Watson of Great Falls saw combat at Rome, Normandy, Southern France, Northern France, the Ardennes, and Central Europe.

Laverne Parrish—Medal of Honor Winner

Medic T-4 Laverne Parrish of Pablo and Ronan served with Company C of the 161st Infantry Regiment, 25th Division. He was born in Missouri in 1919, then moved to Montana in 1934. He enlisted in March 1941 and was stationed at Schofield Barracks when the Japanese attacked Pearl Harbor. The 25th Division relieved the Marines at Guadalcanal, then fought at Munda and New Georgia. Parrish and the rest of the 25th Division landed at San Fabien on the Philippine island of Luzon on January 11, 1945, two days after the initial landing. On January 17th at Binalonan, Parrish rescued two men. On the following day he repeatedly braved intense enemy fire to drag two badly wounded men to safety. His company attacked San Manuel on January 24, but fell back to a ditch under heavy fire, leaving two wounded men in the open. Parrish rescued both men but realized more wounded were lying in the open. He gave first aid to 12 men, and dragged three more to safety. He was tending 37 wounded men lying in the ditch when a mortar shell landed amongst them, and Parrish died of his wounds a few minutes later. Parrish became one of six medics awarded the Medal of Honor, which was given to his parents on August 2, 1945, by Col. A.M. Weyand, the commander of the Fort Missoula Detention Camp at a ceremony held at Missoula High.

February 1945

- February 4. Missoula wastepaper drive yields 50,000 pounds.
- February 9. Great Falls Bisons defeat Flathead Braves 47-46.
- February 10. Missoula Spartans defeat Great Falls Bisons 61-43. Montana Bobcats defeat Gore Field Flyers 44-43.
- February 11. President Roosevelt, Churchill, and Stalin meet at Yalta and sign an agreement splitting Europe into occupation zones.
- February 12. Gore Field Flyers defeat East Base Bombers 11-1 in hockey. Four children, aged 6 months, 3, 4, and 13 die in a fire on the Fort Belknap Reservation. The mother and other children survived.
- February 13. Budapest is occupied by Soviets.
- February 14. Helena Bengals defeat Missoula Spartans 37-36.
- February 15. Anaconda defeats Great Falls Bisons 41-38.
- February 16. U.S. carrier planes attack Iwo Jima with napalm. American paratroopers land on Corregidor. Navy Miners defeat Montana Grizzlies 64-54.
- February 18. Third Army breaches Siegfried line.
- February 19. U.S. Marines land on Iwo Jima. Fred T. Daylis is appointed acting principal of Billings Senior High.
- February 20. Great Falls Bisons defeat Helena Bengals 50-43.
- February 21. A B-24 from the Spokane Air Base crashes 35 miles southwest of Philipsburg en route to Great Falls. The pilot and copilot are killed but one crew member parachutes to safety.
- February 22. Belt defeats Choteau 43-41. Great Falls Bisons defeat Billings Broncs 52-33.
- February 23. U.S. Marine Louis Charlo helps raise the American flag on top of Mt. Suribachi, Iwo Jima.
- February 25. A man dies in a house fire in Great Falls. Great Falls Selects defeat Gore Field Flyers 9-6 to take the city hockey championship.

Donald Ruhl—Medal of Honor Winner

PFC Donald Ruhl was born near Columbus, but during the Great Depression his father roamed the state working as an itinerant blacksmith. Ruhl lived at Pablo and Deer Lodge, and played basketball at Joliet High School before his graduation in May 1942. Four months later he enlisted in the Marines and trained at San Diego, where he received parachute training. He was assigned as a mortar man with the Third Parachute Battalion of the Third Marine Division. In November 1943 he participated in the invasion of Bougainville. Three months later his unit was integrated into the 28th Regiment of the Fifth Marine Division. In February 1945 his unit boarded the combat transport *USS Missoula* for the trip to Iwo Jima. On February 19, 1945 Ruhl's unit, E Company, 2nd Battalion of the 28th Marines, boarded *LST 481*, which landed on the shores of Iwo Jima during the first wave. After landing, Ruhl attacked eight Japanese who had been driven out of a blockhouse, killing two of them, one with a bayonet. On the following day he rescued a wounded marine under fire. According to his lieutenant, Ruhl, "carried the casualty through intense enemy machine gun and mortar fire to the station on the beach three hundred yards away." That night he volunteered to scout out a large Japanese gun emplacement which seven other men had been wounded trying to reach. He reached the emplacement and found no Japanese, but throughout the night he crouched in the position to prevent the Japanese from returning. Three days after the initial landing on Iwo Jima, Ruhl and Sgt. Henry O. Hansen were attacking a Japanese pillbox when a grenade fell between them. Ruhl threw himself on the grenade, thereby saving the life of his sergeant but losing his own life in the process. His company commander called him, "a fine, courageous young man and a good marine." On the day after Ruhl's death, the men of his company, including PFC Louis Charles Charlo of Evaro, raised the flag over Mount Suribachi. Both Charlo and Sergeant Hansen were later killed on Iwo Jima. On January 12, 1947, Ruhl's Medal of Honor was presented to his mother, Mrs. Edith Ruhl in the Community center in Greybull, Wyoming. Ira Hayes and Gene Bradley, two of the men who had helped raise the second flag over Iwo Jima, attended the ceremony. Ruhl is buried near Greybull, and his Medal of Honor, signed by President Truman, is displayed in Billings by the Marine Reserve.

by a popular vote. The Montana House, on the other hand, rejected the convention idea and passed a bill calling for a primary election for O'Connor's successor. Since the two houses of the legislature couldn't agree, Governor Ford and Lester H. Loble, democratic state chairman, asked Attorney General Bottomly to rule on whether or not the governor had the authority to call a special election. Bottomly agreed with the governor, and Ford called for a special election on the fifth of June to elect O'Connor's successor. Three Republicans and three Democrats announced plans to seek the vacant Congressional seat, and the two parties met in mid-April to endorse candidates. Leo C. Graybill, Great Falls city attorney, received the Democratic nomination for Congress, while the GOP picked Wesley D'Ewart over the female candidate, Elva H. Carpenter of Billings.

Senator Wheeler asked the Allies to drop "unconditional surrender" demands and urged the formation of a United States of Europe as "the only basic cure for her ancient ills." In a January speech broadcast by NBC, Wheeler said that if the Allies unconditional surrender demands weren't dropped, "we shall go on blowing Europe and our boys to bits without rhyme or reason, still ignorant of why we fight." Wheeler also denounced FDR's foreign policy and predicted it would lead to war with Russia. In turn, the Soviet press (*Izvestia*) called Wheeler a "profascist" who had been influenced by Nazi propaganda minister Joseph Goebbels.

February saw the "Big Three" (Roosevelt, Churchill, and Stalin) meet at Yalta and sign an historic agreement splitting Europe into occupation zones. The consequences of this agreement were far reaching and played a major part in the beginnings of the Cold War. Hungary, with the specter of the Red Army appearing unstoppable, declared war on former ally Germany, but that didn't stop Soviet troops from occupying Budapest in mid-February. In the Pacific, the Allies opened a land route to China.

The end of the war was nearly in sight, but the length of the daily casualty lists continued to grow. As Patricia E. O'Connell put it, "Life wasn't easy. My favorite boyfriend was over seas. I worried about him. Every six weeks, with bare tires and hoarded gasoline coupons I'd drive across the mountains to visit his mother. Until she called me one chilly winter morning, that is, to tell me he wasn't coming back. Not ever again!"

As the New Year dawned, time had almost run out for the Axis powers. In January, with the island of Leyte firmly in American hands, U.S. troops landed on the Philippine island of Luzon and began advancing on Manila.

In the Pacific, an invasion fleet carrying U.S. Marines steamed towards the tiny island of Iwo Jima. The attack transport *USS Missoula* carried the men of E Company, 28th Marines, including at least two Montanans, Louis Charles Charlo of Evaro and PFC Donald Ruhl of Columbus. When the men of the 28th Regiment left the *Missoula* to board their landing craft, they took with them a small American flag that was destined to make history.

Louis Charlo was a member of the Salish tribe and a great-grandson of Chief Charlo. He enlisted in the Marines in November 1943, one month after he turned 17, then trained at San Diego. He was serving as a radioman on February 23, 1945, when he and three other men reached the top of 546-foot-high Mt. Suribachi and found no resistance. They slid down and reported to Lt. Harold Schrier of Easy Company, then returned to the top of the mountain. Charlo and five other men found a 20-foot piece of pipe, to which they lashed the flag taken from the *USS Missoula*, and raised it over the island. Louis R. Lowery of *Leatherneck Magazine* took a photo of the flag-raising just as a Japanese grenade hit near him, breaking his camera, but leaving the film unhurt. Although Charlo's face cannot be seen in the photo, he is readily identifiable because of the radio on his back.

Since the small flag couldn't be seen from afar, or perhaps because Lt. Col. Chandler Johnson wanted to keep the flag for the 28th Marines, a second flag was raised over the island two hours later. The famous photo of this second flag-raising was flashed worldwide and won Associated Press photographer Joe Rosenthal a Pulitzer Prize. This image, the most famous photograph of World War II, became the logo for a three cent stamp (issued in June 1945), for the seventh war bond drive, and for the Marine Corps War Memorial in Arlington, Virginia, dedicated in 1954.

After Suribachi was captured, a Catholic priest held a mass. A photo taken during the mass showed Louis Charlo. It was the last known photo of the man from Evaro. Charlo was killed in action on March 2, 1945, and his remains were returned to Montana in 1948. After extremely heavy casualties on both sides, Iwo Jima was finally secured on March 17.

15

ᕯ Victory In Europe ᕲ

The 163rd Infantry Regiment landed on Biak to the sound of gunfire. By the time they left Biak almost eight months later, the island boasted a busy airport and that unmistakable sign of civilization, American nurses. Capt. Kenneth Moore of Missoula even met two women from the Bitterroot Valley on Biak, Cpl. Rachel Birrer (WAC), and Florence Kares, a Red Cross worker.

In February, while other elements of the U.S. Army swept through the Philippine island of Luzon and captured Manila and Corregidor, the 163rd left Biak, bound for the Southern Philippines. Other elements of the 41st Division landed on Palawan, while the 163rd was sent to Mindoro. The men of the 41st Division were observing their third anniversary overseas, the longest continuous overseas service of any division except for the 32nd, which had been overseas the same amount of time. Many of the original Montanans in the 163rd had by this time been granted leave, including Colonel Dawley. Dawley was serving on General MacArthur's staff when he got word that he would soon be seeing his home in Montana again. There were still many veterans from the old Montana National Guard, however, and they remained the strong backbone of the 163rd Infantry, which by now had received hundreds of replacements for the casualties they had taken at Sanananda, Aitape, Wakde, and Biak.

On March 8, 1945 the 163rd Regiment left Mindoro for Mindanao, where they were to block any possible escape routes of the fleeing Japanese units. Two days later, after their invasion beach was softened up by naval gunfire and a B-24 strike, they landed near a coconut plantation at San Mateo village on the Zamboanga Peninsula. A few mortar shells fell but resistance was light on the first day. On their second day ashore they were shelled by Japanese artillery, which was quickly dealt with when a field artillery battalion destroyed the Japanese guns. The day after that they ran into a five-mile line of heavily entrenched positions held by Japanese Marines. The Second Battalion's G Company, containing a number of men from Glasgow, was heavily shelled and took many casualties. Aided by tanks, which were of little use in the difficult terrain, two

battalions pushed ahead under heavy fire. On March 13 a huge mine decimated one company of the regiment, creating a crater 200 feet in diameter and blowing debris hundreds of feet in the air. Five men were killed and 38 were wounded by the massive mine. On the following day artillery and another B-24 raid softened the way as the Montana soldiers moved forward.

Eight days after landing most Japanese resistance had ceased, but the 163rd kept battling towards Mt. Pulungbata until they were relieved on March 30. Lt. Jack Todd gave the name of his hometown of Harlowton to a small unnamed town near San Roquet in Zamboanga. He and another son of Harlowton, Colonel Hollister "had a good laugh over it."

On April 2, 1945, the Second Battalion of Montana's 163rd Regiment overran Japanese positions at Sanga Sanga and Bongao in the Sulu Archipelago, halfway between the island of Borneo and the Philippines. A week later, the other two battalions of the regiment left Mindanao and landed at Jolo island, where they began clawing their way up heavily defended Mount Daho, the highest point on the island. In three weeks of combat, the 163rd suffered 37 dead and 191 wounded, but more than 2,600 Japanese fell before their guns. There were only 87 Japanese soldiers alive on Jolo when the Imperial Army surrendered in August.

The Sultan of Jolo, Muhammad Janail Abirin the 2nd, leader of the archipelago's 300,000 Moslems, welcomed Col. William J. Moroney, commander of the 163rd, and promised to help rid the island of Japanese. Earlier in the century, the Sultan had fought General Pershing during the Moro wars and had been sentenced to 15 years imprisonment, but Pershing had gotten him a pardon after only 16 months. Moroney gave the Sultan his .45 pistol because the Japanese had taken guns given to the Sultan by Pershing and Gen. Leonard Wood.

General Eichelberger, now the commander of the Eighth Army, also visited Jolo and met with Moroney, the "thin and hard-bitten commander of the 163rd Infantry, veteran of Sanananda and Biak and other battles, [who] met us, while his soldiers

March 1945

- March 1. Havre Blue Ponies defeat Missoula Spartans 54-36. A government curfew is imposed at midnight on all places of entertainment, taverns, and nightclubs in order to save energy.
- March 2. Bobcats defeat Grizzlies 58-33 in Bozeman after splitting two basketball games in Missoula.
- March 3. Bobcats defeat Grizzlies 48-25.
- March 5. Lewistown is the coldest spot in the nation at minus 34 degrees.
- March 7. U.S. troops seize a bridge over the Rhine at Remagen.
- March 9. Fire-bombing of Tokyo kills more than 100,000.
- March 10. 41st Division lands on the Zamboanga peninsula of Mindanao.
- March 17. U.S. Third Army takes Coblenz.
- March 18. A memorial service is held at Browning for five Blackfeet killed in the war.
- March 20. Mandalay captured.
- March 22. "E" award celebration at Pacific Car and Foundry Co. in Billings.
- March 26. A "war-weary" veteran pilot is arrested after repeatedly buzzing Great Falls at 2 a.m. Remaining Japanese on Iwo Jima mount a futile suicide attack.
- March 28. Hitler fires General Guderian as Chief of the Army General Staff.

Zamboanga and Jolo

- Sgt. Vernon E. Hutchinson of Harlowton, the leader of a machine gun squad on Zamboanga, was awarded the Bronze Star. Under heavy machine gun fire he located a key Japanese position and managed to get his squad into position to destroy the Japanese weapon.
- Master Sgt. Thomas F. Corbally Jr. of Great Falls was the operations sergeant of the 163rd Infantry. He was awarded the Bronze Star for keeping his superiors apprised of the tactical situation at all times during the fighting on Zamboanga.
- Lt. Byron Armstrong of Glasgow, who had previously won two Silver Stars at Sanananda and Wakde, won a Bronze Star on Mindanao, where he acted as battalion executive officer for nine days before. He then took command of the battalion and executed an attack that drove the Japanese from strong positions.
- Maj. Mark D. Holcomb of Whitefish, the regimental surgeon of the 41st Division, already held the Legion of Merit when he was awarded the Bronze Star for his actions on Jolo, where he saved three lives under the most difficult conditions. A makeshift hospital on Jolo was named Holcomb General in honor of the major, and he was also presented with an antique Moro barong (sword) used against two Japanese by a Moro guerrilla. Major Holcomb's dress uniform is on display at the Montana Historical Society in Helena.

kept back the great crowd of Moro spectators who wanted to surge across the airstrip." The Sultan hosted the officers of the 163rd at the village of Parang. Those attending included the 163rd's executive officer, Lt. Col. Leonard A. Wing of Bozeman, and Lt. Col. James R. Kent of Willow Creek, who had been wounded by a mortar on Mindanao. The Americans were entertained by a native girl who chanted the story of two Navy fliers shot down on Jolo and subsequently beheaded by the Japanese in the early days of the war.

After the fight for Jolo, the 163rd was supposed to return to Zamboanga for a rest, but the 24th Division ran into trouble in Davao City, and the Third Battalion moved in to give them a hand.

On Easter Sunday (April 1, 1945) 60,000 U.S. soldiers and Marines landed on the beaches of Okinawa, 750 air miles from Japan. During the first week there was little opposition. The 100,000 Japanese combatants on Okinawa were dug into a strong defensive line in the southern portion of the island. With their air force nearly destroyed and American heavy bomber raids taking a toll against their home islands, the Japanese grew increasingly desperate. One sign of this was a change in tactics, and at Okinawa large numbers of Japanese pilots began crashing their planes into the ships of the U.S. fleet. By mid-April, the battle for Okinawa had turned into one of the bloodiest conflicts of the Pacific war, and it was not until June 21 before organized resistance ended on the island. More than 12,500 Americans died on Okinawa, as did 185,000 Okinawans and Japanese soldiers and civilians.

Just as the fighting on Okinawa was beginning to heat up, the entire nation was shocked by the death of President Roosevelt on the 12th of April, 1945. Radio stations suspended all normal programming and played only somber music until the funeral was over. Vice President Harry S. Truman was quickly sworn in, and Senator Wheeler expressed the opinion that Truman would make a good President. Jefferson Day dinners throughout Montana were canceled because of FDR's death, and Great Falls residents participated in a funeral parade to honor the late President.

In May, Senator Wheeler and four other members of the Senate Interstate Commerce Committee toured Europe, where they met with Winston Churchill and with Gen. Dwight Eisenhower at Rheims. In early June, the Wheeler committee sat down with 500 American soldiers in Rome, and

Wheeler was besieged with criticism from soldiers upset about some of the senator's comments about the Soviets. Nevertheless, Wheeler feared that the Red Army would dominate postwar Europe, and after his return the senator again warned Truman that he had better stand up to the Soviets.

Mansfield predicted that the Soviets would soon join the fight against the Japanese, and he also thought that the Carolines, Marshalls and Marianas Islands should be annexed by the U.S. after the war because Japan had violated the Versailles agreements when they fortified the islands (after the war these islands became part of the Pacific Trust Territories administered by the United States). In other political news during the spring of 1945, Senator Murray co-sponsored a bill to extend social security, and he and Senator Wheeler introduced a bill calling for postwar construction funds for the Alaska Highway.

Water projects were very popular with both the lawmakers and farmers of the arid West, and the postwar period promised to bring a new era of dambuilding to the state. The Reclamation Bureau announced plans to spend $265,000,000 for postwar projects in Montana, and in late April a drilling crew from Grand Coulee Dam arrived in Montana to begin work at the site of the proposed Hungry Horse Dam. After $200,000 was earmarked for the initial construction of Hungry Horse Dam, surveying crews set up camp on the South Fork of the Flathead River and began work in the area. When it was completed in 1953, Hungry Horse Dam was 564 feet high and 2,115 feet long, the fourth tallest dam in the world. As the war ended, the last generators at Fort Peck Dam were installed, several years behind schedule. Construction of Canyon Ferry Dam was planned before the war, but legal wrangling and disagreement among agencies kept the project from beginning until 1949.

During the spring elections, Missoula Mayor Dwight N. Mason was re-elected. Tragically, his son Navy Radioman 3rd class Daniel J. Mason, died of wounds suffered in the Pacific in the waning months of the war. Soon after his re-election, Mayor Mason distributed a questionnaire on postwar planning. He asked citizens to prioritize street lighting, paving, a proposed new city hall and civic center, a new Van Buren Street bridge, and improvements to parks and swimming pools. Shortly after the end of the war, construction crews in Missoula began pouring 15 miles of new sidewalks, while the County Commissioners recommended building a new city jail, an addition to the county poor farm, and a new Van Buren Street Bridge.

The wife of Helena's mayor, Mrs. John J. Haytin, traveled to Quincy, Massachusetts, where on April 28, 1945, she smashed a bottle of champagne against the hull of the new *USS Helena* in front of 5,000 spectators. The new *USS Helena* (the third U.S. Navy ship to bear that name) boasted 8-inch guns. The ship was originally to be named the *USS Des Moines* but was re-named during construction by Bethlehem Steel. Helena residents raised $2,000 to buy a gift for the third *USS Helena*.

The original *Helena* was a gunboat launched January 30, 1896, at Newport News, Virginia. It served in the Spanish-American War, then was decommissioned in 1932 in the Philippines and sold at auction. The silver service of the gunboat *Helena* was eventually sent to the Montana Historical Society.

For Montana's high school students, spring meant the start of track season. The Helena High track team defeated Great Falls, Havre, Ft. Benton and Lewistown to win the Great Falls track meet at the end of April. Two weeks later, 333 athletes attended the annual Missoula track meet, where the home team won the Class A title, and Libby captured the Class B crown. Jimmy Kittell of Missoula took 6 seconds off of previous mile records with a time of 4:27.6 minutes.

Tech. Sgt. Joe Louis, the former heavyweight boxing champion was a big hit at a Great Falls luncheon on April 14. Louis refereed a boxing match for charity, but Troy Evans, the president of the local American Athletic Union (AAU) disqualified 26 amateur boxers because it was not an officially sanctioned match. AAU officials reinstated the boxers and elected a new president, over the protests of Evans, who contended it was an illegal election.

In March 1945, a three-year-old Great Falls girl wandered away from her mother in freezing weather. Five hundred people joined the search, and the girl was located by a soldier from Gore Field who had volunteered for the search. She had been missing for 18 hours in freezing weather. Three Havre boys, aged three to six, also turned up missing but were located unharmed after an all night search. In May, another massive search for a missing child ended tragically when a three-year-old Great Falls boy was found drowned.

During the Easter holiday a blizzard struck the state, killing at least two men. A Livingston resident froze to death when his car stalled five miles from Melville. He tried to walk to Melville but only made it two miles. Similarly, a man froze to death near Zortman after he was thrown from his horse. He told his two companions he would walk back to town while they continued on, but he never made it.

Law enforcement officials were kept busy investigating a number of crimes during the spring of 1945. In early March, Mrs. Mollie Konold of Billings was sentenced to two years in prison for the stabbing death of her uncle. John Smith, a Deer Lodge ranch hand, claimed self defense after he stabbed to death a fellow sheepherder, Verner L. Rhueff. Rhueff, described by witnesses as an unpleasant sort, was killed in an argument over the victim's vicious dog. A soldier at the Great Falls Air Base was found guilty of stealing $1,800 in government property and sentenced to one year in prison. Another soldier was arrested and charged with manslaughter in the hit-and-run death of an elderly Great Falls man. Two men who went on a spending spree in Bozeman were arrested for the April 7th robbery of the Reno Club in Billings, which netted the robbers $5,000. And in late May, two Utah men were arrested in the death of a Butte woman.

Two of the state's more bizarre crimes occurred along the Hi-Line. In Shelby, a badger unearthed an unidentified and dismembered body from underneath a chicken coop, and former tenant farmer Ernest Bowers was arrested and charged with murder. In late May a depressed Glasgow woman hit five of her six children on the head with a hammer and threw them from a 30 foot bridge into the Milk River. She left an incoherent note before also jumping into the water. Her seven-year-old child survived and swam to shore, but the younger children (ages five, four, one, and three weeks) all perished. One other child was staying with an aunt at the time.

An old criminal case in Missoula led to the sale of a major piece of real estate. Mount Jumbo, at the east edge of Missoula, went up for sale at a sheriff's auction on the courthouse lawn. The mountain had previously been owned by George R. Smith, who had killed a deputy sheriff and two other men on March 11, 1941. Smith had been declared insane and had been held at the State Hospital at Warm Springs since the murder. Proceeds of the auction went to the widows of the three victims. The widows, who had already received $2,100 from the sale of other property owned by Smith, wound up buying Mount Jumbo themselves for $869 because the other bids were so

USS Helena (CA-75). MHS 951-402

Mrs. John J. Haytin, wife of Helena's mayor, christens the new *USS Helena* (CA-75) during the spring of 1945. The *Helena* (the third warship to bear the name) was commissioned too late to see action in World War II, but did participate in the Korean War. MHS 951-400

The anchor of the *USS Helena* (CA-75) on display in Last Chance Gulch, Helena.

Okinawa

- Marine Sgt. Paul D. LeClair of Roundup was awarded the Silver Star for his actions on May 14, 1945, on Okinawa. He enlisted December 8, 1941, and served as an anti-aircraft gunner on the *USS Nevada* and *USS North Carolina*. A veteran of Midway and Tarawa, he stood on the bow of an amphibious tractor which was evacuating wounded and guided it out of a narrow defile while shooting several Japanese at close range.
- Staff Sgt. Albert Lave of Billings was awarded the Bronze Star for organizing a patrol to evacuate the wounded under fire.
- 1st Lt. Louis M. Weber of Great Falls was posthumously awarded the Silver Star for taking charge of a shattered medical detachment on April 27, 1945, after the battalion surgeon and his assistant were wounded. Weber was killed a few days later.
- 1st Lt. Ray W. Fenton of Missoula was a 1943 graduate of the University of Montana and was the former editor of the college's newspaper, the *Montana Kaiman*. He served with the First Marine Division on Okinawa, where he was one of the last people to talk to columnist Ernie Pyle shortly before Pyle left for Ie Shima, where he was killed.
- Lt. Bill Lazetich of Anaconda was a veteran of Guam, Bougainville, Saipan, Tarawa, and Iwo Jima when he was wounded in the leg by shrapnel May 15 on Okinawa. He was a former University of Montana Grizzly halfback from 1936-1938, and also played as a forward on the basketball team, where one season he was high scorer on the team. He was also a high jumper and pole vaulter on the Grizzly track team, and earned nine letters at UM before signing with the Cleveland Rams. In 1940 he took a job as a coach at Havre High.
- Lt. Ida Greenwood, a nurse from Terry, was one of 29 people killed in action on April 28, 1945, when a kamikaze plane crashed into the hospital ship *USS Comfort* off Okinawa.

Pacific

- Lawson H.M. Sanderson was promoted to brigadier general, one of 18 Marine Corps aviation generals.
- Major Ben Thrailkill Jr. of Missoula, a University of Montana graduate and former Grizzly football and basketball player, led a Chinese-American patrol from Burma into China and linked up with guerrillas there. He was promoted to lieutenant colonel but was killed in action in Burma on February 1, 1945.
- Lt. John H. Graham of Fife was awarded a Silver Star for singlehandedly wiping out a Japanese machine gun nest.
- Marine Lt. Joseph H. Sanders of Monarch was awarded a Distinguished Flying Cross after destroying a Japanese freighter and floating drydock in the Philippines.
- WAC nurse 2nd Lieutenant Evelyn Gerdrum of Grass Range was killed in a plane crash on the Ledo route into China in March. She was believed to be the first central Montana woman killed in action.
- Sgt. Charles E. Nelson of Missoula was posthumously awarded the Silver Star for his actions on March 2, 1945 while attempting to rescue a wounded man under fire.
- Capt. George C. Hull, a Great Falls doctor serving as an assistant regimental surgeon, was awarded a Bronze Star in the Philippines for his actions from November 1944 to May 1945.
- Navy Signalman 2nd Class Kenneth H. Borosund of Great Falls was awarded the Navy and Marine Corps Medal for his actions on March 18, 1945, when he dove off the bow of a destroyer and rescued an exhausted and nearly unconscious flyer during a Navy bombing raid off the Japanese island of Kyushu.

low. A few months later Mrs. Stringer, the wife of the deputy sheriff slain by Smith, sold 221 acres of Mount Jumbo to two local men.

Housing still remained a big concern in the Great Falls area, and a local housewife who took her curtains down for spring cleaning was inundated by people who thought she was moving and wanted to buy her house. Cities were urged to provide housing for returning vets, and Great Falls was allocated 125 new housing units, while Billings received 75. Ten defense housing units were moved from Anaconda to Drummond to house phosphate miners. Glasgow also experienced a housing shortage.

Dean Arthur L. Stone, founder of the Montana School of Journalism, died in a Missoula hospital on March 19, 1945, at age 79. He first came to Montana in 1888 and joined the staff of the *Anaconda Standard* in 1891. He worked there until 1907, when he became editor and manager of the *Missoulian*, a position he held until 1914. He then established the University of Montana Journalism School in a tent that he borrowed from the Army at Fort Missoula. The tent was pitched on the river near the Hellgate Canyon, but in 1937 he broke ground for a new journalism building on the campus. He wrote *Following Old Trails*, founded the campus cleanup known as Aber Day, was a life member of the Montana Press Association, and retired from the University in 1942. During the last two years of his life he wrote a column for the *Great Falls Tribune*. The Montana Mountaineers requested that Black Butte near Pattee Canyon be renamed Mount Dean Stone, the name it bears today. On April 9, 1945, Representative Mansfield paid his respects to Dean Stone on the floor of the U.S. House. "His passing leaves a void in the heart of Montana and he will long be remembered for his kindness, his courtesy and his consideration for all who came within the ken of his acquaintanceship."

Soviets troops invaded Vienna on the day following President Roosevelt's death, and British and American troops liberated the German concentration camps at Belsen and Buchenwald. Within two weeks, American and Soviet troops met for the first time on the banks of the Elbe River. The Third Reich was on its last legs, and on April 28, deposed Italian dictator Mussolini was executed by Italian partisans.

With his empire in ruins and Soviet troops only a few blocks away, Adolf Hitler married Eva Braun in his bunker underneath the streets of Berlin. The wedding couple then committed suicide, as a macabre party broke out among Hitler's staff. As the German leadership celebrated, Russian shells rained down in the streets outside. The next morning, Hitler's death was announced to the world.

Shortly thereafter, the German armed forces announced their intention to surrender, and on May 8, they signed an unconditional surrender at Rheims, France. It was Victory in Europe Day (VE DAY), and the nation went wild.

Governor Ford declared, "Montana is indeed happy. And Montana is proud of the contribution to the European victory made by valiant fighting men and by her farms, her mines and industry."

The Great Falls City Council, which had been planning for this day since the fall of 1944, adopted a resolution to close all taverns for 24 hours. Although smelters and mines and other vital industries remained open, most businesses closed their doors. The day was relatively quiet, and in Great Falls the local Veterans of Foreign Wars post refused to take part in a VE Day parade, feeling that celebration was premature while the war in the Pacific continued. The European war had cost the American people $185,000,000,000. Nearly 800,000 American men and women had been killed or wounded in the fighting.

Church services were held around the state. The Salish-Kootenai tribe held a silent prayer for the war dead on the shores of Flathead Lake. A VE Day mass was held at the Browning School, and in a more traditional celebration, the Blackfeet danced around their memorial to servicemen in Browning. In Missoula, 1,400 University and high school students gathered at the University student union to hear Dr. Ernest Melby give a VE Day speech.

Dr. Melby, who had arrived at the University only a few months before the Japanese attack on Pearl Harbor, had spent a tumultuous four years in the Treasure State, including a controversial stint as Montana's Chancellor of Higher Education. In April he resigned as executive officer of the State Board of Education, and less than two months later he announced his intention to resign from the presidency of the University in order to become the dean of education at New York University. He expressed the desire to work more closely with students rather than with politics and finances. As he had done many times in the past four years, Melby again blasted the state legislature for failing to unite the University system and for not giving the state Board of Education enough power. The Montana education system,

April 1945

- April 1. Easter Sunday. U.S. troops land on Okinawa, 750 miles from mainland Japan. Meat ration is cut 12 percent.
- April 2. Election day.
- April 7. Japanese battleship *Yamato* sunk by U.S. carrier planes. Governor Ford meets with the governors of Missouri Basin states in Omaha.
- April 9. Two battalions of the 163rd Infantry Regiment land on Jolo Island.
- April 10. Prisoner escapes from Ft. Missoula while unloading new seats for post theater. He is captured in Ravalli County the next day.
- April 12. President Roosevelt dies of a cerebral hemorrhage. Harry Truman is sworn in as President.
- April 13. Vienna falls to the Soviets after a fierce street battle. Nazi concentration camp at Buchenwald is liberated by U.S. forces.
- April 14. Official day of mourning as President Roosevelt is buried.
- April 15. Democrats cancel their Jefferson Day Banquets around the state due to the President's death.
- April 16. Joe Louis referees amateur boxing matches bouts at the Great Falls Civic Center.
- April 18. Correspondent Ernie Pyle is killed on Ie Shima.
- April 21. The citizens of Billings donate 40,000 pounds of clothes for refugees. Soviet tanks reach the outskirts of Berlin.
- April 22. An East Base soldier is arrested by the FBI for stealing $1,800 worth of army supplies and shipping them home to Chicago.
- April 23. Five-day citywide cleanup begins in Billings.
- April 25. U.S. and Soviet troops meet on the Elbe River.
- April 26. Antelope Flour Mill in Plentywood is destroyed by fire, $20,000 damage.
- April 27. Aber Day campus cleanup at University of Montana. Bainville celebrates 140th anniversary of the Lewis and Clark expedition.
- April 28. Benito Mussolini is captured by Italian partisans.
- April 30. Hitler and Eva Braun commit suicide in their bunker.

Cut Bank

One-third of Glacier County's 10,000 residents lived in Cut Bank during the war years. Much of the county was within the borders of the Blackfeet Indian Reservation. The oil industry was the most important industry in the county, and the 5,000,000 barrels of oil produced annually in Glacier County comprised more than 50 percent of the state's output. In 1945 a 90-mile pipeline was completed linking the Cut Bank fields with Great Falls at a cost of $500,000. The county also produced nearly 15 billion cubic feet of natural gas per year.

Agriculture was also important. In 1942 Glacier County produced 900,000 bushels of wheat, 1,500 head of cattle, 8,000 head of sheep and 80,000 pounds of wool. Flax and mustard were among the secondary crops produced. The *Cut Bank Pioneer Press* was the local newspaper. Although many of the residents of Glacier County were themselves impoverished, the community collected 5,500 pounds of used clothing for Russian refugees.

Since the 1930s Cut Bank had hosted a Neighbor Day each July 15, which included a picnic, baseball games, and a foot race. The Cut Bank saddle club was organized in 1943. In a typical year the county boasted 311 births, 98 deaths, 80 marriages, and 50 divorces. During the first year of the war, 352 county residents joined the military. At least 13 of them were killed in the war.

The Cut Bank Air Base, a subsidiary of the much larger Air Force facility at Great Falls, was used to train the crews of heavy bombers, primarily during 1943. A USO club was opened in the basement of the Cut Bank Masonic temple. One of the units training at the Cut Bank Air Base adopted a bear cub mascot, which they obtained from the Red Lodge "See 'em Alive" Zoo. When the squadron was shipped to England, the bear cub, which by then had been named "Victory," was taken overseas. The bear cub was believed to have set an ursine flight record on the trip to England. The air base proved to be a temporary facility, and by 1944 the base had been abandoned and many of the buildings were torn down.

Europe

- PFC Alvin R. Nichols of Butte was awarded the Silver Star after he drove off German fighter planes with the gun on his scout car.
- PFC Robert C. Hallis of Great Falls was awarded the Bronze Star. He served with the 460th Parachute Field Artillery in Europe. While pinned down on the edge of a 1,000 foot precipice for 10 hours by Germans, he rescued vital radio equipment and waited until nightfall, when he slipped back to U.S. lines.
- PFC William H. Stock of Whitefish was awarded the Bronze Star for his actions in Germany with the 106th Cavalry Regiment, Seventh Army at Forest De Parroy.
- PFC Thomas A. Grant Jr., a former smelter worker from Black Eagle, served with the 10th Mountain Division. He was awarded the Silver Star for destroying two German machine gun nests with grenades.
- 2nd Lt. Bill McInnis, a former Great Falls Bison football star, was awarded the Bronze Star for his actions on April 7, 1945. Near Westenfilde, Germany he led an assault on fortified positions, resulting in the capture of many weapons and 24 prisoners.
- Lt. Robert B. Emrick of Conrad, who already had won two Bronze Stars, was awarded the Silver Star for leading a 10-jeep convoy of the 71st Division deep into Germany. They reached Neider Gleink on May 5, 1945, one of the furthest points east reached by any unit of U.S. forces in Europe.
- PFC Joseph Thiebes Jr. of the 104th Division was awarded the Silver Star for his actions on April 17, 1945, in Germany. He and his mortar platoon were trapped in a house which was surrounded by Germans. Armed only with a rifle, he held off the Germans for four hours until help arrived.
- Lt. William D. Lundberg of Billings was awarded the Bronze Star for his service in France and Germany. He was awarded the Silver Star for his actions on March 9, 1945 when he rescued a wounded man from a burning building in Germany. He then removed a large quantity of explosives and flammable material from the building.
- PFC John P. Egan of Great Falls, 413th Field Artillery Battalion, was awarded the Bronze Star for helping a wounded man under fire in Germany on April 29, 1945.
- PFC George H. Cheledinas of Klein was awarded the Silver Star. He was a ferry boat operator who pulled wounded soldiers from the Roer River in Germany.

Germany

- Technical Sgt. Glen C. Flanagan of Cascade, 39th Infantry Regiment, Ninth Division, landed in North Africa in 1942 and was wounded in Bizerte, then fought in Sicily. He landed in Normandy on D-Day and fought through Belgium, crossed the Meuse River into Germany and met the Soviets in Berlin. He was awarded the Silver Star.
- Lt. Col. Robert L. Ashworth of Butte was a member of a Ninth Army glider regiment. He was awarded the Silver Star and the Bronze Star for his role in capturing prominent Nazi and former German Chancellor Franz von Papen on April 10, 1945.
- Sgt. William A. Kipp of Billings was a rodeo rider serving with the Army engineers. He was decorated with the Bronze Star for continuing an engineering project under fire in Germany.
- Technical Sgt. John A. Cote, a former Carroll College faculty member, served in Army Intelligence. He was a veteran of North Africa, Italy, France, and Germany. He was awarded the French Croix de Guerre.
- T-4 Jesse G. Clement of Cut Bank, a medic with the 342nd Infantry Regiment, was awarded the Bronze Star for his actions on April 25, 1945 at Ingolstadt, Germany when he saved two wounded men under fire.
- T-5 Joseph R. Platisha Jr. of Great Falls was with the 11th Armored Division. He was a tanker truck driver who distinguished himself from Bastogne to Austria and was awarded the Bronze Star.
- 1st Lt. Frances L. Grieve of Billings, an Army nurse, was awarded the Bronze Star. She served in Normandy, Northern France, the Ardennes, the Rhineland, and Central Germany. She was a 1940 graduate of St. Vincents Hospital in Billings.
- PFC Harry Hall of Great Falls was awarded the Bronze Star for his actions with the 28th Infantry Division in Germany. At Huertgen Forest he singlehandedly beat off an enemy patrol at night.
- 1st Lt. Lewis C. Archambeault of Fort Peck was awarded the Bronze Star for fighting near the Saar River in which his platoon fought off several German attempts to attack the bridgehead.
- Thirty-three Montana men served with the 82nd Airborne during the occupation of Berlin.

he claimed, "is worse off in relation to the rest of the nation than it was twenty years ago." On the other hand, Melby expressed his "appreciation to Montana people for the cordial goodwill they have shown both to me and to the University."

Dr. R.H. Jesse became vice-president of the University while the school began a nationwide search for a new president. Another radical change hit the campus when the Associated Students of the University of Montana elected their first woman president, Jane Jeffers of Ennis, during the spring of 1945.

Melby was not the only head of a Montana school to step down. At Eastern Montana Normal College in Billings, Dr. L.B. McMullen retired as president, and Dr. A.G. Peterson of Plattsburg, New York took his place. And in Bozeman, Governor Ford installed Dr. Roland R. Renne, who had been acting president since September 1943, as president of Montana State College.

During the spring of 1945, the first three ex-servicemen attended Carroll College under the new G.I. Bill. Carroll College had trained 1,000 Navy students since July 1943. Seven hundred of the students had graduated from the V-12 program and 300 from the V-5 aviation training. The V-12 program continued even after the surrender of Germany.

There were also changes in the state's elementary and high schools. G.A. Ketchum, the principal of Missoula High for the past 33 years, resigned, as did seven other faculty members. Of the 4,694 public school teachers in the state, 1,100 positions were temporarily filled with teachers without certificates, including 300 high school teachers who didn't have a college education. Fourteen percent (734) of the state's teachers left the state in 1945, even though Great Falls teachers won a $200 per year salary increase.

In business news, state retail stores reported a 15 to 30 percent increase in sales during the past year. In fact, retail sales across the state had increased every year during the war. Real estate transactions were also up. In mid-June the Trask Hardware in Deer Lodge, started in 1866, was sold to a local business man, and the following month the equally historic Sherburne Mercantile at Browning, established in 1898, was sold to the F.A. Buttrey Company. In April the Hammond Hotel in Darby was torn down. One of the few original buildings left in Darby, it had been built by the Hammond family of Missoula. As the end of the war neared, many businesses began long-anticipated expansions.

Early in the year the Union Oil Company of California purchased the Glacier Production Co. One hundred new oil wells were planned for the Cut Bank field in 1945, but a new income tax restriction on oil drilling that went into effect in July 1945 was expected to cut production dramatically, and producers warned Congress to either nullify the new law or expect curtailed oil revenues. However, crude production dipped only slightly in 1945. In Glacier County, 125 tons of obsolete oil drilling equipment were added to the scrap heap.

Counties were given permission to donate old records to the paper scrap drive, and by the end of April, 21 tons of paper were shipped from Missoula and 40 tons from Glasgow. During the first six months of 1945, the state shipped 3,700 tons of wastepaper. Even though the war in Europe was over, rationing continued. In mid-May, tire output for civilians was increased by 50 percent, but the sugar ration was cut by a quarter.

In early May 1945, a strike erupted at the Smith Mine and another mine belonging to the Montana Coal and Iron Company at Bearcreek. The strike was precipitated by the firing of a miner. The union demanded the foreman be discharged and the miner reinstated, and the strike lasted for 17 days before management and labor settled.

R.H. Fletcher, a Montana Power Company employee in Butte, wrote the lyrics and music to "Don't Fence Me In," which he had sold to Cole Porter in 1934 for $250. Fletcher was surprised when his song (with a different tune but the same lyrics) turned into a huge hit in the spring of 1945. In other music news, Bing Crosby was voted the most popular male singer, beating out Frank Sinatra in a Downbeat magazine poll. At the 1945 Academy Awards, the best picture was "The Lost Weekend," directed by Billy Wilder (Best Director) and starring Ray Milland (Best Actor). Joan Crawford took the Best Actress award for "Mildred Pierce." "Gung Ho" a film on the Makin Island raid starring Randolph Scott, and "God is my Copilot" made the rounds of Montana theaters. In March 1945 all Missoula theaters donated one week's proceeds to the county Red Cross drive.

As Allied soldiers swept across Europe, thousands of prisoners of war were liberated from German camps, including Missoula flier Col. Hubert Zemke. The news was relayed to Zemke's wife in a telegram from Mike Mansfield. Zemke was destined to spend a few more months in Europe before he could come home, however. As senior officer of

Air War

- Capt. Robert F. Maloney of Butte was credited with downing five German planes. The 8th Air Force flier was a veteran of 400 hours of combat flying and had the Distinguished Flying Cross plus the Air Medal with 9 clusters.
- Master Sgt. Theodore Ritland of Fort Benton, B-24 maintenance crew chief, was awarded the Bronze Star for meritorious achievement for keeping a B-24 in excellent shape through 51 missions.
- Lt. Eddie Doherty of Great Falls was awarded the Silver Star for his actions with the 15th Air Force in Italy. After bombing Blechamer, he was approaching an emergency base when three engines of his plane quit. The rest of the crew bailed out but Doherty and his flight engineer crashed into 12 feet of water. The windshield shattered and both men floated to the surface, where they eventually hailed an Italian fishing boat. They returned to their base five days later.
- Capt. Richard D. Tietjen of Great Falls was a B-17 squadron leader who twice limped crippled bombers back to base after raids over Germany. He was awarded the Distinguished Flying Cross, Bronze Star, and Air Medal with four clusters. He was allowed to return home on leave after 30 missions.
- Lt. Arthur M. Hagan of Redstone was a B-25 pilot with the 12th Air Force. He was awarded the Distinguished Flying Cross, three Bronze Stars and an Air Medal with 2 clusters.
- Capt. Donald H. Smith of Helena was awarded the Bronze Star by General Spaatz. He was the personal pilot to Spaatz and other high-ranking officers.

Railroads

Montana's three major railroads were the Great Northern, the Northern Pacific, and the Milwaukee Road. The Great Northern had 2,639 miles of track in Montana, and needed 400 track workers just to maintain their lines. The Great Northern sent Christmas gifts to each employee in the service, including 200 men from Great Falls. Twenty women were employed at the Great Northern roundhouse and repair shops in Great Falls, which were expanded in 1944 at a cost of $200,000. The Great Northern was planned to build a $381,000 diesel repair shop in Havre and two new tunnels at Belton and Apgar after the war. In 1944 the Great Northern spent $8,000,000 on supplies in Montana.

Despite war-time shortages, the Northern Pacific Railroad completed a $1,450,000 expansion of their shops at Livingston. The Northern Pacific operated brand new Z-8 locomotives between Missoula and Laurel, part of a trend by most railroads to replace their old steam engines with new diesel locomotives. Because of the labor shortage, the NP hired 16-year-old boys at Missoula and Livingston, and by the summer of 1944 there were 150 to 200 high school boys working on the railroad. Several women were also among the 324 Northern Pacific employees at Laurel, and the railroad employed 14 women on section gangs doing light maintenance work on cars in Missoula. The Laurel rebuild shop employed 300 people repairing railroad cars. In 1944, 65 freight trains passed through the Laurel yards every day, and 75 percent of the cargo was destined for the military. The NP's biggest construction project during the war was the drilling of a new tunnel underneath the Bozeman Hill, to replace a smaller existing tunnel. On December 3, 1944 the Northern Pacific railroad finished drilling the 3,105 foot tunnel. The project brought an influx of workers to the area, including at least 40 Italian prisoners from Fort Missoula, who were housed in rail cars because of a serious shortage of housing. The Northern Pacific employed as many as 100 Italians, including 18 carpenters who built bridges and worked on construction crews. The Italian detainees were paid the same rate as regular employees, but they were only allowed a small stipend at one time and the rest of their pay was sent to Fort Missoula, where it was saved for them. Altogether, Montana railroads employed 250 of the Italian detainees from Fort Missoula.

In the early summer of 1943 the Milwaukee Road donated $1,243,000 to the Montana war bond drive. The railroad also began planning a major expansion of their facilities at Harlowton. In the summer of 1944, the Milwaukee Road bought six electric-diesel locomotives to upgrade their equipment.

Stalag Luft I, which was in a zone occupied by the Soviet Red Army, Zemke spent some time trying to track down missing POWs. He was then assigned to oversee the removal of critical equipment and 435 employees and their families from the German Zeiss optical plant at Jena, which was destined to be turned over to Soviet control. While he was busy with that task, a USAAF exposition at the Eiffel Tower in Paris displayed a P-51 Mustang named "Zemke's Wolfpack." In mid-July 1945 Zemke returned to New York by plane, then on to Missoula, where he looked forward to doing some fishing during his 60-day leave. Zemke ranked 20th among American aces, and was ultimately credited with destroying 19.5 enemy planes on the ground and 8.5 in the air. After the war Zemke flew P-80 jets, then returned to Germany where he commanded the 36th Fighter Group from 1949 to 1954. After several other assignments at home and abroad, Zemke retired with 30 years in the service. He later wrote two books about his wartime experiences entitled *Zemke's Wolfpack* and *Zemke's Stalag*.

Dozens of others were also liberated from German POW camps, including Sgt. Lee Varner of Chinook, a B-17 gunner with more than 50 missions when he was shot down April 11, 1944 over Germany. He was awarded the Distinguished Flying Cross and an Air Medal with nine clusters. Glendive alone had six residents who spent time behind German barbed wire, and were freed by Allied troops.

In May 1945 the Italian internees who had previously been held at Fort Missoula received word they were free to return home to Italy, and on May 30 the Red Cross ship *SS Gripsholm* set sail for Europe with 1,150 aliens, many of them the Italian seamen formerly interned at Fort Missoula. More Italians left in July and September by train for Ellis Island, then onto the *SS Gripsholm* and *SD Drottningholm*. Some of the Italians had saved up to $2,000, and they bought scarce items to take home to Italy. Most had been away from home for at least six years.

Several of the Italians interned at Fort Missoula returned to the Garden City after the war, including Umberto Benedetti, a long-time University of Montana employee who received a Masters degree in 1980, and Alfredo Cipolato, who married the daughter of a Missoula grocer who delivered supplies to the fort. As of this writing, 80-year-old Alfredo Cipolato still operates a grocery in downtown Missoula.

Temporary housing for returning war veterans at the University of Montana, Missoula. McKay Collection

16

Peace At Last

By the first of June 1945, Allied occupation troops had taken control of all of Germany. With the war in Europe finished and the invasion of Japan on the drawing board, large numbers of troop were shifted to the Pacific, where the war against the Japanese continued unabated. At home, Whitefish residents remodeled the serviceman's canteen at the Whitefish train depot in anticipation of even more troops heading through town on their way to the Pacific.

Montana newspapers reported in early June that the 41st Division would soon be coming home, but the fight for the Philippines was not yet complete. Beginning on June 4, 1945, the Third Battalion of the 163rd Infantry Regiment, in conjunction with the 24th Infantry Division, fought at Ula-Riverside-Calinan in south-central Mindanao. Much of the fighting was done in thick abaca jungle. Abaca was a cultivated plant used to make rope, but this particular plantation had become overgrown. After three days of fighting, the men of the 163rd forced a crossing over the Talomo River, and on June 10 they captured Riverside, "a clump of ruined huts" according to one of the soldiers. On the following day a U.S. aircraft mistakenly bombed the positions of L Company, killing two and wounded 16 others. From June 14th to the 17th the Third Battalion fought at Calinan and captured the Calinan bridge intact, although they suffered 14 dead and 72 wounded in the process. During the entire Philippine campaign, the 163rd lost 123 dead and 636 wounded and sick. By the 9th of July the entire regiment was reunited at Zamboanga, where they rested and regrouped for the expected November landings on Kyushu, Japan.

In Montana, officials finished last-minute preparations for the special election to choose the late Congressman O'Connor's successor. Democrats Wheeler, Murray, and Mansfield all supported the candidacy of Leo Graybill, and Mansfield and Murray both toured the state and spoke at rallies on Graybill's behalf. During the campaign, Mansfield announced that the Truman administration planned on building a $1,300,000 veteran hospital in eastern Montana, and a Republican Congressman charged that this was an attempt by Truman to influence the special Montana Congressional race.

Governor Ford supported Wesley A. D'Ewart, a Wilsall rancher running on the Republican ticket. Although Graybill ran a high profile campaign and received the vast majority of the media coverage, only 40 percent of Montana's 130,259 registered voters showed up at the polls, and they went overwhelming for the Republican candidate. Official election returns showed that D'Ewart received 26,158 votes, compared to 22,126 for Graybill. Robert Yellowtail, the Crow Reservation superintendent, also ran for the open Congressional seat as an independent. Much of his support came from the state's Indians, and he tallied 3,417 votes. Socialist candidate E. Spriggs received only 200 votes.

The first Republican elected from the eastern district in more than 20 years, D'Ewart claimed his election reflected an anti-MVA stand. Soon after taking his seat in Washington, D'Ewart was appointed to the House Irrigation, Mining, Public Lands and Indian Affairs committees, while Mike Mansfield returned to the House Foreign Affairs Committee.

Congress approved several projects involving Montana, including a bill to provide land for the expansion of the Yellow Bay biological station at Flathead Lake. Work was started on the Big Flat irrigation ditch in Missoula, and across the state 1,200 men were employed in highway repair crews.

Spring weather brought out the gardeners, and two subdivisions in Great Falls held a contest to see which could grow the best Victory garden. Prizes of $5 and $10 were awarded for the best-looking gardens, and as an added incentive, Victory gardeners were eligible for more gasoline coupons.

Although the snowpack during the spring of 1945 had been lighter than usual, cool weather and early summer rains eliminated any fears of drought. On the other hand, the rain and cold slowed the growth of the sugar beet crop. Farmers also had to contend with an outbreak of army worms and alfalfa weevils. Hail storms during the first week of July damaged crops throughout central Montana, and an August 11 hailstorm in the Malta area destroyed 800 acres of sugar beets and thousands of acres of grain.

Approximately 4,243 prisoners of war and 3,800

Mexicans worked on Montana ranches, fields and forests in 1945. By 1945, so many people had left the state that harvesting the 83,250 acres of sugar beets under cultivation would have been an impossible task without the aid of the prisoners and foreign workers, who represented 85 percent of the available labor for Montana farmers. Hundreds of Mexican farm workers first arrived in the state during March. Many helped ranchers with spring lambing, while nearly 1,000 of the migrant workers were employed by the Forest Service until the beet crop needed thinning. Although Mexicans made up the bulk of the foreign workers in the state, 225 Jamaicans also came to the state, and were housed in a former CCC camp between Fairview and Sidney. After the beet work, many of the Mexicans went back to work for the Forest Service, while others worked on the reconstruction of the Sun River Dam (Pishkun Reservoir).

The first POWs arrived in the state in late May. Three hundred of the prisoners were sent to Miles City, where local farmers had converted the Eastern Montana Fairgrounds into a temporary POW camp. The prisoners slept in the fair exhibition hall while mess tents were erected next door. The 45 officers and enlisted men of the guard detail were quartered in the 4-H building, while Booth 1 and Booth 2 served as office and messhall. The 250 POWs stationed at Malta had less spacious accommodations. The Utah-Idaho Sugar Company purchased 35 government-owned granaries, each of which was 14 by 24 feet, and remodeled them to serve as barracks at the Malta facility, which was on the site of an old CCC camp near the Milk River. Granaries were also used to house prisoners at Chinook and Harlem.

The 450 POWs sent to Glasgow were quartered at the abandoned Glasgow Air Base, and one-third of them were available for any kind of work. Strict rules governed the use of prisoner labor, and farmers were required to read and sign off on the rules, which included an eight-hour workday (not including meals, breaks, or transportation). Prisoners were not supposed to work on farms more than 25 miles from their camps, but in the wide open spaces of eastern Montana this rule was generally ignored. POWs were paid $.80 per day, and no other workers were allowed to be in the fields at the same time. Besides the guards, only the farmer who owned the land was allowed to talk with the prisoners.

Fort Shaw received 234 POWs, who were housed at the local school's gymnasium. When the harvest was complete at Fort Shaw, these men were transferred to a temporary tent camp set up at Vaughn, just outside of Great Falls. POWs were also sent to Chinook (500), Bridger (200), Ballantine (350), Billings (400), Harlem, and Fairfield. In all, some 865,000 tons of beets were picked, the largest crop since 1942. Although the yield of sugar beets was about the same as it had been in 1939, the value to farmers had doubled in just six years. After the harvest was in many POWs were sent to Oregon and others were sent to Victor at the request of fruit growers in Ravalli County, who had asked that 250 POWs be sent to the Bitterroot Valley.

Apple production dropped sharply during the war but cherry production nearly quadrupled as the trees near Flathead Lake matured. The Flathead Lake cherry orchards shipped 500,000 pounds of fruit in 1945.

Agriculture accounted for 51 percent of the state's total income in 1945 (cattle and sheep accounted for 25 percent and dairy six percent). A harvest of more than 30,000,000 bushels of winter wheat was anticipated in 1945, despite a cutworm infestation which hit wheat fields in central Montana. Farmers across the state also reported a harvest of 41,200,000 bushels of spring wheat, 17,200,000 bushels of barley, and 12,100,000 bushels of oats. The harvest of spring wheat and oats remained about the same as in previous years, but the yield of winter wheat had increased substantially. Barley production had almost quadrupled in the past six years, and the price paid to farmers was more than 10 times the levels of 1939. Values of all agricultural crops had gone up during the war, and the value of many farms doubled in just four years.

Hay production remained about the same as prewar levels, but more and more farmers began planting alfalfa. Montana ranges held a record 1,770,000 cattle in 1945. This represented a trend towards larger herds that continued for several years. Beef production nearly doubled during the war, and the industry retained its strength during the postwar era. During the summer of 1945, a group of eight Wyoming and Idaho men purchased the Great Falls stockyards. Wool production in 1945 dropped 15 percent from the previous year, continuing the steady decline of the sheep industry during the war years. The number of sheep and the amount of wool produced in the state dropped nearly in half in the decade after the war. In response to the plight of wool growers, Senator Wheeler asked for a hearing

Pacific

· Lt. Robert Saldin of Missoula was awarded the Distinguished Service Cross. With remnants of his platoon and another under-strength platoon of the 25th Division, he found an abandoned machine gun and set up a defensive line on Luzon. They held off an attack by 20 Japanese tanks, destroying 11, but Saldin was wounded in the chest. A veteran of Munda and New Georgia, he also had the Silver Star.

· Col. Roy B. Arnold of Big Sandy was a veteran of World War I and the 1916 Mexican incursion. He was original plans and training officer of the 163rd Infantry, then transferred to the Signal Corps. He was decorated with the Bronze Star.

· Staff Sgt. James F. Lynch of Roundup was an A-20 gunner with the 5th Air Force in the Philippines. He was awarded the Silver Star for a low-level bombing and strafing mission on Formosa. At the time he was a veteran of 23 combat mission over New Guinea and the Philippines.

· Theodore Farrell of Havre joined the merchant marine at age 15 and traveled all over the Pacific. He manned a 20mm anti-aircraft gun aboard a ship at Iwo Jima. At age 17 he returned to Butte and promptly enlisted in the Marines.

June 1945

· June 1. A new bus station opens in Billings. University of Montana graduation. Three hundred German POWs arrive in Glasgow.

· June 2. An 11-year-old Butte boy drowns in ice pond near Butte. Heavy bomber crashes on runway at Gore Field, three injured. Flyers baseball team defeats Bombers 6-0.

· June 4. Five hundred B-29s drop incendiary bombs on Kobe, Japan.

· June 5. Special election to choose eastern district Congressman.

· June 8. Three-day Montana Boy Scout camp-out begins in Missoula.

· June 9. Billings Go-Western parade. Non-com club opens at East Base.

· June 10. East Base Gunners defeat Bombers 2-1.

· June 12. Two rooms of Commercial Hotel in Billings gutted by fire, $1,000 damage. Abner Decker, first white child born in the Gallatin Valley, dies in Bozeman at age 81.

· June 14. Occidental Elevator Co. grain and feed mill in Billings is destroyed by a fire.

· June 15. Senator Murray speaks at MVA meeting in Omaha.

· June 16. An Army officer is electrocuted at Gore Field.

· June 18. Miles City bucking horse sale. Four-day Thirst Dance dedicated to Indians in the service begins in Bearpaw Mountains on the Rocky Boys Reservation. A 7th Ferrying Group pilot dies in a crash 18 miles from Fairfield.

· June 19. Butte man is found murdered in the Big Hole River.

· June 21. Japanese resistance on Okinawa ends.

· June 23. Rangerider's reunion and rodeo begins in Miles City.

· June 24. Augusta rodeo begins.

· June 25. Yellowstone River rises to 48 inches above normal at Livingston.

· June 26. Midnight curfew on bars is lifted. Fifty nations sign United Nation's Charter in San Francisco.

· June 27. Arthur Brother's Circus performs in Great Falls.

· June 28. General MacArthur reports organized resistance on Luzon has ended.

· June 30. A train carrying 300 delegates from the San Francisco conference stops in Glacier Park.

on wool freight rates, which he thought were too high.

Hog production more than doubled during the war, then began to drop slowly off. Egg production increased, as did the number of chickens raised in the state, and by 1945 poultry growers received almost double the price they had been paid just a few years before.

Although the number of acres planted in flax was substantially higher in 1945 than the year before, the yield was actually smaller than 1944, and barely a third of the record 1943 crop. A new mustard and flax seed mill opened in Great Falls in July. It had cost $100,000 to build and employed 25 people initially. The mill produced linseed oil and feed cake from a portion of the 28,000,000 pounds of mustard seed and 1,300,000 bushels of flax harvested in the state in 1945. The production of both mustard and flax had skyrocketed during the war.

Montana's university system was on the brink of unprecedented expansion by the spring of 1945, but enrollment figures did not reflect the coming boom. The University of Montana graduated 115 students during the spring of 1945, and announced soon after that 111 UM students were known to have died in the war so far. Veteran James A. McCain was chosen as the new president of the University, replacing Dr. Ernest Melby. The Missoula Mercantile and the Alumni Challenge Athletic Field Corporation, founded in 1923 to finance a new football field, donated land on the south bank of the Clark Fork River (where the UM fieldhouse now sits) to the school. The University of Montana had 400 students enroll for their summer session while Montana State College had 479 students during the summer.

Montana State College graduated 56 students during the spring quarter, and the College announced that their war training courses would end in July. A total of 900 aviation cadets were trained at Montana State College during the war years. In Butte, the Montana School of Mines had already resumed normal classes, although some of the Navy engineering students remained.

A complete eclipse of the sun occurred at 6:14 a.m. on July 9, 1945. The eclipse brought many of the nation's pre-eminent astronomers to Montana. University of Montana professors observed the eclipse near Saco, while faculty from Montana State College journeyed to Butte to observe the solar event from the campus of the Montana School of Mines. Butte also served as a base of operations for astrono-

mers from Hayden Planetarium in New York. A Life magazine photographer arrived in Butte to make the first color movies of a total eclipse, and NBC radio broadcast the eclipse progress from the Mining City. Scientists from Mount Wilson Observatory in California viewed the eclipse at Opheim, while astronomers from Princeton University set up camp at Malta and enlisted local residents to read instruments. They also asked 60 Forest Service fire lookouts to make observations. Clouds marred the view of the eclipse at Malta, but the overcast broke just in time to allow astronomers 11 minutes of observations during totality.

In July, Lt. Col. Kermit R. Hatt, the commander of the 7th Ferrying Group, was transferred from East Base to the Pacific, where he piloted one of the first C-47 cargo planes to land in Tokyo. Hatt was replaced by Col. Floyd E. Evans, who had previously commanded an ATC base in Tunisia. As the war wound down, the base at Great Falls was given additional duties, including the Air Force's only school for winterizing planes. The base also became a divisional headquarters of the Air Force Search and Rescue Command, and had jurisdiction over an area ranging from Minnesota in the east down to Tucson and Galveston in the south.

Early in June, Montana ranked second in the seventh war bond drive, behind Mississippi and ahead of Alabama, but the Treasure State soon captured first place and was the first state in the union to meet the seventh war bond quota of $35,000,000 in individual contributions. The state soon pledged 119.8 percent of the state's seventh war loan quota. Including corporate donations, Montana pledged a total of $61,511,000. From December 1941 and through eight subsequent war bond drives, Montanans led the nation in buying bonds as a function of per capita income, and over-subscribed to every single bond drive. Disabled soldiers in convalescent hospitals built 56 model jeeps which were awarded to the most successful bond salesmen in each county in Montana.

The generosity of Montanans was not limited to the war bond drives. Montanans also donated goods to refugees from war-torn areas of Europe. Although there was a fear of clothes rationing in the U.S., a clothing drive was held for destitute Greeks while Lewistown residents collected costume jewelry. One of the best-organized campaigns provided clothing and books for the Soviet Union. As early as September 1944, a drive was mounted in Great Falls to collect shoes and clothes for the Russians. Ten thousand pounds of goods were collected, then sorted at the Ice Arena. Russian War Relief Inc. opened an office in Great Falls, and soon began distributing yarn in the hopes that local women would knit garments for Russian refugees. Eighty Montana communities collected some 626,527 pounds of clothes for refugees, which were shipped to Europe on the Red Cross ship *SS Gripsholm*.

Although the United States was spared the hardships that so many other countries faced in 1945, contagious diseases remained a very real threat. In March an outbreak of mumps swept Great Falls, and by the following month Cascade County was struck by more than 100 cases of contagious jaundice. Scarlet fever struck Plentywood, and six children died and 13 others became sick after a diarrhea outbreak at Shodair Hospital in Helena. Modern medicine put in an appearance when penicillin went on sale at drugstores for the first time. Two spotted fever cases, one fatal, occurred in 1945, the lowest year on record for spotted fever. In 1944 there had been six cases, three of which were fatal. A four-year-old Fairfield boy, Larry Roe, was flown to the Mayo Clinic in Rochester, Minnesota, by a C-47 of the 7th Ferrying Group on June 22, 1945, after he was accidently shot in the head by a playmate. He had been in a coma for a week prior to the flight, but regained consciousness once he reached Rochester. His story made national news, and he returned to Montana with only slightly impaired hearing and sight on his left side, even though the fragmented .22 bullet remained in his brain.

In late July the U.S. Senate ratified the United Nations Charter by a vote of 89-2. Eighteen official delegates and 200 diplomats from 16 different nations then left the two-month-long United Nations conference in San Francisco and traveled on an 18-car Victory train to New York. They passed through Montana and stopped at the Glacier Park Hotel, where members of the Blackfeet tribe held a dance and exhibitions. Five delegates (an Iranian, an Indian, the French Foreign minister, Rep. Sol Bloom from New York, and U.S. Navy Commander Harold Stassen) were inducted into the Blackfeet tribe. That old isolationist, Senator Wheeler, found fault with the U.N. Charter but vowed not to organize a fight against it and even expressed reluctant support for it. Wheeler did urge that the draft be stopped and that the soldiers in Europe be immediately brought home.

Although the war was about over, rationing was not. Eggs continued to be hard to find, as did men's shirts. Ration points for restaurants were cut on July 1, raising an outcry among restaurant owners state-wide, and causing several to temporarily shut their doors. Once Japan surrendered, most price controls were removed, and rationing ended on many items, including some food, although not sugar. Sugar was the first food item rationed and the last to be taken off the list. The ban on sales of most types of firearms was lifted, but controls were kept on .38 special revolvers (much in demand by police) and 12-gauge shotguns (which farmers needed for predator control).

During the summer of 1945, the Forest Service trained rescue crews from the Canadian Pacific Railroad and Coast Guardsmen from Alaska at Camp Paxson (Seeley Lake). Personnel at Camp Paxson also experimented with the parachuting of dog sled teams into remote areas, using canine parachute harnesses designed at the Army War Dog Training Center at Camp Rimini. Injuries among the airborne dogs were unacceptably high, however, and the parachute harnesses were dropped in favor of padded crates.

The Absaroka National Forest was merged into the Gallatin National Forest during the summer, and several Region One forests experimented with aerial fire patrol. The Forest Service also planned 500 miles of new roads around the state at a cost of $1,700,000.

The Forest Service's labor shortage had restricted the number of available timber sales, and during April of 1945, the ACM mill at Bonner shut down several times because of a shortage of logs. The shortage did not seem to bother the Idaho-Montana Pulp and Paper Company however, and the company announced plans to reopen mills at Columbia Falls and Polson. The production of telephone poles in Montana plants increased tenfold in the years right after the war, and small loggers from the Pacific Northwest began moving into western Montana.

The 1945 fire season, while not as bad as the previous year, was worse than the 1943 season. Since there was an acute lack of firefighters protecting the western forests, some lumber mills in Montana agreed to send their mill-workers to fight fires if the need arose. The forests also planned to use 350 of the Fort Missoula prisoners as emergency firefighters, but they were not needed. One hundred smokejumpers were trained in 1944, 18 of whom had been kept on since the previous summer. In July, the Forest Ser-

Hamilton

The seat of Ravalli County had a population of 2,282 in 1940, and had the highest proportion of retired people of any community in the state. The Bitterroot Valley was the original home of the Salish Indians and was the first area of Montana settled by whites. During the war years, agriculture and livestock raising were the predominant industries in the valley. Harvesting of sugar beets and apples brought a variety of foreign farm laborers to the valley, including Nisei, Mexicans, Italian detainees and German prisoners of war. The Daly Stock Farm, founded by copper king Marcus Daly, raised championship horses and was an important part of the valley's economy. Hamilton was a service, finance, and transportation center for the smaller communities of the Bitterroot. The town was home to the Rocky Mountain Spotted Fever Laboratory, and served as headquarters of the Bitterroot National Forest. By the mid-1940s, the timber industry in the Bitterroot was more than 100 years old, yet still played an important part of the valley's economy, and ACM operated a large sawmill at Hamilton. Sixty-five Ravalli County men died while serving with the armed forces during the war.

July 1945

· July 1. Three-year ban is lifted on the production of passenger cars, refrigerators, stoves, bicycles, lawn mowers, and many other household goods. Gold mining ban is dropped, and more ration points are allotted to western miners.

· July 2. An 11-year-old boy is killed by a train at Livingston, and an 11-year-old girl is killed by lightning while swimming at Hogeland. Sixteen Northern Pacific freight cars derail at Gold Creek.

· July 3. Rodeos begin in Browning and Drummond, horse races in Glendive. Days of '49 celebration in Roundup begins.

· July 9. Astronomers converge on Montana to view total eclipse of sun at 6:14 a.m.

· July 10. One thousand carrier planes bomb Tokyo. Missoula Rose Society holds first rose show.

· July 11. Representative Mansfield delivers a speech on the Japanese economy on the floor of the U.S. House.

· July 14. Cooke City highway opens for season.

· July 15. Fifty tons of paper and three tons of tin are collected in weekend drive in Missoula. The *SS Great Falls Victory* is launched at Richmond, California. Bozeman residents celebrate 140th Lewis & Clark anniversary with a parade featuring Boy Scouts and Campfire Girls.

· July 17. Truman, Churchill, and Stalin meet at Potsdam conference.

· July 18. A major wind and hailstorm at Poplar and Sidney smashes windows and trees and rips the copper roof from the Sidney post office. A sheepherder is killed near Glasgow when high winds tip over his wagon and it rolls 400 feet into a ravine.

· July 24. Blackfeet tribe hosts a Lewis & Clark anniversary celebration.

· July 25. Lewis & Clark pageant in Great Falls features cowboys and Indians, bands and military displays.

· July 26. Potsdam Declaration broadcast calls for the unconditional surrender of Japan. Clement Atlee becomes Prime Minister of Britain. Gore Field Flyers baseball team defeats East Base Gunners 1-0 in front of a record 2,600 fans. Flyers win 1945 League championship.

· July 27. Last balloon bomb in Montana is found near Babb. Northern Pacific Bozeman tunnel opens for use.

· July 28. Great Northern passenger train collides with freight train near Stanford, injuring nine.

· July 31. Two men are arrested in Billings for robbing Windmill restaurant and cracking safe.

vice dropped the largest number of smokejumpers used to that point. Forty Missoula smokejumpers and 52 Army paratroopers jumped on a 200-acre blaze in Idaho. The blaze quickly grew to 4,788 acres, and more than 1,000 firefighters, including migrant workers from Mexico, fought it. Many smaller fires cropped up, including an 800-acre fire at Libby and a 600-acre range fire near Belt. In August, eight smokejumpers parachuted into the scene of a backcountry fire near Darby and spent 12 hours carrying out a badly burned firefighter. Carrying a stretcher, it took the eight men 12 hours to cover the 15 miles to a road.

In early August, three small Missoula boys playing with matches on Madeline Avenue at the base of Mount Sentinel started a fire that blackened much of the hill. The fire raced to top of the mountain and reached 400 acres before 100 firefighters managed to subdue it. Dozens of fires broke out all over the state in August. Forty Army paratroopers from Oregon were dropped on a fire in very rough country near Plains, which burned more than 2,000 acres before being controlled. The paratroopers were members of the 555th Parachute Infantry Battalion, America's first and only unit of black paratroopers. Known as the "Triple Nickels," the 555th also jumped on large fires in the Cabinet and Bitterroot mountains.

As they had throughout the war, National Park officials discouraged travel to Yellowstone and Glacier Parks because of a lack of facilities (travel in the parks rose sharply just after VJ Day, and the state recorded its best tourist year since the war began). The 1945 Montana State Fair was again canceled because of manpower and travel restrictions. In Missoula, a fishing pond at Cold Springs slough was named the Garden City Children's Fishing Pond, and was open to all grade school children. Sponsored by the Western Montana Fish and Game Association, the pond was stocked with rainbow and brook trout, and opening day was attended by 432 children.

Capt. Cecil Rhodes of Kalispell, a Pacific veteran who had been awarded the Silver Star and Purple Heart, headed up a group which staged an infantry demonstration entitled "Here's Your Infantry." Forty-nine veterans demonstrated infantry weapons and re-enacted an attack on a Japanese pillbox. The show was put on in Kalispell, Missoula, Helena, Anaconda, Butte, Billings, Miles City, and Sidney. There were also several performances in Wyoming. In Sidney, 4,000 to 5,000 people watched the show, including 400 German POW farm laborers who watched from a stockade at the other end of the fairgrounds.

In Missoula, the War Department held a meeting in the Florence Hotel in late July to explain the progress of the war to citizens. A film was shown and officers and enlisted men from Europe and the Pacific spoke and answered questions. A lunch of K-rations was served, presumably to demonstrate the hardships that America's fighting men had to endure.

It was a quiet Fourth of July in Great Falls, but there was more than a little holiday excitement in Whitehall, where federal officials confiscated 40 gallons of moonshine whiskey and arrested two men. In Billings the holiday was marred by a fire at the Great Western sugar warehouse which destroyed 10 rail cars loaded with sugar beet seed and caused an estimated $150,000 damage. Thirty German prisoners of war helped carry bags of sugar out of danger.

During the summer of 1945, the state also celebrated the 140th Anniversary of the Lewis and Clark expedition, and cities all along the expedition's route hosted a variety of events. The state boasted 68 chapters of the Montana Council of American Pioneer Trails Association, which coordinated the anniversary. Early in July, the citizens of Missoula and the Salish-Kootenai tribe celebrated the journey of Meriwether Lewis through Missoula, and a temporary marker was erected just east of Missoula. Later in the month the American Pioneer Trails Association hosted events in Butte, Browning, Helena, and Three Forks. A picnic was held at the Gates of the Mountains on July 26, and 6,000 people attended a pageant at the Northern Montana Fairgrounds in Great Falls. Entitled the, "Cavalcade of the Great Northwest," the program highlighted Montana history from the Lewis and Clark expedition to the coming of the railroads.

Guy Owen of Cut Bank was crowned the 1945 men's state golf champion in August, while Edean Anderson retained the woman's crown. The shortage of golf equipment became so severe that even professional golfers were forced to use old golf balls made before the war. The prewar golf balls sold for as much as $10 apiece, five times their value by weight in silver.

Perhaps the most active baseball town in Montana was Great Falls, where the city baseball league announced a 64 game schedule. The military again fielded teams such as the Gore Field Flyers, the

Bombers, the Gunners, and the Army Medics. They played teams like the City Bar of Great Falls, the East Helena Smelterites, and a team from Sunburst. With 11 victories apiece, the Flyers and the Bombers tied for the city championship. The Gunners were a couple of games back, and the City Bar and the Medics occupied the cellar in the city league. The Bombers defeated City Bar 8-6 in the last league game of season. A baseball team from Fort Missoula traveled to Fort Douglas, Utah, where they were defeated 8-2. Two of the most active teams playing American Legion ball were the Miles City Cowboys and Missoula. Miles City went undefeated in the regional tourney in Billings, where they defeated Aberdeen, South Dakota 8-4. The Cowboys hosted the next round of the playoffs in Miles City, where they lost to a team from Stockton, California.

Although the crime rate throughout the state had declined during the war years, it had not disappeared altogether. A Helena man was fined $15 for riding while intoxicated after he and his horse were found cavorting on the lawn of the police station. A forest fire 35 miles west of Kalispell precipitated a murder when a rancher's wife fatally wounded her husband after he refused firefighters access to his property. Although the coroner's jury ruled it was a justifiable homicide, Mrs. Nellie Giffin was charged with second degree murder. In late June, Albert J. Ball, who had murdered his wife in Butte in 1938, escaped from the Montana State Prison. Although authorities feared he might be headed for Mexico, he was recaptured in Idaho the following month.

Authorities continued to have trouble with the Army Detention Center at Fort Missoula. Two prisoners escaped from Fort Missoula in late May, but were recaptured in the Bitterroot Valley on the following day. Later in the summer a disturbance left one prisoner stabbed to death, another seriously injured and several others hurt in a free-for-all among the prisoners. Charles Goddard was charged with the fatal stabbing of his fellow prisoner.

In late August the Army Detention Center experienced yet another rash of escapes. Two escapees led off by stealing an army truck, which was later found abandoned at Lolo. By the end of the week 13 prisoners were on the loose. One was recaptured as far away as Los Angeles. Five more Fort Missoula internees escaped from a Spokane hospital where they had been taken for medical treatment. Two were immediately recaptured and a third was found dead after he hid in a house that was being fumigated with cyanide. Two of the prisoners from Fort Missoula who didn't escape had been given the death sentence after being found guilty of a rape in California. Their scheduled execution date was set for August, but they were given a last-minute stay, and the executions never took place.

On July 26, 1945, President Truman, Winston Churchill, and Joseph Stalin issued the Potsdam Declaration, preparing the way for peace in Europe and calling for the unconditional surrender of Japan. The Japanese Imperial forces, having lost nearly all of the territory they had captured in the early part of the war, desperately prepared to repel the expected American invasion of their home islands, an invasion which American military planners estimated would cost 1,000,000 U.S. casualties and many times that number of Japanese casualties. The meticulously prepared invasion plans would never be needed however. A secret new weapon was on its way to the Pacific, and on August 6, 1945, the world entered the nuclear age when a lone B-29 dropped a single crude atom bomb on the Japanese city of Hiroshima. Estimates of the number of people killed at Hiroshima ranged from 80,000 to more than twice that number. Two days later the Soviet Union declared war on Japan and 1,500,000 Red Army soldiers attacked the Japanese Kwantung Army in Manchuria. On August 9, a second, more sophisticated, atomic bomb was dropped on Nagasaki, killing at least 40,000 Japanese. On August 15, Hirohito, the stunned Emperor of Japan, broadcast an appeal to his countrymen to lay down their arms.

On the morning of August 15, 1945, the headline of the *Daily Missoulian* blared out "JAPS QUIT" in huge red letters. The headline which so many people had looked forward to for so long, was set with wooden resurrection type, type too big to be set on a machine and called that because most editors felt it was only appropriate for the second coming of Christ.

Governor Ford was in Great Falls at the time and immediately proclaimed a two-day holiday. He requested (unsuccessfully) that all bars and stores close their doors.

Patricia E. O'Connell of Missoula wrote, "Early in the afternoon of the day we all knew the war had ended people poured out of offices and stores onto Higgins Avenue. Going home. Contrary to what some reports say, there was no immediate celebrating. Instead the mob of people who surged down Higgins Avenue were SILENT and GLASSY-EYED. Strange! The heavy burden they'd carried for four

August 1945

- August 1. Air Force Day.
- August 2. Allies issue Potsdam Declaration preparing for peace in Europe. Miners Field Day in Butte.
- August 5. Shelby rodeo begins, but the celebration is marred when a Shelby man is killed in a hit-and-run. Miles City Cowboys win Montana Legion title by defeating Missoula 5-4. In Cascade County, 165 city and county workers walk off the job. They return to work two days later while negotiations resume.
- August 6. U.S. drops an atomic bomb on Hiroshima.
- August 8. Soviets declare war on Japan.
- August 9. U.S. drops an atomic bomb on Nagasaki. More than 1,000,000 Soviet soldiers attack the Japanese Kwantung Army in Manchuria. North Dakota train wreck kills 34 and leaves 50 injured. Nine of the injured and at least eight of the dead are from Montana. Most were servicemen stationed at Gore Field. Great Falls rodeo begins.
- August 10. Thirty-four smokejumpers drop on fires all over Region One.
- August 11. Regional baseball finals in Billings. Flyers defeat Bombers 1-0 in playoff game.
- August 12. A false news story on the UPI wire causes premature VJ day celebration in Great Falls.
- August 14. Emperor Hirohito decides to surrender. All restrictions on sales of passenger cars and many other goods are lifted by WPB.
- August 15. VJ Day. Emperor Hirohito broadcasts his decision to surrender to the Japanese people.
- August 18. Kalispell rodeo begins. Two Washington men are hurt in a plane crash near Helena.
- August 19. Three are injured in freight train wreck at Geraldine. A grass fire burns 500 acres west of Great Falls.
- August 22. Japanese Kwantung Army surrenders to the Soviets.
- August 24. Controls on books, magazines, and penicillin are lifted.
- August 27. U.S. and British warships anchor in Tokyo Bay. Glacier National Park has 31 lightning fires burning at once.
- August 28. Western Montana fair in Missoula opens.

years had suddenly been lifted from their backs. It would take a while to get used to. Of course, later that evening there was laughing and dancing, hugging and kissing, quite a bit of drinking and lots and lots of celebrating." Fifty years later she added, "My memories of WWII are uneasy ones. Tell me it won't happen again."

Prisoners of War

American troops in the Philippines liberated a number of prisoner of war camps housing several hundred American survivors of the Bataan Death March, as well as U.S. citizens captured when the Japanese landed. Although many American prisoners had been moved to Japan and Manchuria, 1,447 POWs were liberated in the Philippines, including at least 44 Montanan servicemen and a number of civilians.

Among those civilians released were Mr. and Mrs. Byron Kerns of Stevensville, Dr. Elmer W. Herold of Missoula, as well as his wife and two children, Miss Margaret Wickes McDonald, also of Missoula, and five or six other Montana women. Many of them had been interned at the Santo Tomas camp in the Philippines throughout the war.

· Technician 4th Class George Wicks of Poplar spent three years hiding from the Japanese in the hills of the Philippines.
· PFC Ben Steele of Roundup was among those liberated in the Philippines. A survivor of the Death March and subsequent maltreatment by the Japanese, Steele later became chairman of the art department at Eastern Montana College from 1970 to 1980. He and his wife Shirley were awarded the Governor's Award for Distinguished Achievement in the Arts in 1992.
· Samuel Winn of Bozeman was captured in the Philippines and died at Camp Tanagawa on Honshu Island, Japan, in January 1943. Fellow POW John Fisher, also of Bozeman, was with him when he died. Winn's Prisoner of War medal was awarded to his widow Lora Winn at a Bozeman retirement home in 1989.
· Stevensville resident Greg Rodriguez Jr. worked tirelessly to achieve more VA benefits for POWs held by the Japanese in World War II. His father was captured in the Philippines, and was held in captivity for three-and-a-half years, much of the time at a camp at Mukden, Manchuria, where he was subjected to biological warfare tests. Rodriguez Jr. has organized reunions of the survivors of Bataan and Corregidor, and has interviewed hundreds of the former prisoners of war. In 1979 he founded Ex-POW Vision Quest, an organization that lobbied for veteran's rights and sponsored seminars for ex-POWs in several Western states.
· Staff Sgt. Hayes Bolitho of Butte was captured in the Philippines and spent two-and-a-half years as a captive. He escaped from the Japanese when a transport he was on was torpedoed. The Japanese crew fired machine guns and threw grenades at the men in the hold, and Bolitho was wounded but managed to crawl out the torpedo hole. At least 11 Montanan's died on the "Hell Ship" which was torpedoed October 24, 1944. Another Montanan was killed in the sinking of a "Hell Ship" at Subic Bay, December 13, 1944.

MARK RATION EXPIRATION DATES ON CALENDAR

HARDWARE
HOUSEWARES
GIFT GOODS

SOUTH SIDE HDWE.
BUTTE, MONTANA

17

☞ Aftermath ☜

As the news of peace spread, major celebrations broke out in virtually every community in the state. Cars bedecked with flags cruised the streets, horns blowing. Firecrackers, banned during Fourth of July celebrations throughout the war, were fired off by the thousands. Churches and bars were equally crowded. Central Avenue in Great Falls was the scene of a wild celebration, and women kissed every serviceman they met. In Great Falls, almost 40 people were arrested for public drunkenness.

On August 30, 1945, 1st Lt. William Lazetich, still wearing a bandage from a wound sustained on Okinawa, became one of the first Montanans to set foot in defeated Japan. "I went this far and wanted to be sure to be in on the final chapter." Lazetich, who had survived some of the toughest battles of the Pacific, returned to Montana after the war and became the long-time football coach at Billings Senior High.

On September 2, Japanese envoys signed the surrender aboard the *USS Missouri*. In the ensuing days, Japanese troops on dozens of isolated islands and in China and Southeast Asia surrendered. Surrender of one of the Japanese garrisons was particularly sweet to Brig. Gen. Lawson Sanderson and his fliers of the Fourth Marine Aircraft Wing, who flew into Wake Island to take the Japanese surrender there. In the days after Pearl Harbor, Marine aviators at Wake had put up a valiant but ultimately futile defense of the tiny island.

On September 6, the Second Battalion of Montana's 163rd Infantry landed at Hiro, Japan (near the flattened rubble of Hiroshima), where they were put to work destroying Japanese military equipment at the Kure Naval Base. According to the 163rd's historian, Dr. Hargis Westerfield, the unit that the Japanese had called the Bloody Butchers of Sanananda "quickly made friends of the delightful Japanese people." Few original members of the 163rd spent any time in Japan, however, because they were quickly rotated back to the United States. The last Billings man serving with the 163rd was discharged in September.

The 163rd Infantry Regiment, like the rest of the 41st Division, was deactivated without fanfare at the end of 1945. The unit that had begun as the Montana National Guard contained barely 20 percent Montanans at the end of the war, more than five years after the Montana National Guard had been inducted. Although the 163rd was one of the first American units sent overseas and had lost 360 dead and 1,491 wounded, of the Montana men in the regiment only 39 had been killed in action, 10 died of wounds, and 10 others died of non-combat causes. The 41st Division claimed to have inflicted 19 casualties for every one they had taken.

In 1947 the 163rd was reactivated as the Montana National Guard with Col. W.R. Rankin and Lt. Col. Byron Armstrong (both veterans of the fighting in the Southwest Pacific) in charge.

In 1991, 3,424 Montanans from 27 communities across the state were members of the 163rd Armored Brigade, although Pentagon cutbacks threatened to drastically reduce that number. Another 1,080 Montanans served as members of the Montana Air National Guard, headquartered in Great Falls.

After the war, Maj. Jesse E. DeFrance of Laurel was active in the Billings Air Force Reserve unit. He was an ace who had been captured by the Germans and who was awarded a Distinguished Flying Cross while he was a prisoner of war. Another man active in the Air Force Reserve in Billings was Lt. Col. Chester K. Shore, who took command of the unit in 1954. Shore later wrote *Montana in the Wars*, an important source for this book.

Soon after the war, 50 to 60 men were being discharged daily at East Base. The Air Force had spent $10,000,000 on the facilities at Gore Field and another $20,000,000 on the construction of East Base. Thousands of workers, many of them women, had been stationed at Gore Field and East Base. The Soviet Union had received more than $8,500,000,000 worth of Lend-Lease aid, much of which had passed through Great Falls. Although the figures do not reflect every plane that passed through Montana on the way to the Soviet Union, from January 1, 1943, to September 3, 1945, more than 7,600 warplanes left Great Falls bound for Alaska and the Soviet Union. In 1943, 2,500 planes were flown to the Soviet Union, 3,000 the following year, and 2,100 in 1945.

During the same period Western Airlines had flown 22,000,000 pounds of military cargo from Great Falls to Nome, Alaska. An additional 5,891 Flying Fortresses passed through Great Falls on their way from the Boeing factory at Seattle to Denver.

The city of Great Falls, which had done everything possible to facilitate the Air Force's activity during the war, filed suit against the military in order to recover $19,370 in street damage incurred during the past three years. The 7th Ferrying Group was deactivated November 15, 1945, and most of the 1,600 enlisted men and 800 officers were discharged from the Air Force. The Soviet contingent left Great Falls soon after the formal Japanese surrender, and the Air Force base through which the Soviets had funneled so much vital information and equipment became, ironically, one of the front-line bases deterring the Soviet nuclear threat. In 1956 East Base was renamed Malmstrom Air Force Base after a flier killed in a training accident. By the 1990s the Base was home to two squadrons of KC-135 aerial tankers as well as the 341st Missile Wing, in charge of 200 Minuteman III nuclear missiles.

In September 1945, General Frederick visited Helena, where several veterans of his First Special Service Force met him. Many of the Forcemen who had trained at Helena returned there after the war, including Mark Radcliffe, Herb Goodwin, Roy Hudson, John Marshall, Robert Durkee, and James Wines, who eventually became the police chief of Helena. A number of ex-Forcemen still live in Montana's capital city.

By August 1945, 11,015 veterans had been released in Montana, and veteran's offices were opened in Great Falls, Missoula, and Bozeman. Veterans were afforded many benefits, although as one celebrity found out, these could sometimes backfire. Comedian Red Skelton was visiting his in-laws in Kalispell when he was fined $100 for shooting an elk without a license. He had tried to buy a license but the clerk told him they were free for returning servicemen, which was true for Montana residents, but not for Skelton, who was visiting from out of state.

Fort William Henry Harrison reverted to the Veterans Administration in 1948. The original hospital, built in 1932 and rebuilt after the 1935 Helena earthquake, was augmented by a new 160-bed hospital in 1963. Since the Veterans Hospital at Fort Harrison could not adequately serve the tens of thousands of Montana World War II veterans, in 1951 the Veteran's Administration opened a new facility at Miles City. In July 1993 the U.S. Department of Veterans Affairs estimated that there were still 29,400 World War II veterans living in the state.

An estimated 55,000,000 people had perished during World War II. The War Department's Official Honor List of Dead and Missing (compiled in 1945) lists the names of 1,553 Montanans known to have died in the war, but it is not complete. The most accurate listing of Montanans killed in the war was compiled by the Montana Historical Society. This list contains the names of 1,869 Montanans (317 of them sailors and Marines) killed during the war, however the actual total of dead and missing from Montana is probably closer to 2,500. After the war, it was determined that Montana had the highest percentage of combat deaths of any state except New Mexico.

Approximately 57,000 Montanans joined the armed forces during World War II, while 69,000 others left the state for defense work. Montana's population dropped dramatically during the war, Deer Lodge County gained 4,000 residents, Cascade County remained even, and nearly every other county in the state lost population. Rural counties like Valley and Broadwater experienced population losses as high as 35 percent. However, as soon as the war ended, tens of thousands of veterans came flooding back to the state. That and the subsequent baby boom soon brought the population back to prewar levels.

Those killed in action included the entire 11-man starting lineup of the 1940-41 Montana State College football team, the only American college football team to lose its entire starting line-up. By the fall of 1946 Montana State College had nearly 3,600 students, double the enrollment of five years before. In 1947 several large frame buildings from the chrome mines near Columbus were brought to Bozeman for classroom space. Military trailers, prefab buildings, Quonset huts and a large Hudson dormitory were also brought to the campus to house the returning veterans. A $5,000,000 mill levy for the colleges passed in 1948 to deal with the record enrollments.

Cmdr. James McCain took over the presidency of the University of Montana during the fall quarter of 1945. Lt. Col. William G. Kelly, who had served with the 163rd Infantry Regiment and had been wounded at Sanananda, took a post at the University as professor of Military Science. During the fall of

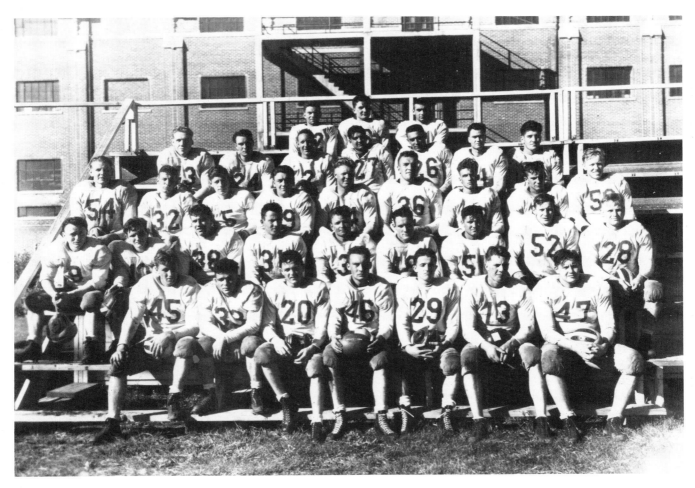

Montana State College football team, 1940-41. MONTANA STATE UNIVERSITY ARCHIVES

September 1945

· September 2. Japan signs surrender aboard the *USS Missouri*. *USS Helena* dedicated in Boston.
· September 4. Forest fire in Lewis & Clark National Forest burns 5,500 acres near Sun River Canyon.
· September 6. 163rd Infantry Regiment goes ashore near Hiroshima, Japan.
· September 12. Japanese troops in Southeast Asia surrender. Cheese rationing ends. ABC and NBC workers go on strike.
· September 15. Moose season opens in Beartooth Mountains.
· September 21. Missoula Spartans football team defeats Kalispell Braves 33-0 in Great Falls.
· September 30. Some meat rationing ends. War time ends.

Montana State College 1940-1941 Football Team

· Capt. John F. Burke, a Montana State College football player on the 1941 team, was a tackle killed in action in Italy on January 7, 1944. Burke was given a written commendation by Eisenhower for salvaging armored vehicles under fire.
· Dana Bradford, end, killed in plane crash.
· John Hall, Jr., end, killed in plane crash.
· Albert Zupin, center, killed in plane crash.
· Newell Burke, tackle, killed in New Guinea.
· Bernard Cluzen, guard, killed in South Pacific.
· Joseph McGreever, guard, killed in Germany.
· Wendell Scabad, backfield, killed in action,
· John Phelan, backfield, killed in action.
· Alton Zempel, quarterback, killed in plane crash.
· Rich Roman, backfield, killed in Germany.

Families

- Seven Varner boys of Chinook served during World War II. Sgt. Lee Varner was a B-17 gunner who spent a year in POW camps in Europe. His brother PFC Frank Varner was killed in action at Okinawa.
- Seven Hruska boys of Lewistown served during World War II.
- Seven Carey brothers of Richey served during WWII.
- Seven Murphy brothers of Great Falls were in the service. Marine PFC Charles Murphy was killed in action on the *USS Indianapolis*, sunk July 30, 1945, after delivering the first atomic bomb to Tinian.
- Six Hopkins brothers of Roundup served during World War II.
- Five members of the Meredith family, Forsyth, were in the service, two in the army, one in the Navy, one WAC and one WAVE.
- The four Hutchinson brothers of Harlowton all served in the Pacific, one with the Marines in the Solomons, one in the Navy, and two in the 163rd Infantry Regiment.
- Four children of the Dahl Family of Bozeman served in World War II. S. Sgt. Charles Raymond Dahl was a B-24 bombardier shot down over Germany May 29, 1944. His brother Lt. Eldon H. Dahl was a B-17 pilot shot down over Italy August 25, 1943, and captured. He escaped and made his way back to U.S. lines. Their sister Mary E. Dahl was a 2nd Lt. who served as an Army nurse, while brother John B. Dahl graduated from the Navy V-12 program and became an officer. Their mother, Mrs. Emil H. Dahl christened the ship *SS Victory Bozeman* on December 19, 1944.
- The LaFromboise family of Great Falls lost one son who died in a Japanese prison camp, one missing in action in Italy, and one wounded in action.
- Five boys of the Dickson family of Geyser served in the armed forces.

Havre

Situated on the Milk River, Havre was founded as a railroading town when the Great Northern line was built across Montana's Hi-Line. The seat of Hill County, Havre had a population of 6,372 in 1940. Governed by longtime mayor Joseph A. Wright, the city was a division point and stock shipping center for the Great Northern Railroad, as well as being an agricultural, trade, and service center. The Grand Hotel served visitors, and an annual music festival was held every May. A $500,000 airport was completed in 1943 and the city began planning for a new sewage plant.

The Department of Agriculture operated an agriculture experiment station at the site of the frontier military post at Fort Assiniboine, eight miles south of Havre. The Rocky Boys Reservation was also nearby.

The four brick buildings which comprised Northern Montana College were barely more than a decade old when the war began. In addition to the normal prewar courses in liberal arts and pre-professional studies, Northern added classes in chemical and electrical engineering and secretarial skills to meet the war-time demand for those specialties. Like most other state institutions, Northern suffered a precipitous drop in enrollment due to the war. The college, which had 221 students in 1942, had only 112 students by the following year. By the fall of 1944 the school had only 105 students (16 men and 89 women). The high school had nearly as many students as the college, and in 1945, 116 students graduated from Havre High.

Two earlier graduates of Havre High, Cpl. William Livesay and Cpl. Ralph Shawlee, who hadn't seen each other in two years, met up on the island of Bougainville when they dove into the same foxhole during an artillery barrage. Lt. Cmdr. L.T. Sussex, formerly a doctor in Havre, directed Navy corpsmen on Guadalcanal and Tarawa. On the other side of the world, 16 former Havre residents held a reunion in a Red Cross club in London late in 1944. Havre women also did their part for the war effort, and in a six-month period they turned out 125,000 surgical dressings for the Red Cross. At least 40 men from Hill County lost their lives in the war, as did WAC 2nd Lt. Vera Bruder. Havre is the site of the little-known Montana World War II memorial.

GREAT FALLS TRIBUNE, Monday, January 29, 1945

Girls of Montana, You Are Needed

to Serve Your Country as Nurses

20,000 Additional Students are Urgently Needed to Fill the Quota for 1945

THE COLUMBUS HOSPITAL

Where Students of the Columbus Hospital School of Nursing Receive Clinical Experience

Hospital Fully Approved by American College of Surgeons
School of Nursing Fully Approved by State Board of Nurse Examiners
School Fully Approved by U.S.P.H.S. for Training Cadet Nurses
Affiliated With Great Falls College of Education and Montana State Tuberculosis Hospital

NEXT CLASS BEGINS MARCH 26, 1945

1945 registration at the University of Montana (1,091) increased 35 percent from the year before. The GI Bill provided an opportunity for veterans to receive a college education, and by the fall of 1946, there were 3,300 people enrolled at the University of Montana, 1,400 more than the campus could comfortably handle. The forestry school was particularly popular because a nationwide housing shortage caused a boom in the lumber industry.

The Montana Grizzlies again bowed out of the Pacific Coast Conference for 1945. Since Maj. Doug Fessenden was still coaching an Air Force Training Command football team in Fort Worth (he returned to the head coach position in 1946), assistant coach "Jiggs" Dahlberg coached the five games of the University's 1945 football season. During his long career at the University, Dahlberg wrote an unpublished 1,000 page handwritten work entitled the "Red Book," the definitive history of Grizzly athletics. The basketball court at Harry Adams Field House in Missoula is now named Dahlberg Arena. Jiggs Dahlberg passed away in 1993, shortly after being inducted into the Grizzly Hall of Fame. Grizzly players Eso Naranche, Bill O'Donnell, Norman Streit, Bill Holt, and Walt Fitzmaurice were all killed in the war.

The Missoula Spartans, reigning state champions, started off another winning football season in 1945 by defeating the Butte Bulldogs 34-6 and shutting out the Great Falls Bisons in two consecutive games.

Fort Missoula remained a U.S. Army Detention Center, but some of the prisoners were transferred to Fort Leavenworth as early as October 1946. By April 18, 1947, all prisoners had been transferred and the camp was closed. Fort Missoula today is used by a number of different groups. The Army Reserve and the Montana National Guard utilize buildings at the fort, as does the University of Montana, the Forest Service, and the Historical Museum at Fort Missoula. In 1994 the University of Montana Foundation sold the site of the former Fort Missoula Detention Camp to land developers, despite a petition drive by thousands of Missoula citizens seeking to preserve the area as public property.

The war brought tremendous changes to the state's economy, industry, agriculture, and work force. Roads, airports, and telephone lines had all been improved, and electricity had finally reached the most isolated areas of the state. Even so, at the end of the war there were still 30,743 Montana farms without electricity. In a four-year span, businesses in the state of Montana were awarded $74,300,000 in war contracts for supplies and facilities. On the other hand, the war had done little to diversify the state's economy, and Montana remained dependent on the same industries (agriculture, mining, and timber) as before the war.

However, the state's heavy industries (mining, smelting, and milling) became increasingly important to the nation's economy, and by 1947 the state boasted 7,000 more manufacturing jobs than it had in 1939.

High food prices proved to be a boon to farmers and ranchers for several years after the war, and property values for agricultural land soared. The average size of Montana farms and ranches grew by 400 acres during the war. Between 1940 and 1948 the value of Montana ranches increased 188 percent. As the size of ranches and farms grew larger, the percentage of Montanans making a living off that land grew smaller. In 1940, more than 30 percent of Montana's population was employed in agriculture. Ten years later that percentage had dropped to less than 25 percent.

The United Nations was established in October 1945, and many people hoped that lasting peace was finally at hand. Pundits predicted that the production of atomic powered locomotives, two-way radio phones for cars, and rockets capable of flying between New York and Chicago in three minutes would revolutionize society. Those with a more practical bent simply wanted to replace their bald tires.

Although gasoline rationing was halted upon news of Japan's surrender, the 35 mile per hour speed limit was kept in effect until most drivers had an opportunity to buy new tires. Great Falls residents held hearings on the possibility of introducing parking meters and parallel parking, and by the following year the first parking meters were also being tried in Billings.

Throughout the first few weeks of October 1945, Billings was gripped by a polio epidemic, and several high school football games were canceled. As the epidemic progressed, all public places in Billings were quarantined. The quarantine was lifted October 21 after 54 people had contracted the disease and nine had died. After the war, Billings also experienced a major boom in population and the fastest growth of any city in Montana, which soon made it the state's largest city.

The state began a building boom after the war

ended. In 1949 a home for senile men and women was established at Lewistown, and a new science building was constructed at Eastern Montana Normal College. Many more buildings were built at state institutions in the 1950s. The number of radio stations in the state more than doubled in the postwar years and in 1953 several television stations began broadcasting in the state.

Sen. James Murray, elected in 1935, served 26 years, the longest senate term of any Montanan. He was a delegate to the London United Nations conference and attended the first UNESCO meeting in Paris in 1946.

Mike Mansfield served five terms in the House of Representatives, then defeated incumbent Zales Ecton for his U.S. Senate seat in 1952. Mansfield rose to serve as senate majority leader during the Kennedy, Johnson, Nixon, and Ford administrations, and then was appointed U.S. Ambassador to Japan.

Wesley D'Ewart served out the remainder of Representative O'Connor's term and was elected to four more terms in the House.

Jeannette Rankin remained a lifelong advocate for peace, and protested American military involvement overseas up until the Vietnam war. The Jeannette Rankin Peace Resource Center in Missoula honors her lifelong commitment to world harmony.

Democrat John W. Bonner, formerly a colonel serving on the staff of Gen. Omar Bradley in Europe and an assistant staff judge advocate with the First Army, won election to the governor's office in 1948, serving one term. Bonner was awarded the French Croix de Guerre and a Bronze Star for his actions in Europe. In 1962, Donald G. Nutter, a veteran of the China-Burma-India theater, was elected governor of Montana. Nutter, a former B-24 pilot who had conducted 62 combat missions against the Japanese, was killed in a plane crash just a year after his inauguration. Nutter was succeeded by Lt. Gov. Tim Babcock, formerly a staff sergeant with the 99th Division. Babcock had fought at the Battle of the Bulge and the Ludendorff Bridge at Remagen.

2nd Lt. Lee Metcalf of Stevensville served as an army prosecutor in Germany. In his first case he prosecuted a German civilian who was given three months in jail for disobeying an American Military Policeman. After the war Metcalf served on the Montana Supreme Court and was elected to the U.S. House of Representatives in 1952, where he served four terms before succeeding James Murray in the U.S. Senate.

Five years after Senator Wheeler leaked the Victory Program to the press, his political career came to an end. Wheeler's prewar isolationist stand and his alienation of the farm labor groups, who turned against him as he moved to the right, led to his defeat by Leif Erickson during the 1946 primary, and a conservative Republican, Zales Ecton, won the November election. Despite Wheeler's defeat, according to his biographer Richard Ruetten, "No one, before or since, wielded such political power in Montana as did Burton K. Wheeler."

Gov. Sam Ford buys the first war bond on the first day of the Victory Bond Drive from Frank Murray, bond drive chairman, 1945. MHS 74-89.1

October

- October 1. AFL printers strike newspapers in Butte, Helena, Missoula, and Anaconda. The strike lasted for several weeks.
- October 9. Two Great Falls men die in train wreck 10 miles north of Great Falls.
- October 10. Detroit Tigers defeat Chicago Cubs in seventh game to win World Series.
- October 16. Bud Linderman of Red Lodge wins bareback riding at New York rodeo. He was out on bail for manslaughter charges.
- October 24. United Nations charter takes effect.
- October 25. Vice Admiral Hoover, deputy commander of the Pacific Fleet, is guest of honor at Navy day in Great Falls.
- October 29. Eighth war bond drive begins with a statewide quota of $25,000,000 dollars.

Postwar Years

- December 8, 1945. A C-47 bound for Seattle from Newark and loaded with veterans who were being discharged catches a wing in trees on Poly Drive in Billings. The plane crashes and burns near Virginia Lane. Of 23 men on board, 19 were killed instantly and two died later at a Billings hospital.
- January 1, 1946. 163rd Infantry Regiment is deactivated.
- April 18, 1947. Fort Missoula Detention Camp is closed.
- October 17, 1948. Ground-breaking at Miles City VA Hospital.
- 1948. Billings Mustangs baseball team plays first season.
- August 19, 1951. New veterans hospital at Miles City is dedicated.
- 1953. Canyon Ferry Dam is completed. KXLF in Butte broadcasts first television signal in Montana.

Memorials

Although few people are aware of its existence, the Montana State World War II memorial is located in Havre.

A memorial near the Lewis and Clark County Library in Last Chance Gulch in Helena honors the four U.S. Navy warships to bear the name *USS Helena.*

At nearby Memorial Park in Helena stands a memorial to the First Special Service Force, which was dedicated August 15, 1948, at a ceremony attended by U.S. and Canadian members of the Force. This monument was paid for in part by the $5,000 anteed up by the Forcemen on their way to Kiska, when they heard of the sinking of the *USS Helena.* They sent the money to Helena to be used as a memorial for the ship, but the mayor saved it in order to honor the Forcemen.

Soldiers Chapel at Lone Mountain was built in 1955 by Velma and Nelson Story III of Bozeman as a memorial to the fallen members of the 163rd Infantry Regiment, Montana National Guard. A stained glass window depicts a dying soldier in the tropics lifting one hand to God. The 163rd's buffalo skull with regimental crest on it is also displayed there, as is the Regimental Memorial Monument with the names of the original members of the regiment who fell in action.

The Doughboy statue in Missoula lists 166 Missoula County men killed in the war. The 43 bells of the carillon housed in the University of Montana Main Hall commemorate the University students who lost their lives in the war. In January 1944, the Daughters of Union Veterans of the Civil War suggested a memorial park be built on Brooks Street in Missoula, and today 2,500 roses honor Montana's war dead. This park is also the site of the Montana Vietnam Veterans Monument.

Even the tiny town of Hinsdale erected a war memorial, and buried underneath it a time capsule containing newspapers, magazines, books and letters from servicemen. The American Legion in Whitefish erected a native rock memorial honoring veterans of both World Wars. In Great Falls VFW post 1087 erected a memorial at Margaret Park honoring the men and women of the Electric City who served in the armed forces.

A state highway marker stands before the remains of the Smith Mine near Red Lodge, and in nearby Coal Miner's Park, 74 trees commemorate the miners who were killed in the state's worst coal mining disaster.

⋐ Honor Roll ⋑

Montanan's Awarded Significant Decorations For Combat During World War II

This is neither an official nor a complete list of those Montanan's who won medals during World War II. It is, however, an attempt to recognize the many men and women whose contribution might otherwise be forgotten. The awarding of medals was at best an imperfect method of evaluating a soldier's actions on the battlefield (in the European theater 82 percent of all decorations went to the Air Force, while the infantry won less than 10 percent of the medals given) and many fine soldiers received little or no recognition. Most of the information in this list comes from articles printed in the *Great Falls Tribune* from 1942 to the end of 1945. Many World War II medals were awarded years after the end of the war, and recipients of those awards are not included here. This list also does not include most of the people whose stories are told in more detail in the text.

CONGRESSIONAL MEDAL OF HONOR. The highest and rarest U.S. military award. Given only for acts of conspicuous bravery while at risk of losing one's life.
- William Galt (posthumous).
- Laverne Parrish (posthumous).
- Leo Power.
- Donald Ruhl (posthumous).
- Henry Schauer.

NAVY CROSS. Awarded to Navy and Marine personnel for extraordinary heroism.
- 1st Lt. Henry E. Clark of Billings, Avenger pilot on the *USS Hornet.* He also had a Silver Star and two Distinguished Flying Crosses.
- Marine Thomas C. Mather of Great Falls, UM journalism graduate.
- Cmdr. Justin Miller of Missoula. He commanded a Navy patrol bomber in the Philippines, and also had the DFC.
- Lt. Cmdr. Lee S. Pancake, (posthumous).
- Ens. James Shelton, (posthumous).
- Lt. Stanley Vejtasa.

DISTINGUISHED SERVICE CROSS (DSC). Awarded to Army personnel for extraordinary heroism in combat.
- Pvt. Charles Ball of Fort Belknap.
- Lt. Rex Cantrell of Billings, a navigator in an 8th AF B-17.
- Lt. Phillip R. Clark of Polson, a bombardier based in England.
- Lt. Luther S. Gustafson, (posthumous).
- PFC Lawrence T. Levandowski of Stockett. He stepped on a mine while trying to rescue two wounded men. The mine blew his foot off but he gave first aid to the wounded men before tending his own wound.

LEGION OF MERIT. Awarded for exceptionally meritorious service.
- T. Sgt. Benhart H. Kero of Roberts, for "exceptionally meritorious conduct in the performance of outstanding service" in the Southwest Pacific area from April 1942 to September 1943.
- Col. Raymond W. Curtis of Fort Benton, plans and operations officer of IV Corps, 5th Army, Italy. He also had the Silver Star.
- T. Sgt. Gerald F. Corrigan of Great Falls, Austria.
- Lt. J.O. Gehrett of Laurel, Southwest Pacific theater.
- Sgt. John A. Heisler of Billings, Pearl Harbor.
- Capt. James D. O'Brien of Billings, 24th Division, Pearl Harbor.
- Col. Lawson H.M. Sanderson, USMC, first Montanan to win Legion of Merit.
- Sgt. Herbert T. Warren of Suffolk, Southwest Pacific theater.

SILVER STAR. Awarded to military personnel for extraordinary heroism in combat.
- Pvt. Raymond A. Ackerman of Fraser, New Guinea.
- PFC Wesley M. Alrick of Ferdig, November 28, 1944, in Germany.
- Capt. William C. Benson of Billings, New Guinea.
- PFC Edward Dennehy of Butte.

- Lt. Eddie Doherty of Great Falls, B-24 pilot, 15th AF, Italy. He also had the DFC and Air Medal with cluster for 35 missions.
- PFC Floyd A. Durfey of Richey, Guadalcanal.
- Capt. Conway L. Ellers of Shepherd, New Guinea.
- Pvt. Norman Enberg of Butte, Anzio.
- Sgt. LaVerne Flournoy of Butte, Anzio.
- Capt. John H. Gerneraad of Billings. He also had DFC.
- Sgt. Richard Vander Hagen of Castle Butte, tank battalion, Europe.
- Pvt. Harold Halvorsen of Great Falls, 41st Division, Biak.
- PFC Dwight Hutchins of Billings, for rescuing a wounded man under fire in Luzon, 43rd Division.
- 2nd Lt. Stanley W. Johnson of Lewistown, missing in action since November 7, 1943.
- Cpl. Michael Kilwine of Billings, for helping the wounded under fire in Europe.
- S. Sgt. Chester V. Larson of Forsyth, Naples.
- Lt. Daniel G. Massing of Moulton, New Guinea.
- Sgt. Robert N. Mitchell of Poplar, New Guinea.
- Capt. Boyd Myhr of Malta, 163rd Infantry, South Pacific.
- Capt. James T. Murphy of Roundup, New Guinea.
- 2nd Lt. Arthur D. Nebel of Neihart, France.
- 1st Lt. Ralph H. Rinker of Lewistown, mechanized cavalry, Third Army, France.
- S. Sgt. Oliver J. Russell of Dupuyer, 15th AF.
- Col. Barton M. Russell of Billings, commander of a fighter group.
- 1st Lt. Richard J. Satran of Whitefish, Pacific theater.
- 1st Lt. Herman U. Schrader of Browning, Pacific theater.
- PFC Robert L. Scott of Great Falls, 12th Armored Div., Breymuhl, France.
- Sgt. Theodore Thayer of Helena, Fifth Army in Italy.
- Capt. Henry J. Vandal, Luzon.
- 1st Lt. Benny Stephens of Great Falls, Bastogne.

DISTINGUISHED FLYING CROSS. Awarded for heroism or extraordinary achievement in the air. (AF stands for Air Force. Cluster represents the awarding of a second medal)
- Capt. George R. Barker of Livingston, 20 Bomber Command, India.
- S. Sgt. Franklin H. Banjamain of Billings, 8th AF.
- Lt. Kenneth W. Beckstrom of Vaughn, Southwest Pacific.
- T. Sgt. Dell S. Benson of Ekalaka, 9th AF, Europe, 25 missions.
- S. Sgt. Irving J. Biesinger of Havre, Southwest Pacific.
- Sgt. Irwin J. Blessinger of Helena, Southwest Pacific.
- S. Sgt. Warren W. Bondy of Richland, Southwest Pacific.
- S. Sgt. Willis L. Brainerd of Chinook, 9th AF, Europe, 25 missions.
- S. Sgt. Lewis B. Brisco of Sun River, 8th AF, B-17 waist gunner.
- T. Sgt. A.N. Brown of Great Falls. 8th AF, B-17 pilot with 22 missions.
- Lt. (jg) Ralph Brownell, European theater.
- 1st Lt. Richard F. Burns of Chinook, 73rd Bombardment Group, a B-29 unit based in Saipan.
- Lt. (jg) Francis O. Buron of Billings. He bombed a Japanese cruiser in the Solomons.
- Lt. Merrill O. Burton of Harlem (missing in action since May 30, 1944).
- T. Sgt. Grant L. Butcher of Miles City.
- 2nd Lt. George R. Carpenter of Hamilton, 8th AF.
- Lt. Gale Chase of Great Falls, (posthumous). He was a transport pilot who crashed in the jungle after more than 50 missions.
- Capt. John W. Clapper of Billings, Southwest Pacific.
- 1st Lt. Claude N. Cory of Helena, 8th AF.
- Lt. Frank A. Crockwell of Roundup, Southwest Pacific.
- Capt. Ralph W. Cummings of Great Falls, declared dead after a November 11, 1943, raid over Bremen.
- 1st Lt. Burton K. Davis of Butte, 8th AF.
- Sgt. John Dea Jr. of Great Falls, South Pacific for actions between March 23, 1943, and November 19, 1943.
- Lt. (jg) Arthur Doherty of Great Falls, a Hellcat pilot with Air Group Two, Pacific theater.
- Sgt. John K. Dunne of Billings, B-29 gunner.

- S. Sgt. James Dye of Kalispell.
- Maj. Gordon Eaton of Great Falls, 20th Bomber Command, India.
- 1st Lt. Malcolm W. Enman of Drummond, 7th AF.
- S. Sgt. Kenneth von Eschen of Billings.
- T. Sgt. John H. Fitzsimmons of Sarpy, Southwest Pacific.
- S. Sgt. Edwin Fugman of Missoula.
- 1st Lt. John J. Goggins of Butte, 10th AF.
- Lt. Lawrence J. Gregor of Eureka, 8th AF.
- 2nd Lt. Donald E. Grovac of Great Falls, India Air Transport Command.
- 1st Lt. Howard G. Hammond of Kremlin, 8th AF.
- Lt. Waino W. Hannukela of Geyser.
- Sgt. John R. Hanratty of Butte. Southwest Pacific.
- Lt. Phillip G. Haugland of Watkins, 9th AF, Europe, 25 missions.
- Lt. Walter H. Heiseman of Billings, 50 missions.
- Ens. Charles B. Hiigel of Missoula. Air Group Two, Hellcat pilot aboard a carrier in the Pacific.
- Lt. (jg) Robert J. Humphrey of Billings. He was a carrier pilot with DFC and cluster, plus the Air Medal with 5 gold stars.
- F.O. Wilbur Hyland of Great Falls, India-China Air Transport Command.
- S. Sgt. George Ingebo of Winnett. He was an aerial photographer and gunner in the Southwest Pacific.
- S. Sgt. Anton M. Jochim of Inverness.
- Flight Officer Harry E. Jones of Roundup, pilot in China-Burma-India theater.
- 1st Lt. Clayton A. Johnston of Billings, cluster.
- Lt. Stanley W. Johnson of Lewistown, Southwest Pacific.
- Sgt. Tom Kelly of Great Falls, B-29 gunner with DFC and cluster for 35 missions over Japan.
- Flight Officer Alvin A. King of Havre, B-29 engineer.
- 1st Lt. Thomas O. Kliev of Whitefish, 8th AF.
- Capt. Arnold C. Koenning of Missoula.
- 2nd Lt. Luke Kunkerly of Glendive, 8th AF.
- Capt. Robert E. Lamb of Laurel, 8th AF.
- 1st Lt. Robert Lammers of Hedgesville, 9th AF, B-26 bombardier. He was killed in action February 25, 1944 in Europe.
- Lt. Arnold V. Larson of Billings.
- Albert E. Liddicoat of Butte, 50 missions over Europe.
- S. Sgt. Allen W. Mack of Billings, 8th AF.
- 1st Lt. Clarke G. McCarthy of Missoula, 8th AF.
- Sgt. Jack M. McDonald of Kevin, 8th AF, B-17 waist gunner.
- Lt. John A. Miller of Chinook, he was a transport pilot in the China-Burma-India theater.
- Lt. Delbert F. Milliron of Larslan.
- T. Sgt. Clyde R. Mitchell of Billings, 10th AF.
- Lt. Charles Perry Moore of Harlowton, DFC and cluster, 341st Bomber Squadron, 97th Bomber Group, Mediterranean.
- T. Sgt. Robert Morton of Anaconda.
- Lt. John F. Mufich of Butte, Southwest Pacific
- 1st Lt. Andy S. Muri of Cartersville, Southwest Pacific.
- T. Sgt. Francis J. Murphy of Helena, B-29 gunner based on Guam.
- 1st. Lt. James T. Murphy of Roundup.
- Machinists Mate 1st Class George W. Myers.
- 2nd Lt. Gerald W. Nagle of Anaconda.
- Lt. Glenn A. Nelson of Whitefish, Southwest Pacific and 5th AF, cluster.
- Sgt. Archie J. Nichols of Great Falls, India Air Transport Command.
- Lt. Stanley Olson of Glendive, 8th AF, B-17 bombardier.
- Capt. George T. Orvis Jr. of Missoula, cluster.
- Lt. Donald G. Overose of Great Falls, Southwest Pacific.
- 1st Lt. George J. Peterson of Bozeman, Gallatin High and MSC graduate. B-24 navigator in Europe.
- Lt. John Phelan of Butte, 8th AF.
- Lt. John Power of Helena, China-Burma-India theater.

- T. Sgt. Everett R. Pratt of Wolf Creek, 7th AF, cluster.
- 1st Lt. Perry E. Raster of Custer, cluster.
- Capt. Jeffrey B. Roberts of Simms, 15th AF, B-24 commander.
- S. Sgt. Edward J. Roth of Baker, 15th AF.
- Capt. Warren H. Sands of Zurich, 7th AF, cluster.
- Lt. Francis Sauer of Billings, Pacific.
- 1st. Lt. Neil D. Sharp of Hysham, 10th AF.
- S. Sgt. Charles E. Shaw of Lodge Grass. He shot down two Japanese planes over New Guinea.
- S. Sgt. Thomas E. Schoonen of Hinsdale, B-24 missions over Europe, Italy, and N. Africa. He also held the Air Medal with three clusters.
- T. Sgt. W.D. Siler of Sunburst, radioman/gunner on a B-24 with 30 missions over Europe. He had the Air Medal with two clusters.
- T. Sgt. Clement M. Simmons of Manhattan.
- Lt. Paul Smith of Billings, P-61 pilot and first night fighter ace.
- Sgt. Frank Spindler,(posthumous), veteran of North Africa and Italy.
- Maj. Albert E. Steensland of Missoula.
- Lt. James A. Stokes of Belt, 102 B-24 flights in China-Burma-India theater, cluster.
- Lt. Frederick J. Stone of Great Falls, 300 hours in China-Burma-India theater.
- Capt. Frederick J. Telecky of Great Falls, 300 flying hours in India branch of Air Transport Command.
- PFC Donald Tomcheck of Helena, (posthumous), India-China division of ATC.
- Sgt. Frank L. Underhill of Deer Lodge, B-29 radio operator in Pacific.
- Sgt. James F. Walsh of Shelby, Southwest Pacific.
- Lt. Robert Weldon of Lewistown, Normandy.
- T. Sgt. Arthur C. Welsh of Miles City, Southwest Pacific.
- S. Sgt. Emanuel Wenz of Billings, 9th AF, 25 missions over Europe.
- 1st Lt. David O. Wilcox of Augusta, 8th AF.
- 1st Lt. Robert B. Wiley of Wyola, 8th AF.
- Sgt. Robert E. Williams of Miles City.

BRONZE STAR. Awarded for heroic or meritorious achievement while engaged in combat.
- Lt. Col. Arthur K. Amos of Helena.
- Sgt. Herbert F. Base of Froid, Fifth Army radioman.
- Sgt. Jim Birkett of Roundup, Normandy invasion.
- T-3 Raymond W. Bundtrock of Great Falls, 54th Ordnance Group, August to November 1944 in France. He was a veteran of Africa, France, and Germany.
- S. Sgt. Daniel I. Burbank of Great Falls. He had a Bronze Star each for Leyte and Okinawa.
- Lt. Floyd W. Chapman of Great Falls, 372nd MP unit, France and Germany.
- Maj. Betty Clague, WAC, former head of women's physical education at UM, China-Burma-India theater.
- Sgt. Frank J. Coleman of Great Falls, 58th Bombardment Wing, China and India.
- Cpl. Kenneth A. Connelly, Jr., of Billings, chaplain's assistant with Ninth Army.
- Sgt. Donald Conolly of Valentine, ground mechanic, 15th AF.
- Sgt. Thomas B Craver of Butte, Pacific theater.
- PFC. Earl R. Cripps of Giltedge, 175th Infantry Regiment in Europe.
- Cpl. Vernon L. Dobeck of Plevna.
- Capt. John H. Duncan of Helena.
- T. Sgt. Roy M. Duff of Whitefish, Pacific theater.
- Lt. Col. Harold F. Dyer of Lewistown, Army engineer and former Fergus County surveyor.
- S. Sgt. Clarence Ecker of Stanford. He was with the provost marshall's office in Europe.
- Capt. Addison S. Farrell of Polson.
- Pvt. Frank E. Flaherty Jr., 104th Division, Normandy, Antwerp, Aachen.
- Lt. Albert J. Gates of Lewistown, European theater, cluster.
- Marine Sgt. Edwin Gieschen of West Yellowstone, Pacific theater.
- Col. Walter R. Graham of Bozeman, France.
- Capt. F. Orville Gray of Great Falls, 28th Regiment, 8th Division. After his superior was wounded in France, he took command of his unit.
- Chief machinists mate John P. Gutensohn of Whitefish, for maintaining vital equipment aboard a submarine.

- Sgt. Maurice Hain of Cohagen.
- PFC John R. Halseth of Great Falls, medic, 407th Infantry, Ninth Army, Germany.
- S. Sgt. Elmer E. Holliday of Roundup, Third Army in Luxemburg.
- S. Sgt. James J. Jensen of Choteau, 349th Infantry, 88th Division, 5th Army, Italy.
- Capt. Frank S. Kambic of Roundup, 4th Armored Division. Presented by General John S. Wood.
- Maj. Patrick Kirk of Froid, telegraph and telephone officer at Colmar during January and February 1945.
- T-5 Clifford Komar, ambulance driver with 9th Medical Battalion, Germany.
- 1st Sgt. Raleigh E. Kraft of Billings, a veteran of France, Belgium, Germany, and Czechoslovakia.
- Sgt. George A. Larson of Scobey. He had 100 missions with the 67th tactical reconnaissance group of the 9th AF.
- S. Sgt. Margaret Leuschen of Jordan, Europe.
- M. Sgt. Joseph R Linnane of Great Falls, 186th Infantry, 41st Division.
- PFC George B. Linville of Billings, 5th Army, Italy.
- Gunnery Sgt. Allan J. Madding of Livingston, Pacific theater.
- PFC Allen L. McCann of Great Falls.
- Tech. 3 Garnett E. McCollim of Whitehall.
- Maj. H.E. McIntyre of Billings, medical unit in Philippines. On May 4, 1945, he aided a wounded man under fire.
- Sgt. Gilbert A. Mestdagh of Roundup, 41st Division, cluster.
- Pvt. William B. Miller of Billings, Europe.
- T-3 Albert A. Miron of Billings.
- Pvt. William C. Moorefield of Roundup, 9th Infantry rifleman, Germany.
- S. Sgt. Elmer L. Morgan of Lewistown, (posthumous), Fifth Army, Italy.
- 1st Lt. Leonard E. Morrow of Great Falls. He was a forward mortar observer with the Sixth Army on Luzon, and also fought at Bougainville.
- S. Sgt. Olaf M. Olsen of Great Falls, Italy, cluster.
- Tom Olsen of Glaston.
- S. Sgt. Oswald J. Olson of Grass Range, European theater.
- Capt. Woodrow W. Overcast of Zurich, armament officer with the 58th Bombardment Wing, India and China.
- PFC Charles E. Peterson of Lewistown, North Africa and Italy.
- Sgt. Thomas Pistoria, 5th Armored Division.
- PFC Eugene D. Reichelt of Big Sandy, combat engineer, Fifth Army, Italy.
- Lt. Col. Lawrence B. Rhodes of Billings. He was Provost Marshall, Air Force Service Command, Italy, from December 1944 to May 1945.
- Sgt. Jack E. Rich of Lewistown, 805th Tank Destroyer Battalion, 88th Division, Fifth Army, Italy.
- PFC Calvin W. Perman of Billings, medical detachment, 351 Regiment, 88th Division, Fifth Army.
- Maj. Carl A. Peterson of Waltham, plans and operations officer of 194th Glider Infantry, 82nd Airborne. He was a veteran of the Bulge, Ruhr, and Roer rivers, as well as the occupation of Berlin.
- S. Sgt. Edwin G. Pfeifle of Great Falls, 41st Division, Biak.
- M. Sgt. Raymond L. Richard of Great Falls, B-17 crewmember in Italy.
- PFC Leo Richardson of Harlowton, 163rd Infantry, two clusters.
- M. Sgt. Patrick Rogers of Miles City, 20th Bomber Command, India.
- Cpl. George M. Smith of Great Falls, 741st Tank Battalion, Europe.
- S. Sgt. Virgil L. Spradlin of Monarch, Europe and Mideast.
- S. Sgt. Julian K. Stenson of Choteau, 5th Armored Division, Germany.
- 1st Lt. Frank D. Strong of Bozeman.
- T. Sgt. Alvis L. Taylor of Columbia Falls, 20th Bomber Command, India and Western China.
- PFC William J. Talvi of Great Falls, (posthumous), Leyte.
- Sgt. Myles E. Ventling of Billings, 1st Infantry Division, Luzon.
- PFC Walter C. Vogel of Hinsdale, 362 Infantry, 91st Division. Fifth Army.
- Sgt. Steve J. Vranish of Roundup, 33rd Infantry Division.
- S. Sgt. James Wallette of Wolf Point, 7th Infantry Division.
- S. Sgt. John H. Whittle of Glasgow, 3rd Division, Italy.
- PFC Fred M. Wilson of Billings, 100th Division, Seventh Army, Germany, cluster.
- S. Sgt. Lester E. Wiprud of Dutton, 9th Armored Division through France, Belgium, Luxemburg, and Germany.
- 1st Lt. Raymond E. Wise of Great Falls, 325th Glider Infantry, Battle of the Bulge.
- Sgt. Kerridge W. Wright of Lewistown, 4th Armored Division, Germany. He also had the Presidential Unit Citation.
- T. Sgt. Leland E. Yarbrough of Hamilton, aircraft mechanic with 58th Bombardment Wing, India and China.

☞ Select Bibliography ☜

BOOKS

Adleman, Robert, and Col. George Walton. *The Devil's Brigade*. New York: Bantam Books. 1966.

Bosworth, Allan R. *America's Concentration Camps*. New York: Bantam Books. 1967.

Burhans, Lt. Col. Robert D. *The First Special Service Force: A War History of the North Americans*. Washington Infantry Journal Press. 1947.

Burlingame, Merrill G. *A History—Montana State University, Bozeman Montana*. Bozeman: Office of Information Publication. 1968.

Cohen, Stan. *The Forgotten War*. Four volumes. Missoula: Pictorial Histories Publishing Co. 1981.

-----------. *V For Victory*. Missoula: Pictorial Histories Publishing Co. 1991.

Eichelberger, Robert L. *Our Jungle Road to Tokyo*. New York: Viking Press. 1950.

Giles, Kevin S. *Flight of the Dove: The Story of Jeannette Rankin*. Beaverton Oregon: Touchstone Press. 1980.

Gilluly, Bob. ed. *The Grizzly Gridiron*. Missoula: Montana State University. 1960.

Guth, A. Richard, and Stan Cohen. *Northern Region: A Pictorial History of the U.S. Forest Service 1891-1945*. Missoula: Pictorial Histories Publishing Company. 1991.

Hammel, Eric. *Guadalcanal: Decision at Sea*. New York: Crown Publishers. 1988.

-------------. *Guadalcanal: Starvation Island*. New York: Crown Publishers. 1987.

Haugland, Vern. *Letter From New Guinea*. New York and Toronto: Farrar and Rinehart, Inc. 1943.

Howard, Joseph Kinsey. *Montana: High, Wide, and Handsome*. New Haven: Yale University Press. 1943.

Jordan, George Racey. *From Major Jordan's Diaries*. New York: Harcourt, Brace and Company. 1952.

Josephson, Hannah. *First Lady in Congress, Jeannette Rankin*. Indianapolis and New York: Bobbs-Merrill Inc. 1974.

Kenney, William. The Crucial Years, 1940-1945. New York: McFadden Books. 1962.

Kent, Graeme. *Guadalcanal: Island Ordeal*. New York: Ballantine Books. 1971.

Lacey, Richard. *Montana Militia, A History of Montana's Volunteer Forces. 1867-1976*. Dillon: Dillon Tribune Examiner Press. 1976.

Lowery, Geraldine. *The American Legion in Montana 1919-1963*. American Legion, Montana Department. 1965.

Malone, Michael P., Roeder, Richard B., Lang, William L., *Montana: A History of Two Centuries*. revised edition. Seattle and London: University of Washington Press. 1991.

Mast, Gerald. *A Short History of the Movies*. Indianapolis and New York: The Bobbs-Merrill Co. 1971.

McCombs, Don and Fred Worth. *World War II Superfacts*. New York: Warner Books. 1983.

Merriam, H.G., *The University of Montana: A History*. Missoula: University of Montana Press. 1970.

Montana State University. *The Montana Almanac 1959-60*. Missoula: Montana State University.

Morris, Lt. C.G., with Hugh B. Cave. *The Fightin'est Ship: The Story of the Cruiser* Helena. New York: Dodd, Mead and Co. 1944.

Morrison, Samuel Elliot. *The Two-Ocean War*. Boston: Atlantic Monthly Press. 1963.

-----------------------. *History of US Naval Operations in World War II, vol. 5. The Struggle for Guadalcanal, August 1942- February 1943*. Boston: Little Brown and Co. 1949.

Paladin, Vivian, and Jean Baucus. *Helena, An Illustrated History*. Norfolk, Virginia: The Donning Company. 1983.

Polenberg, Richard. *America at War*. Englewood Hills, N.J.: Prentice Hall, Inc. 1968.

Saiki, Patsy Sumie. *Ganbare! An Example of Japanese Spirit*. Honolulu: Kisaku, Inc. 1982.

Shore, Chester K. *Montana in the Wars*. Compiled for the American Legion and Auxiliary of Montana. Miles City: Star Printing. 1973.

Sommerville, Donald. *World War II, Day by Day*. Dorset Press. Greenwich, Ct. 1989.

Spritzer, Donald E. *Senator James E. Murray and the Limits of Post-War Liberalism*. New York and London: Garland Publishing Inc. 1985.

Toole, John. *Battle Diary*. Missoula: Vigilante Press. 1978.

-----------. *Red Ribbons, A Story of Missoula and Its Newspaper*. Lee Enterprises. 1987.

Toole, K. Ross. *Twentieth Century Montana, A State of Extremes*. Norman: University of Oklahoma Press. 1972.

U.S. Forest Service. *History of Smokejumping*. Missoula: USDA Forest Service Northern Region. 1976.

U.S. Navy. *Dictionary of American Naval Fighting Ships*. Washington, D.C: Office of Chief of Naval Operation, Naval

History Dept. 1969.

Vader, John. *New Guinea, The Tide is Stemmed.* New York: Ballantine Books Inc. 1971.

Werth, Alexander. *Russia At War, 1941-1945.* New York: Avon Books. 1964.

Westerfield, Hargis. *41st Infantry—The Fighting Jungleers.* 41st Infantry Division Association. 1980.

Wheeler, Burton K. and Healy, Paul F. *Yankee From the West.* New York: Doubleday and Co. Garden City. 1962.

Zemke, Hubert. *Zemke's Wolf Pack.* as told to Roger Freeman, New York: Orion Books. 1989.

Zemke, Hubert, and Roger Freeman. *Zemke's Stalag.* Washington, D.C. and London. Smithsonian Institution Press. 1991.

PERIODICALS

The *Billings Gazette*. 1941-1945.

The *Great Falls Tribune*. 1941-1945

The *Missoulian*. 1941-1945, 1984-1994

Fischer, Karen. "Training Sled Dogs at Camp Rimini, 1942-1944." *Montana, the Magazine of Western History*. Winter 1984.

Gordon, Dennis. "Black Monday—A Liberator Falls." The *Montana Journal*. December 15, 1987.

THESIS

Van Valkenburg, Carol. "An Alien Place: The Fort Missoula, Montana Detention Camp, 1941-1944." Unpublished Master's Thesis, University of Montana 1988.

Loken, Scott C. "Montana During World War II." Unpublished Master's Thesis, University of Montana 1993.

☞ About the Author ☜

A fourth-generation Montanan, Gary Glynn grew up in Billings, where he graduated from West High in 1975. He attended the University of Montana and received a B.S. in Forestry in 1980. He has worked as a timber cruiser for the U.S. Forest Service, as a carpenter, and as a leathercraftsman. Since 1991 he has written a regular feature for the *Missoulian* newspaper. His work has also appeared in *American History Illustrated, World War II* magazine, *America's Civil War*, the *Montana Journal*, and the *Great Falls Tribune*. He lives in Missoula with his wife Mary, daughter Kelsey and son Connor.

MARY LYNDES PHOTO

INDEX